Basilisk

ORIGINAL STORY BY FŪTARO YAMADA

BASED ON THE KODANSHA NOVEL *THE KOUGA NINJA SCROLLS*

MANGA BY MASAKI SEGAWA

TRANSLATED AND ADAPTED BY DAVID URY
LETTERED BY FOLTZ DESIGN

BALLANTINE BOOKS, NEW YORK

sR

A Del Rey Trade Paperback Original

Basilisk volume 3 copyright © 2003 by Fūtaro Yamada and Masaki Segawa
English translation copyright © 2006 by Fūtaro Yamada and Masaki Segawa
Excerpt from *The Kouga Ninja Scrolls* copyright © 2006 by Fūtaro Yamada

Published in the United States by Del Rey Books, an imprint of The Random House Publishing Group, a division of Random House, Inc., New York.

DEL REY is a registered trademark and the Del Rey colophon is a trademark of Random House, Inc.

Publication rights arranged through Kodansha Ltd.

First published in Japan in 2003 by Kodansha Ltd., Tokyo.

ISBN-10 0-345-48272-7
ISBN-13 978-0-345-48272-3

Printed in the United States of America

www.delreymanga.com

9 8 7 6 5 4

Translator and adaptor: David Ury
Lettering: Foltz Design

Contents

Honorifics Explained

Throughout the Del Rey Manga books, you will find Japanese honorifics left intact in the translations. For those not familiar with how the Japanese use honorifics, and, more important, how they differ from American honorifics, we present this brief overview.

Politeness has always been a critical facet of Japanese culture. Ever since the feudal era, when Japan was a highly stratified society, use of honorifics—which can be defined as polite speech that indicates relationship or status—has played an essential role in the Japanese language. When addressing someone in Japanese, an honorific usually takes the form of a suffix attached to one's name (example: "Asuna-san"), as a title at the end of one's name, or in place of the name itself (example: "Negi-sensei," or simply "Sensei!").

Honorifics can be expressions of respect or endearment. In the context of manga and anime, honorifics give insight into the nature of the relationship between characters. Many English translations leave out these important honorifics, and therefore distort the feel of the original Japanese. Because Japanese honorifics contain nuances that English honorifics lack, it is our policy at Del Rey not to translate them. Here, instead, is a guide to some of the honorifics you may encounter in Del Rey Manga.

-SAN: This is the most common honorific and is equivalent to Mr., Miss, Ms., or Mrs. It is the all-purpose honorific and can be used in any situation where politeness is required.

-SAMA: This is one level higher than "-san" and is used to confer great respect.

-DONO: This comes from the word "tono," which means "lord." It is an even higher level than "-sama" and confers utmost respect.

-KUN: This suffix is used at the end of boys' names to express familiarity or endearment. It is also sometimes used by men among friends, or when addressing someone younger or of a lower station.

-CHAN: This is used to express endearment, mostly toward girls. It is also used for little boys, pets, and even among lovers. It gives a sense of childish cuteness.

BOZU: This is an informal way to refer to a boy, similar to the English terms "kid" or "squirt."

SEMPAI/
SENPAI: This title suggests that the addressee is one's senior in a group or organization. It is most often used in a school setting, where underclassmen refer to their upperclassmen as "sempai." It can also be used in the workplace, such as when a newer employee addresses an employee who has seniority in the company.

KOHAI: This is the opposite of "-sempai" and is used toward underclassmen in school or newcomers in the workplace. It connotes that the addressee is of a lower station.

SENSEI: Literally meaning "one who has come before," this title is used for teachers, doctors, or masters of any profession or art.

-[BLANK]: This is usually forgotten on these lists, but it is perhaps the most significant difference between Japanese and English. The lack of honorific means that the speaker has permission to address the person in a very intimate way. Usually, only family, spouses, or very close friends have this kind of permission. Known as *yobisute,* it can be gratifying when someone who has earned the intimacy starts to call one by one's name without an honorific. But when that intimacy hasn't been earned, it can be very insulting.

Basilisk
3

THE TEN COMBATANTS OF THE IGA CLAN

OGEN

OBORO

YASHAMARU

ROUSAI AZUKI

JINGOROU AMAYO

KOSHIROU CHIKUMA

NENKI MINO

HOTARUBI

TENZEN YAKUSHIJI

AKEGINU

THE TEN COMBATANTS OF THE KOUGA CLAN

DANJOU KOUGA

GENNOSUKE KOUGA

JUUBEI JIMUSHI

SHOUGEN KAZAMACHI

GYOUBU KASUMI

JOUSUKE UDONO

SAEMON KISARAGI

HYOUMA MUROGA

KAGEROU

OKOI

Chapters

Summary

THE STORY SO FAR...

UNDER THE ORDER OF RULER IEYASU TOKUGAWA, THE THIRD TOKUGAWA SHOGUN SHALL BE DECIDED BY A BATTLE OF 10 VS 10 BETWEEN THE KOUGA AND THE IGA NINJA. THE BLOODBATH BETWEEN THESE TWO NINJA CLANS BEGINS WHEN THE TWO CLAN LEADERS, OGEN OF IGA AND DANJOU OF THE KOUGA CLAN TAKE EACH OTHER'S LIVES. SOON AFTER, JUUBEI JIMUSHI, SHOUGEN KAZAMACHI, JOUSUKE UDONO AND OKOI OF THE KOUGA CLAN ALSO MEET THEIR DEMISE. ONLY AFTER THE DEATHS OF THESE KOUGA NINJA DOES THE REST OF THE KOUGA CLAN LEARN THAT THE IGA/KOUGA TRUCE HAS BEEN DISSOLVED. THE KOUGA CLAN BEGINS TO STRIKE BACK IMMEDIATELY BY KILLING IGA CLAN MEMBERS YASHAMARU AND ROUSAI AZUKI. MEANWHILE, BOTH GENNOSUKE KOUGA AND OBORO OF IGA HAVE LEARNED ABOUT THE BATTLE BETWEEN THEIR CLANS. GENNOSUKE LEAVES IGA TSUBAGAKURE TERRITORY IMMEDIATELY. OBORO OF IGA, FILLED WITH WORRY AND SORROW, SPLASHES A BLINDING POTION UPON HER OWN EYES. THE BATTLE BETWEEN THE IGA AND THE KOUGA CONTINUES...

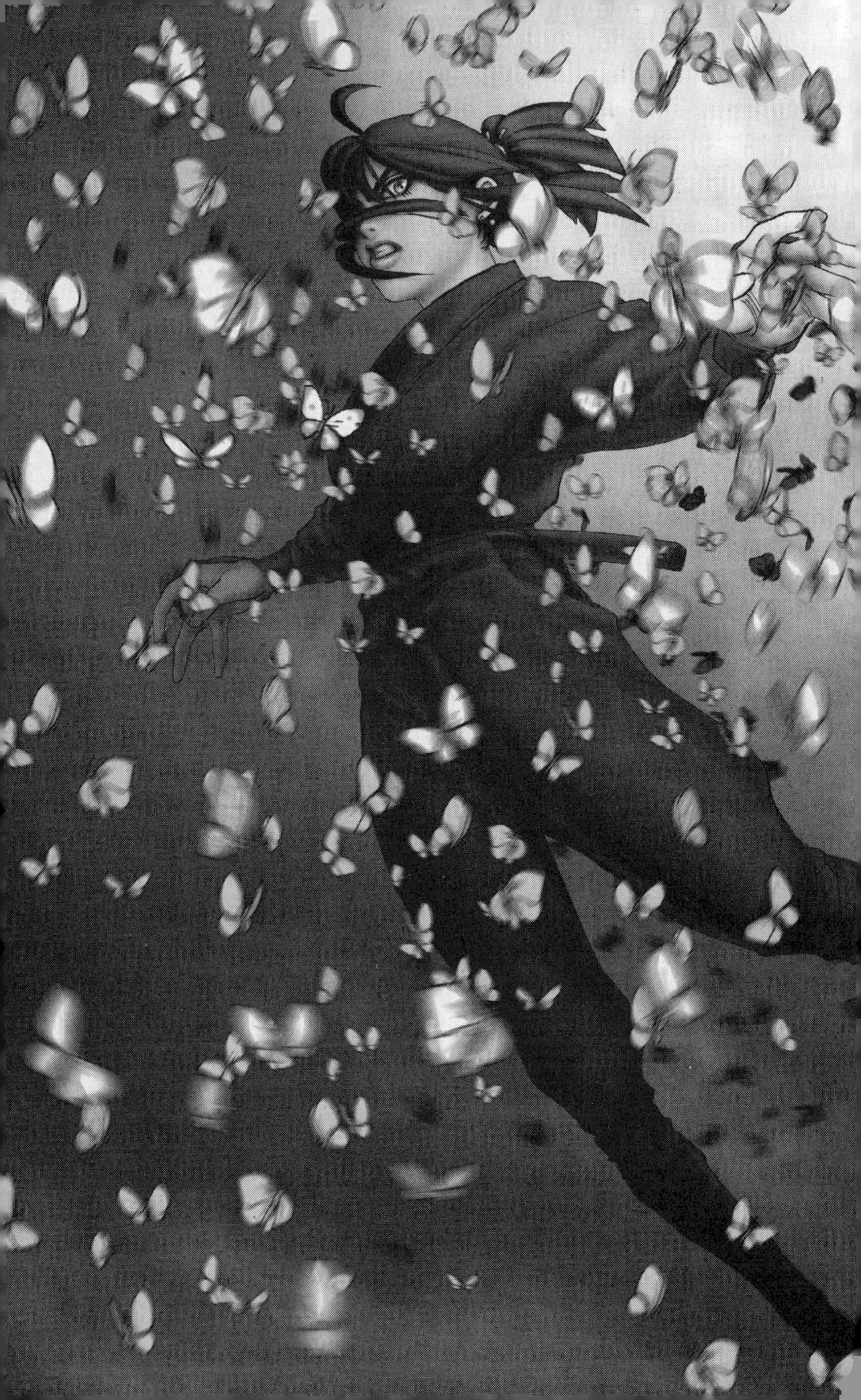

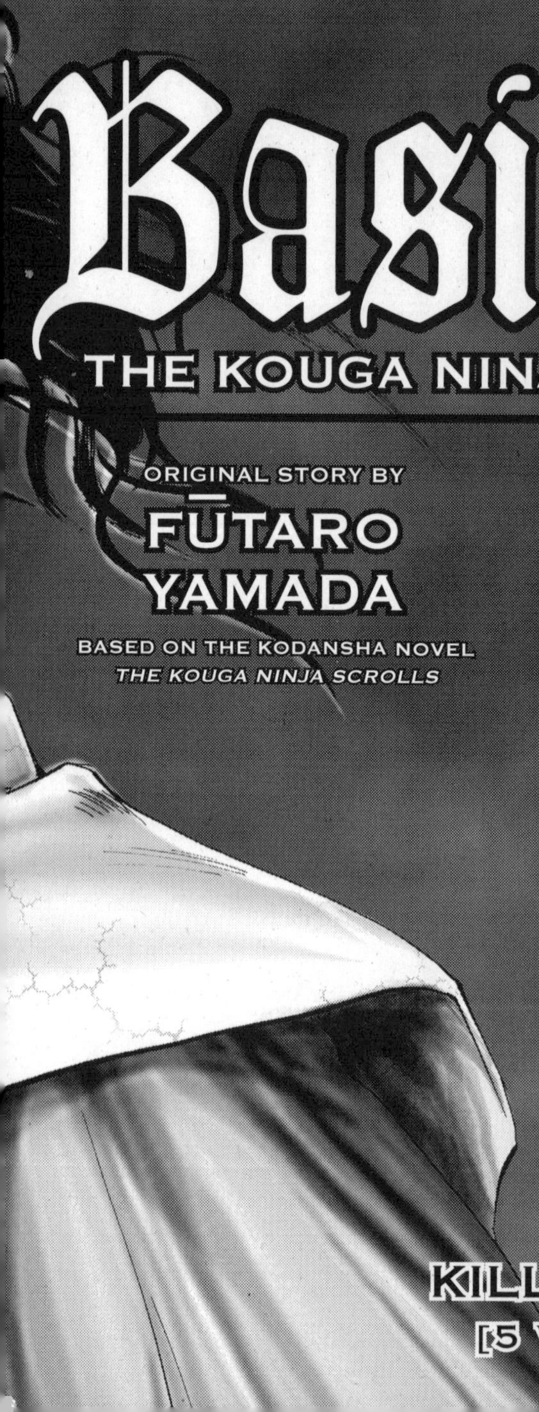

Basilisk

THE KOUGA NINJA SCROLLS

ORIGINAL STORY BY
FŪTARO YAMADA

MANGA BY
MASAKI SEGAWA

BASED ON THE KODANSHA NOVEL
THE KOUGA NINJA SCROLLS

KILL NUMBER 14
[5 VS 7 (PART 3)]

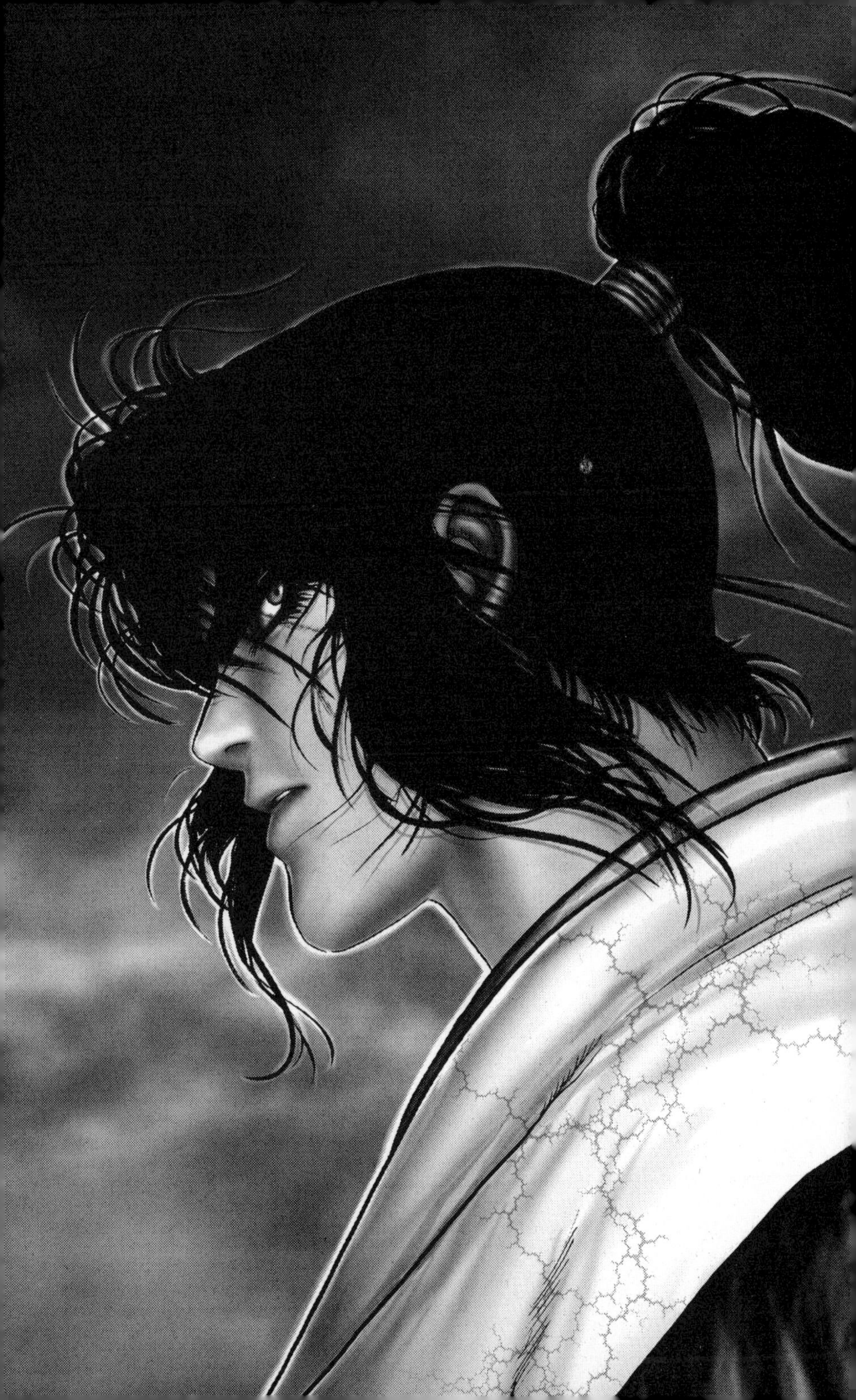

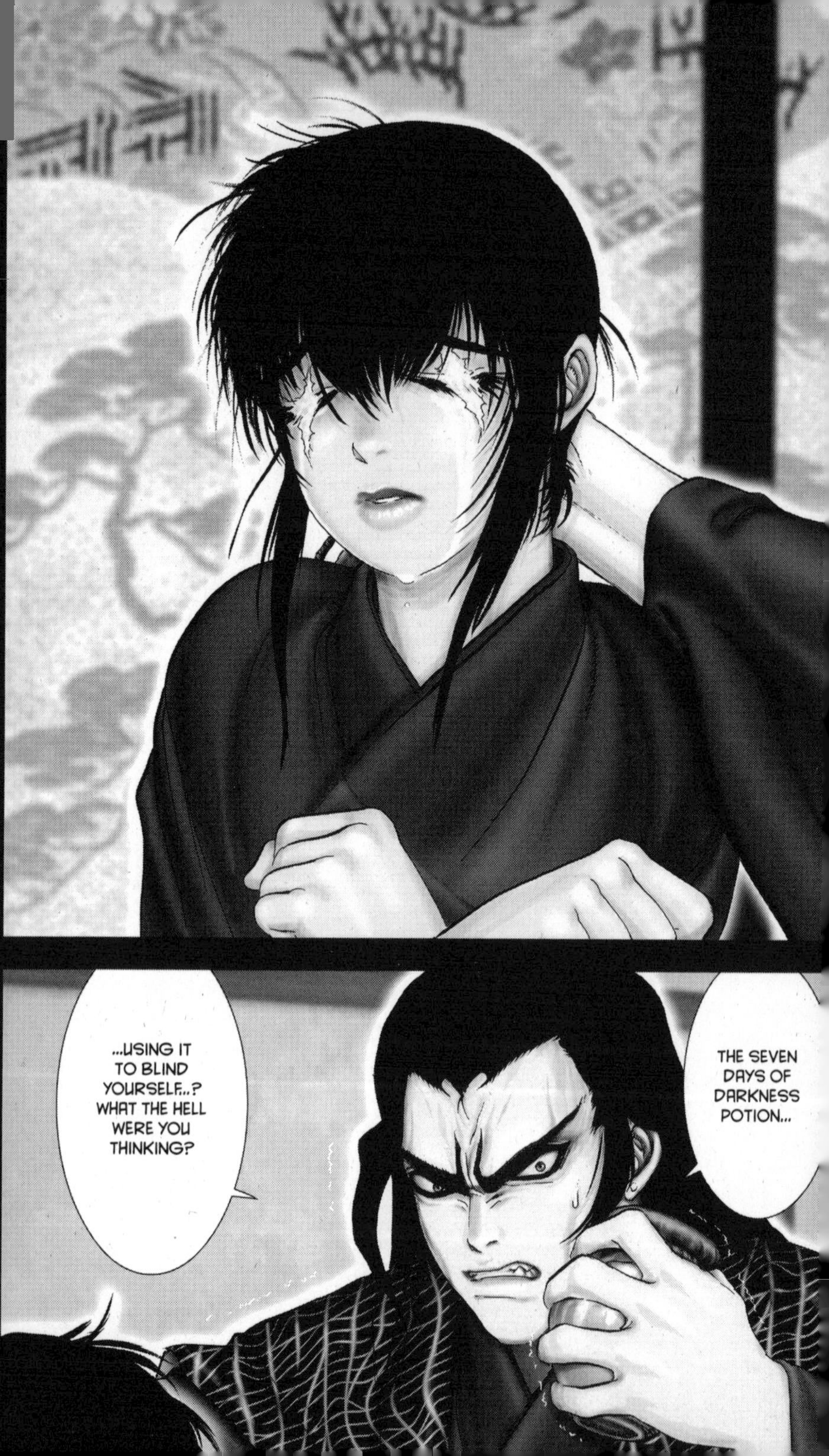
THE SEVEN DAYS OF DARKNESS POTION...
...USING IT TO BLIND YOURSELF...? WHAT THE HELL WERE YOU THINKING?

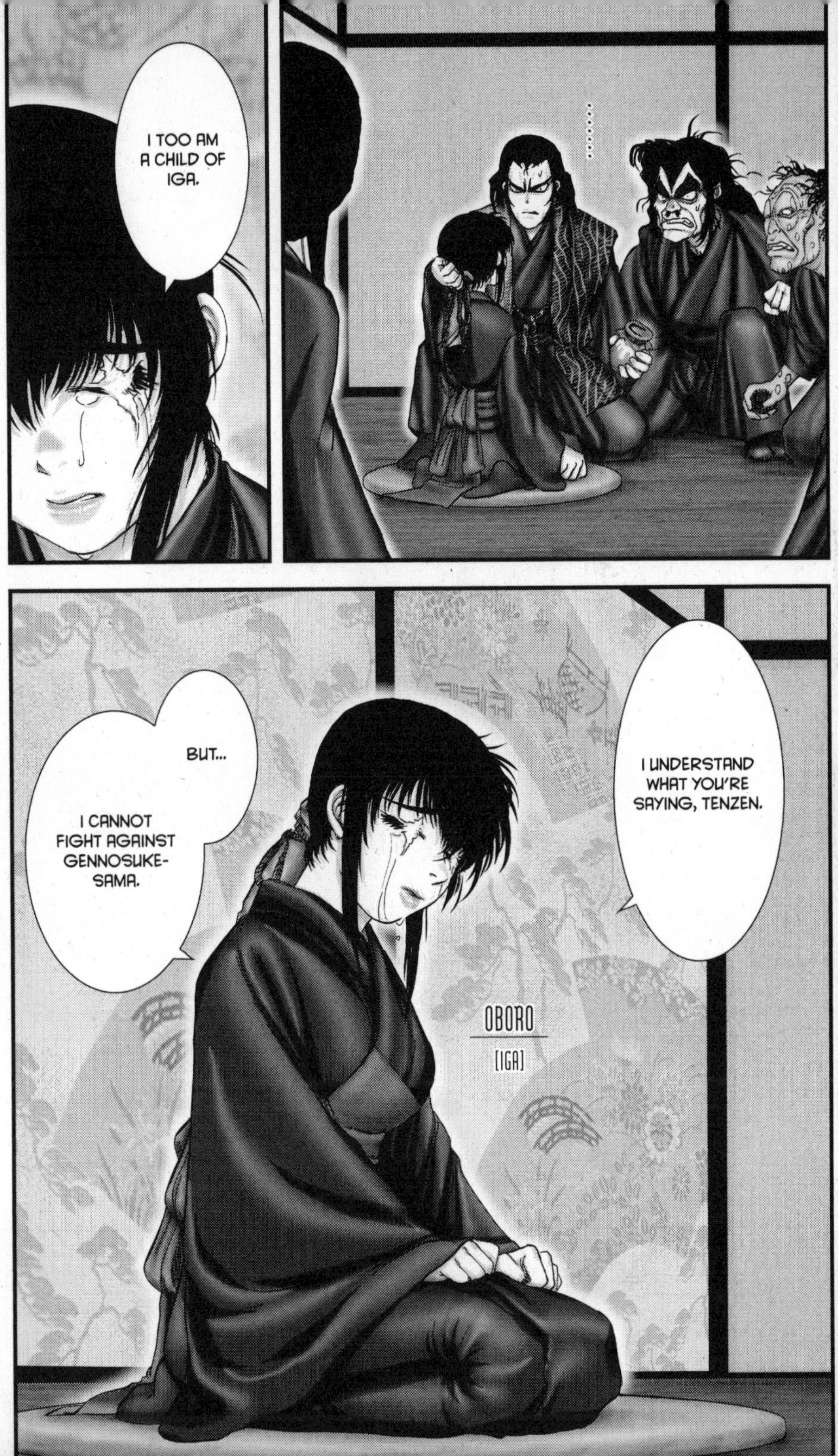
....
I TOO AM A CHILD OF IGA.
I UNDERSTAND WHAT YOU'RE SAYING, TENZEN.
BUT...
I CANNOT FIGHT AGAINST GENNOSUKE-SAMA.
OBORO
[IGA]

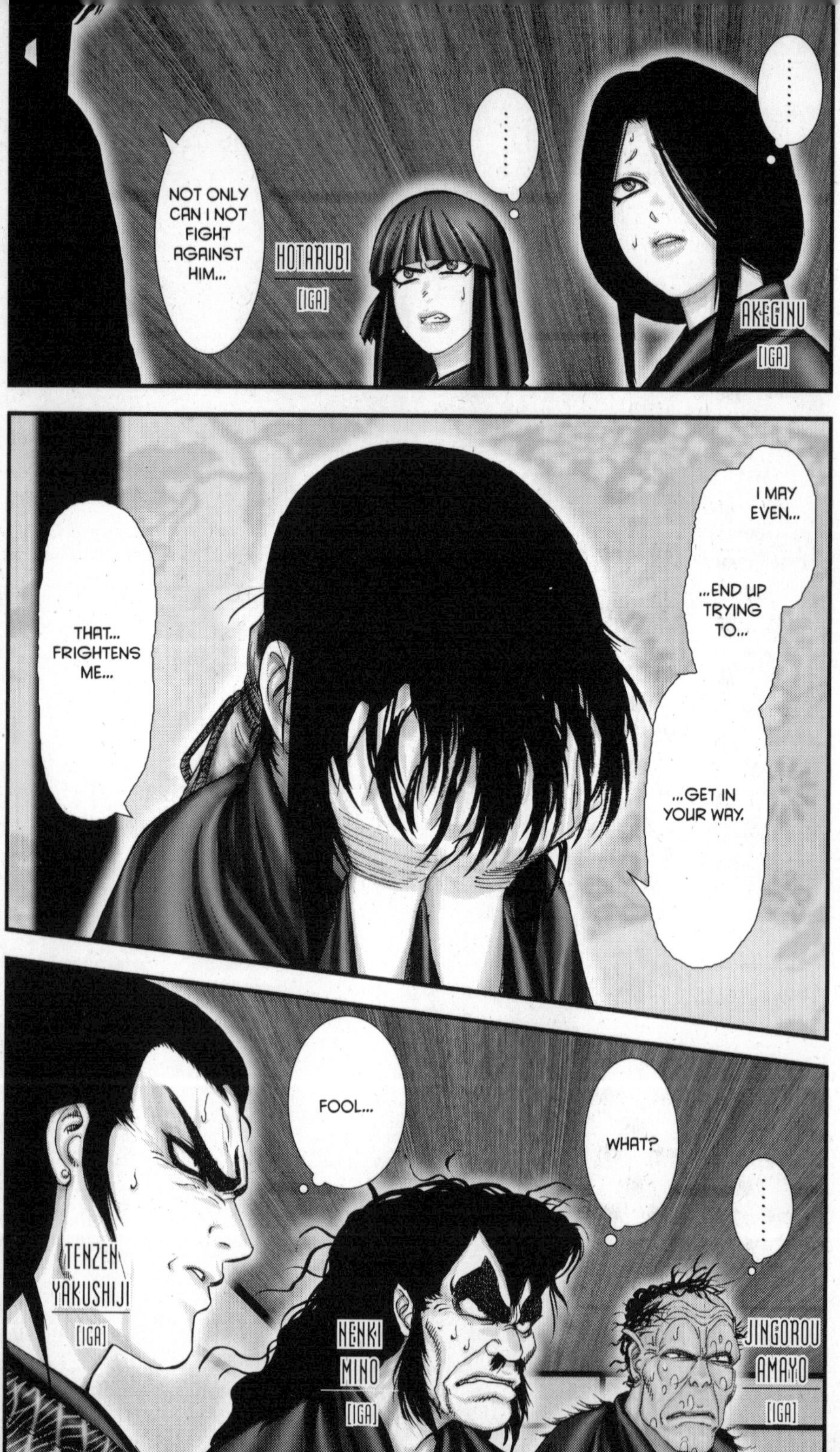
......
......
NOT ONLY CAN I NOT FIGHT AGAINST HIM...
AKEGINU
[IGA]
HOTARUBI
[IGA]
I MAY EVEN...
...END UP TRYING TO...
...GET IN YOUR WAY.
THAT... FRIGHTENS ME...
......
WHAT?
FOOL...
JINGOROU AMAYO
[IGA]
NENKI MINO
[IGA]
TENZEN YAKUSHIJI
[IGA]

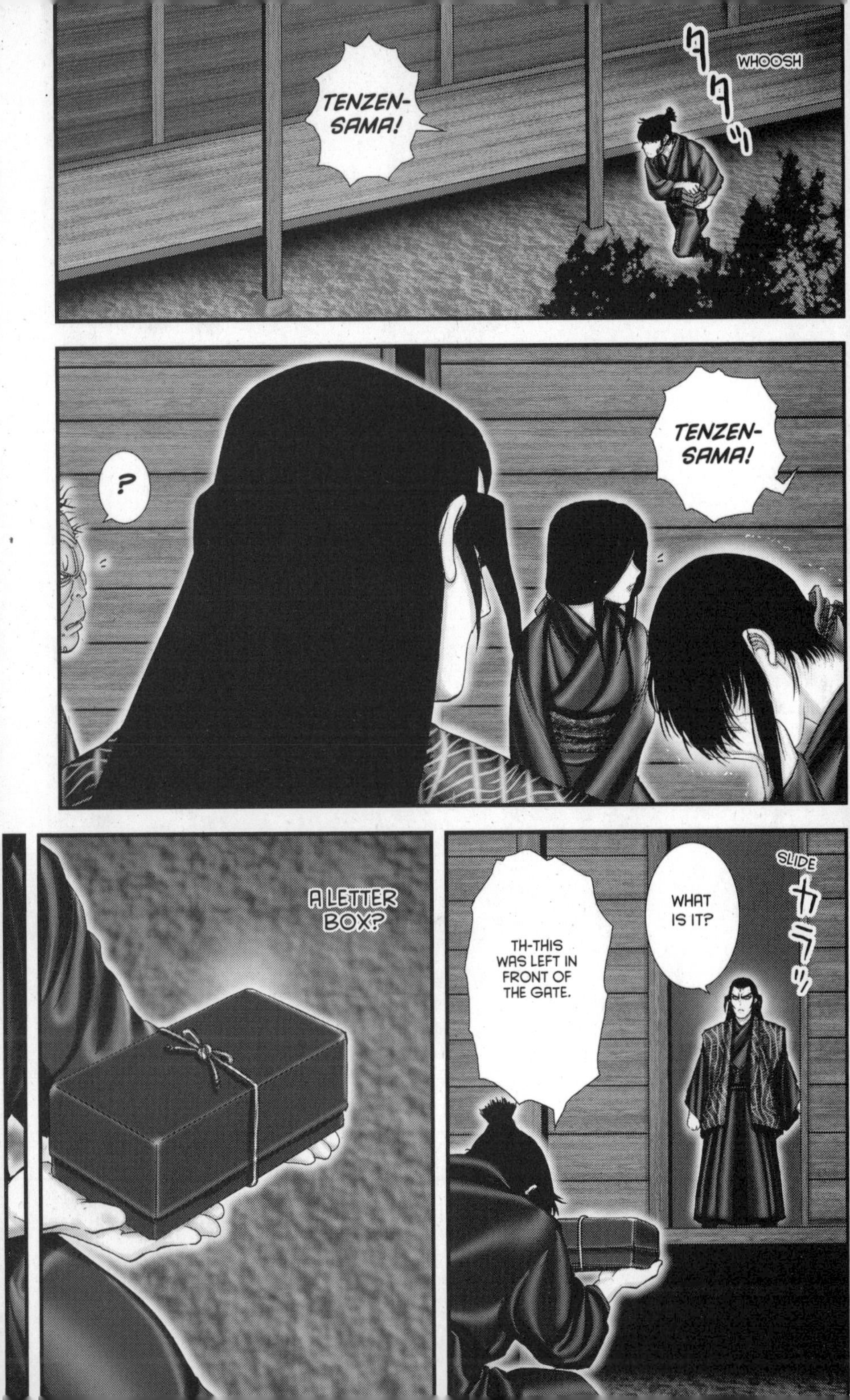
WHOOSH
TENZEN-SAMA!
TENZEN-SAMA!
?
SLIDE
WHAT IS IT?
TH-THIS WAS LEFT IN FRONT OF THE GATE.
A LETTER BOX?

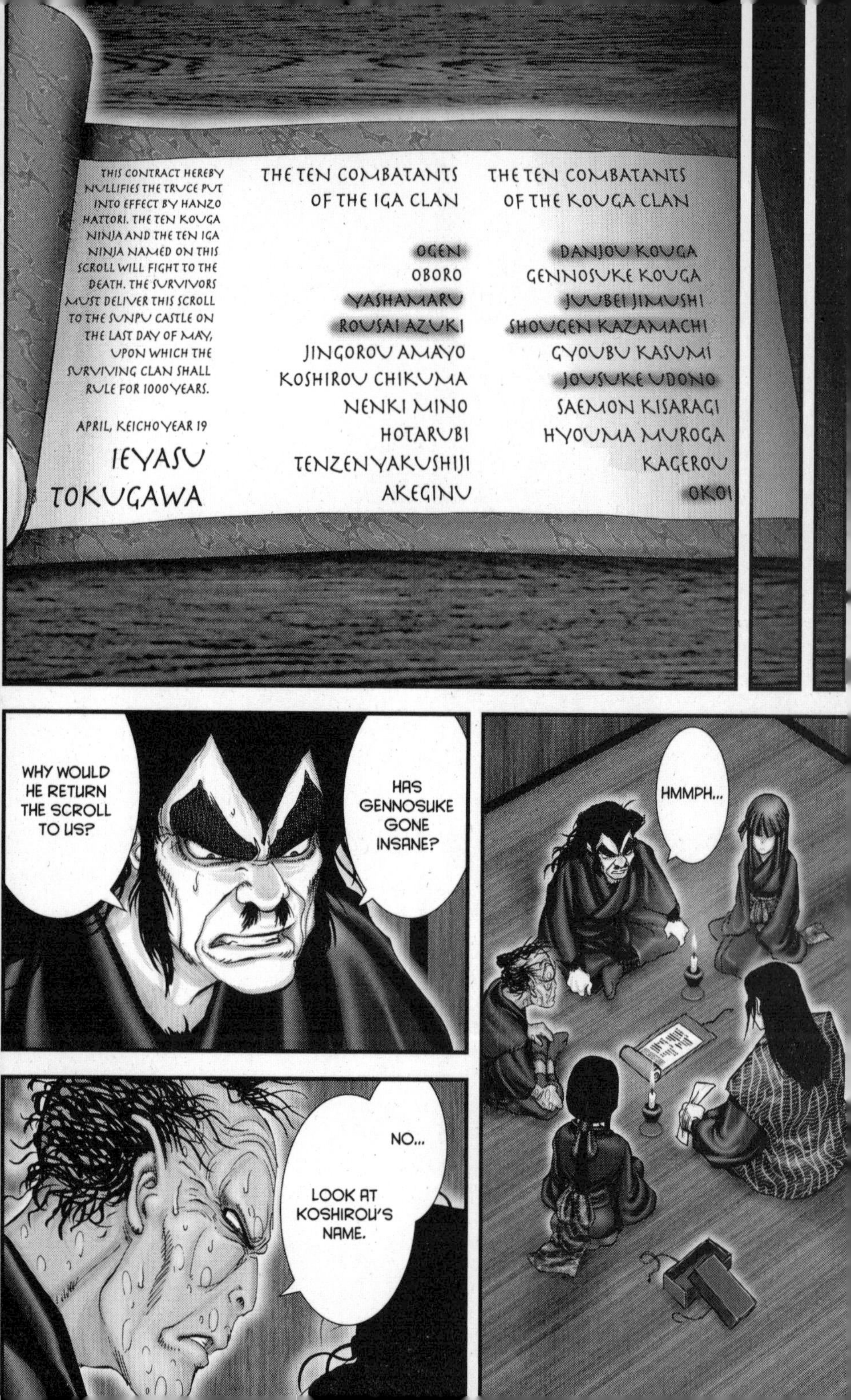
THE TEN COMBATANTS OF THE KOUGA CLAN
DANJOU KOUGA
GENNOSUKE KOUGA
JUUBEI JIMUSHI
SHOUGEN KAZAMACHI
GYOUBU KASUMI
JOUSUKE UDONO
SAEMON KISARAGI
HYOUMA MUROGA
KAGEROU
OKOI
THE TEN COMBATANTS OF THE IGA CLAN
OGEN
OBORO
YASHAMARU
ROUSAI AZUKI
JINGOROU AMAYO
KOSHIROU CHIKUMA
NENKI MINO
HOTARUBI
TENZEN YAKUSHIJI
AKEGINU
THIS CONTRACT HEREBY NULLIFIES THE TRUCE PUT INTO EFFECT BY HANZO HATTORI. THE TEN KOUGA NINJA AND THE TEN IGA NINJA NAMED ON THIS SCROLL WILL FIGHT TO THE DEATH. THE SURVIVORS MUST DELIVER THIS SCROLL TO THE SUNPU CASTLE ON THE LAST DAY OF MAY, UPON WHICH THE SURVIVING CLAN SHALL RULE FOR 1000 YEARS.
APRIL, KEICHO YEAR 19
IEYASU TOKUGAWA
HMMPH...
HAS GENNOSUKE GONE INSANE?
WHY WOULD HE RETURN THE SCROLL TO US?
NO...
LOOK AT KOSHIROU'S NAME.

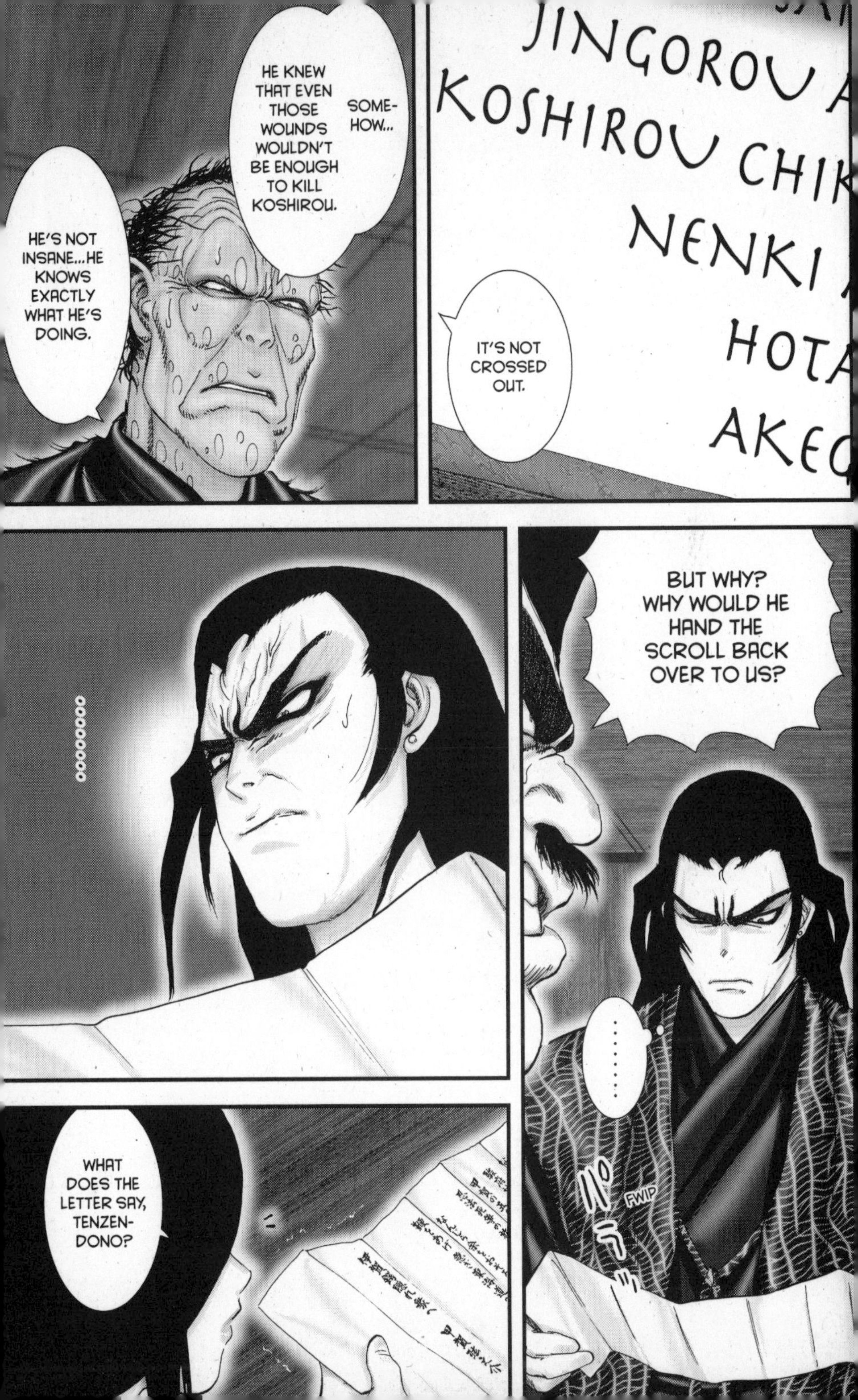
JINGOROU
KOSHIROU CHIK
NENKI
HOTA
AKEG
IT'S NOT CROSSED OUT.
SOME-HOW...
HE KNEW THAT EVEN THOSE WOUNDS WOULDN'T BE ENOUGH TO KILL KOSHIROU.
HE'S NOT INSANE...HE KNOWS EXACTLY WHAT HE'S DOING.
BUT WHY? WHY WOULD HE HAND THE SCROLL BACK OVER TO US?
......
FWIP
WHAT DOES THE LETTER SAY, TENZEN-DONO?

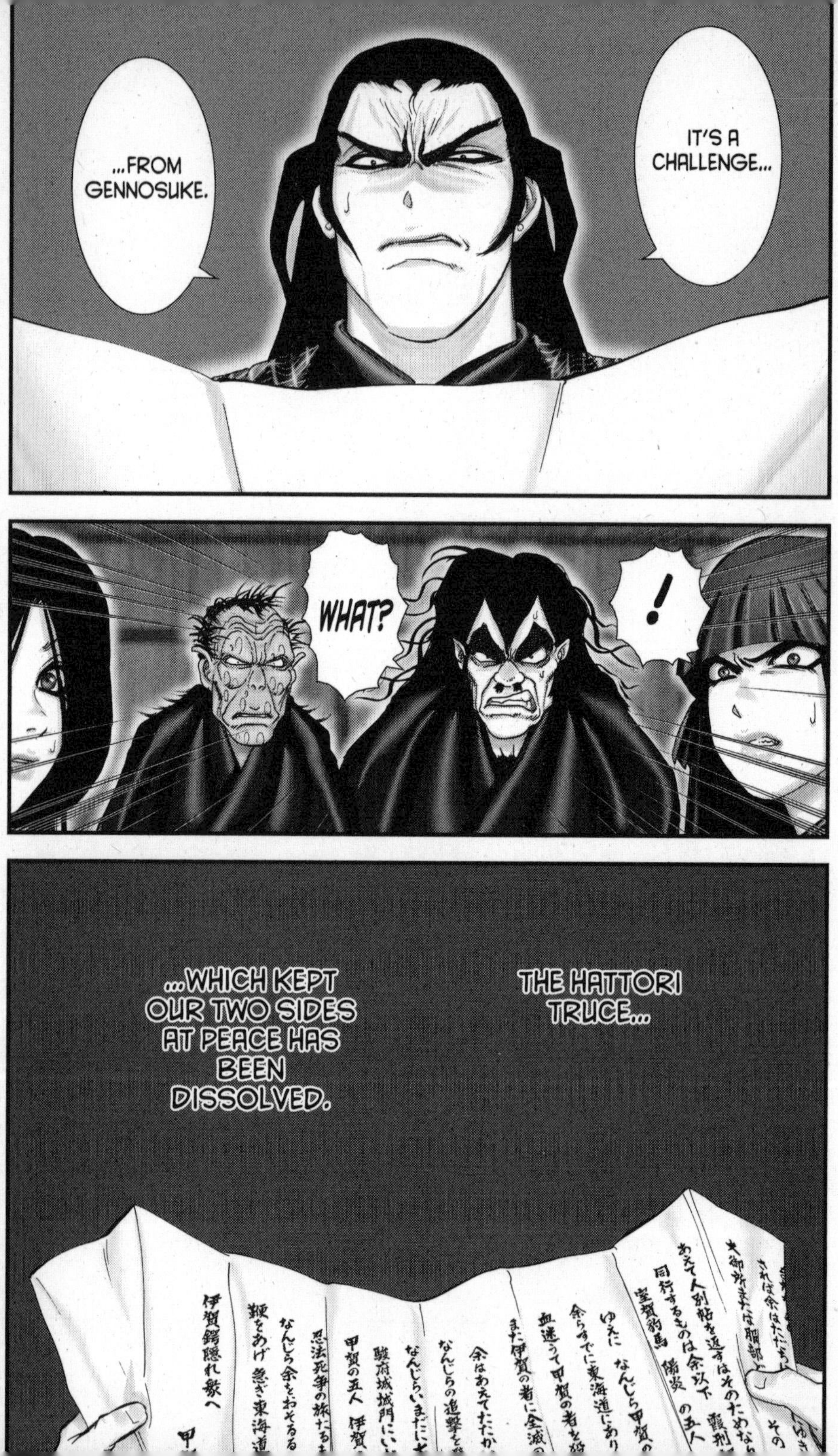
IT'S A CHALLENGE...
...FROM GENNOSUKE.
!
WHAT?
THE HATTORI TRUCE...
...WHICH KEPT OUR TWO SIDES AT PEACE HAS BEEN DISSOLVED.

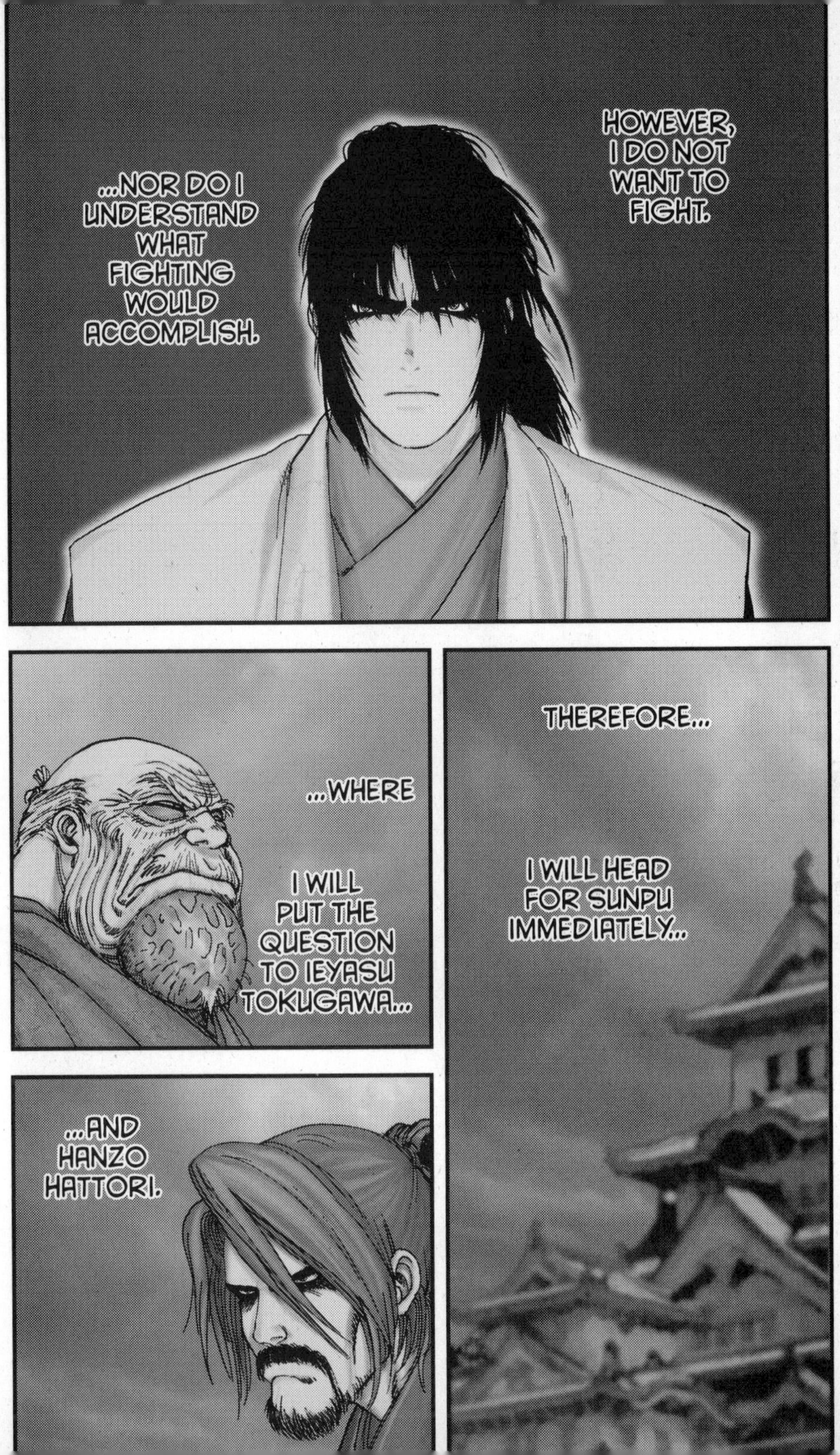
HOWEVER, I DO NOT WANT TO FIGHT.
...NOR DO I UNDERSTAND WHAT FIGHTING WOULD ACCOMPLISH.
THEREFORE...
I WILL HEAD FOR SUNPU IMMEDIATELY...
...WHERE
I WILL PUT THE QUESTION TO IEYASU TOKUGAWA...
...AND HANZO HATTORI.

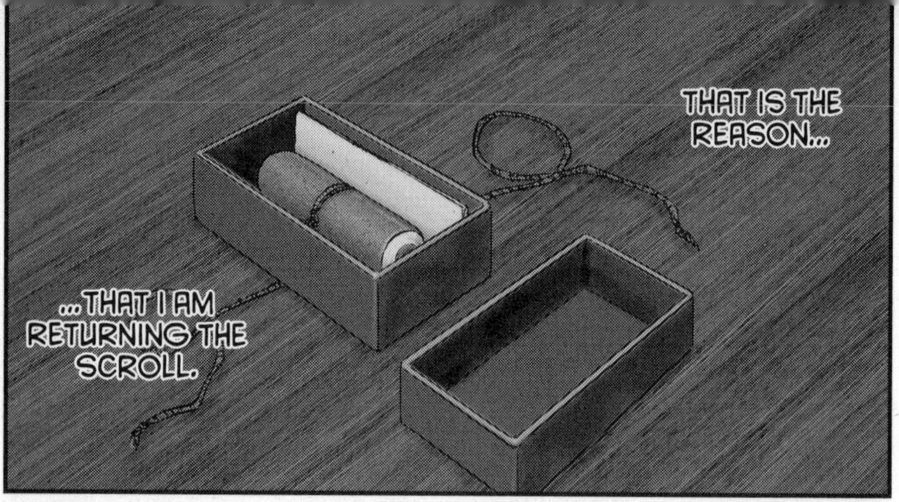
THAT IS THE REASON...
...THAT I AM RETURNING THE SCROLL.
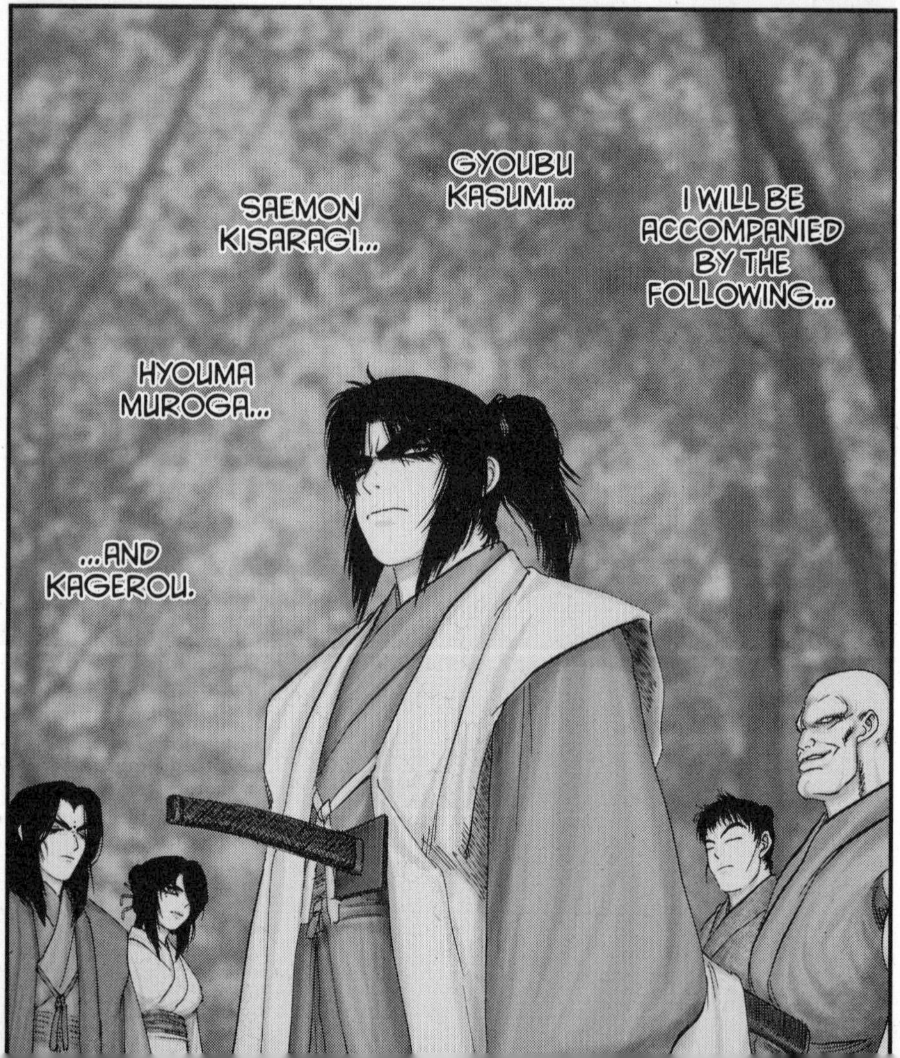
I WILL BE ACCOMPANIED BY THE FOLLOWING...
GYOUBU KASUMI...
SAEMON KISARAGI...
HYOUMA MUROGA...
...AND KAGEROU.

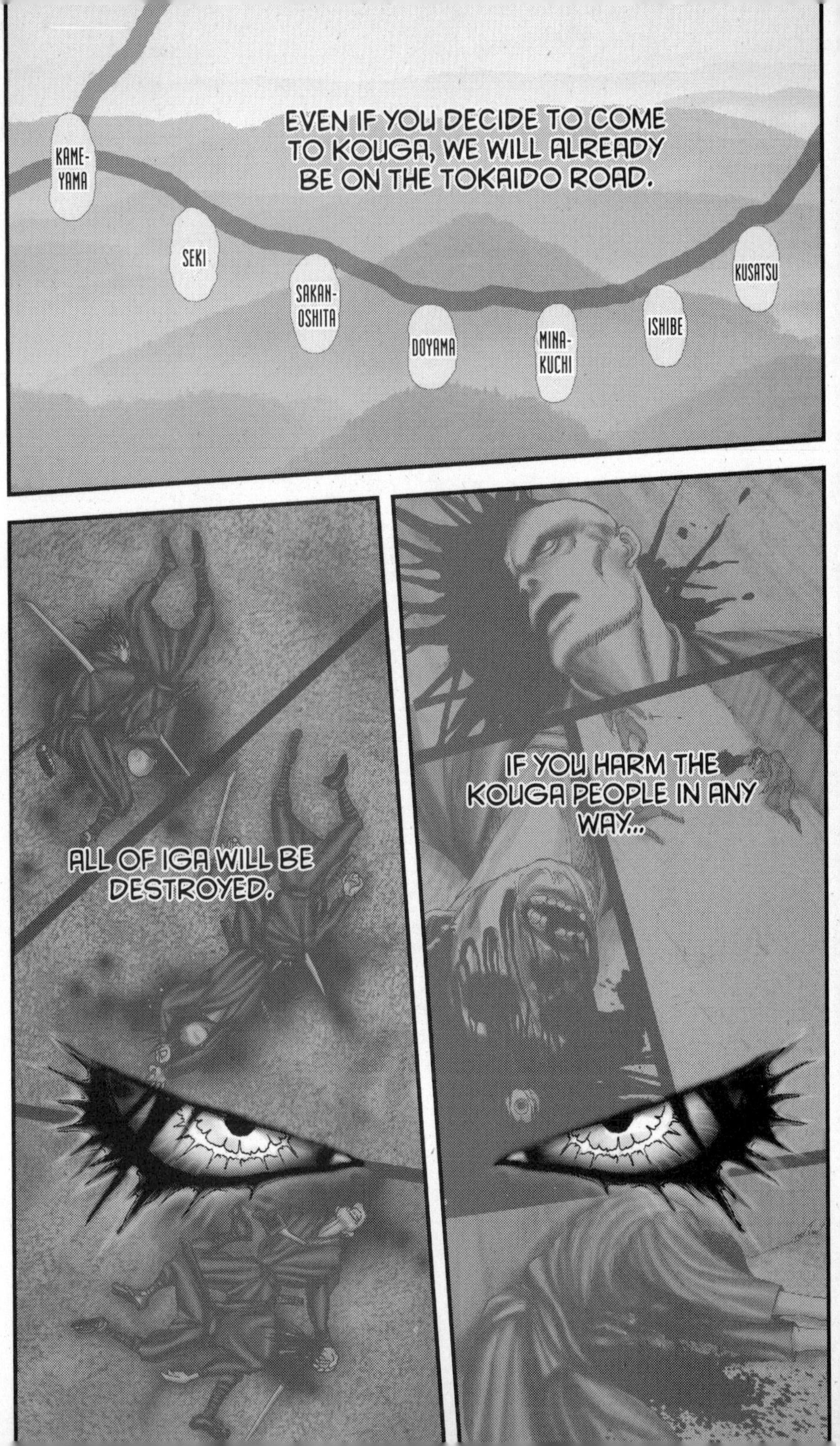
EVEN IF YOU DECIDE TO COME TO KOUGA, WE WILL ALREADY BE ON THE TOKAIDO ROAD.
KUSATSU
ISHIBE
MINA-KUCHI
DOYAMA
SAKAN-OSHITA
SEKI
KAME-YAMA
IF YOU HARM THE KOUGA PEOPLE IN ANY WAY...
ALL OF IGA WILL BE DESTROYED.

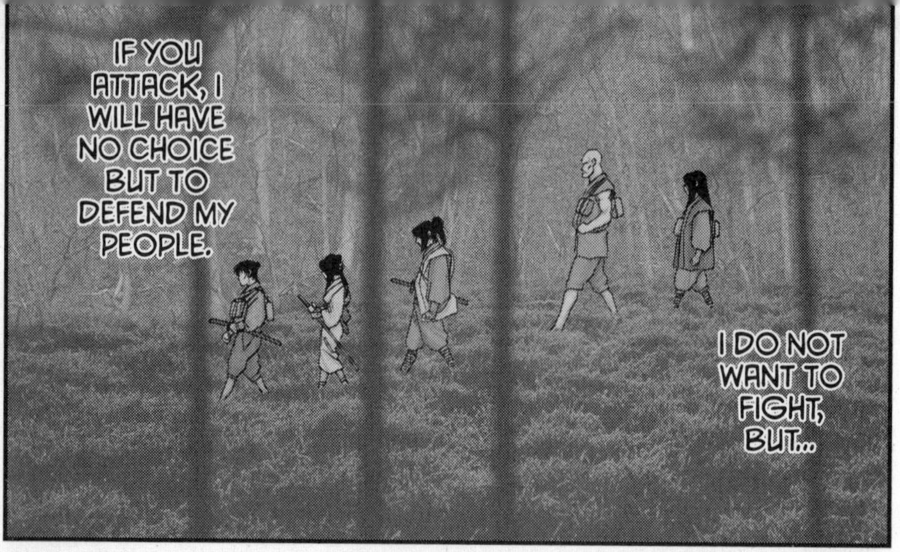
I DO NOT WANT TO FIGHT, BUT...
IF YOU ATTACK, I WILL HAVE NO CHOICE BUT TO DEFEND MY PEOPLE.

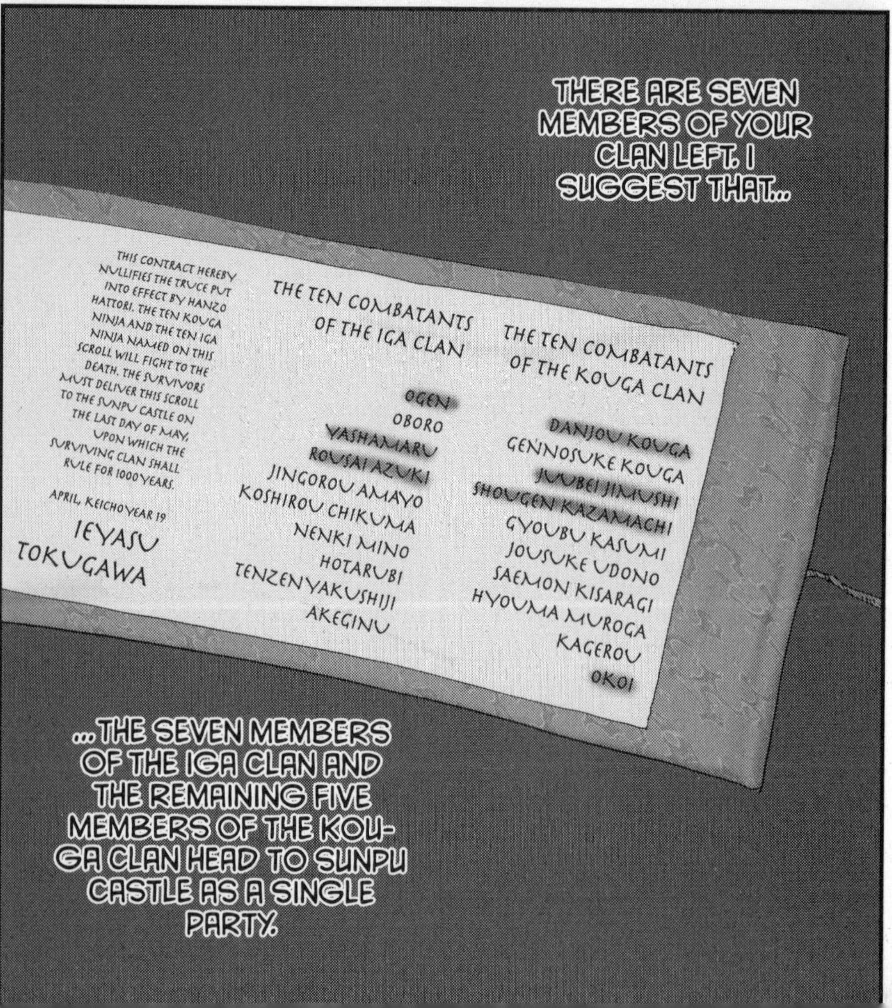
THERE ARE SEVEN MEMBERS OF YOUR CLAN LEFT. I SUGGEST THAT...
THIS CONTRACT HEREBY NULLIFIES THE TRUCE PUT INTO EFFECT BY HANZO HATTORI. THE TEN KOUGA NINJA AND THE TEN IGA NINJA NAMED ON THIS SCROLL WILL FIGHT TO THE DEATH. THE SURVIVORS MUST DELIVER THIS SCROLL TO THE SUNPU CASTLE ON THE LAST DAY OF MAY, UPON WHICH THE SURVIVING CLAN SHALL RULE FOR 1000 YEARS.
APRIL, KEICHO YEAR 19
IEYASU TOKUGAWA
THE TEN COMBATANTS OF THE IGA CLAN
OGEN
OBORO
YASHAMARU
ROUSAI AZUKI
JINGOROU AMAYO
KOSHIROU CHIKUMA
NENKI MINO
HOTARUBI
TENZEN YAKUSHIJI
AKEGINU
THE TEN COMBATANTS OF THE KOUGA CLAN
DANJOU KOUGA
GENNOSUKE KOUGA
JUUBEI JIMUSHI
SHOUGEN KAZAMACHI
GYOUBU KASUMI
JOUSUKE UDONO
SAEMON KISARAGI
HYOUMA MUROGA
KAGEROU
OKOI
...THE SEVEN MEMBERS OF THE IGA CLAN AND THE REMAINING FIVE MEMBERS OF THE KOU-GA CLAN HEAD TO SUNPU CASTLE AS A SINGLE PARTY.

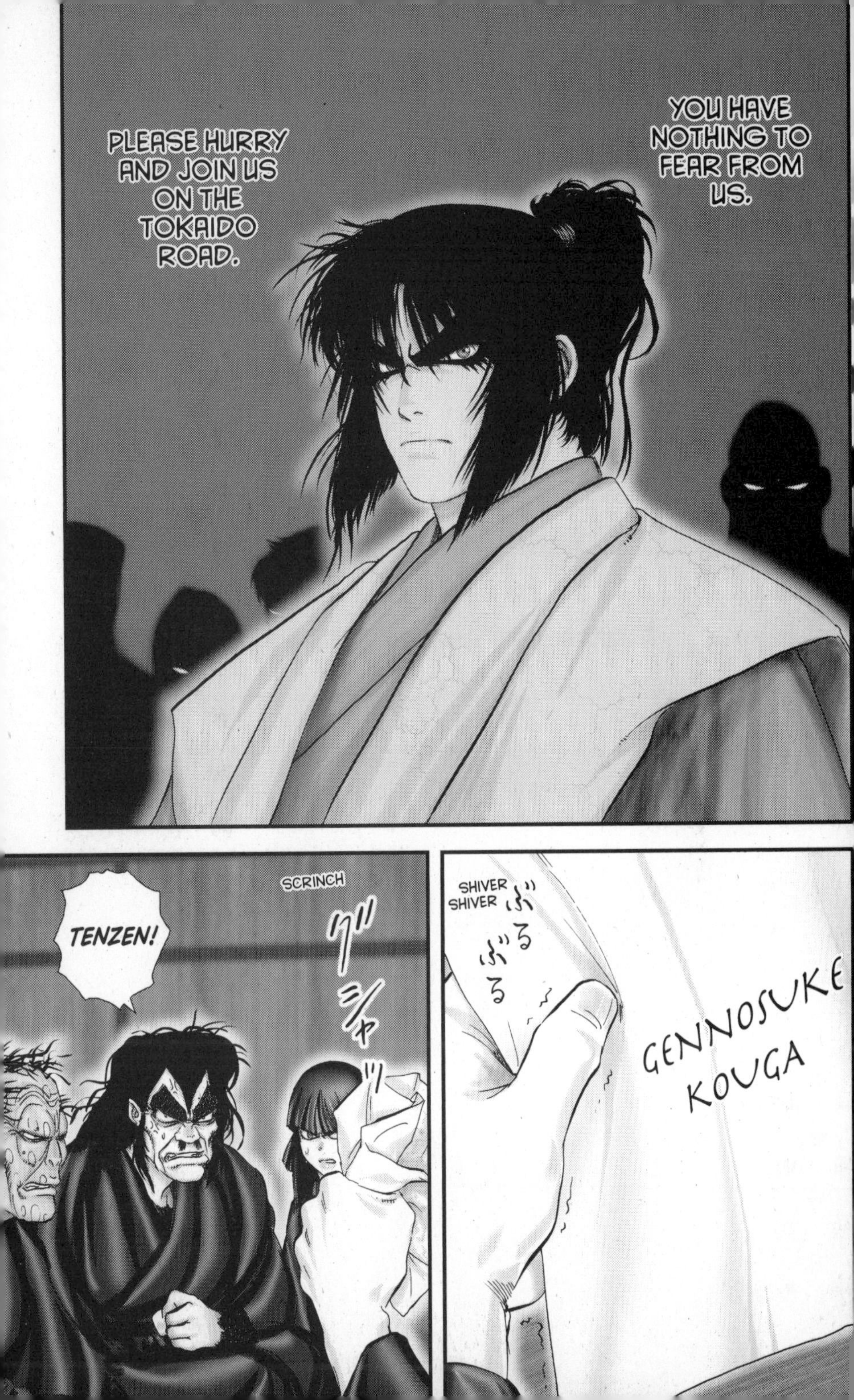
YOU HAVE NOTHING TO FEAR FROM US.
PLEASE HURRY AND JOIN US ON THE TOKAIDO ROAD.
SHIVER SHIVER
ぶるぶるぶる
GENNOSUKE KOUGA
SCRINCH
グシャリ
TENZEN!

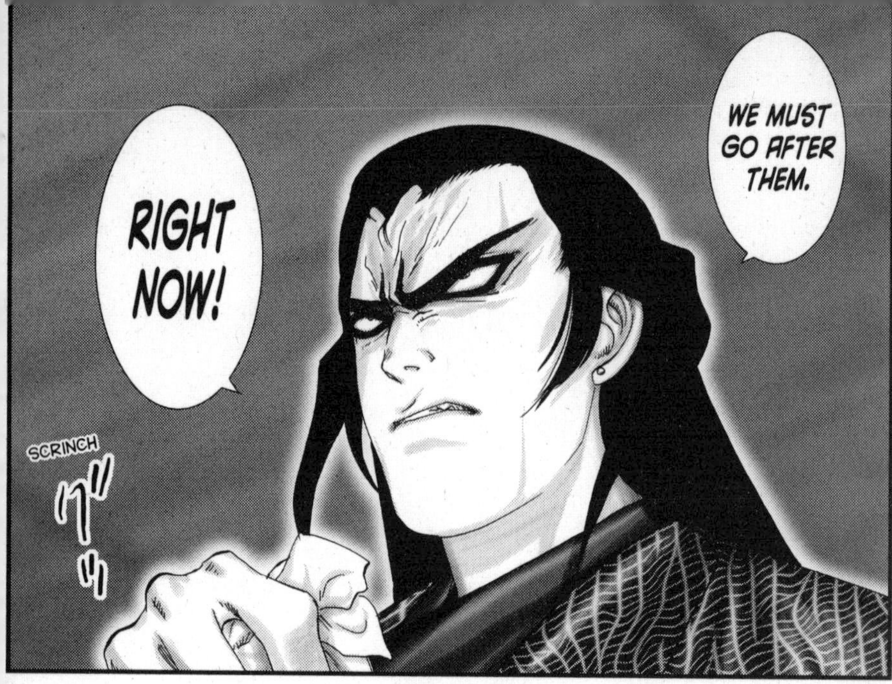
WE MUST GO AFTER THEM.
RIGHT NOW!
SCRINCH

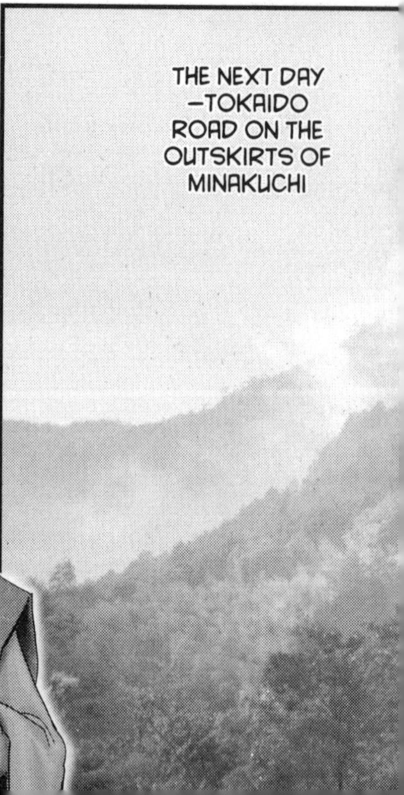
THE NEXT DAY —TOKAIDO ROAD ON THE OUTSKIRTS OF MINAKUCHI

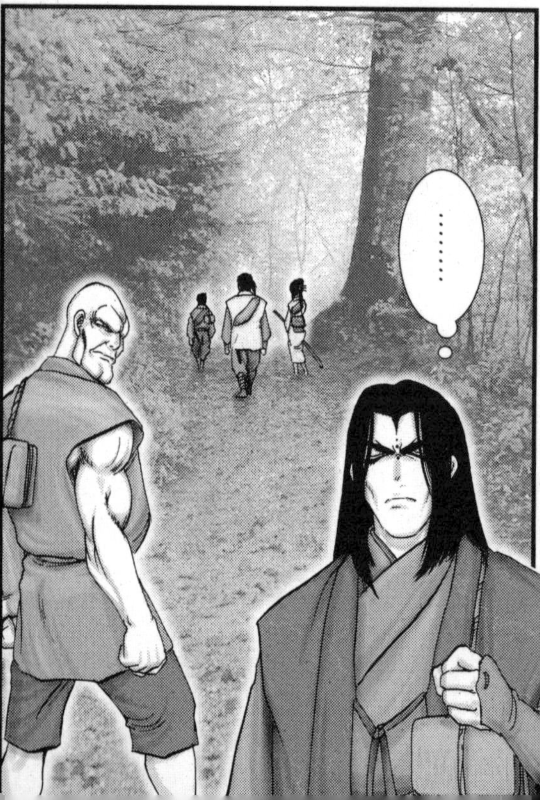
....

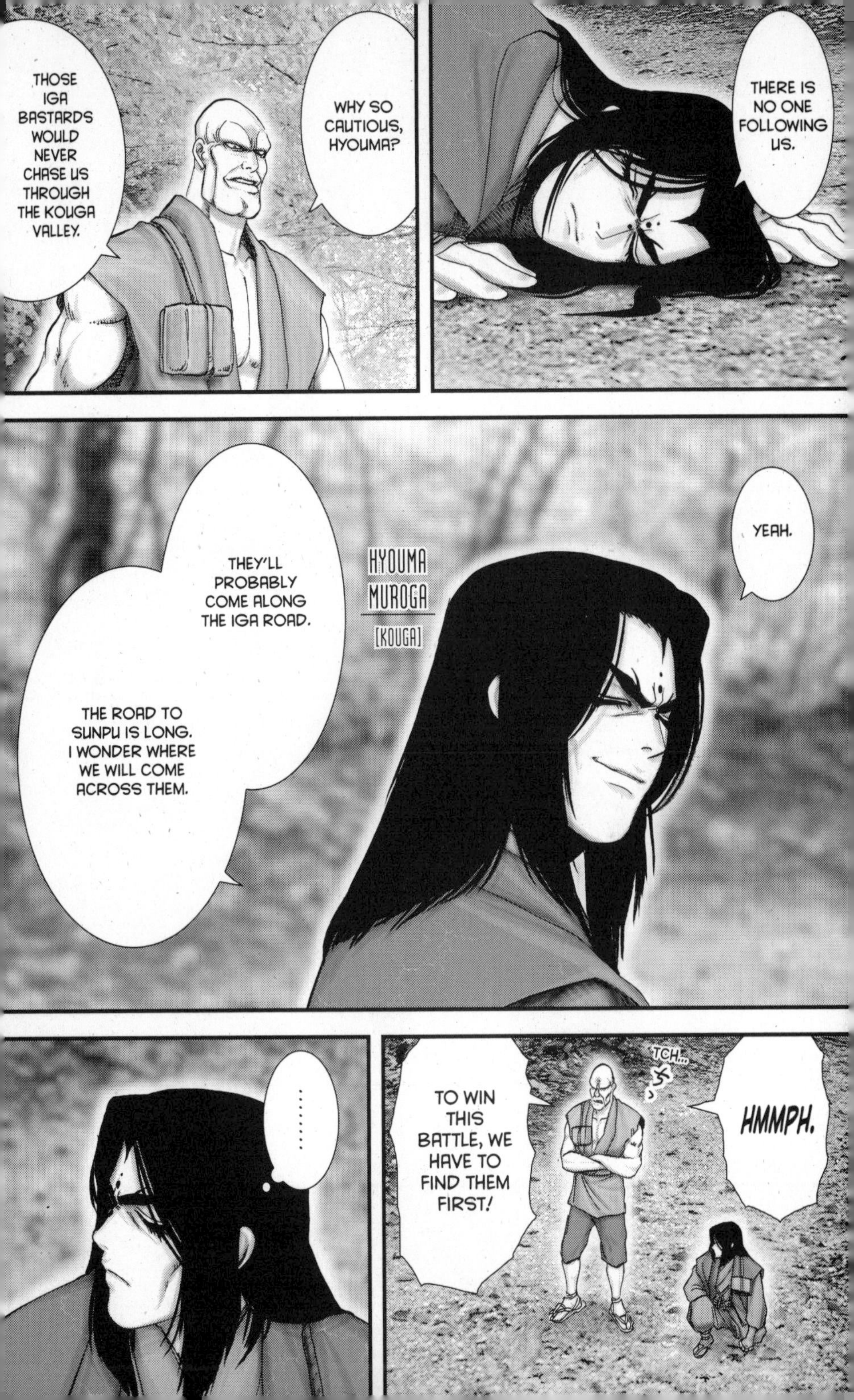
THERE IS NO ONE FOLLOWING US.
WHY SO CAUTIOUS, HYOUMA?
THOSE IGA BASTARDS WOULD NEVER CHASE US THROUGH THE KOUGA VALLEY.
YEAH.
HYOUMA MUROGA
[KOUGA]
THEY'LL PROBABLY COME ALONG THE IGA ROAD.
THE ROAD TO SUNPU IS LONG. I WONDER WHERE WE WILL COME ACROSS THEM.
HMMPH.
TCH...
TO WIN THIS BATTLE, WE HAVE TO FIND THEM FIRST!
......

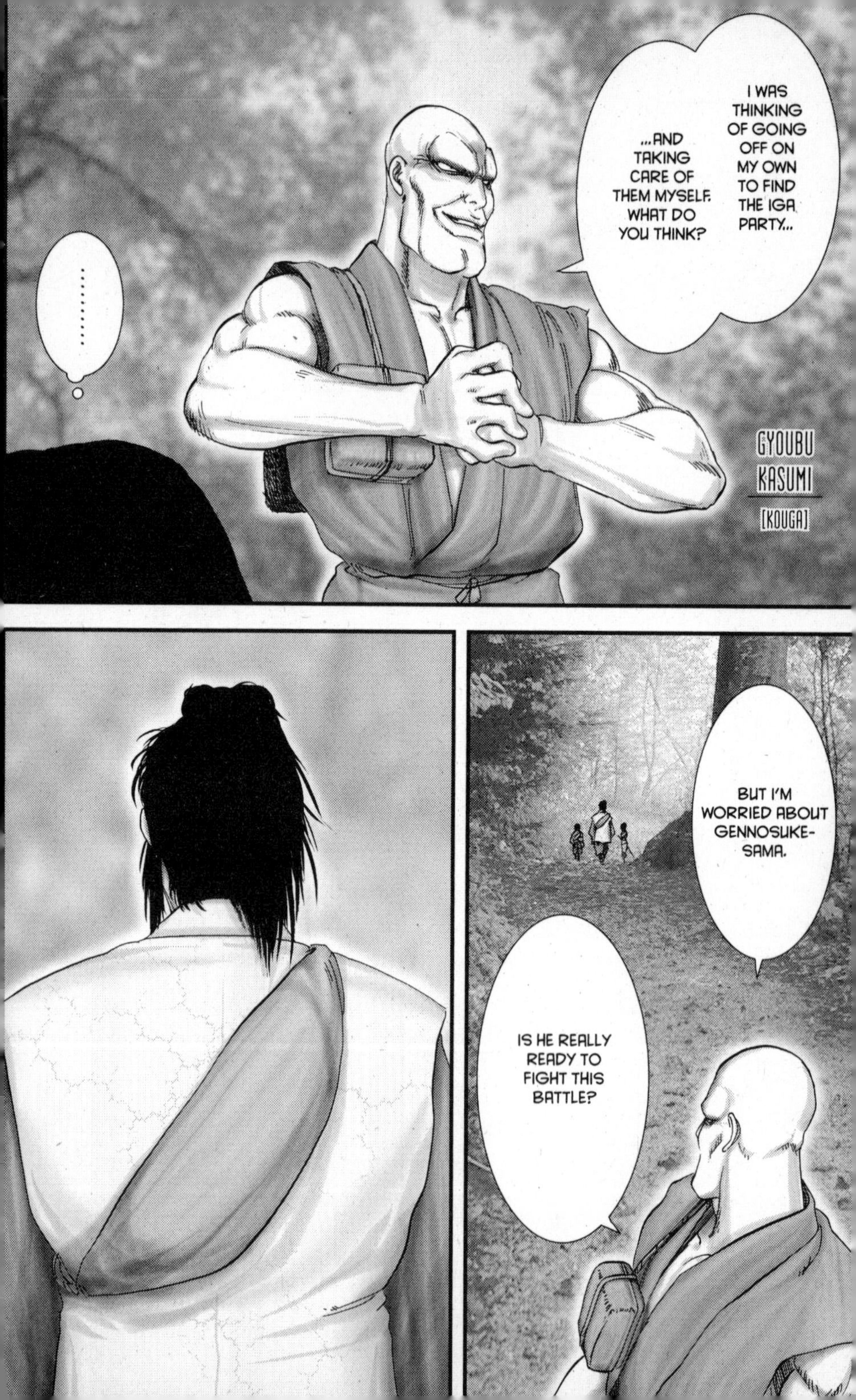
I WAS THINKING OF GOING OFF ON MY OWN TO FIND THE IGA PARTY...
...AND TAKING CARE OF THEM MYSELF. WHAT DO YOU THINK?
......
GYOUBU KASUMI
[KOUGA]
BUT I'M WORRIED ABOUT GENNOSUKE-SAMA.
IS HE REALLY READY TO FIGHT THIS BATTLE?

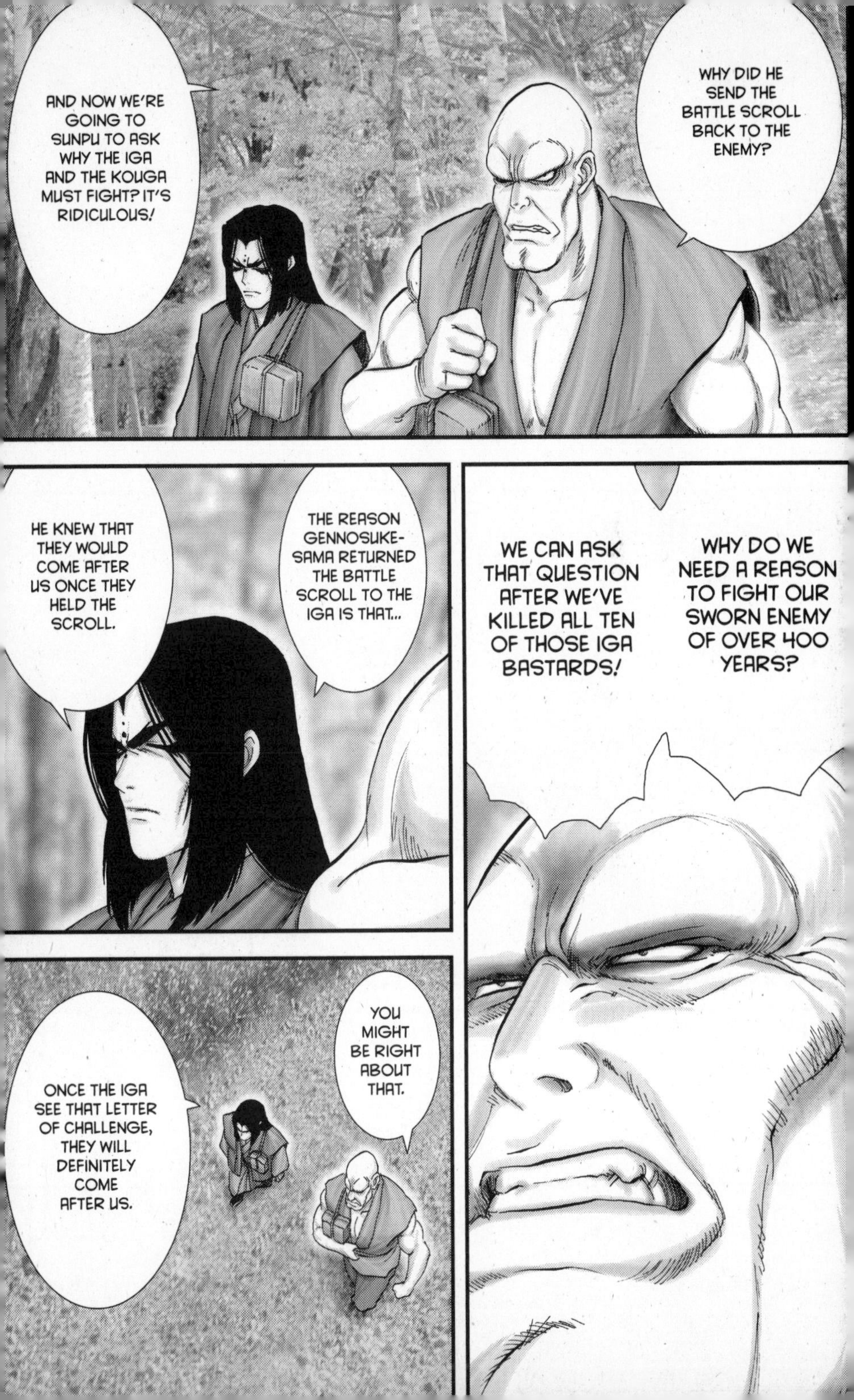
WHY DID HE SEND THE BATTLE SCROLL BACK TO THE ENEMY?
AND NOW WE'RE GOING TO SUNPU TO ASK WHY THE IGA AND THE KOUGA MUST FIGHT? IT'S RIDICULOUS!
WHY DO WE NEED A REASON TO FIGHT OUR SWORN ENEMY OF OVER 400 YEARS?
WE CAN ASK THAT QUESTION AFTER WE'VE KILLED ALL TEN OF THOSE IGA BASTARDS!
THE REASON GENNOSUKE-SAMA RETURNED THE BATTLE SCROLL TO THE IGA IS THAT...
HE KNEW THAT THEY WOULD COME AFTER US ONCE THEY HELD THE SCROLL.
YOU MIGHT BE RIGHT ABOUT THAT.
ONCE THE IGA SEE THAT LETTER OF CHALLENGE, THEY WILL DEFINITELY COME AFTER US.

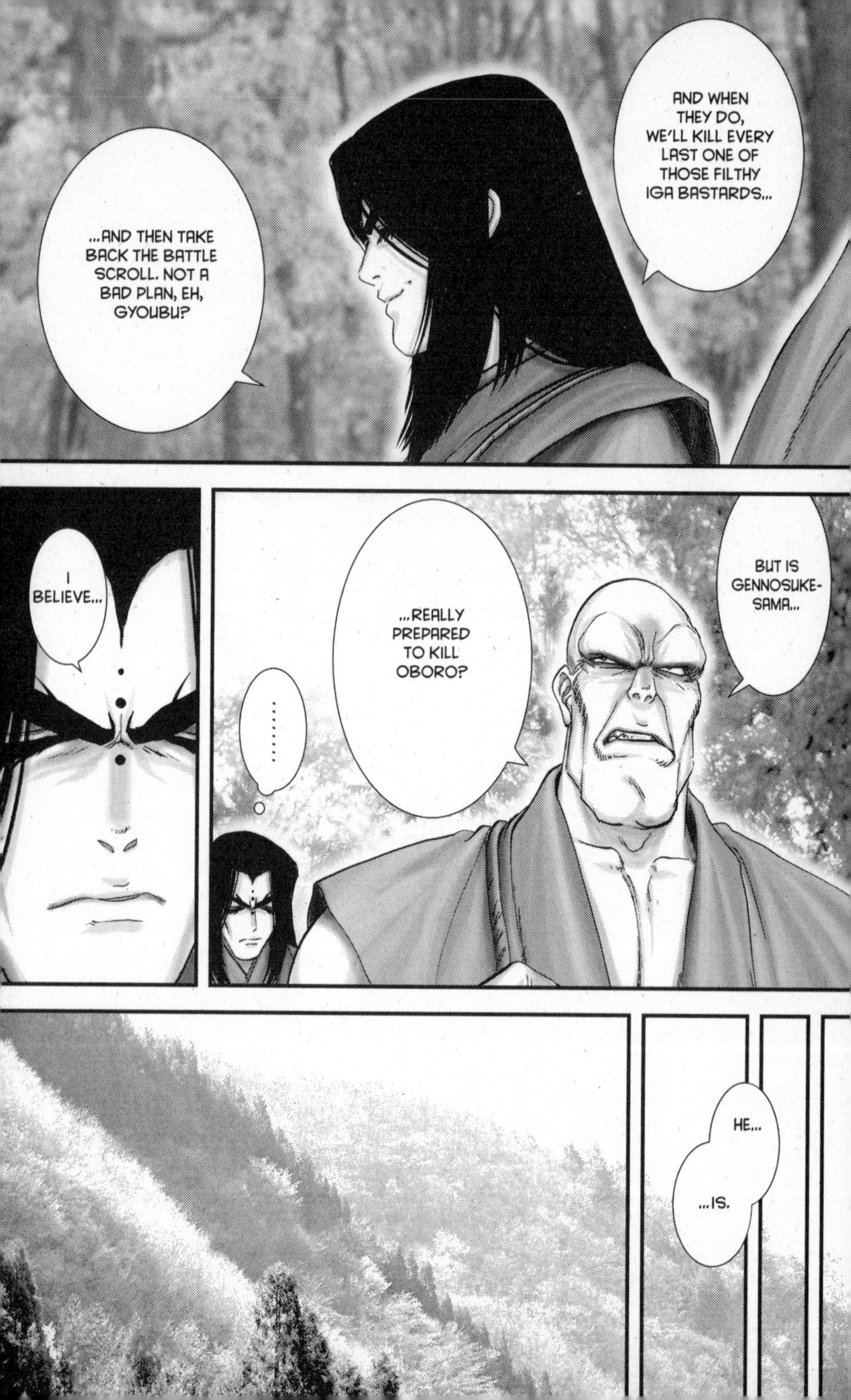
AND WHEN THEY DO, WE'LL KILL EVERY LAST ONE OF THOSE FILTHY IGA BASTARDS...
...AND THEN TAKE BACK THE BATTLE SCROLL. NOT A BAD PLAN, EH, GYOUBU?
BUT IS GENNOSUKE-SAMA...
...REALLY PREPARED TO KILL OBORO?
......
I BELIEVE...
HE...
...IS.

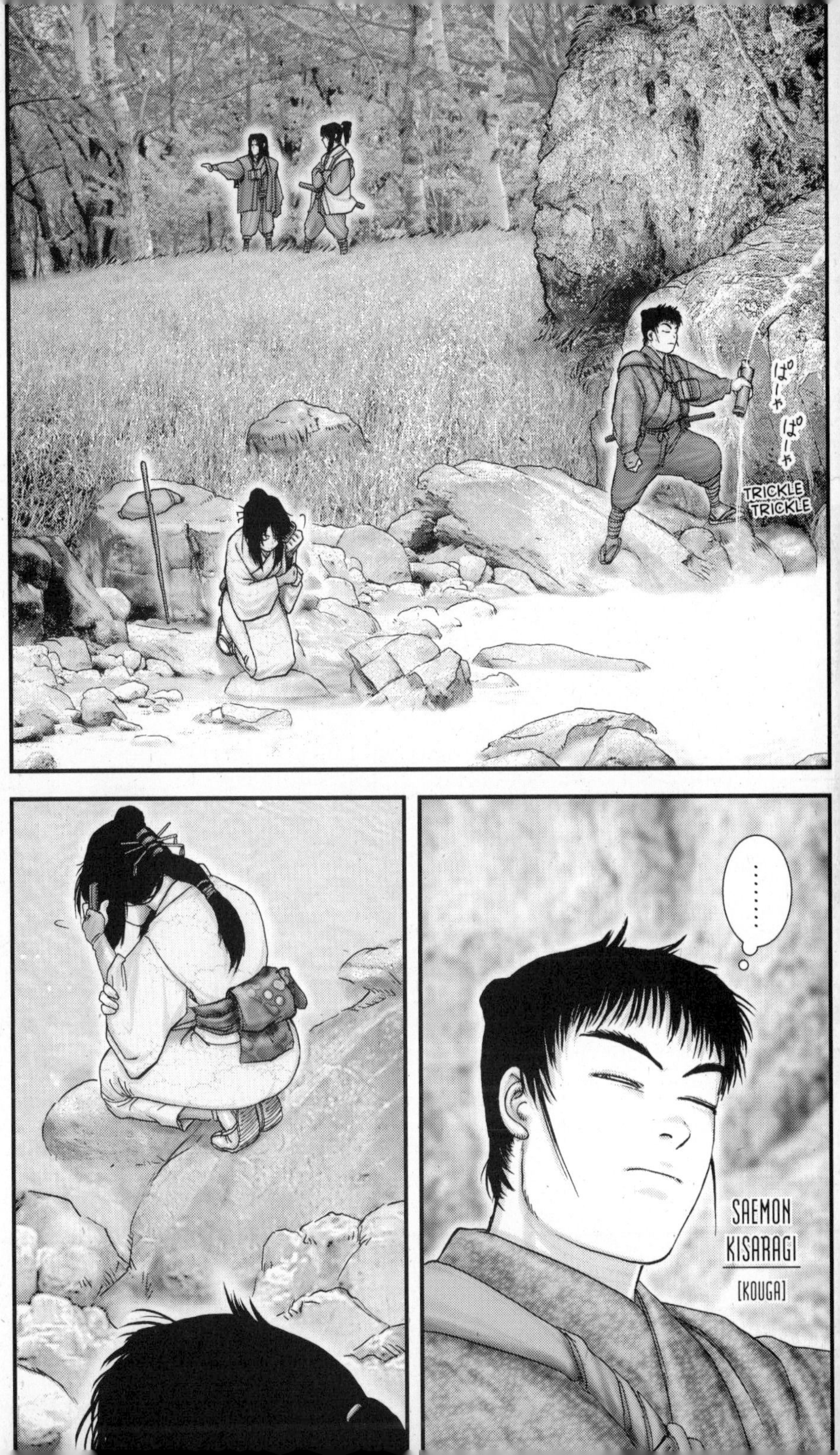
ぱーゃ ぱーゃ
TRICKLE TRICKLE
......
SAEMON KISARAGI
[KOUGA]

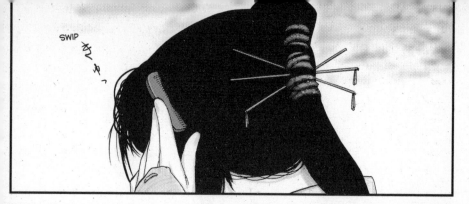

SWIP

KAGEROU
[KOUGA]

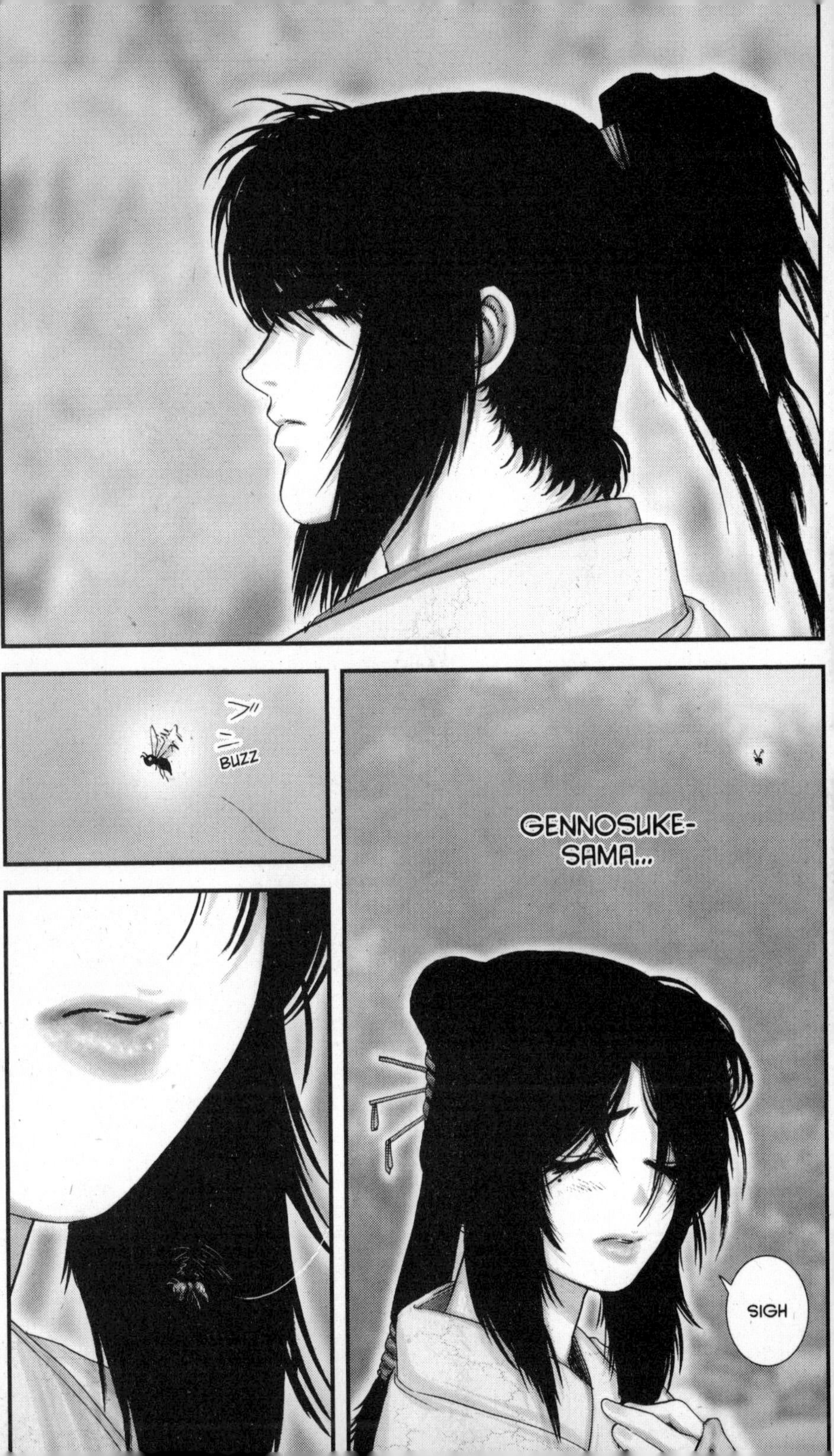
GENNOSUKE-SAMA...
SIGH
BUZZ

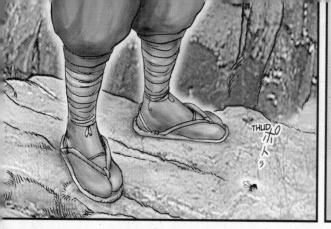

FWISH
スラッ・・
THUD
ポトッ
TRICKLE TRICKLE
ぱしゃ ぱしゃ
......
I HAVEN'T SEEN GYOUBU FOR A WHILE.
WHAT HAPPENED TO HIM?

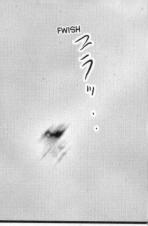

MAYBE HE MELTED INTO THE SHADOWS AGAIN...

WHAT?

HE ISN'T HERE?

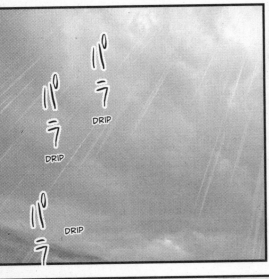

パラ DRIP

パラ DRIP

パラ DRIP

DRIP

HUH?

YOU WENT OFF ON YOUR OWN, DIDN'T YOU, GYOUBU?

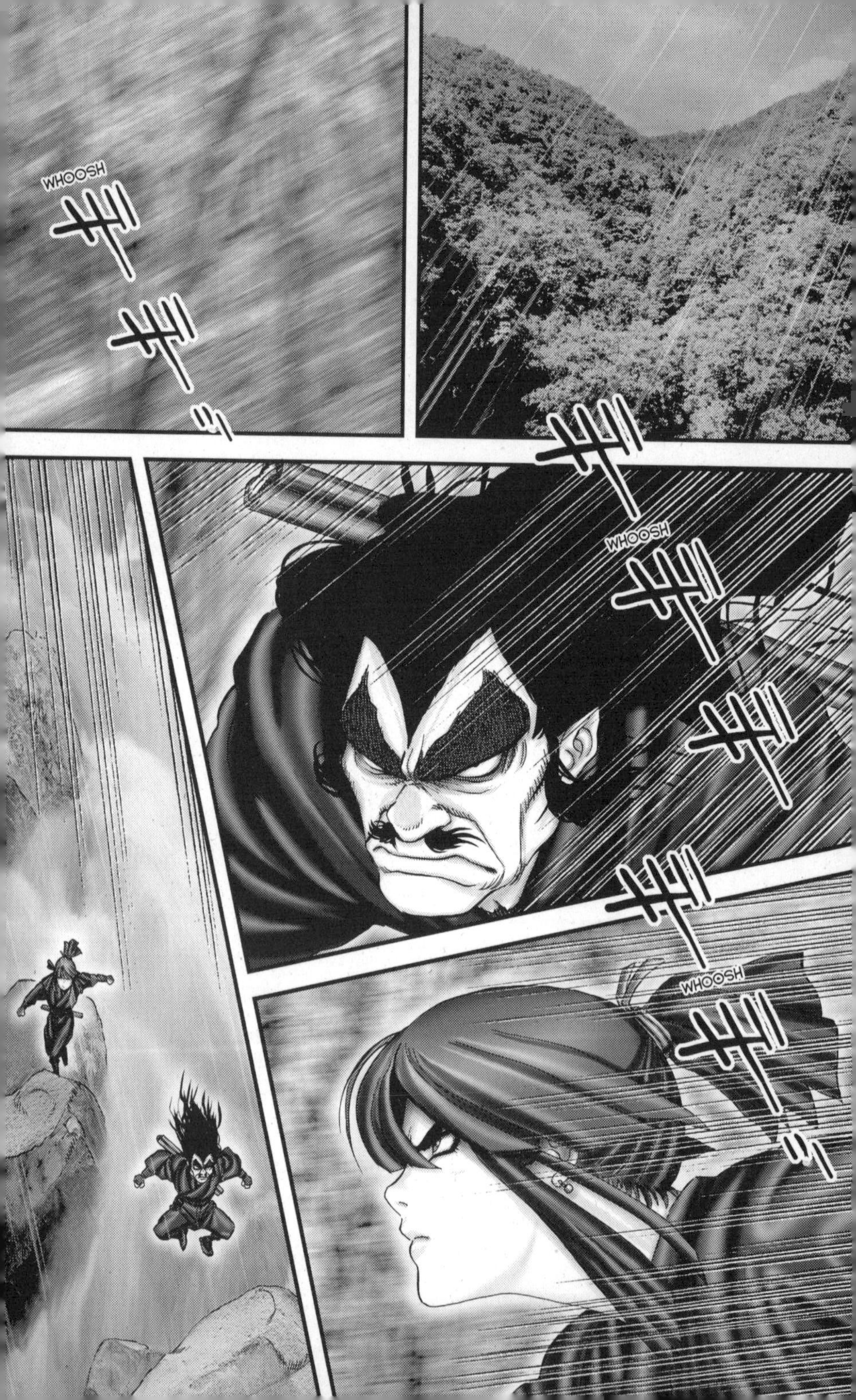
WHOOSH
WHOOSH
WHOOSH

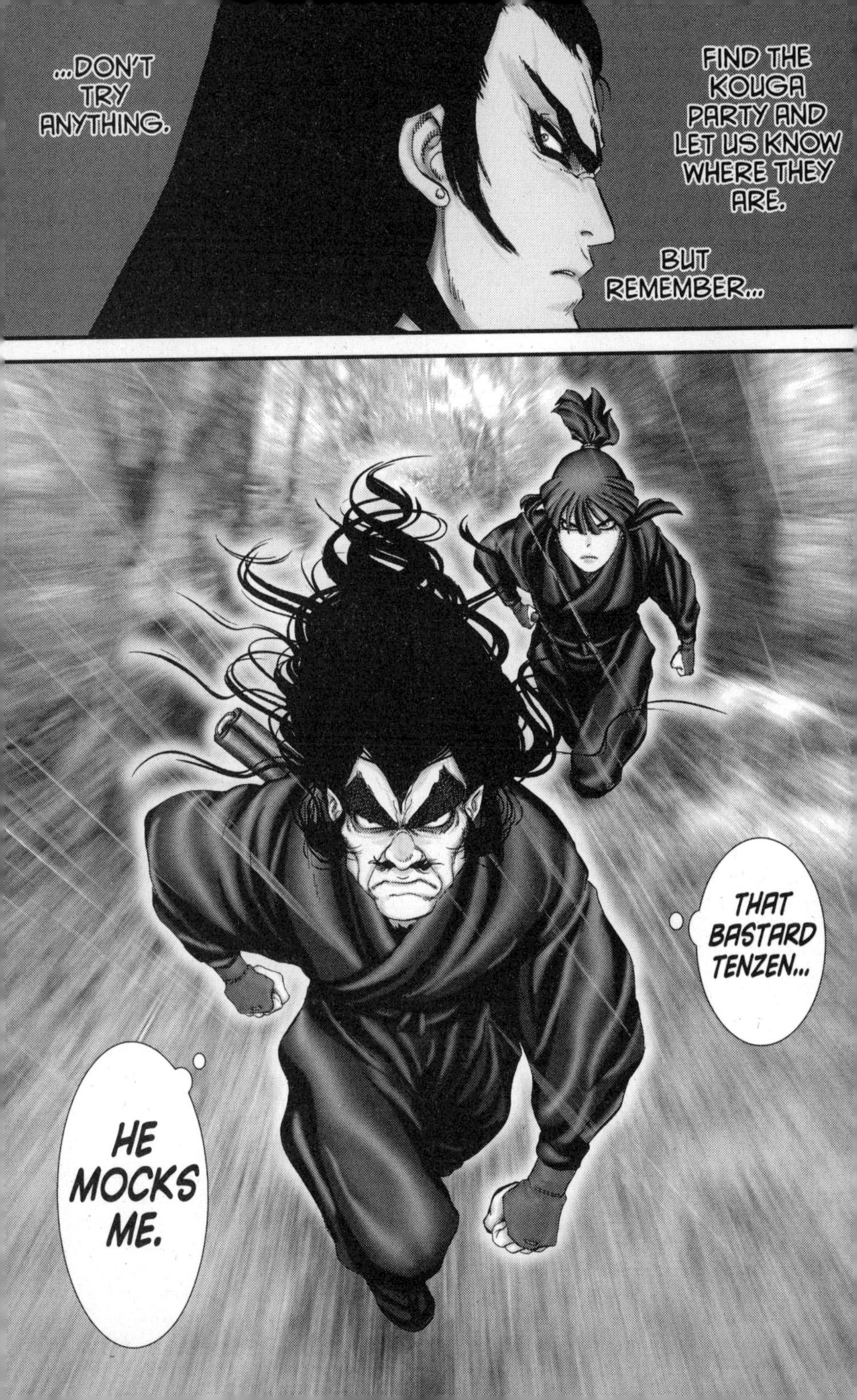
FIND THE KOUGA PARTY AND LET US KNOW WHERE THEY ARE.
BUT REMEMBER...
...DON'T TRY ANYTHING.
THAT BASTARD TENZEN...
HE MOCKS ME.

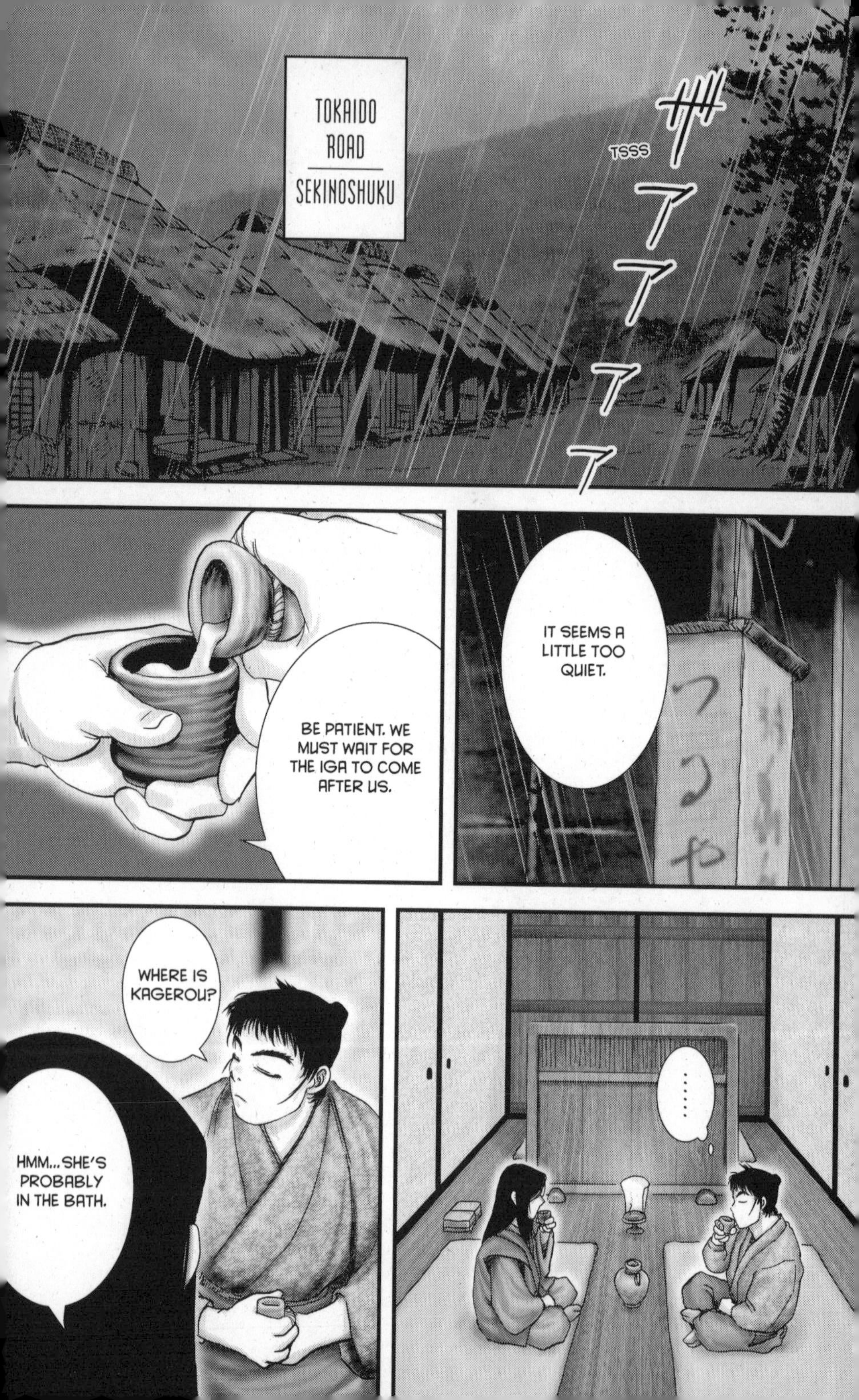
TOKAIDO ROAD
SEKINOSHUKU
ザァァァァ
TSSS
IT SEEMS A LITTLE TOO QUIET.
BE PATIENT. WE MUST WAIT FOR THE IGA TO COME AFTER US.
......
WHERE IS KAGEROU?
HMM...SHE'S PROBABLY IN THE BATH.

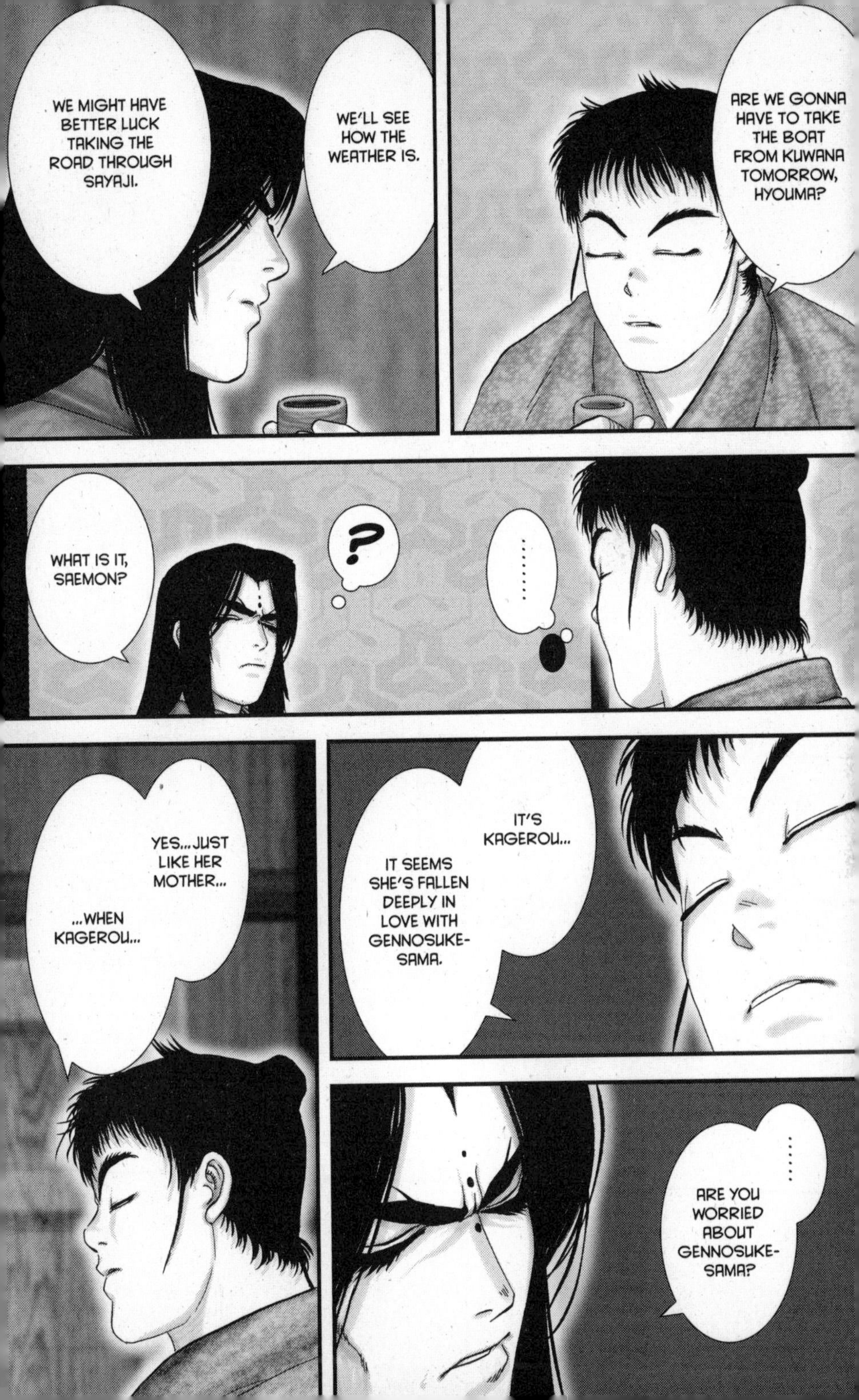
ARE WE GONNA HAVE TO TAKE THE BOAT FROM KUWANA TOMORROW, HYOUMA?
WE'LL SEE HOW THE WEATHER IS.
WE MIGHT HAVE BETTER LUCK TAKING THE ROAD THROUGH SAYAJI.
......
?
WHAT IS IT, SAEMON?
IT'S KAGEROU...
IT SEEMS SHE'S FALLEN DEEPLY IN LOVE WITH GENNOSUKE-SAMA.
......
ARE YOU WORRIED ABOUT GENNOSUKE-SAMA?
YES...JUST LIKE HER MOTHER...
...WHEN KAGEROU...

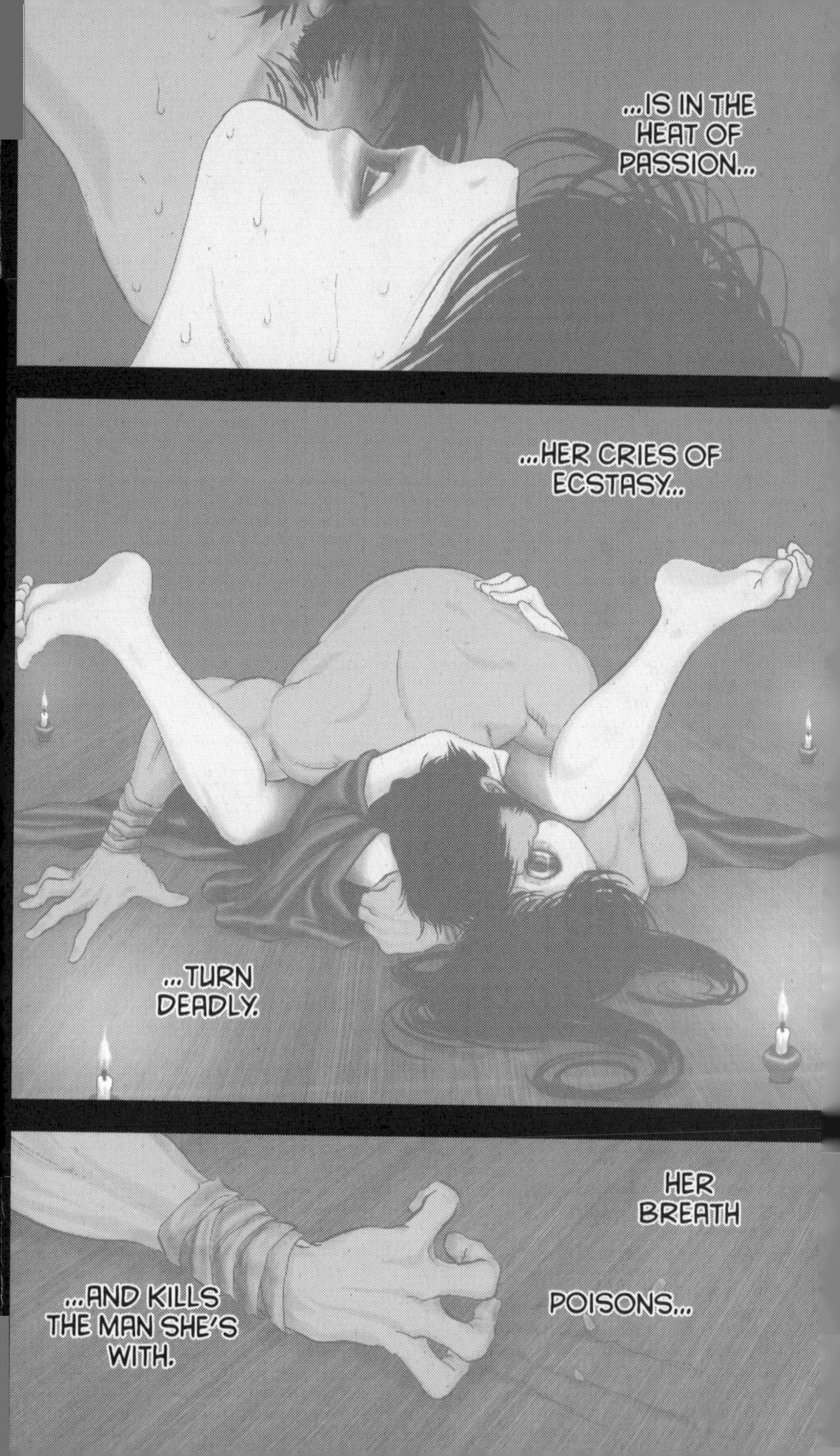
...IS IN THE HEAT OF PASSION...
...HER CRIES OF ECSTASY...
...TURN DEADLY.
HER BREATH
POISONS...
...AND KILLS THE MAN SHE'S WITH.

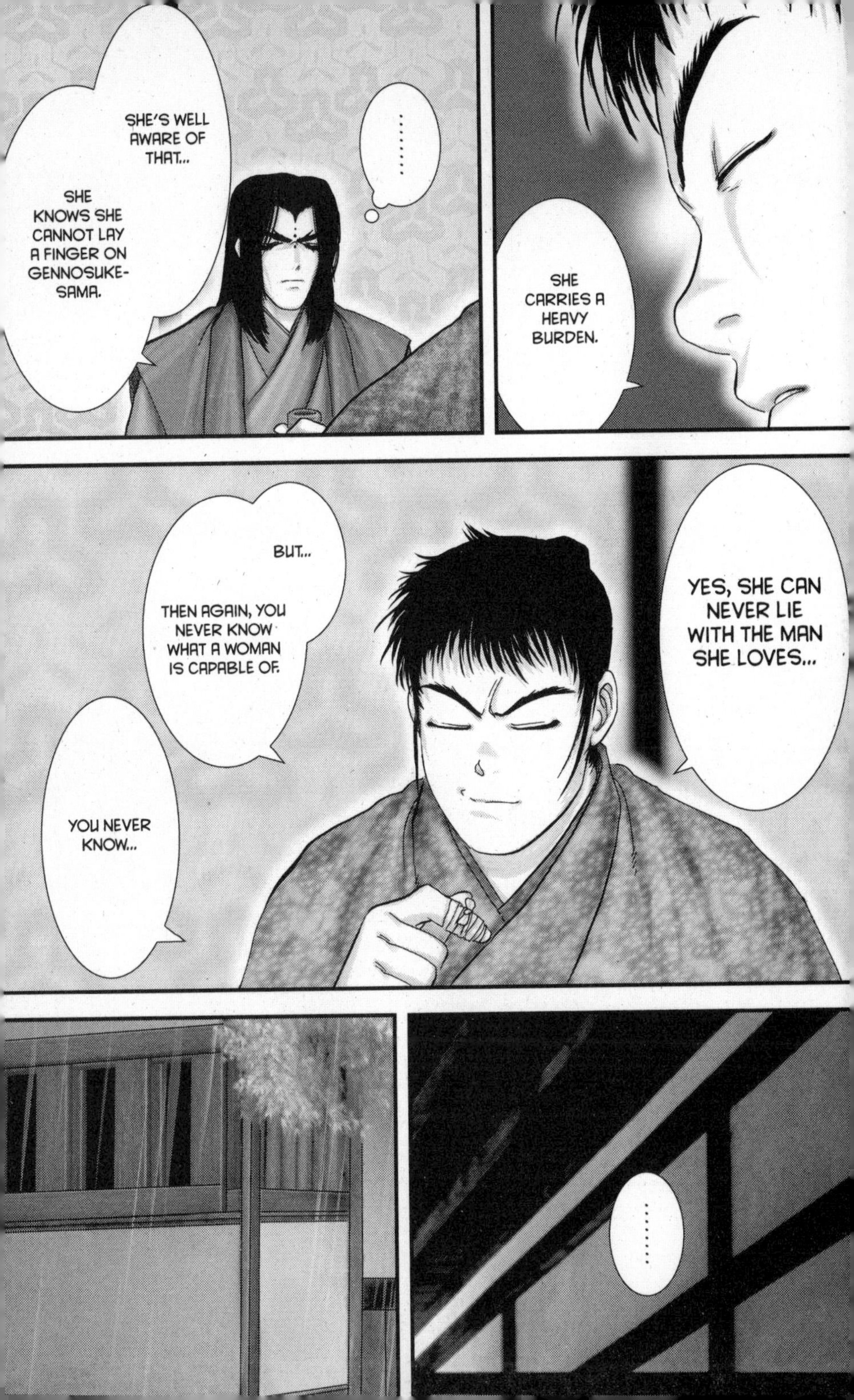
SHE CARRIES A HEAVY BURDEN.
....
SHE'S WELL AWARE OF THAT...
SHE KNOWS SHE CANNOT LAY A FINGER ON GENNOSUKE-SAMA.
YES, SHE CAN NEVER LIE WITH THE MAN SHE LOVES...
BUT...
THEN AGAIN, YOU NEVER KNOW WHAT A WOMAN IS CAPABLE OF.
YOU NEVER KNOW...
....

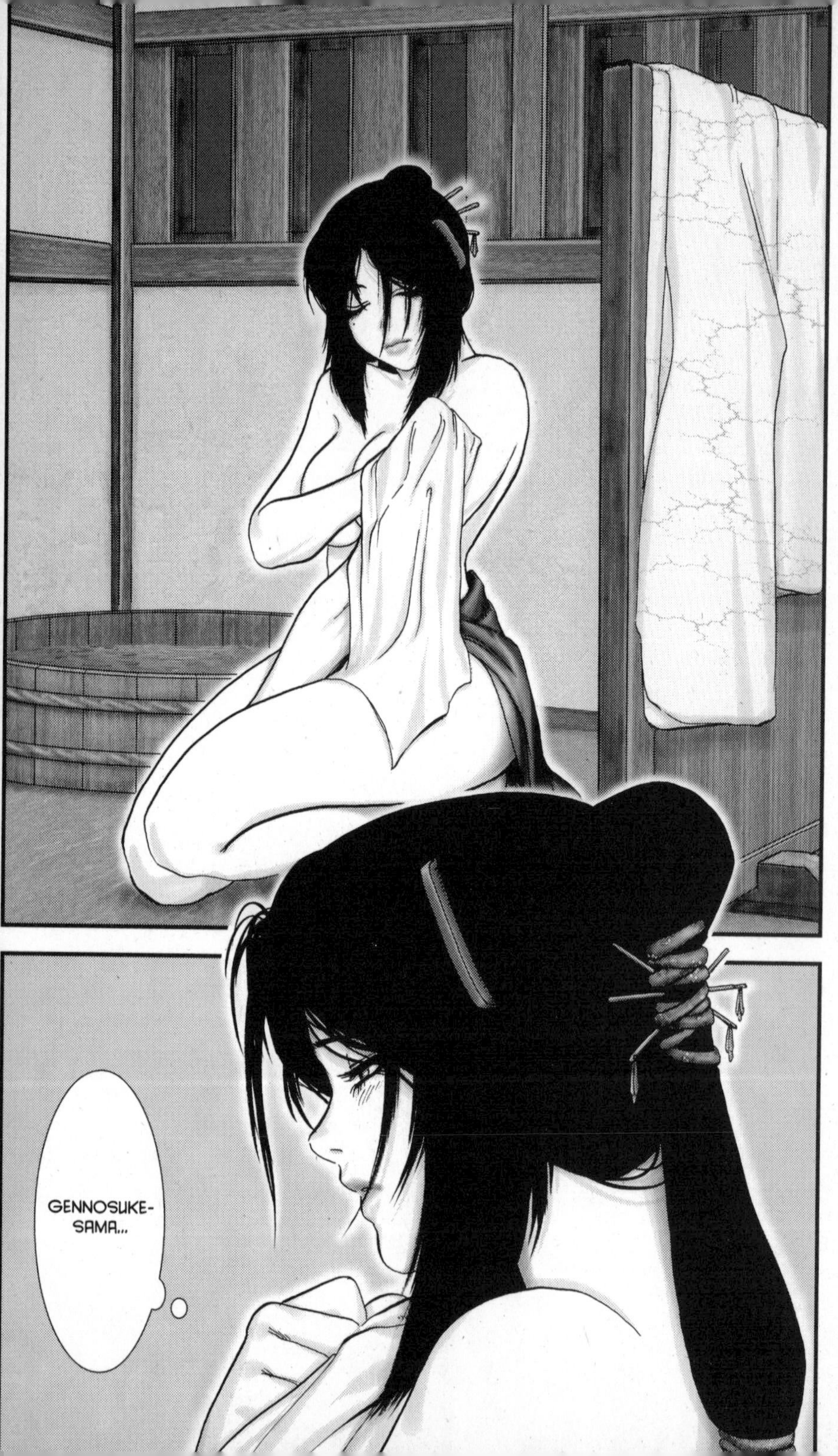
GENNOSUKE-SAMA...

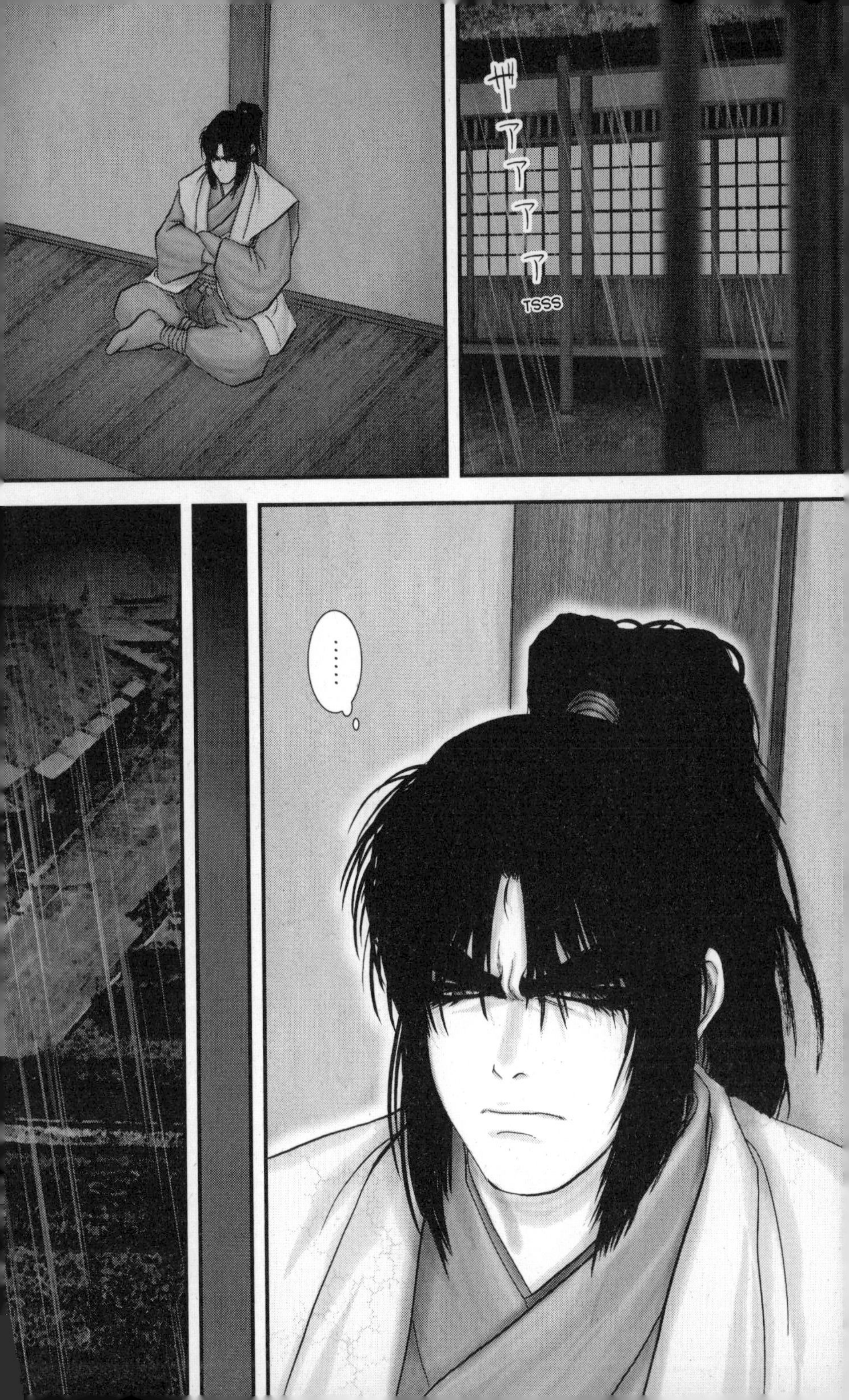
ザアアアア
TSSS
......

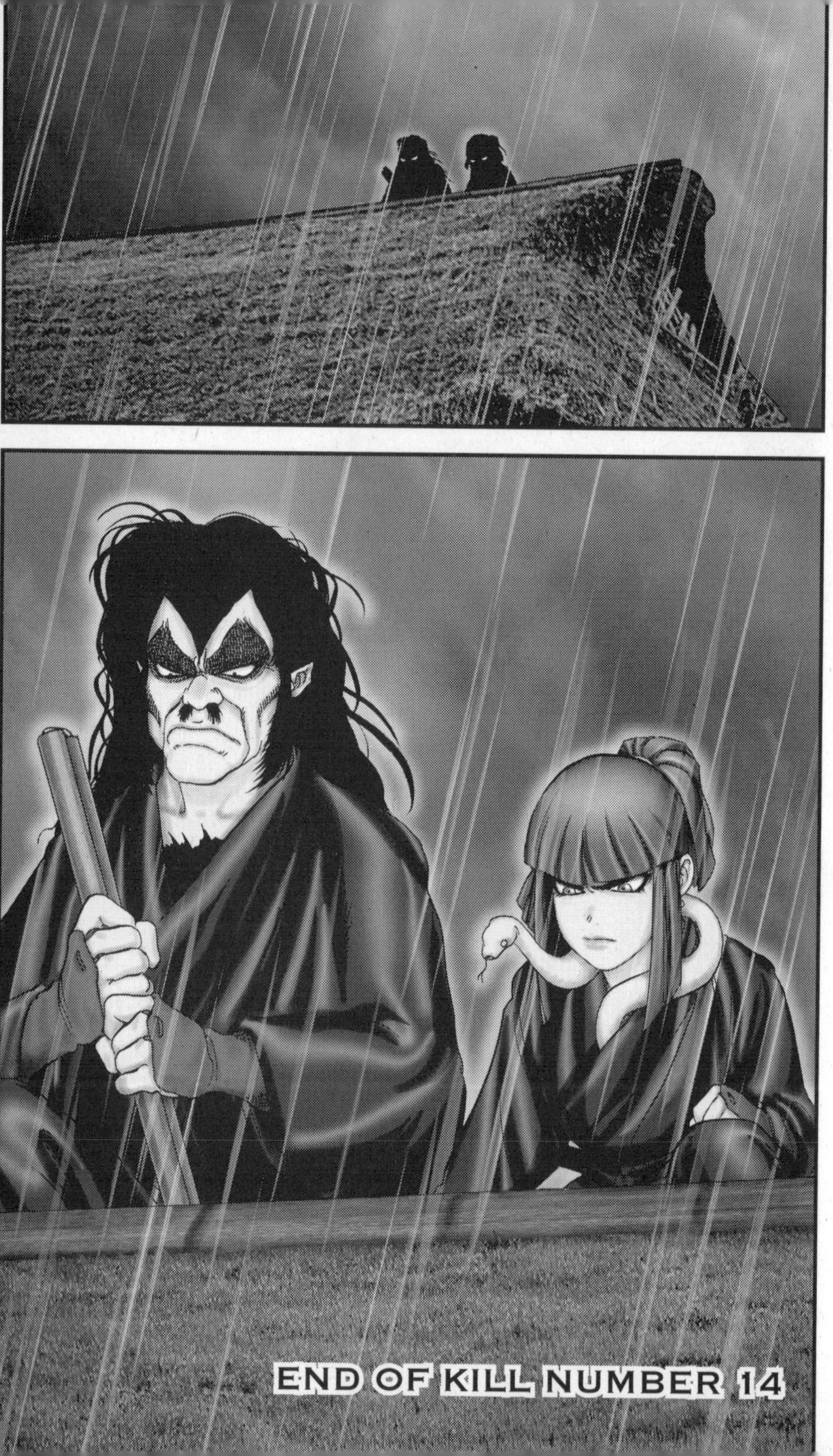
END OF KILL NUMBER 14

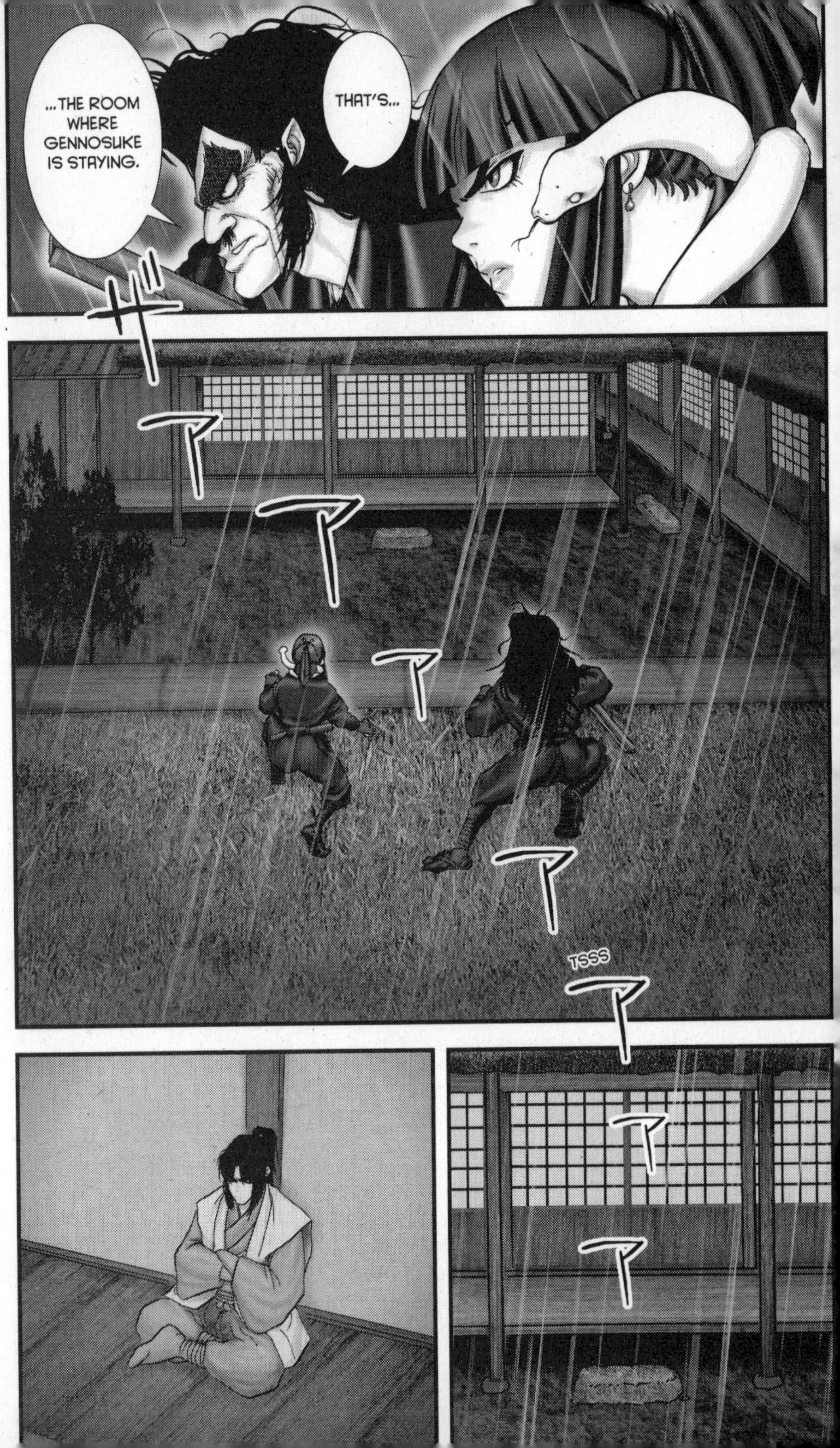
THAT'S...
...THE ROOM WHERE GENNOSUKE IS STAYING.
ザアアアアアアア
TSSS

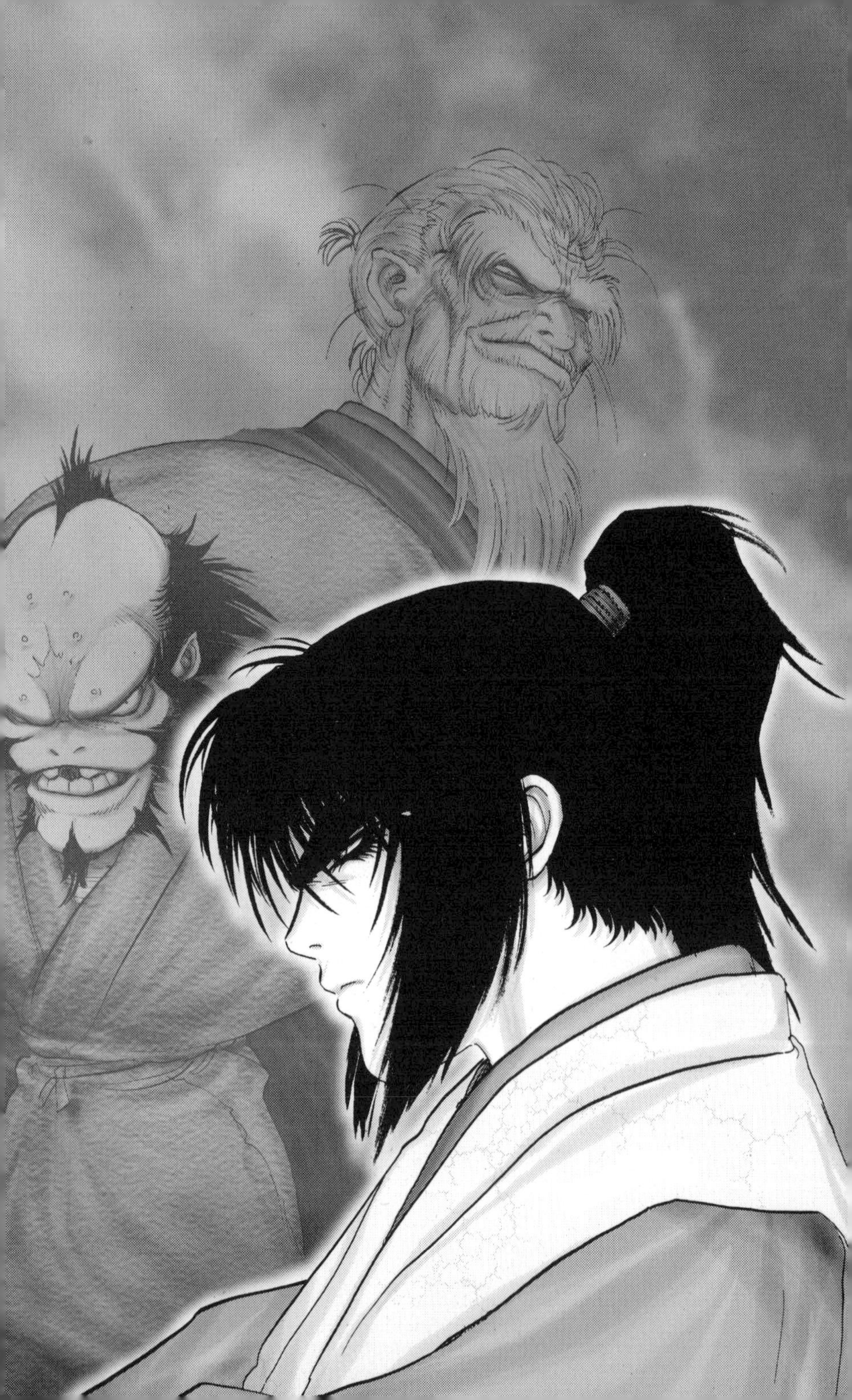

KILL NUMBER 15
[5 VS 7 (PART 4)]

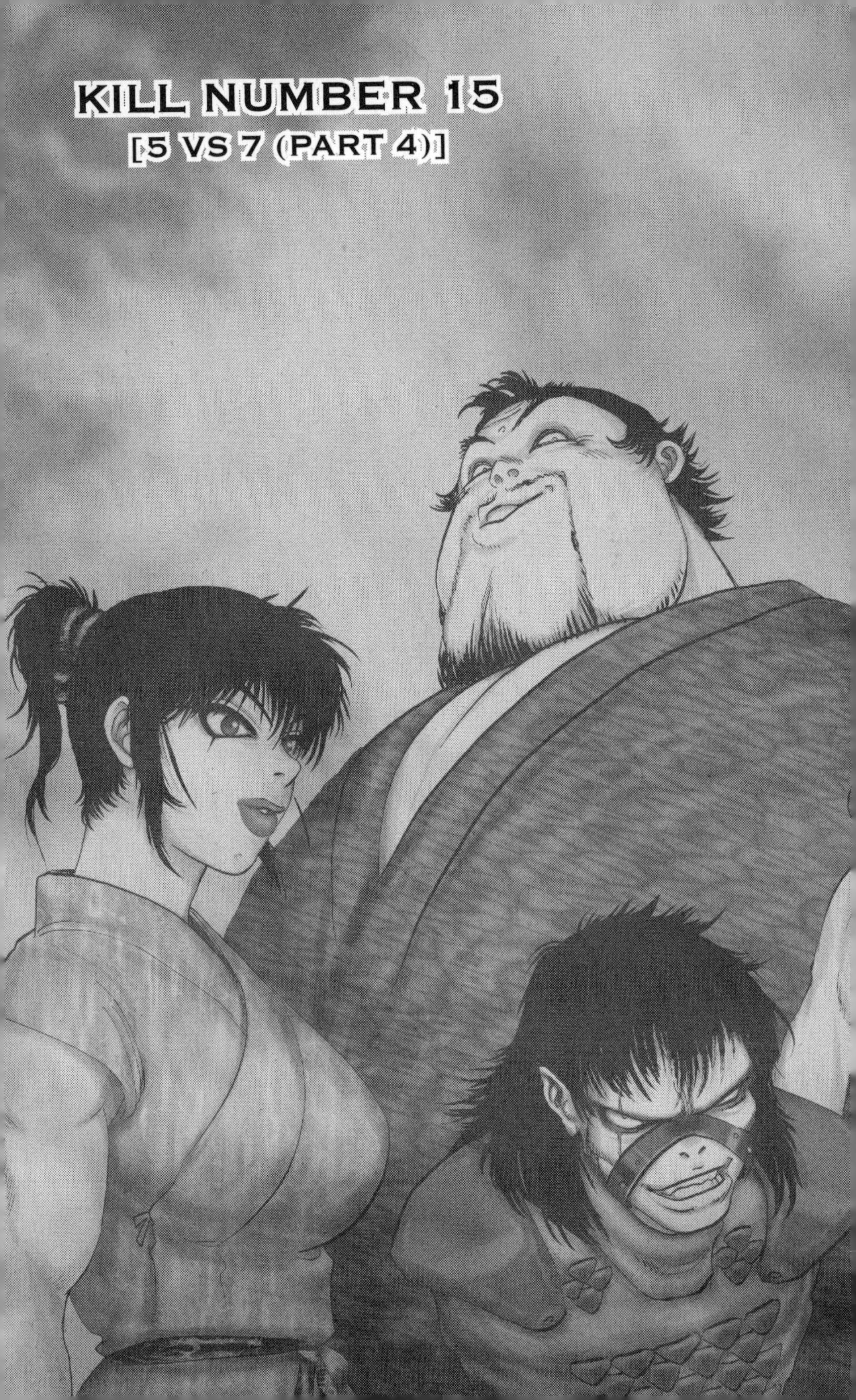

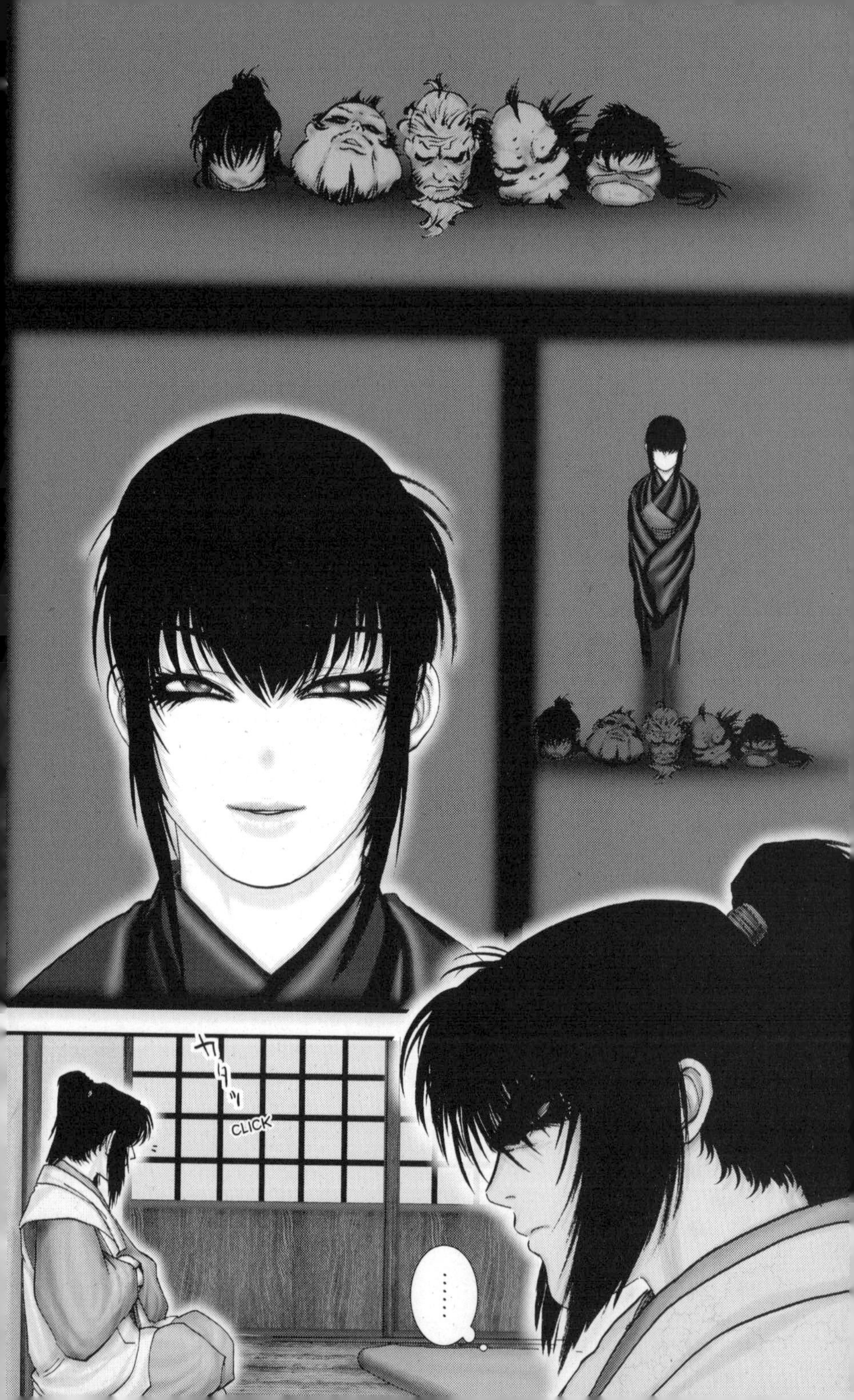

カチャッ
CLICK
......

SWIP

WHO IS IT?

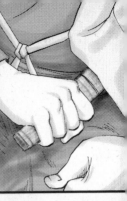

KAGEROU?

WHAT HAPPENED? IS SOMETHING WRONG?

．．．．．．

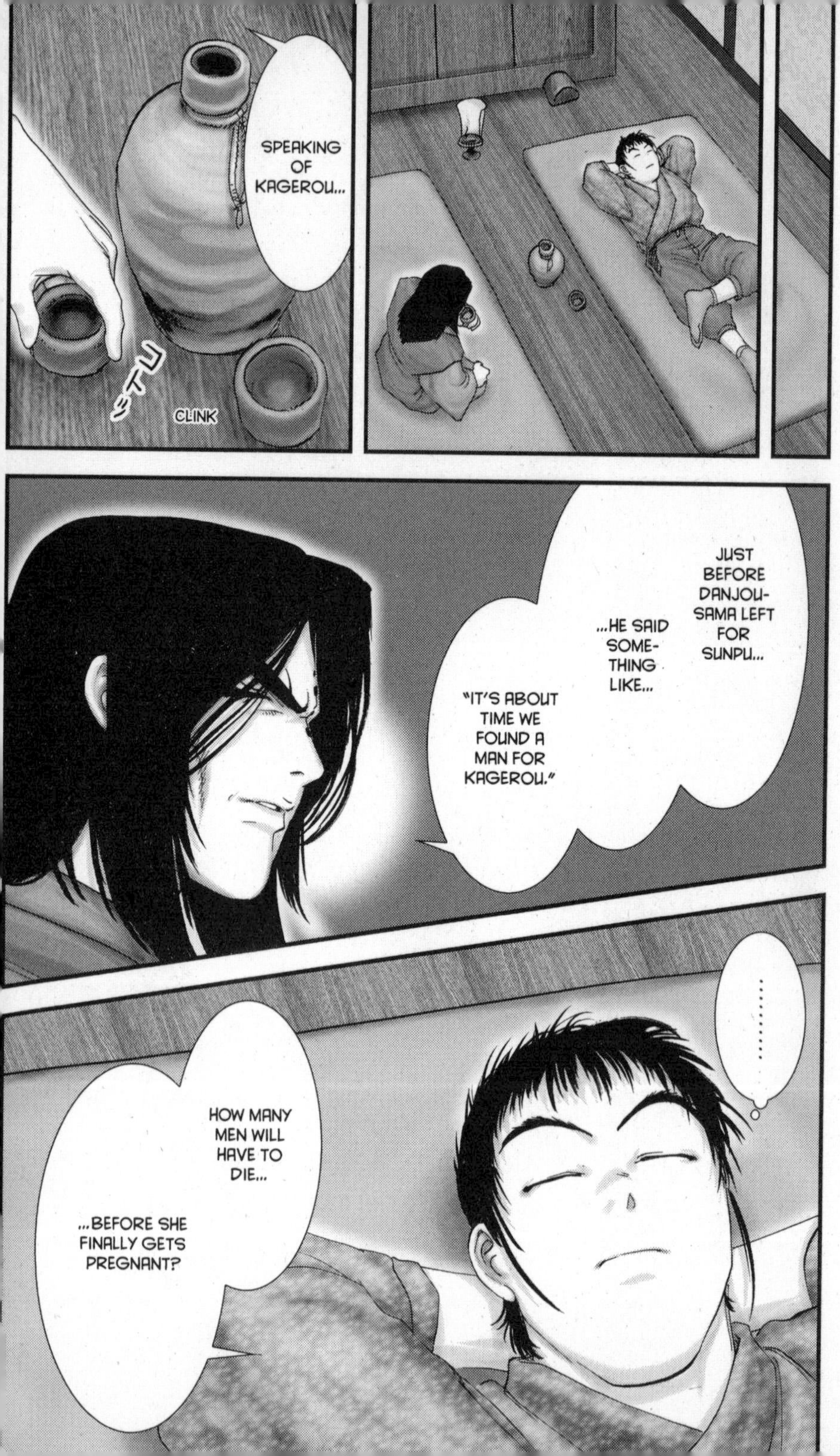
SPEAKING OF KAGEROU...
CLINK
JUST BEFORE DANJOU-SAMA LEFT FOR SUNPU...
...HE SAID SOMETHING LIKE...
"IT'S ABOUT TIME WE FOUND A MAN FOR KAGEROU."
......
HOW MANY MEN WILL HAVE TO DIE...
...BEFORE SHE FINALLY GETS PREGNANT?

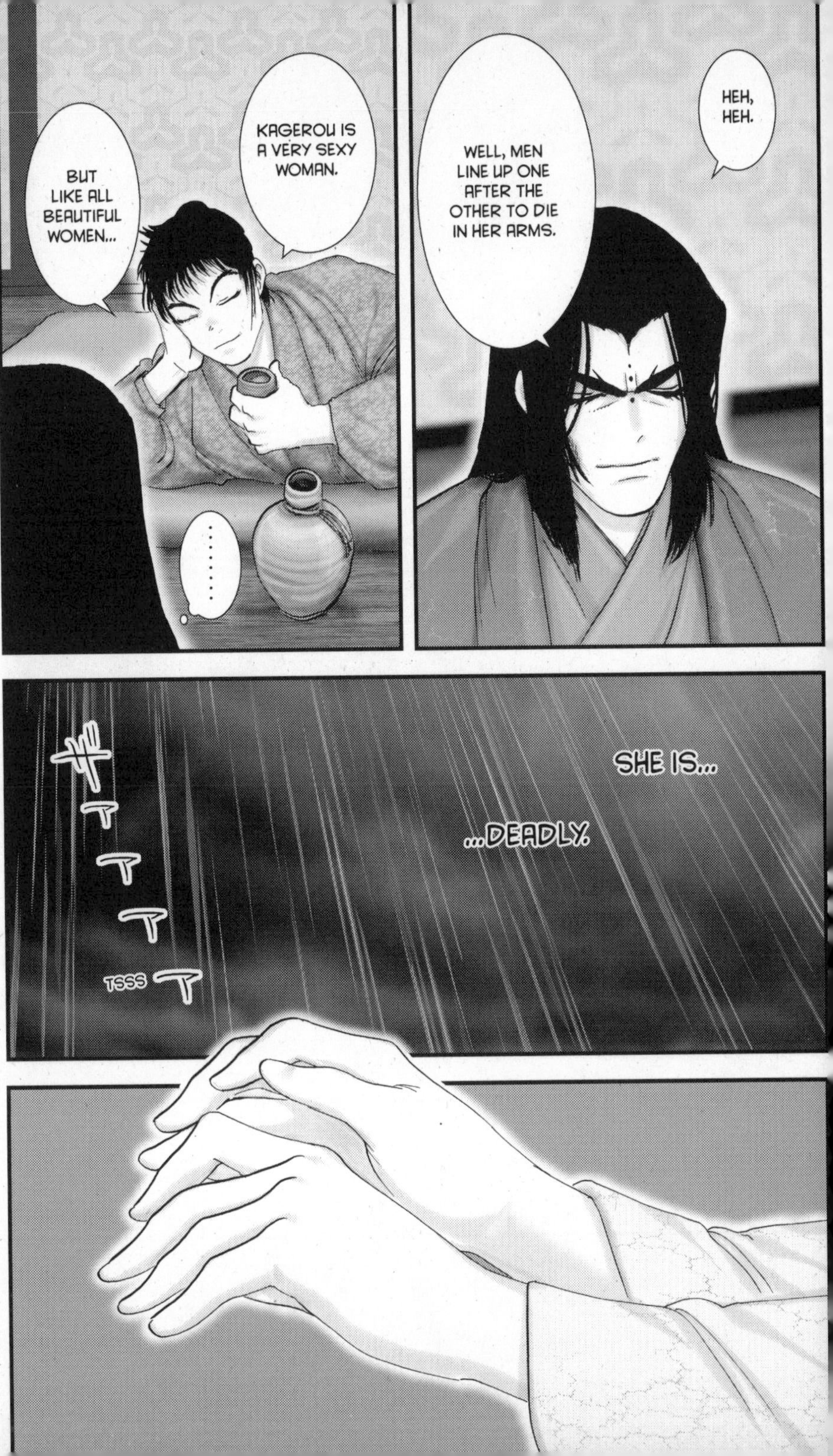
HEH, HEH.
WELL, MEN LINE UP ONE AFTER THE OTHER TO DIE IN HER ARMS.
KAGEROU IS A VERY SEXY WOMAN.
BUT LIKE ALL BEAUTIFUL WOMEN...
......
SHE IS...
...DEADLY.
TSSS

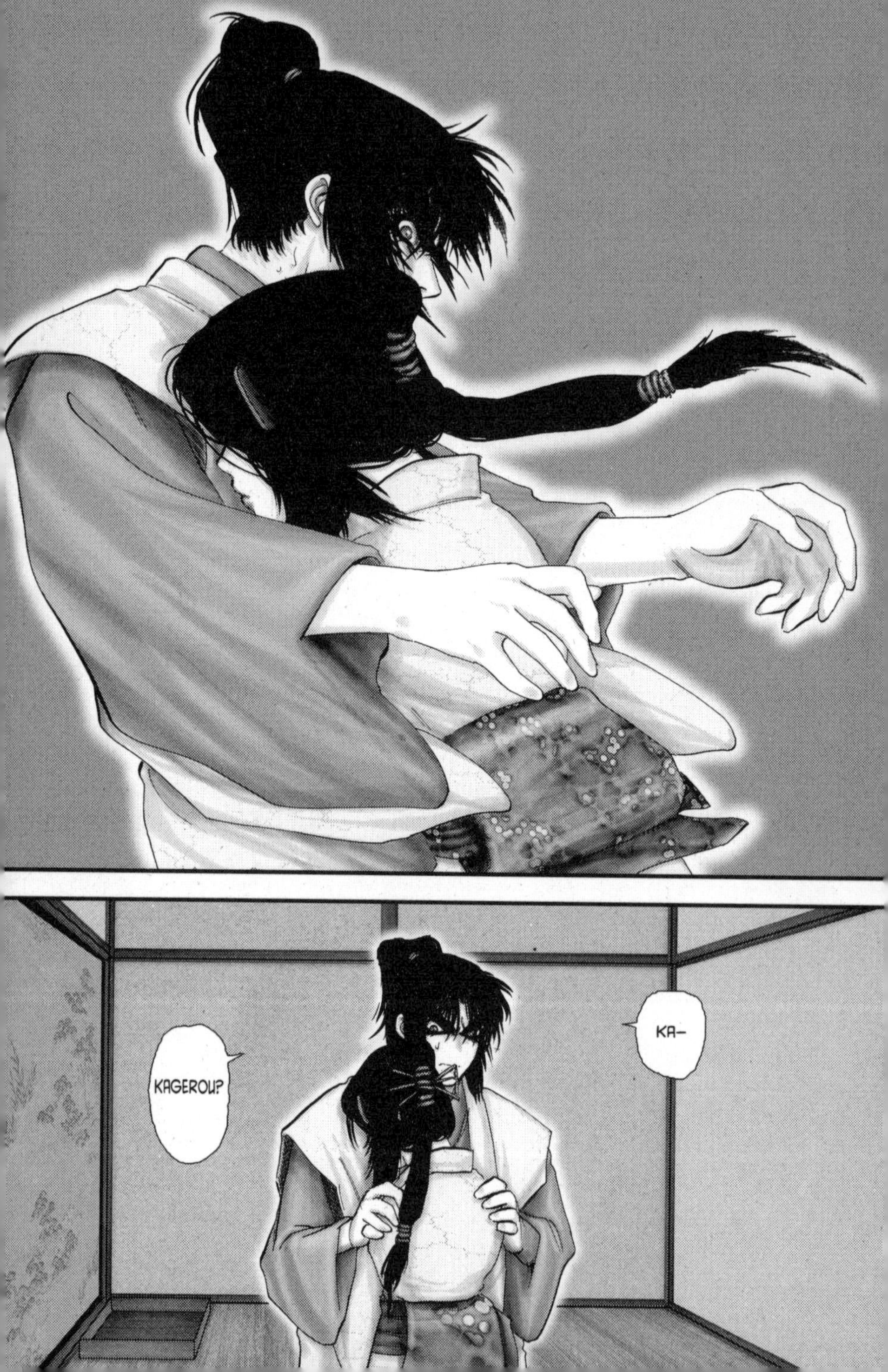
KA–
KAGEROU?

I LOVE YOU...

GENNOSUKE-SAMA.

!

......

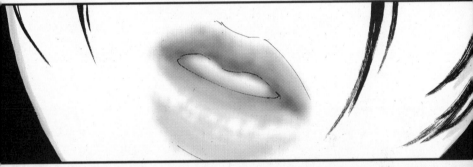

YANK

YANK

SQUINCH

UNG...

URGGH...

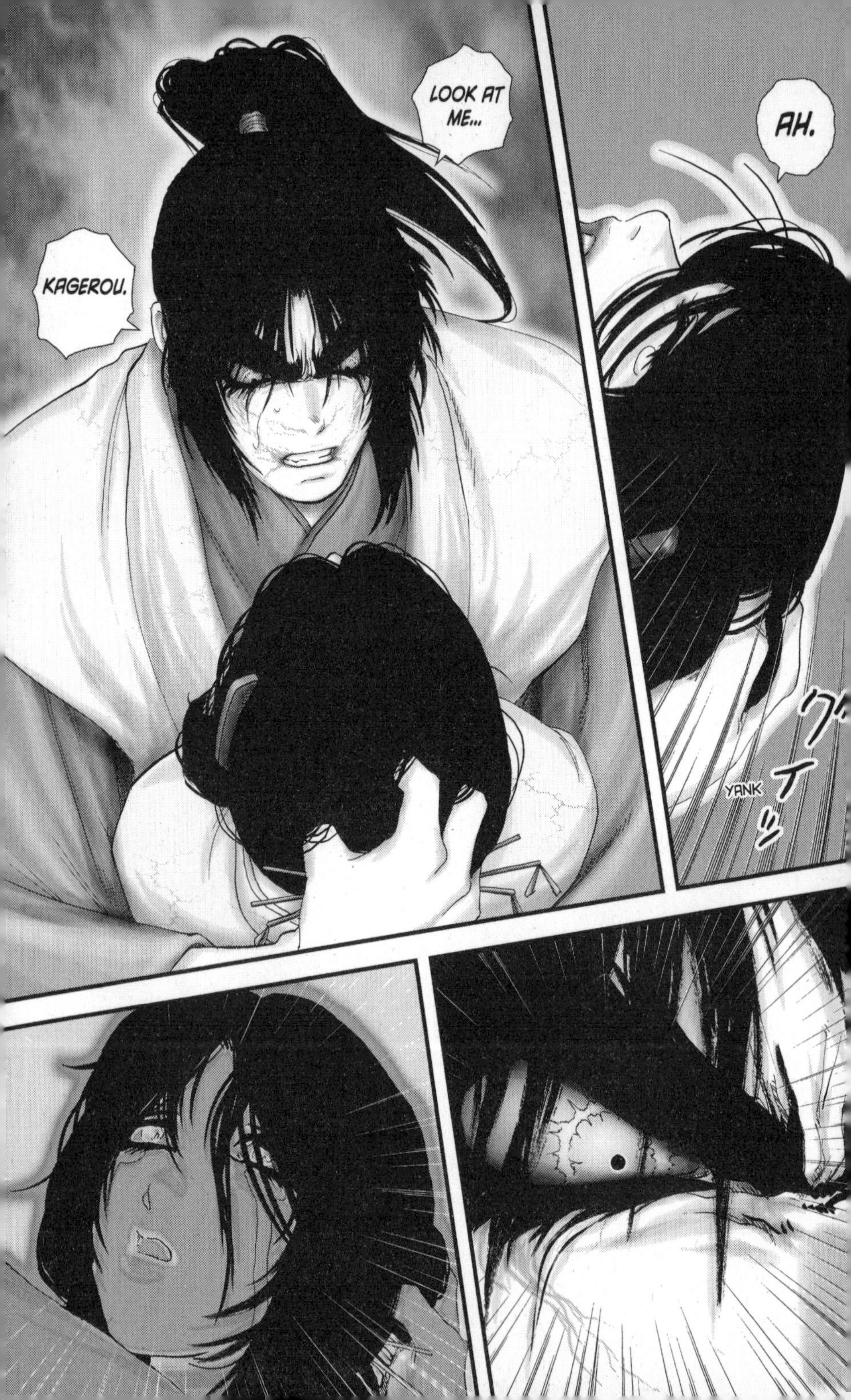
AH.
グイッ
YANK
LOOK AT ME...
KAGEROU.

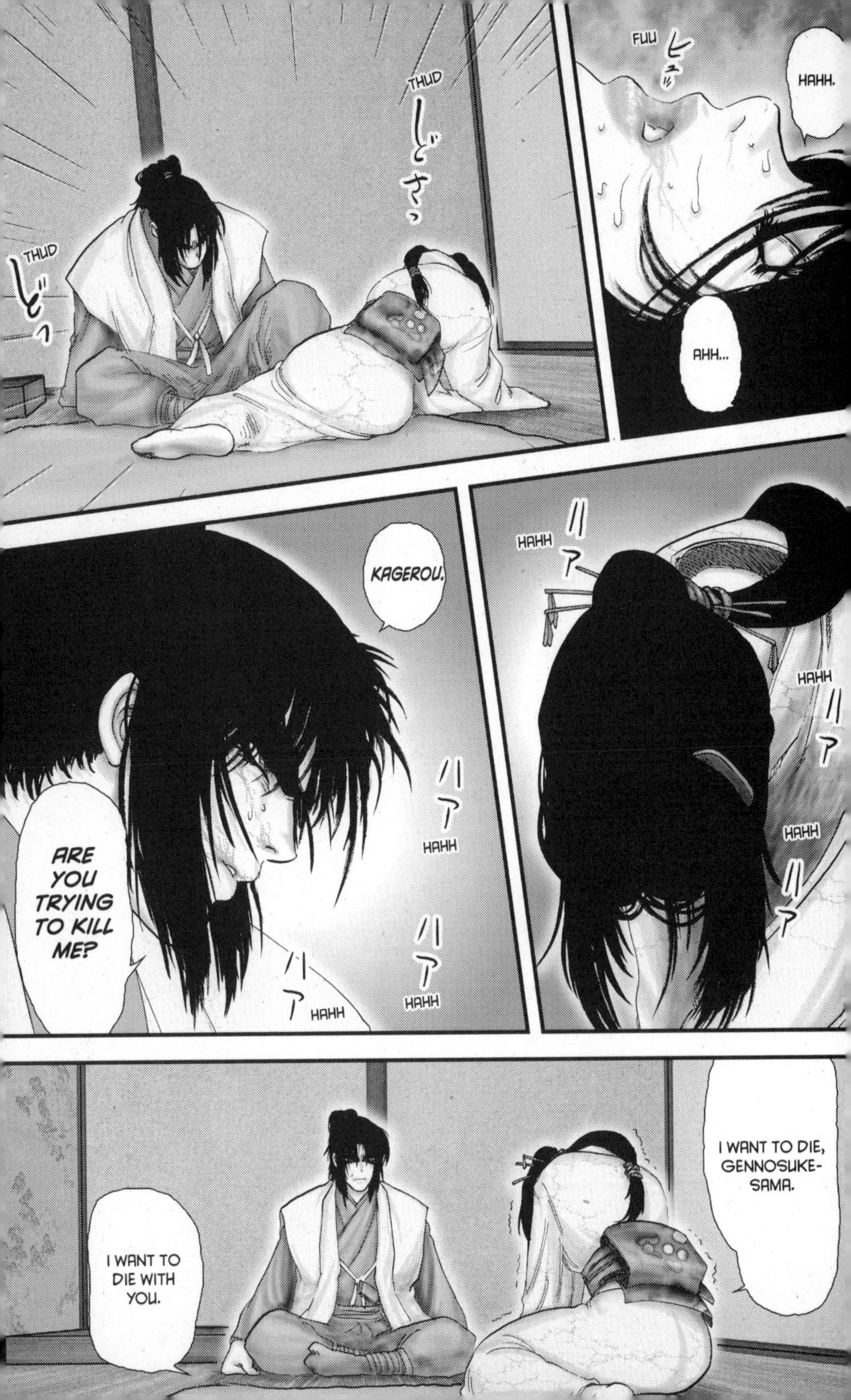

FUU
ヒュ
HAHH.
AHH...
THUD
じどさっ
THUD
じっ
HAHH
ハア
HAHH
ハア
HAHH
ハア
KAGEROU.
ハア
HAHH
ハア
HAHH
ハア
HAHH
ARE YOU TRYING TO KILL ME?
I WANT TO DIE, GENNOSUKE-SAMA.
I WANT TO DIE WITH YOU.

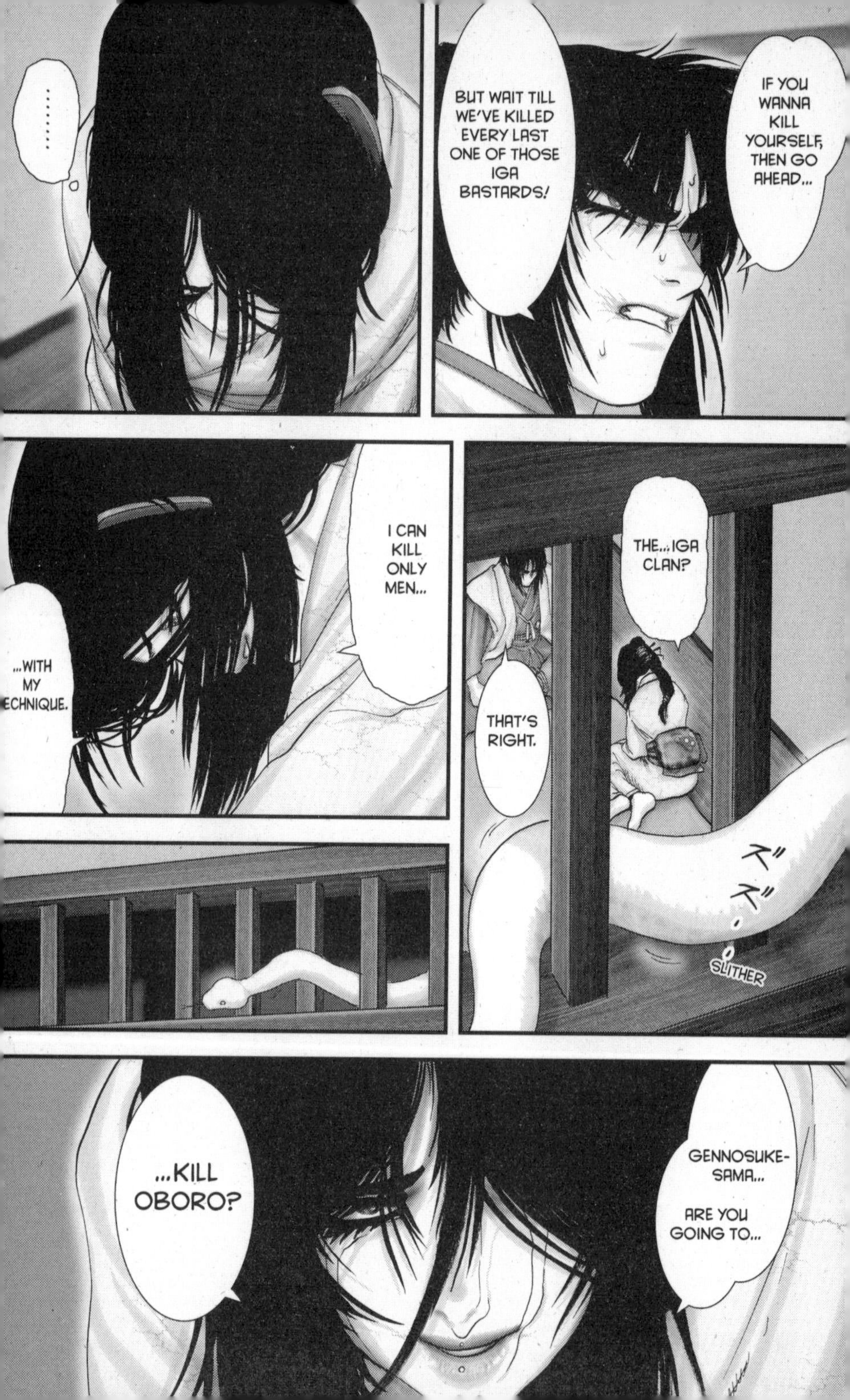
IF YOU WANNA KILL YOURSELF, THEN GO AHEAD...
BUT WAIT TILL WE'VE KILLED EVERY LAST ONE OF THOSE IGA BASTARDS!
....
THE... IGA CLAN?
THAT'S RIGHT.
ズズ
SLITHER
I CAN KILL ONLY MEN...
...WITH MY ECHNIQUE.
GENNOSUKE-SAMA...
ARE YOU GOING TO...
...KILL OBORO?

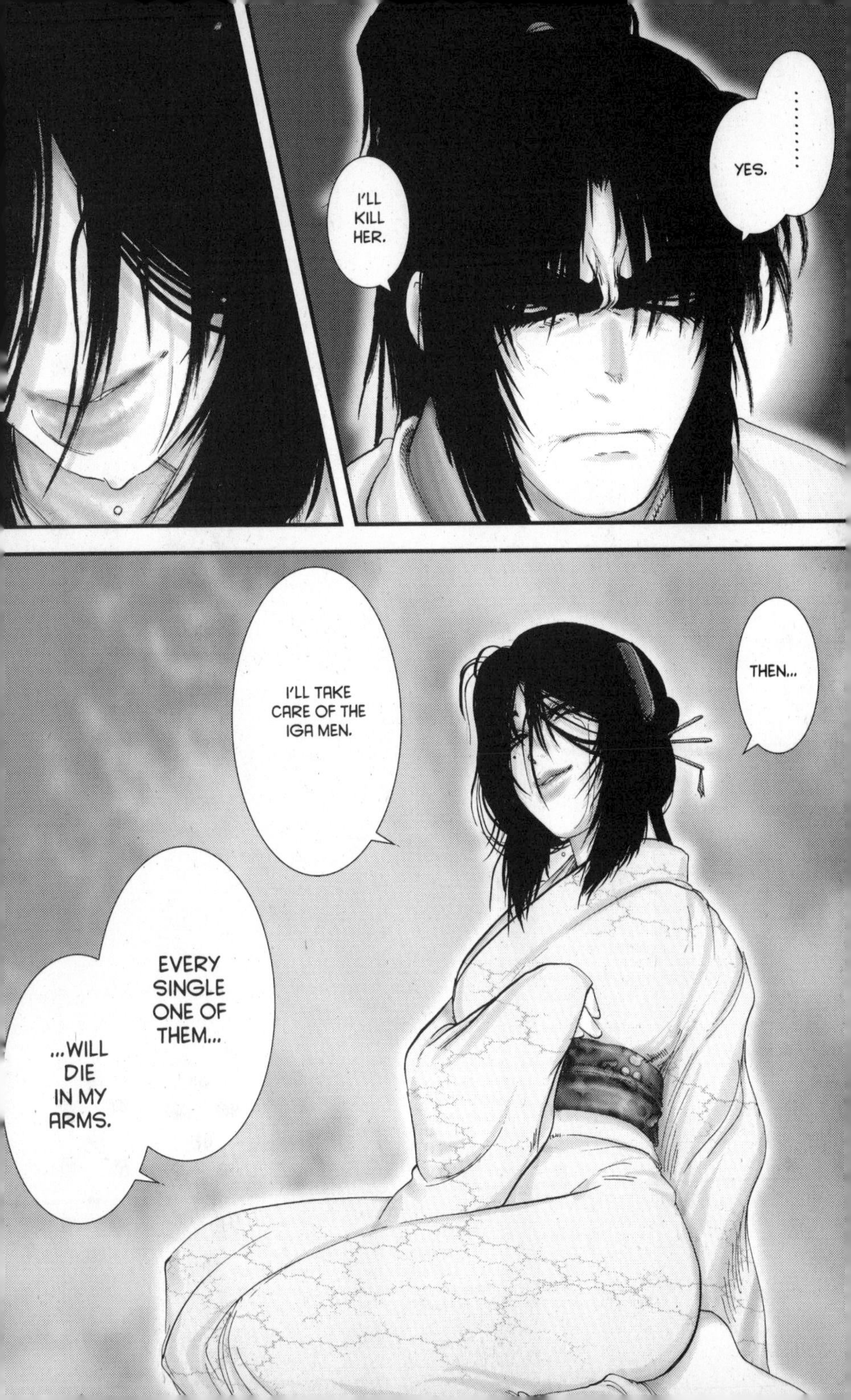
......
YES.
I'LL KILL HER.
THEN...
I'LL TAKE CARE OF THE IGA MEN.
EVERY SINGLE ONE OF THEM...
...WILL DIE IN MY ARMS.

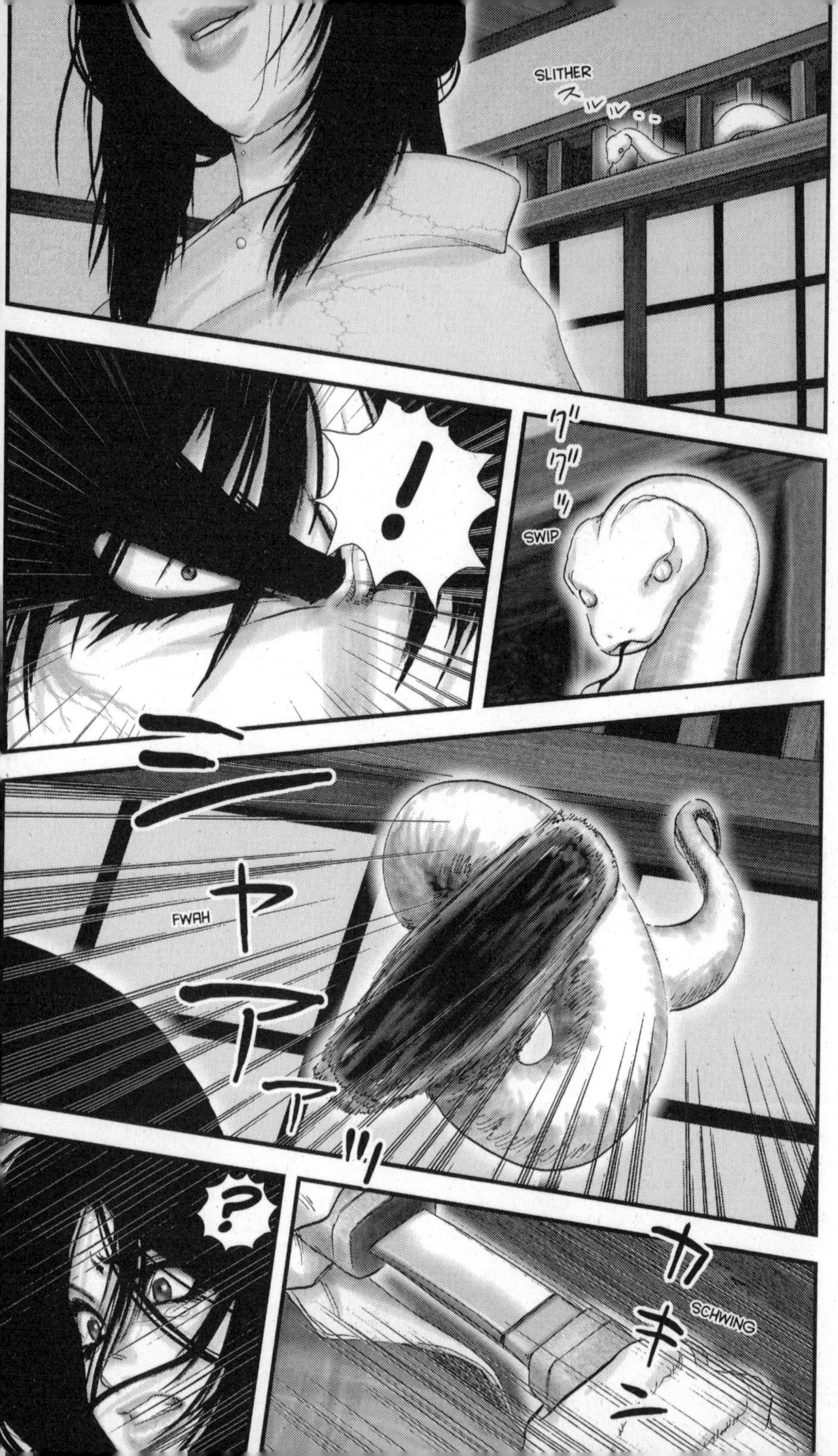
SLITHER
スルッ..
グググッ
SWIP
!
FWAH
SCHWING
カキン
?

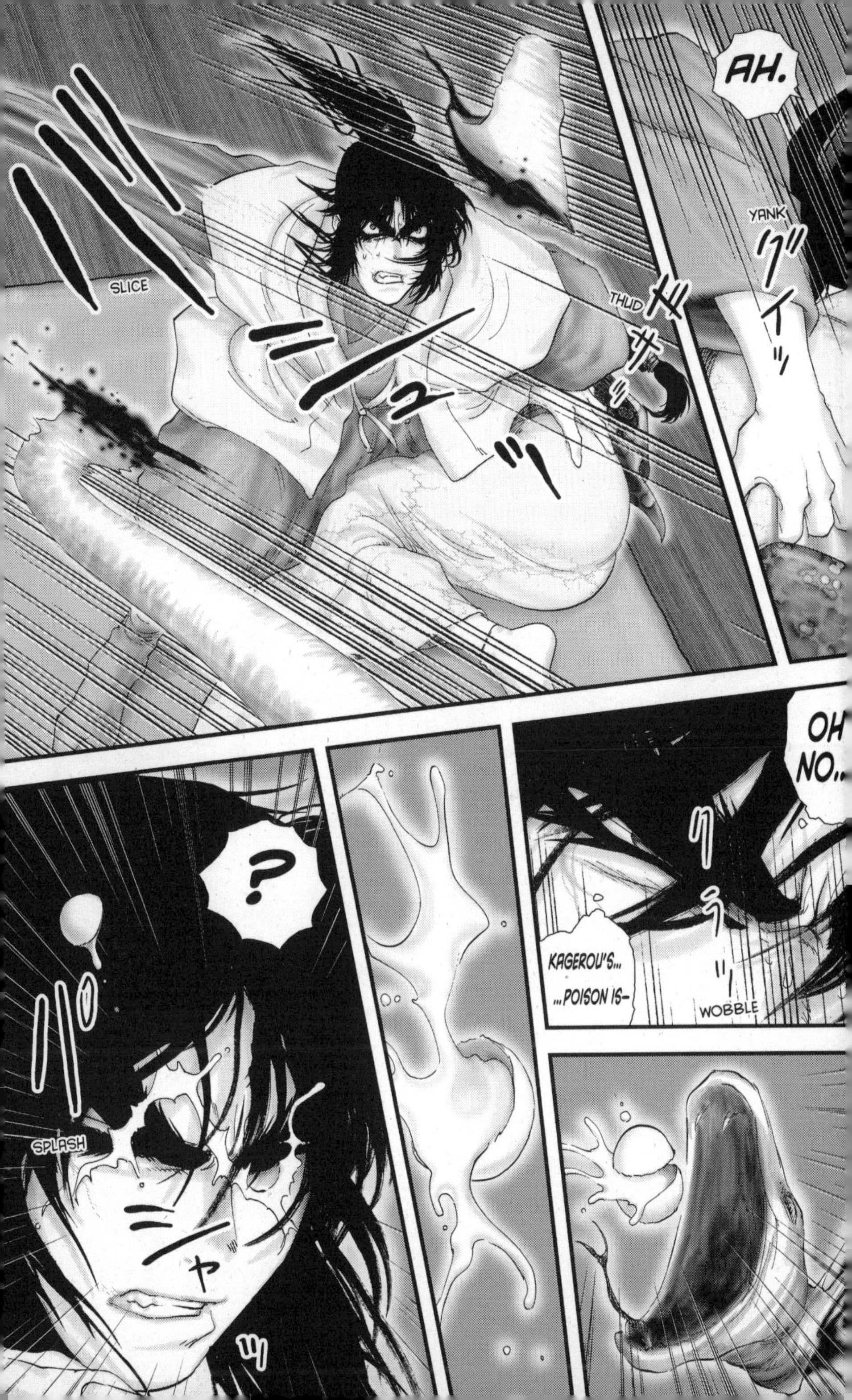
AH.
YANK
THUD
SLICE
OH NO..
KAGEROU'S...
...POISON IS-
WOBBLE
?
SPLASH

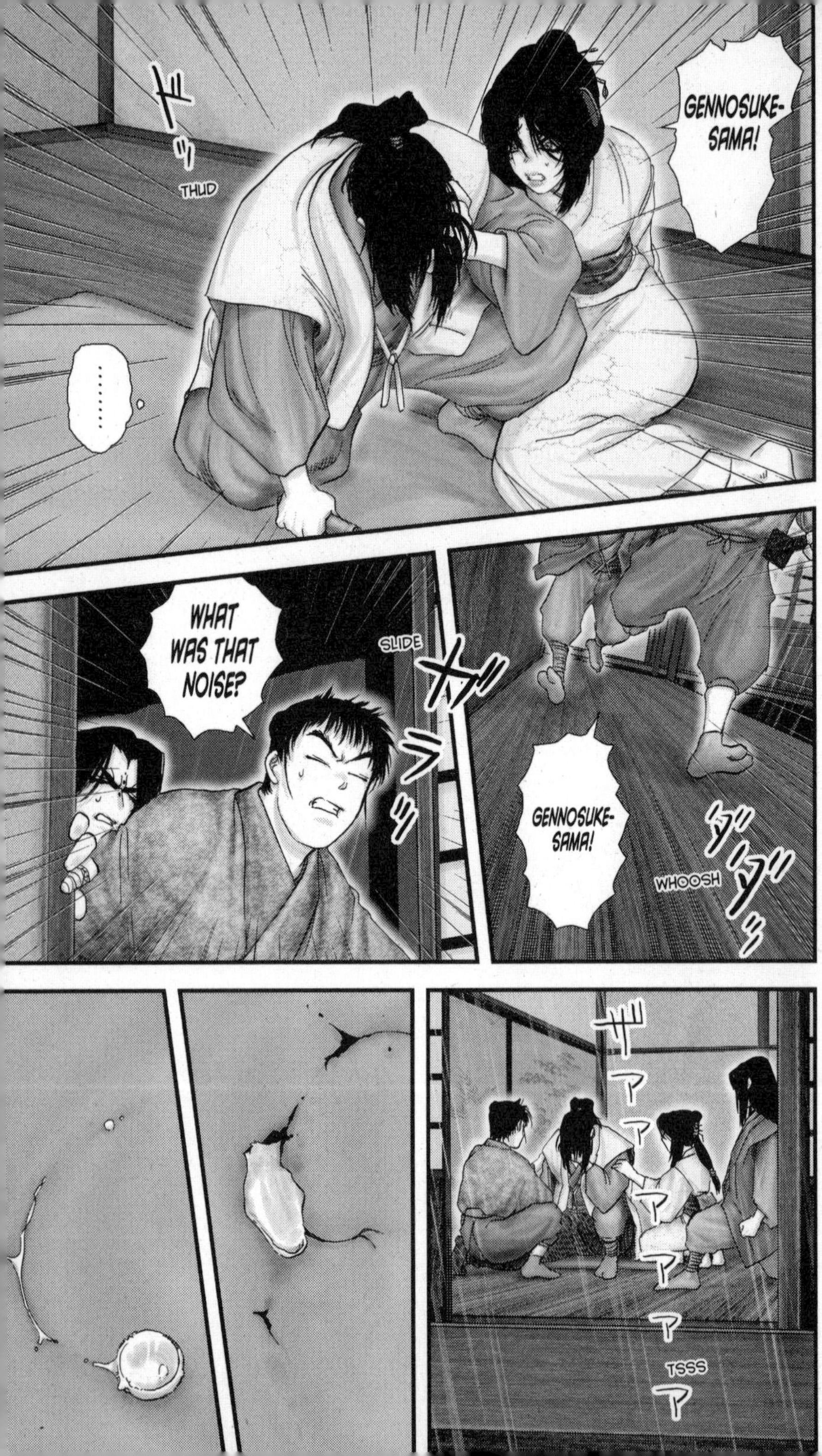
GENNOSUKE-SAMA!
THUD
......
GENNOSUKE-SAMA!
WHOOSH
WHAT WAS THAT NOISE?
SLIDE
TSSS

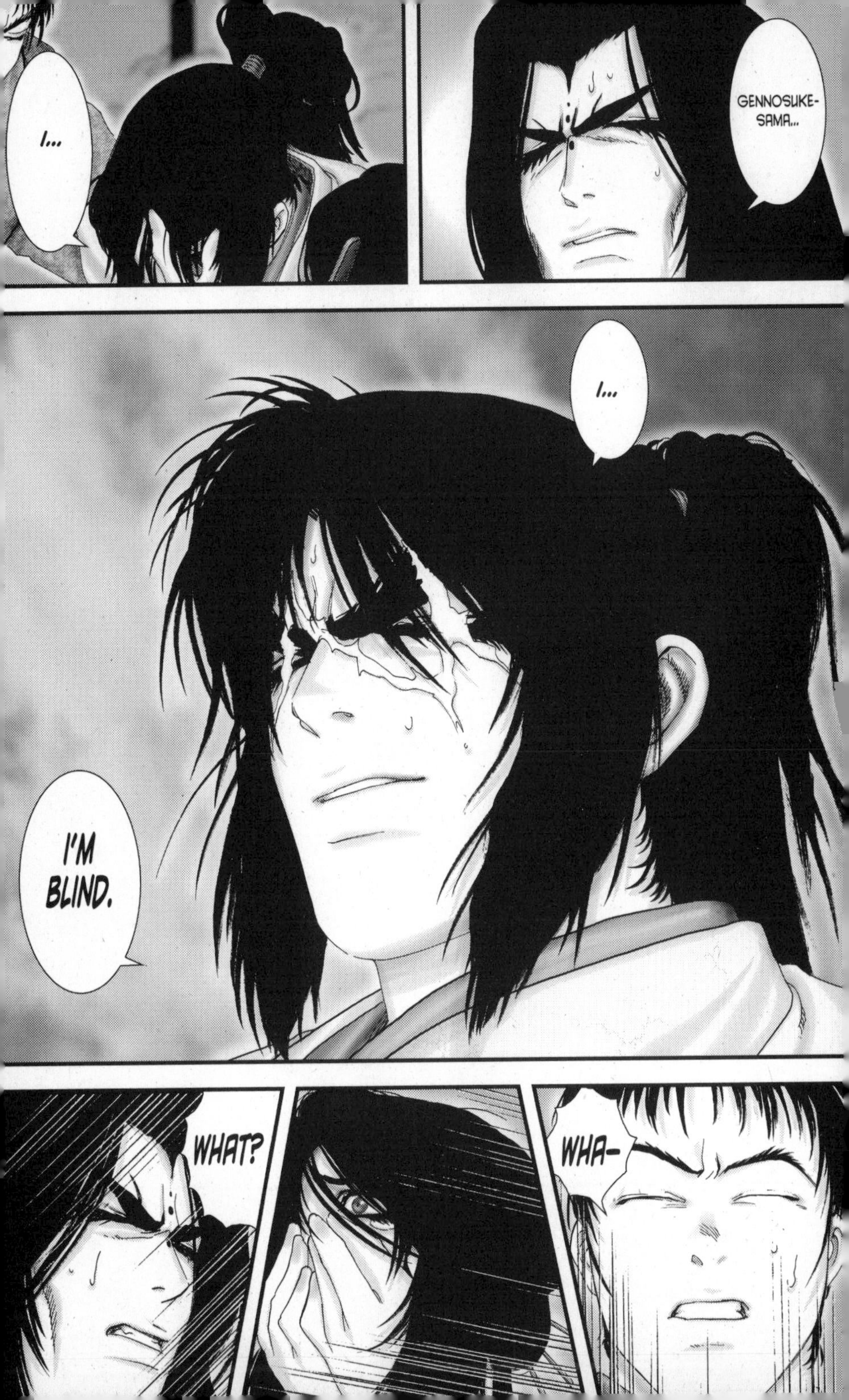
GENNOSUKE-SAMA...
I...
I...
I'M BLIND.
WHA-
WHAT?

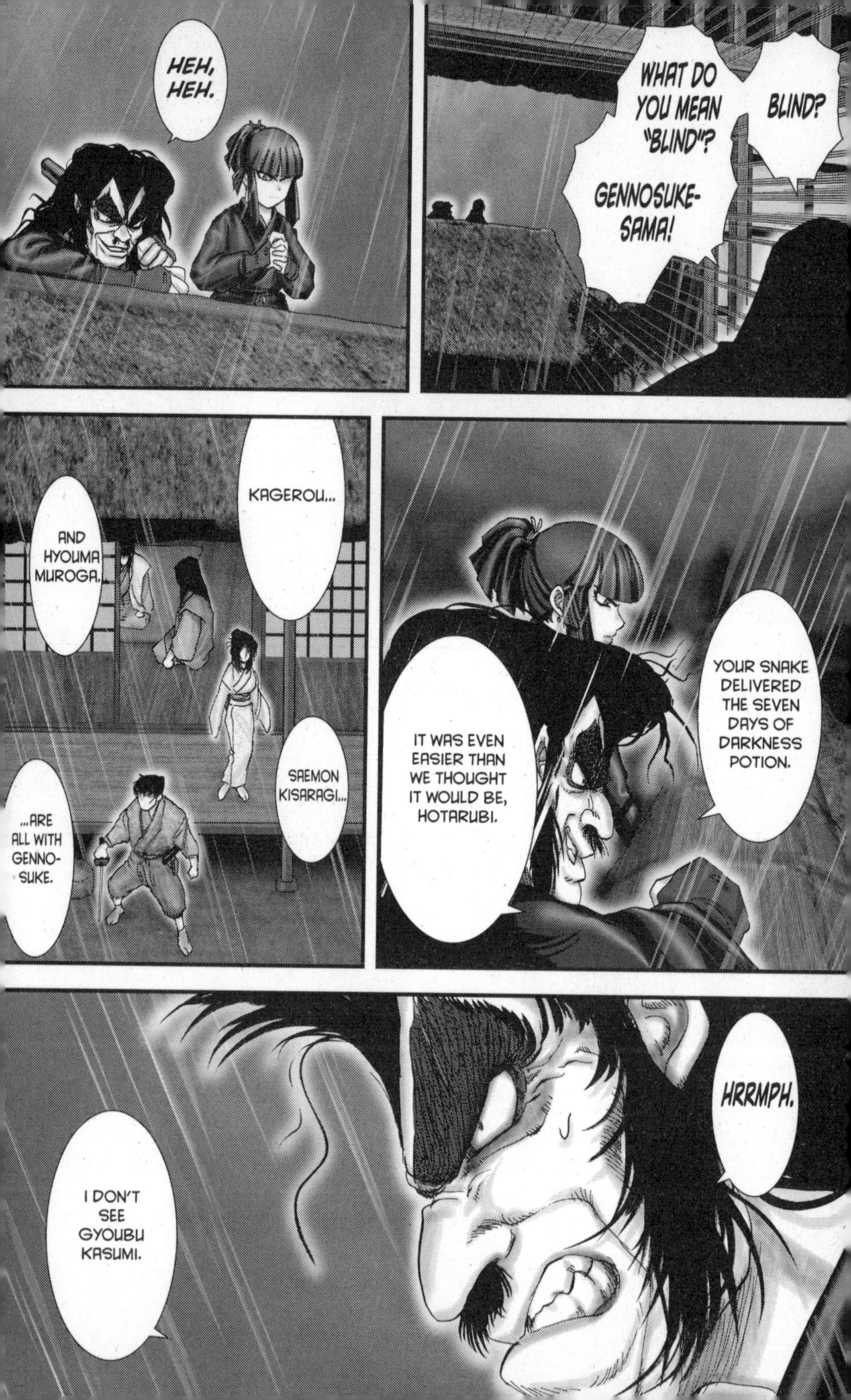
BLIND?
WHAT DO YOU MEAN "BLIND"?
GENNOSUKE-SAMA!
HEH, HEH.
YOUR SNAKE DELIVERED THE SEVEN DAYS OF DARKNESS POTION.
IT WAS EVEN EASIER THAN WE THOUGHT IT WOULD BE, HOTARUBI.
KAGEROU...
AND HYOUMA MUROGA...
SAEMON KISARAGI...
...ARE ALL WITH GENNOSUKE.
HRRMPH.
I DON'T SEE GYOUBU KASUMI.

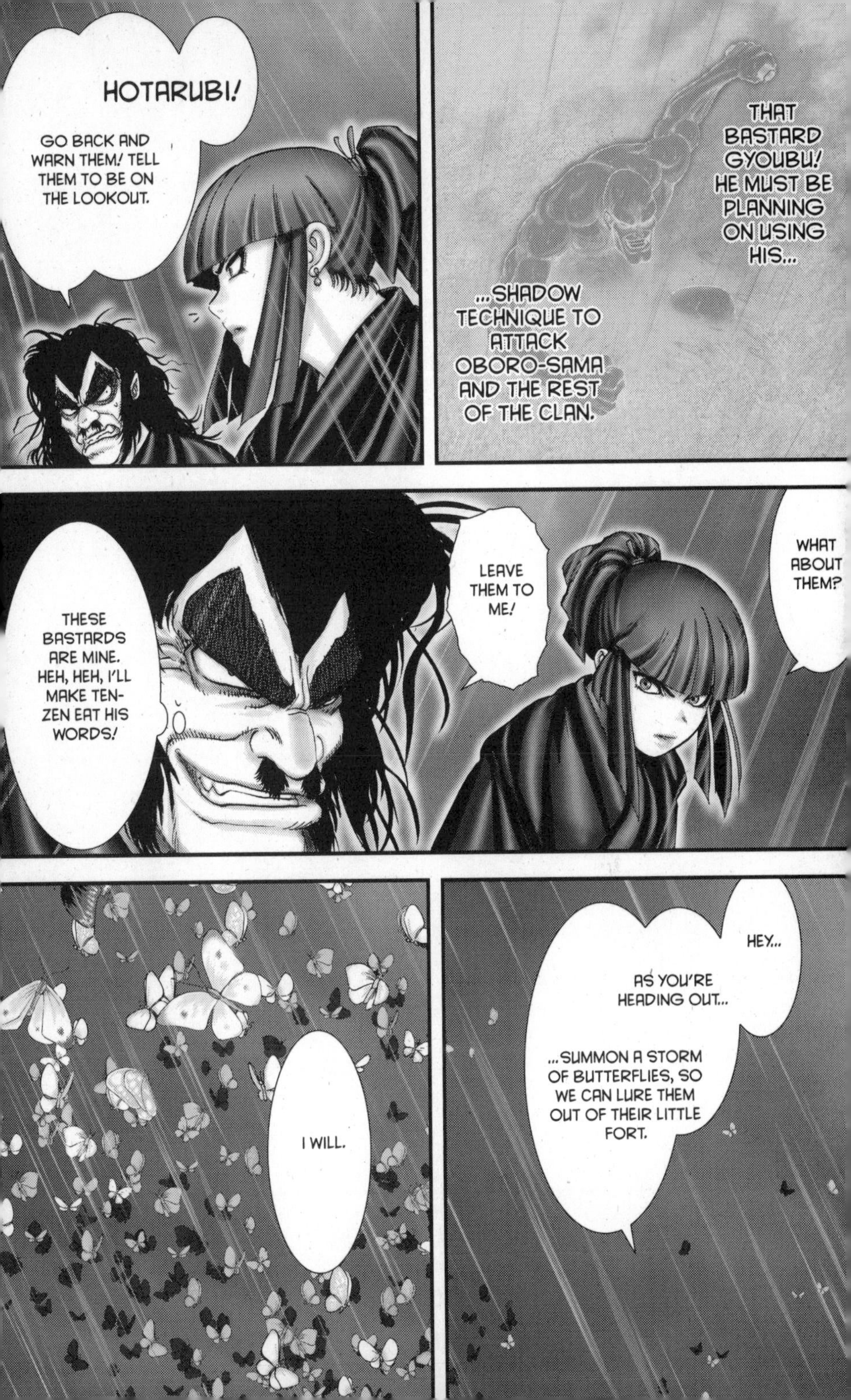
THAT BASTARD GYOUBU! HE MUST BE PLANNING ON USING HIS...
...SHADOW TECHNIQUE TO ATTACK OBORO-SAMA AND THE REST OF THE CLAN.
HOTARUBI!
GO BACK AND WARN THEM! TELL THEM TO BE ON THE LOOKOUT.
WHAT ABOUT THEM?
LEAVE THEM TO ME!
THESE BASTARDS ARE MINE. HEH, HEH, I'LL MAKE TEN-ZEN EAT HIS WORDS!
HEY...
AS YOU'RE HEADING OUT...
...SUMMON A STORM OF BUTTERFLIES, SO WE CAN LURE THEM OUT OF THEIR LITTLE FORT.
I WILL.

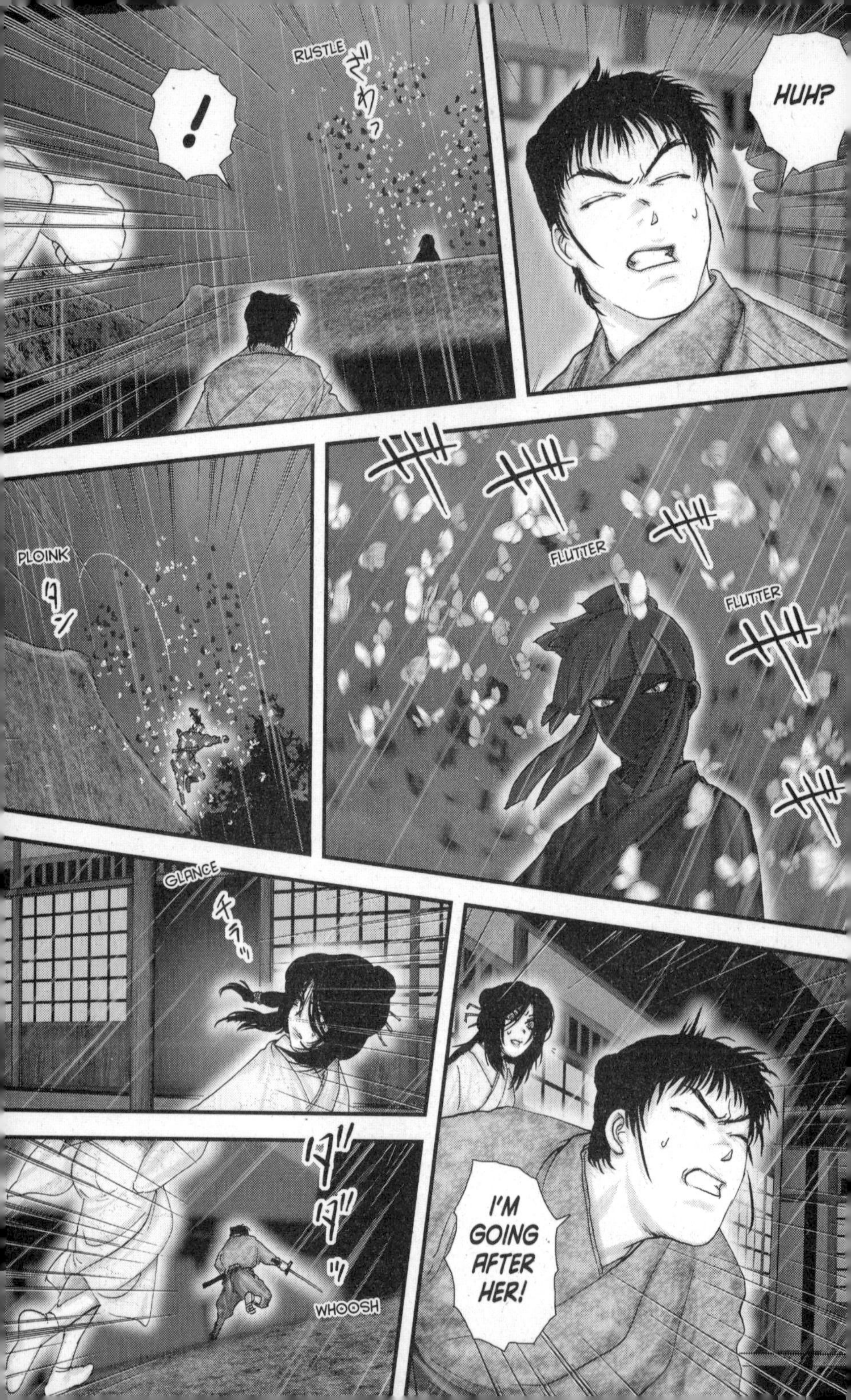
HUH?
RUSTLE
ざわっ
!
FLUTTER
FLUTTER
PLOINK
I'M GOING AFTER HER!
GLANCE
チラッ
ダダッ
WHOOSH

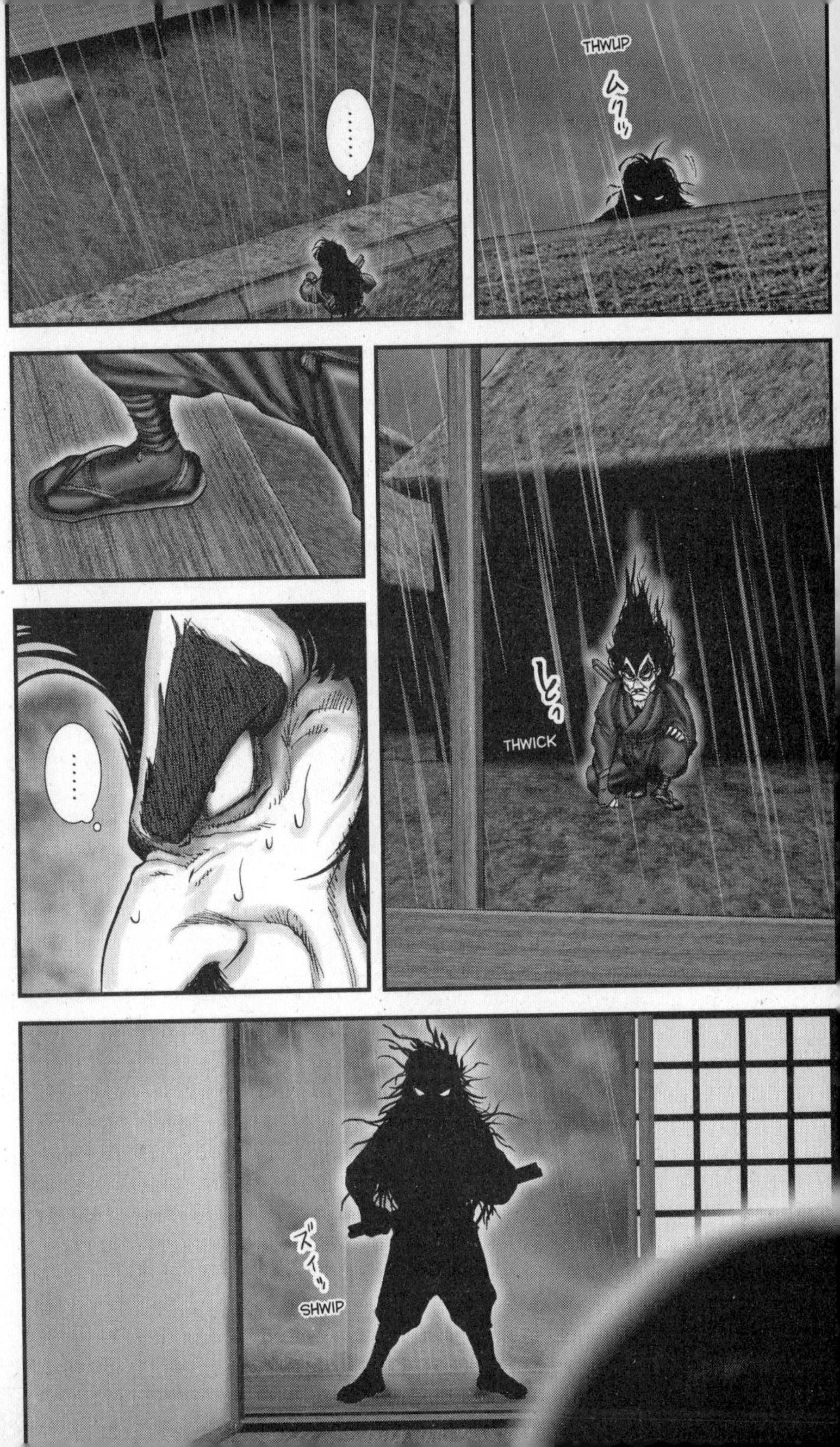
THWUP
ムクッ
……
THWICK
……
ズイッ
SHWIP

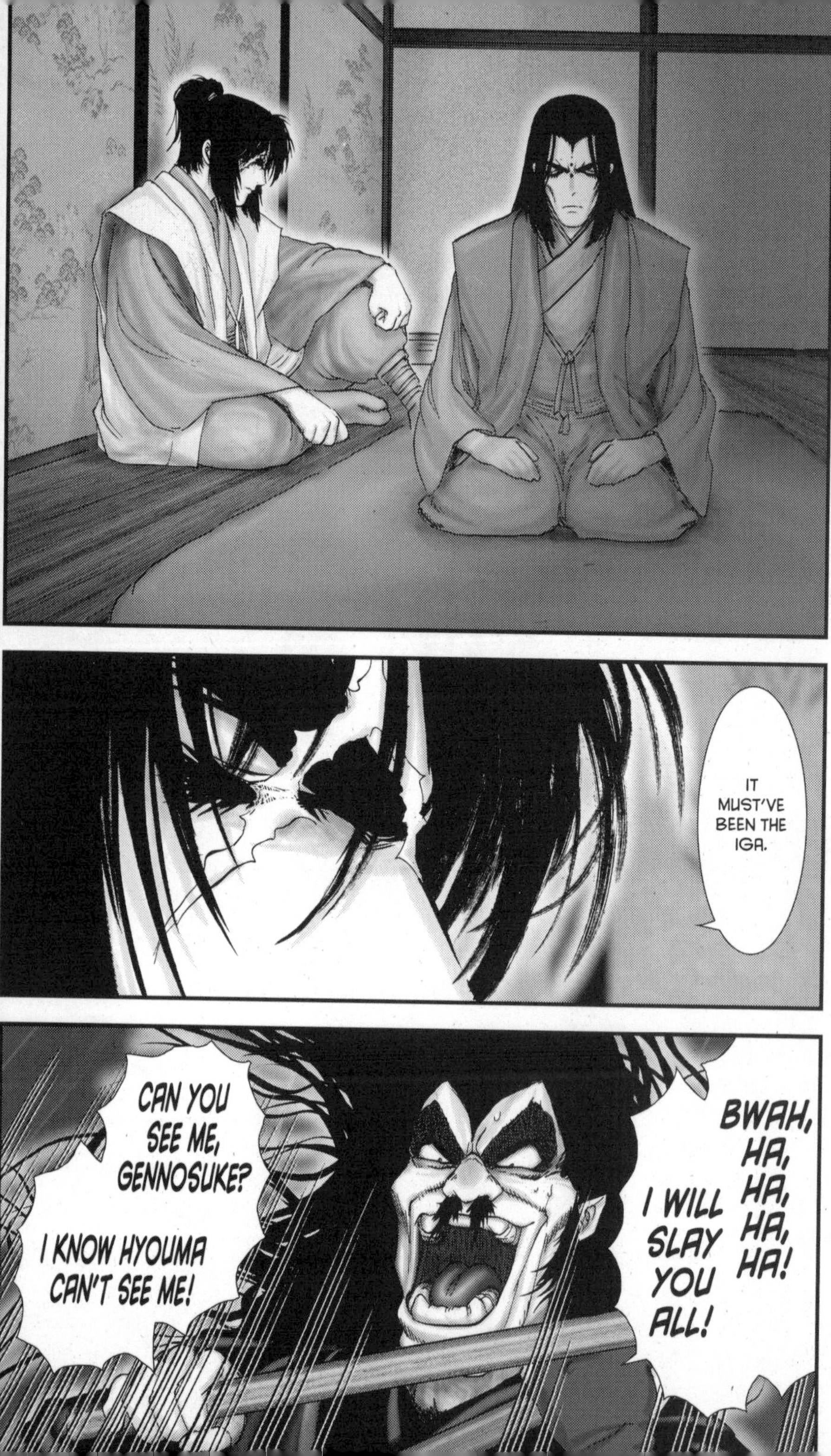
IT MUST'VE BEEN THE IGA.
BWAH, HA, HA, HA, HA!
I WILL SLAY YOU ALL!
CAN YOU SEE ME, GENNOSUKE?
I KNOW HYOUMA CAN'T SEE ME!

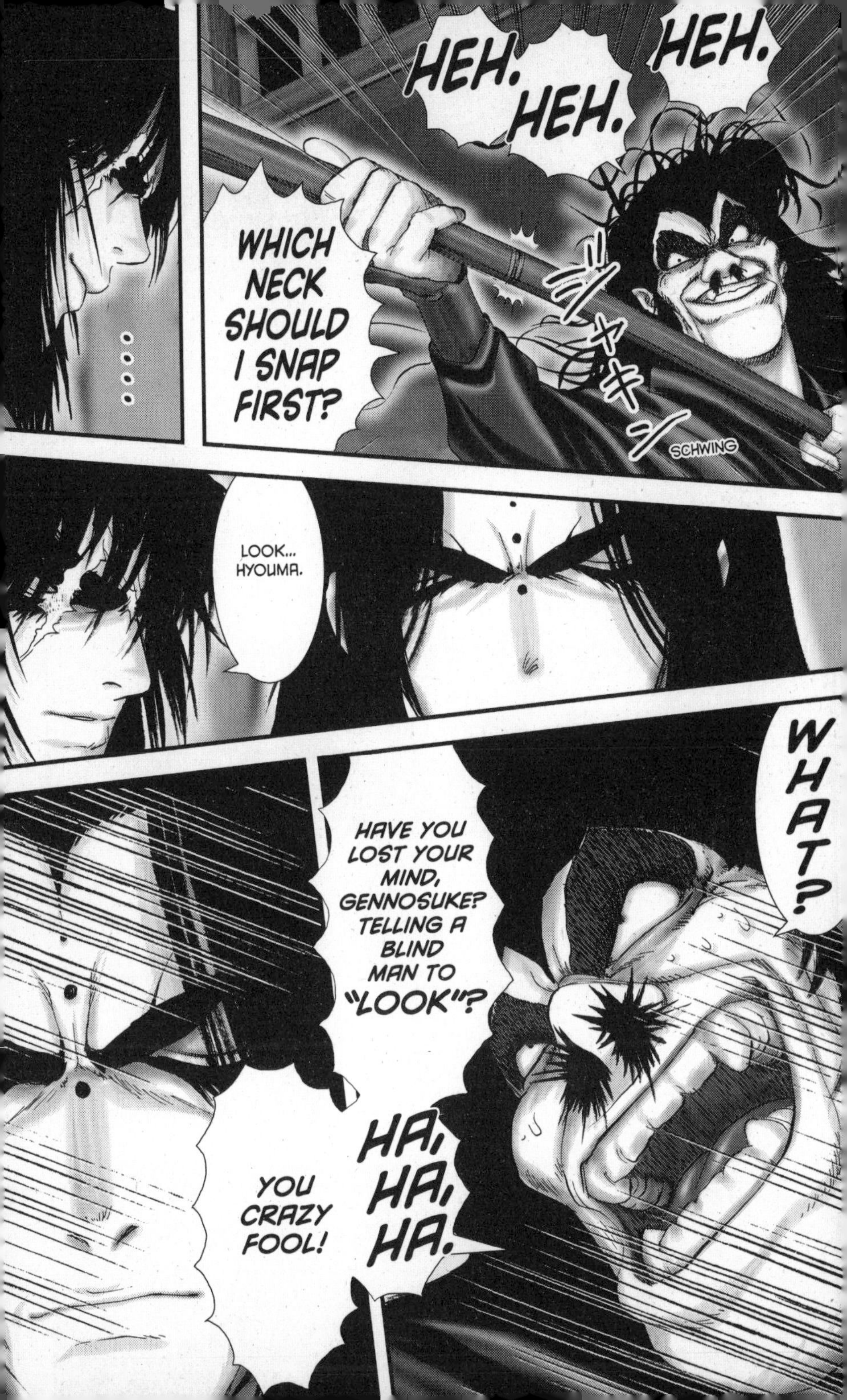
HEH.
HEH.
HEH.
WHICH NECK SHOULD I SNAP FIRST?
SCHWING
....
LOOK... HYOUMA.
WHAT?
HAVE YOU LOST YOUR MIND, GENNOSUKE? TELLING A BLIND MAN TO "LOOK"?
HA, HA, HA.
YOU CRAZY FOOL!

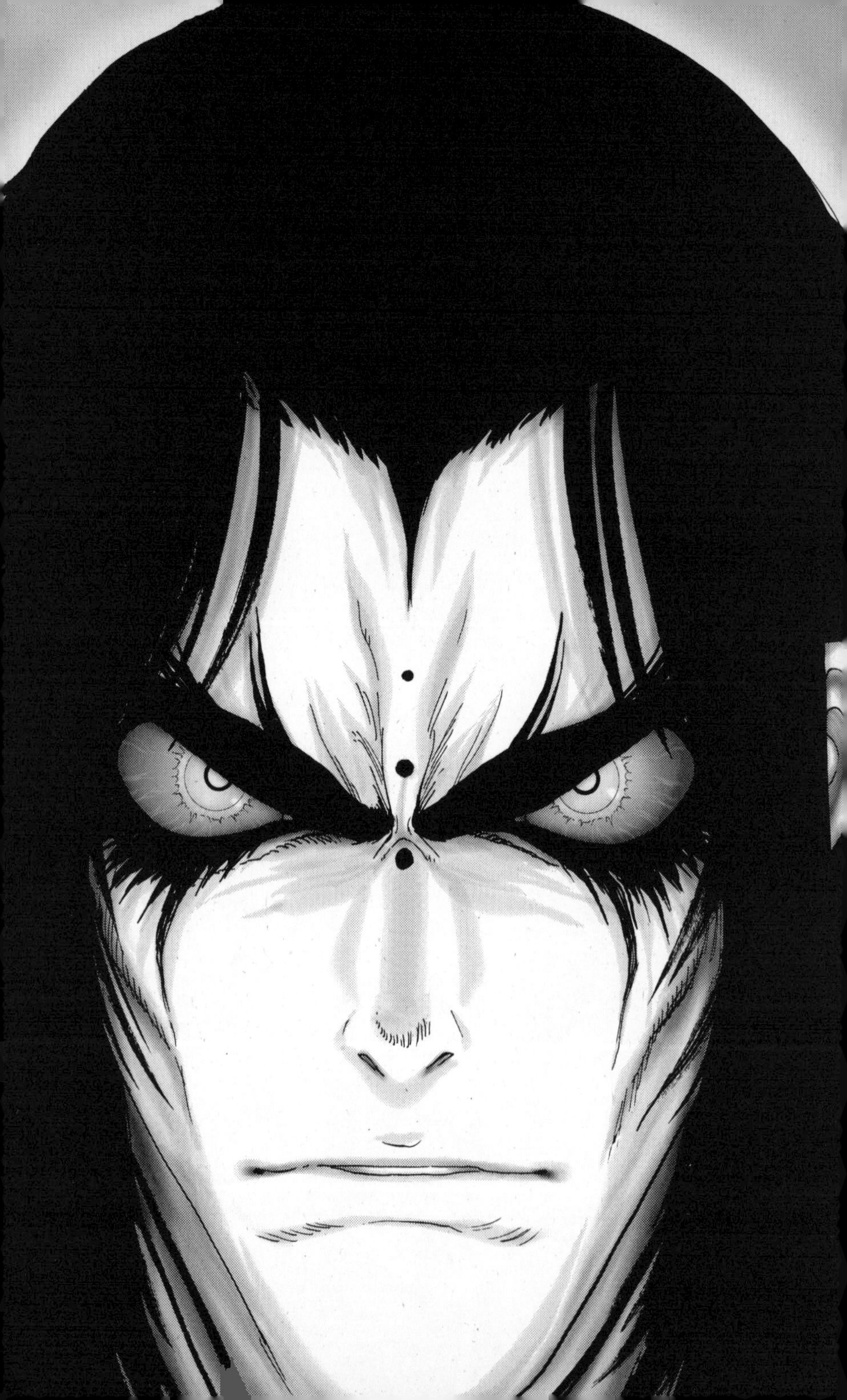

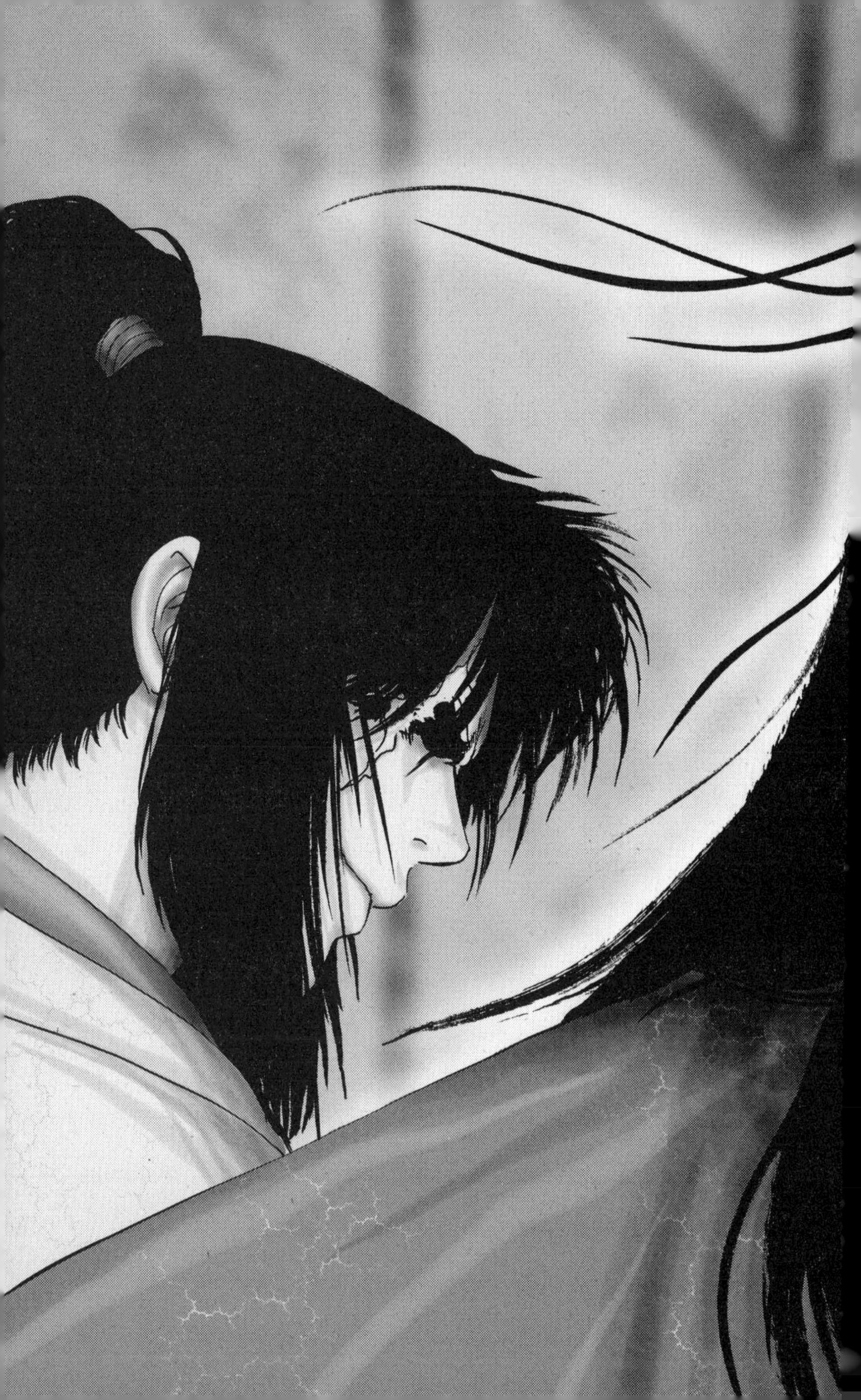

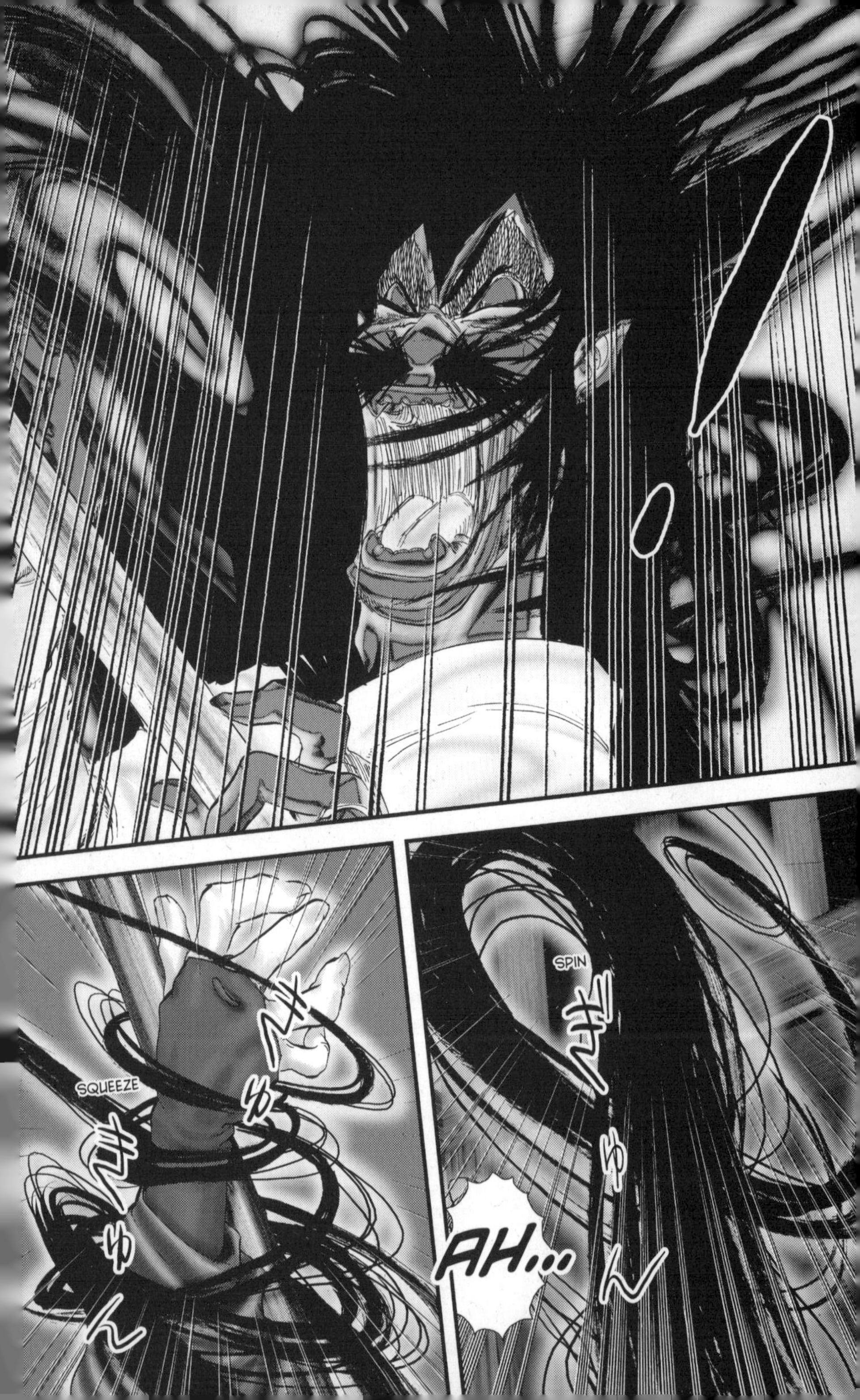
SPIN
AH...
SQUEEZE

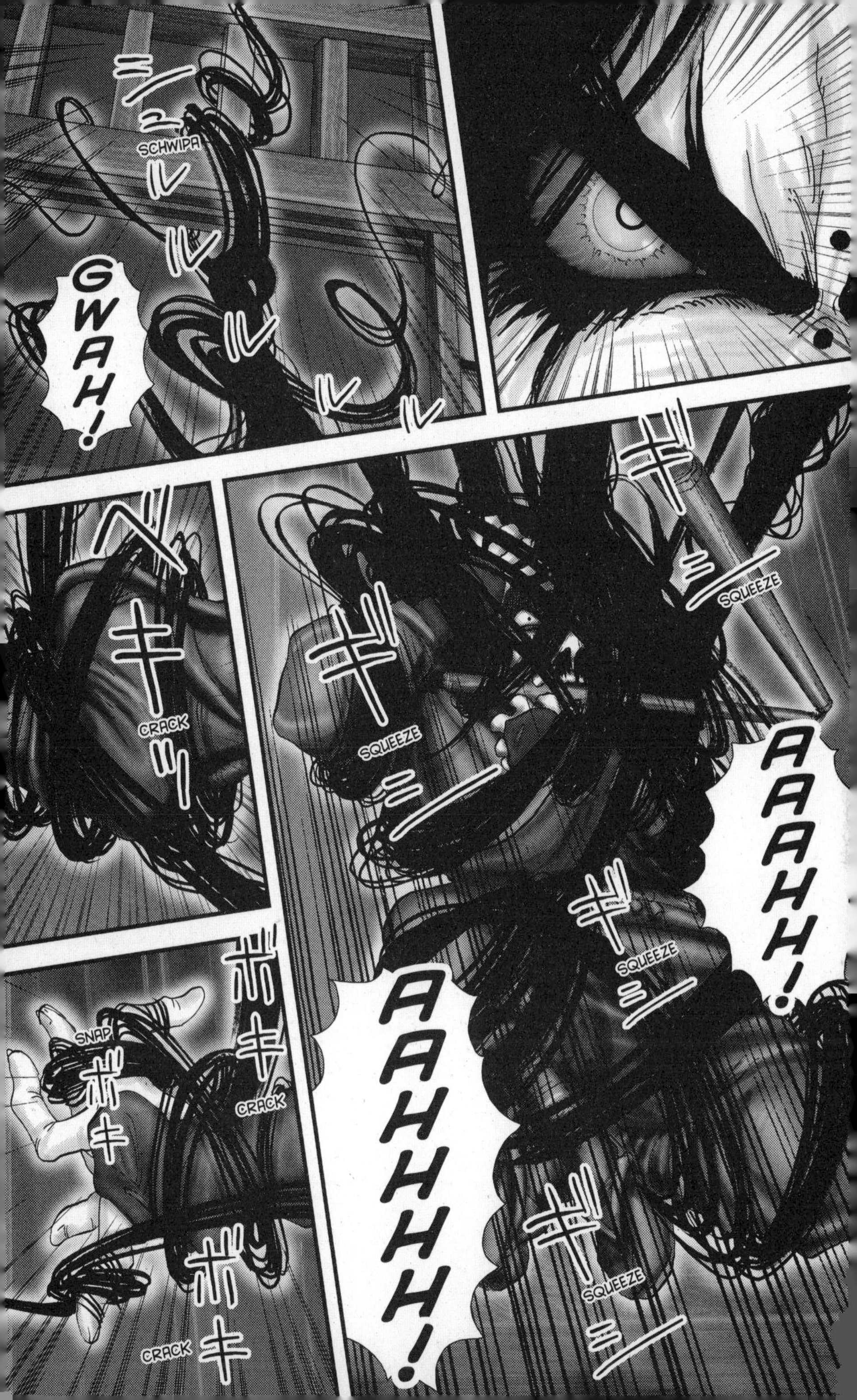
SCHWIPA
GWAH!
SQUEEZE
AAAAHH!
SQUEEZE
SQUEEZE
AAHHHHH!
SQUEEZE
CRACK
SNAP
CRACK
CRACK

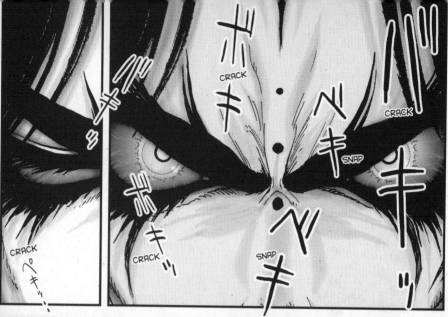

CRACK

CRACK

CRACK

SNAP

CRACK

CRACK

SNAP

...BE CAUSING ANY MORE TROUBLE.

HE WON'T...

GOOD.

YOU'RE AS POWER-FUL AS THE DAY YOU TAUGHT ME MY FIRST LESSON. WELL DONE.

IT IS AN HONOR TO HEAR SUCH WORDS FROM YOU.

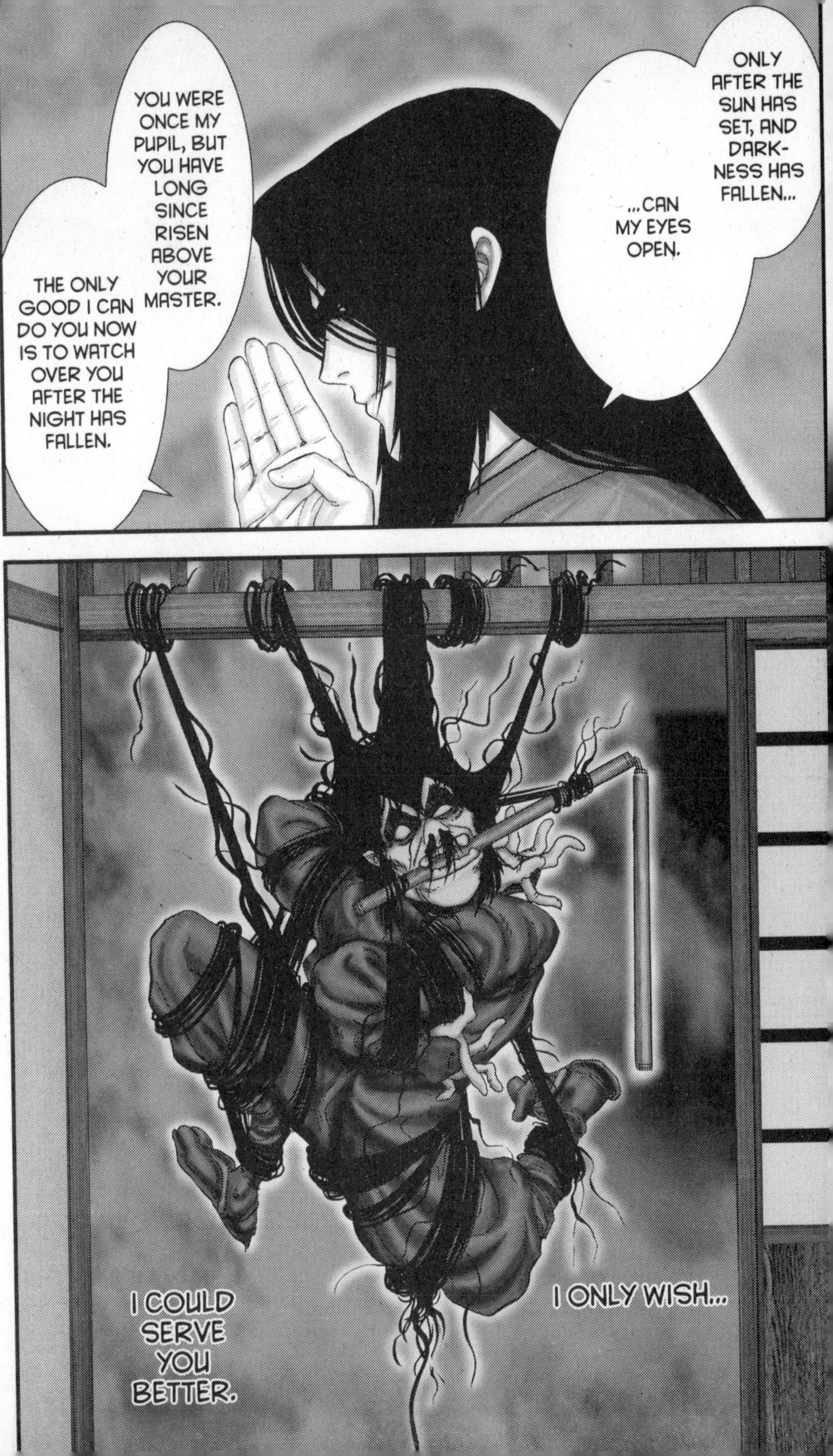
ONLY AFTER THE SUN HAS SET, AND DARKNESS HAS FALLEN...
...CAN MY EYES OPEN.
YOU WERE ONCE MY PUPIL, BUT YOU HAVE LONG SINCE RISEN ABOVE YOUR MASTER.
THE ONLY GOOD I CAN DO YOU NOW IS TO WATCH OVER YOU AFTER THE NIGHT HAS FALLEN.
I ONLY WISH...
I COULD SERVE YOU BETTER.

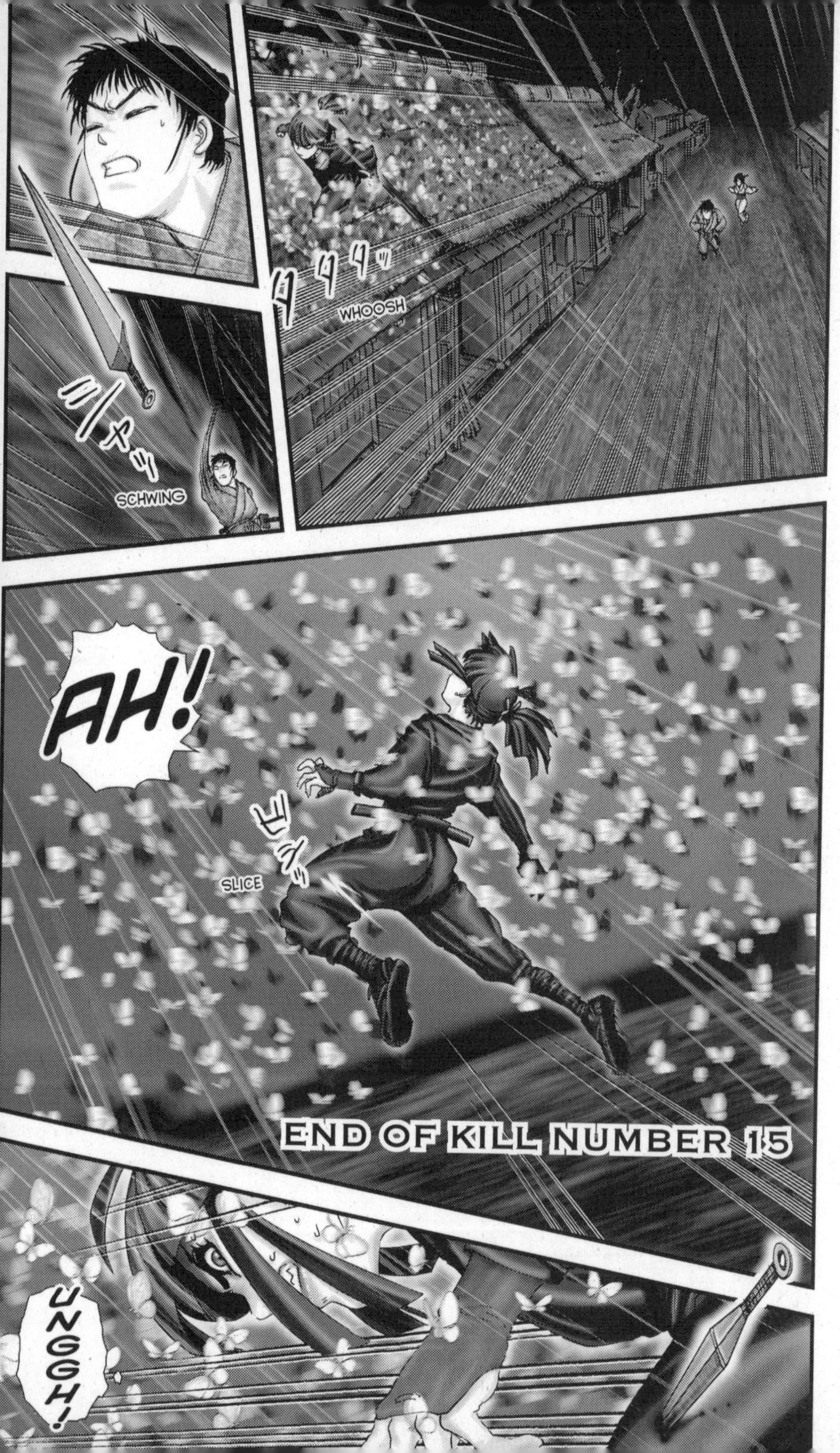
WHOOSH
SCHWING
AH!
SLICE
END OF KILL NUMBER 15
UNGGH!

服部半蔵
霞刑部
解かれ了んぬ
じ闘して殺すべし
駿府城へまかり
勝たば一族
雨夜陣五郎
筑摩小四郎
蓑念鬼
蛍火
朱絹

右甲賀十人衆伊賀十人衆たがいにあい闘
のこれるものこの秘巻をたずさえ五月晦日駿
出ずべきことその数多きを勝ちとなし勝た
永禄あらん
甲賀組十人衆
甲賀弾正
甲賀弦之介
地虫十兵衛
風待将監

徳川家
鵜殿丈助
如月左衛門
室賀豹馬
陽炎

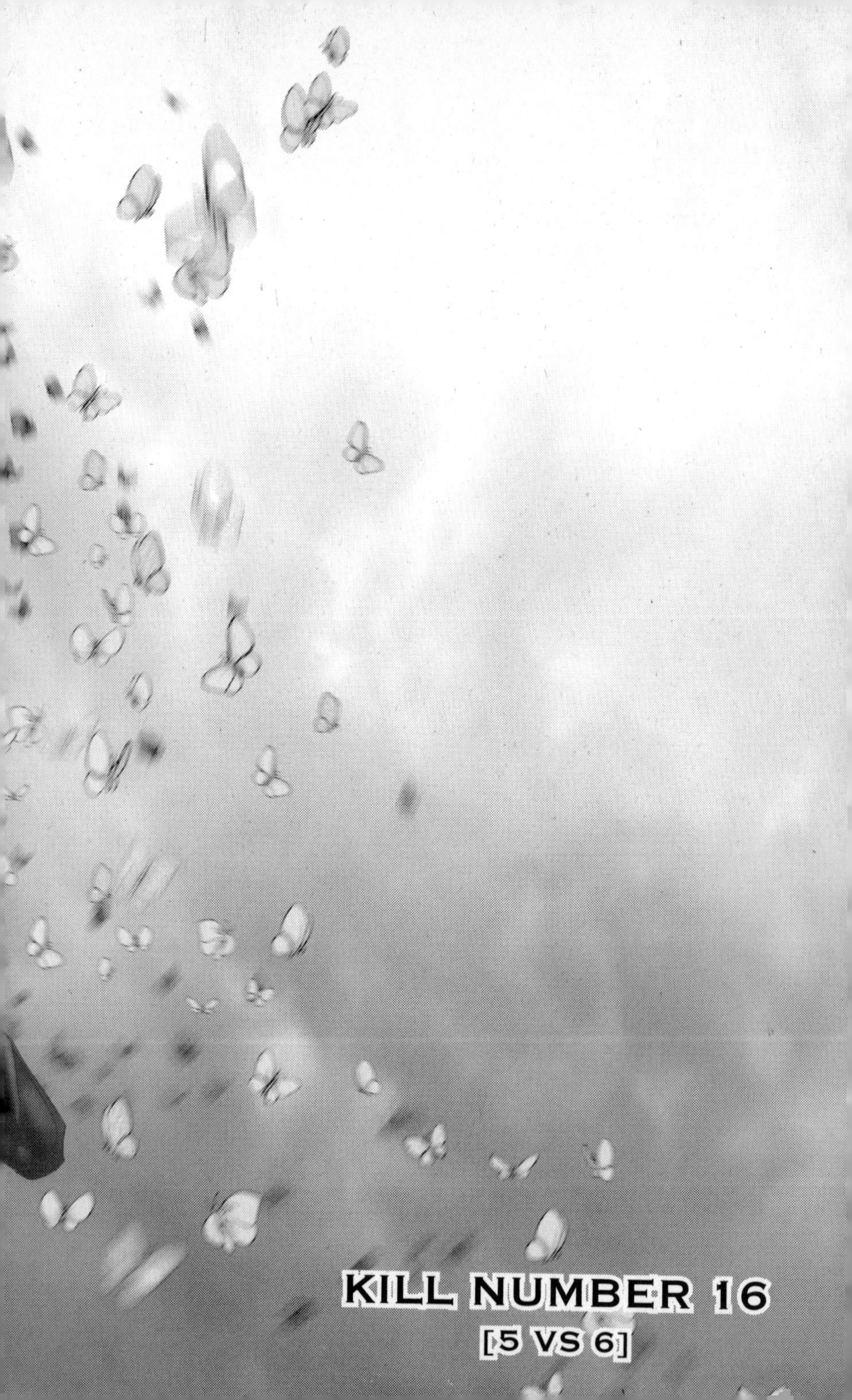
KILL NUMBER 16
[5 VS 6]

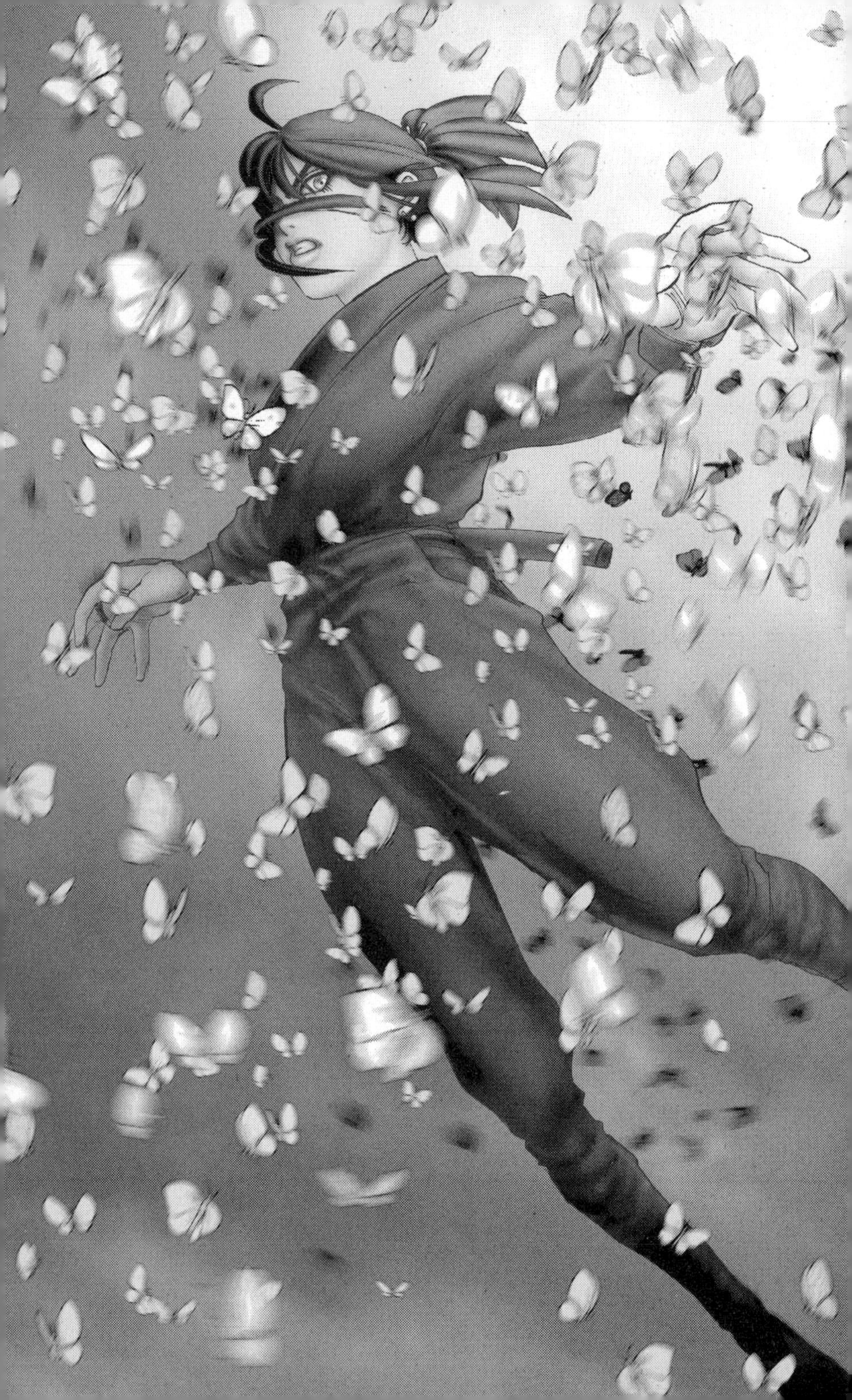

右甲賀十人衆　伊賀十人衆たがひに

胡夷

賀豹馬

月左衛門

伊賀　蝋袮　へとこと　秘巻をたずさえ

おゝ幻楽禄りん

朧

夜陣五郎

夜叉丸

慶長十九年四月

雨夜陣五郎

筑摩小四郎

徳

蝋斉

蓑念鬼

螢火

摩小巴郎

薬師寺天膳

朱絹

蓑念鬼

服部半蔵との約定

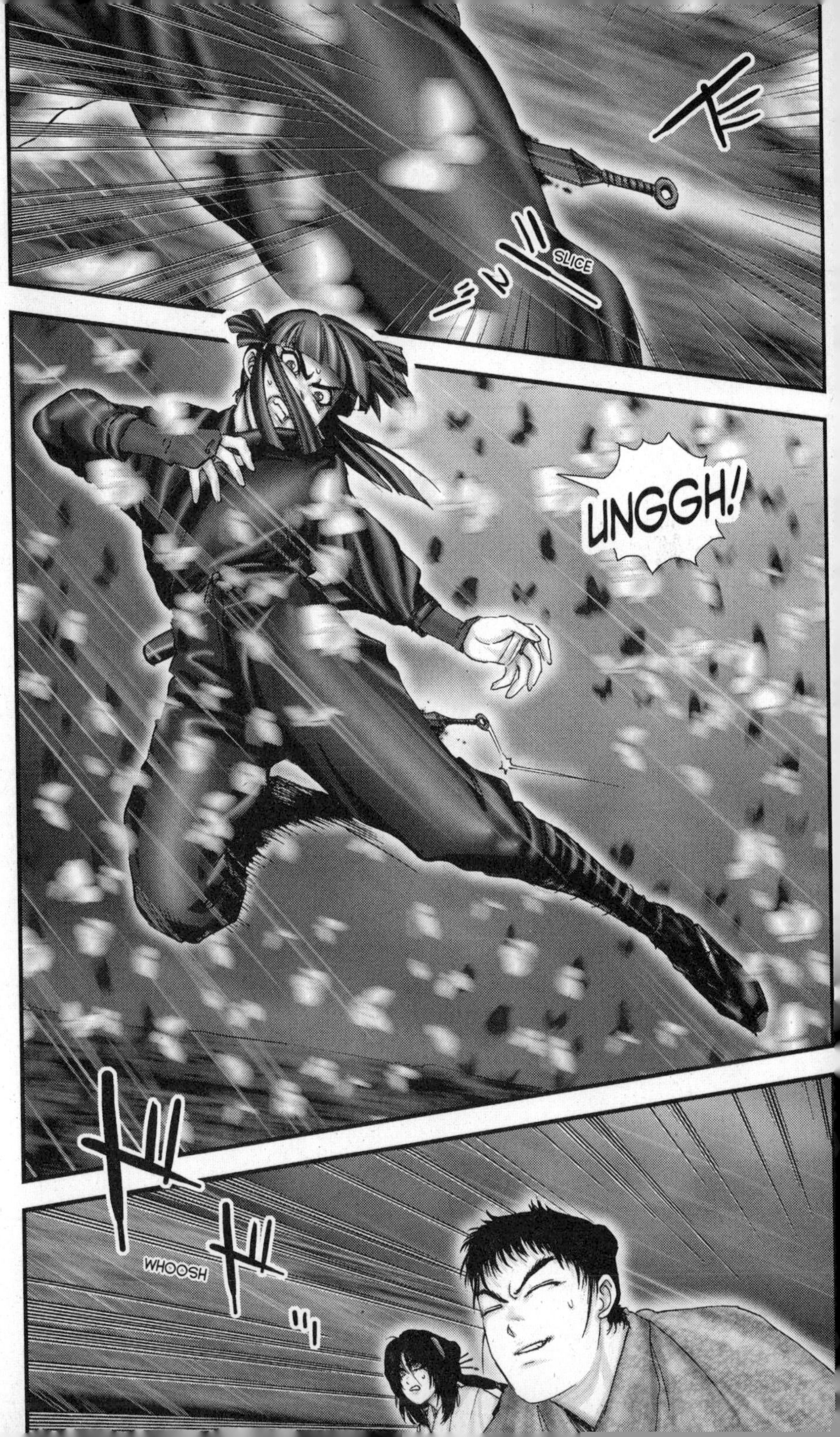
SLICE
UNGGH!
WHOOSH

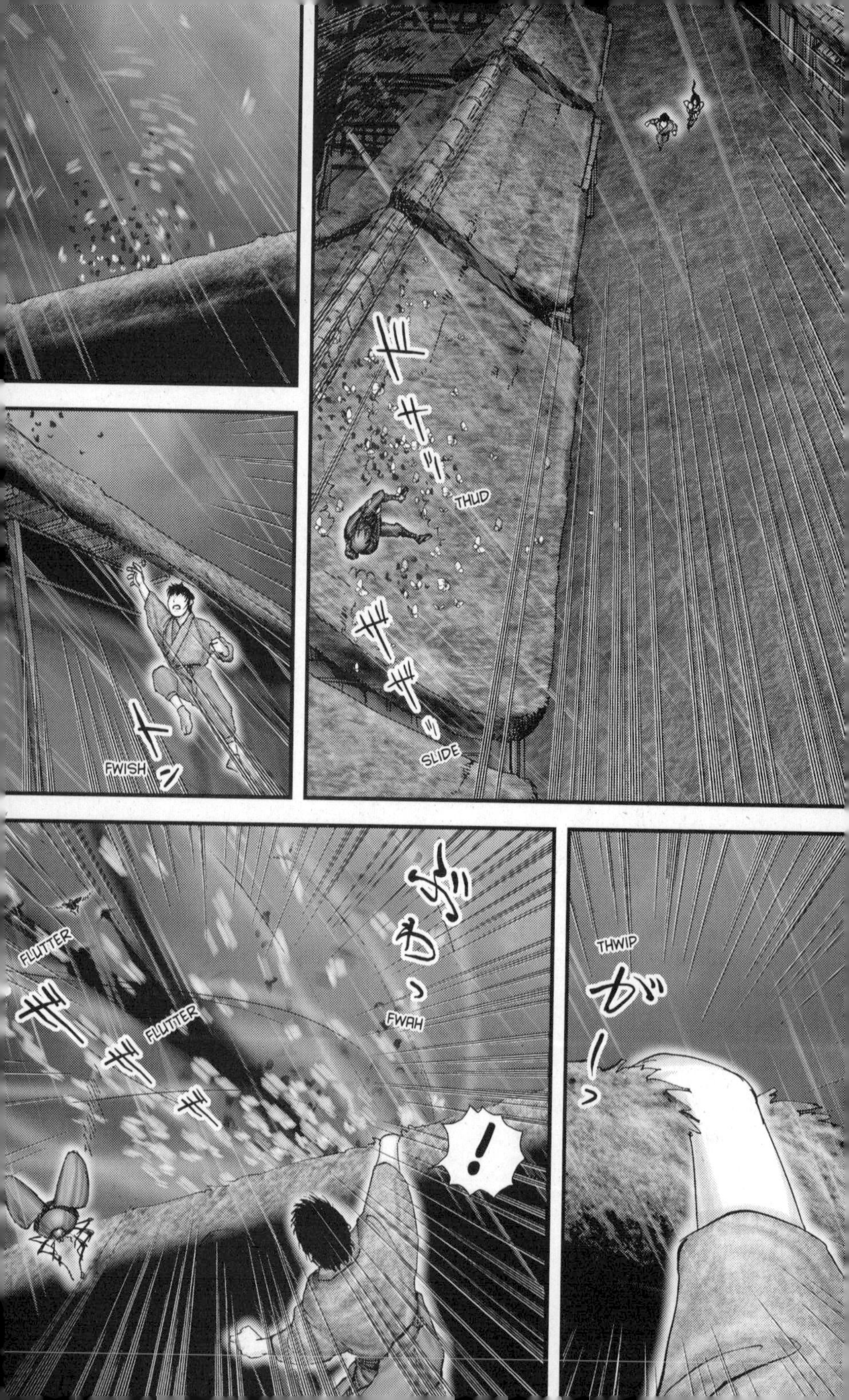
THUD
SLIDE
FWISH
THWIP
FWAH
FLUTTER
FLUTTER
!

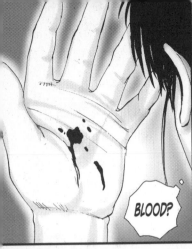

BLOOD?

DRIP

THWUP

WHOOSH

I WON'T LET HER GET AWAY!

SHE'S HURT!

SAEMON DONO.

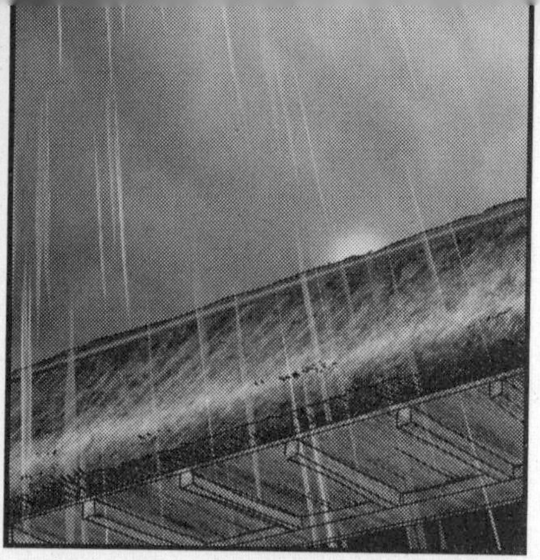

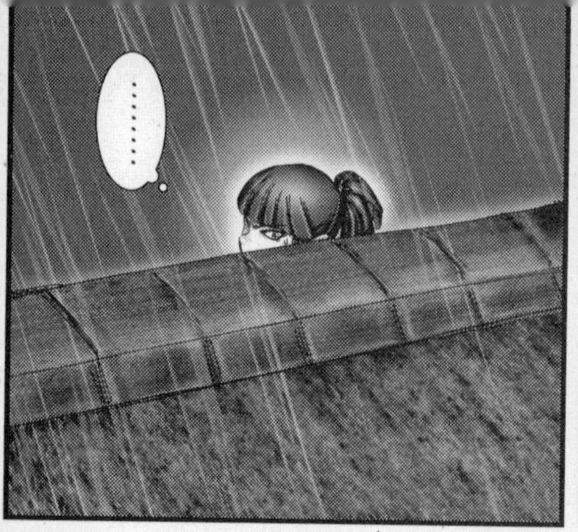

......

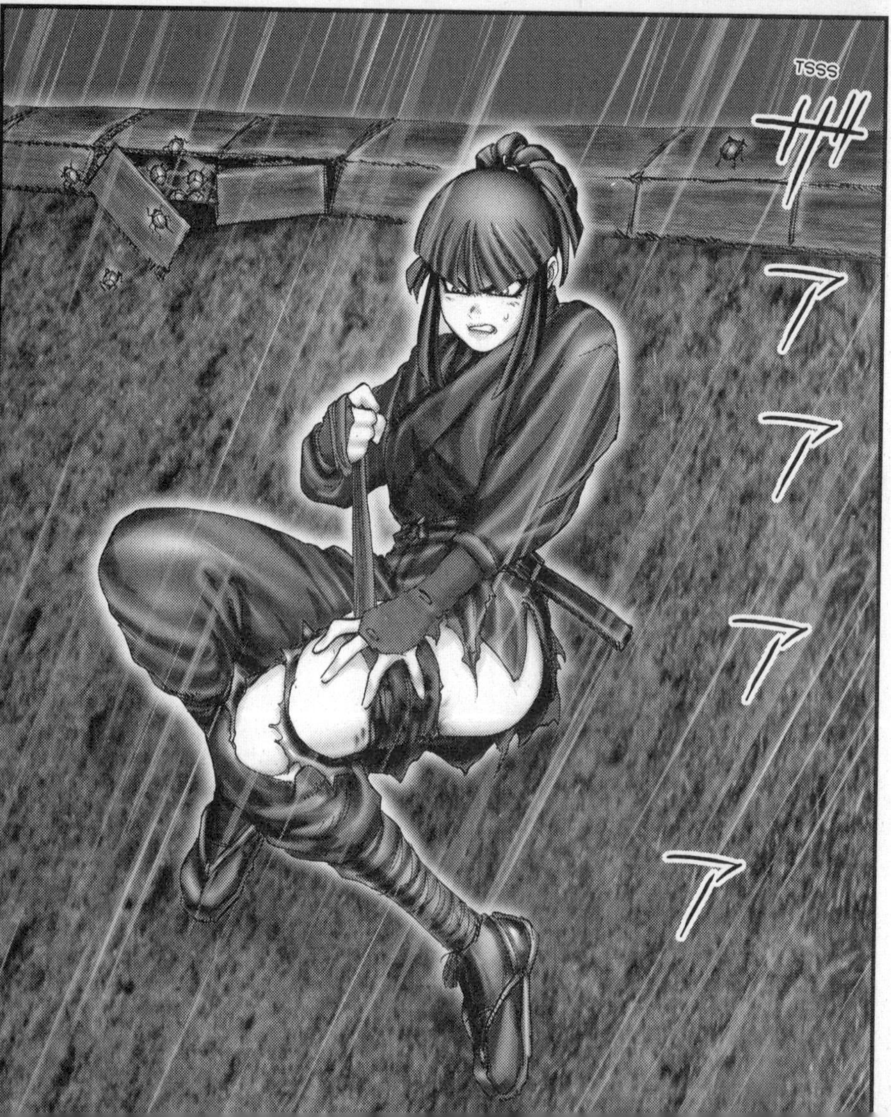

TSSS
ザアアアア

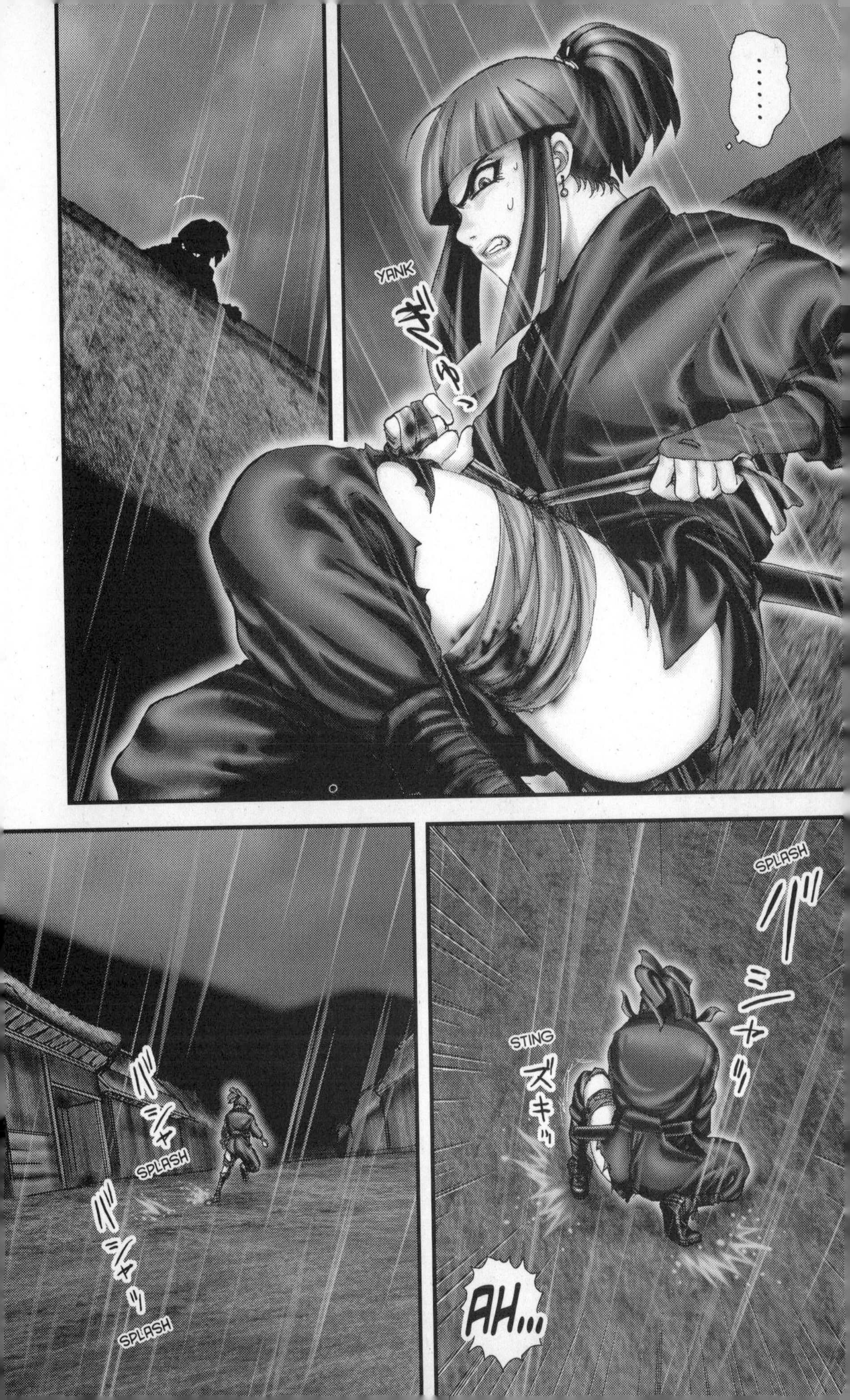
......
YANK
ぎゅっ
SPLASH
STING
ズキッ
AH...
バシャ
SPLASH
バシャッ
SPLASH

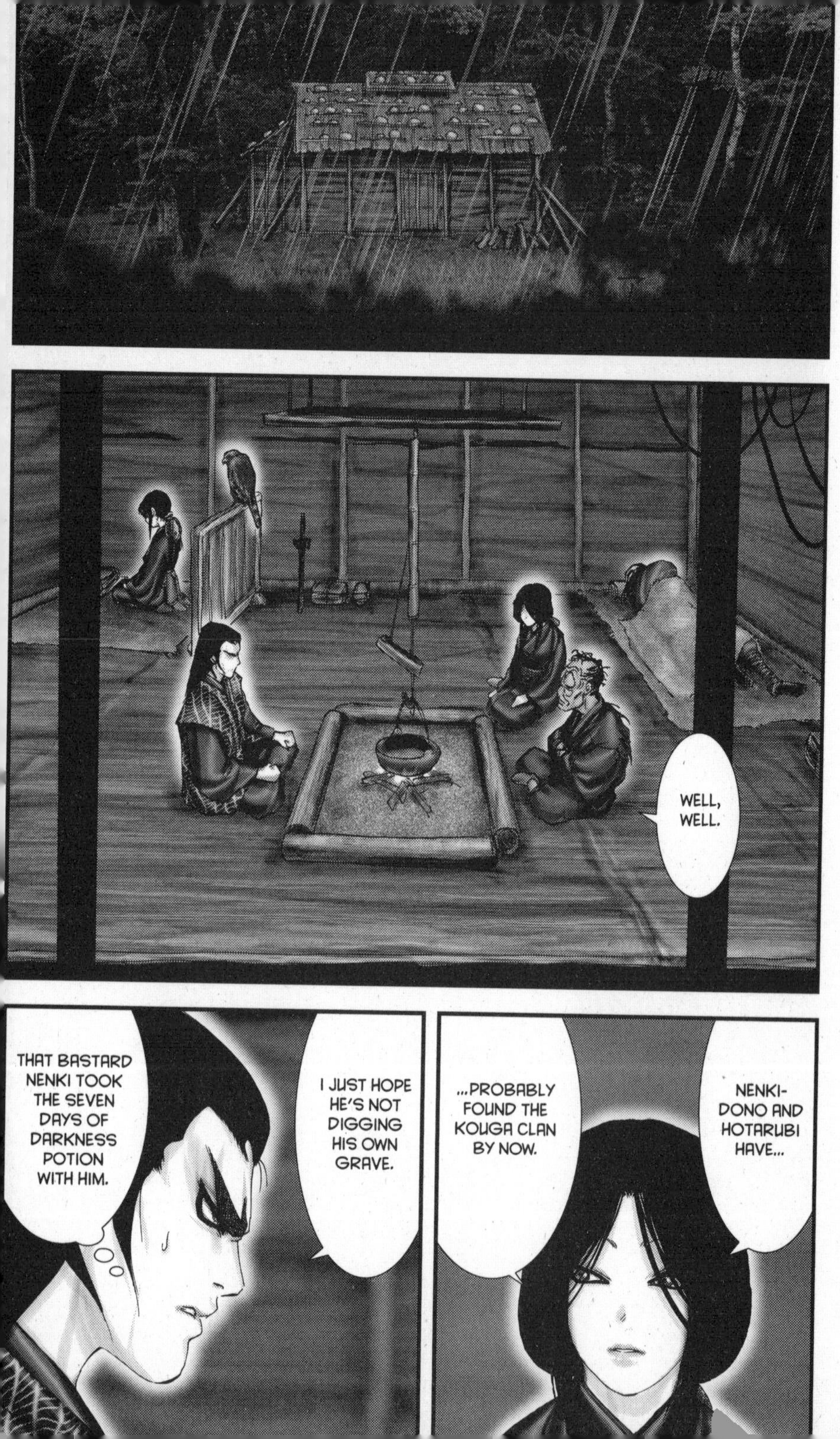
WELL, WELL.
NENKI-DONO AND HOTARUBI HAVE...
...PROBABLY FOUND THE KOUGA CLAN BY NOW.
I JUST HOPE HE'S NOT DIGGING HIS OWN GRAVE.
THAT BASTARD NENKI TOOK THE SEVEN DAYS OF DARKNESS POTION WITH HIM.

IN ANY CASE, THERE'S NO WAY THAT OBORO-SAMA AND KOSHIROU CAN GO OUT IN THIS RAIN-STORM.

WE'LL HAVE TO MEET BACK UP WITH THEM TOMORROW.

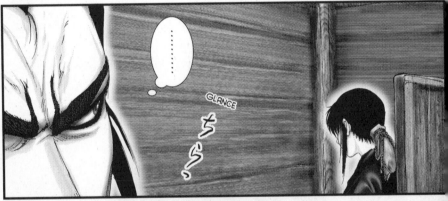

· · · · · · · · ·

GLANCE

ちらっ

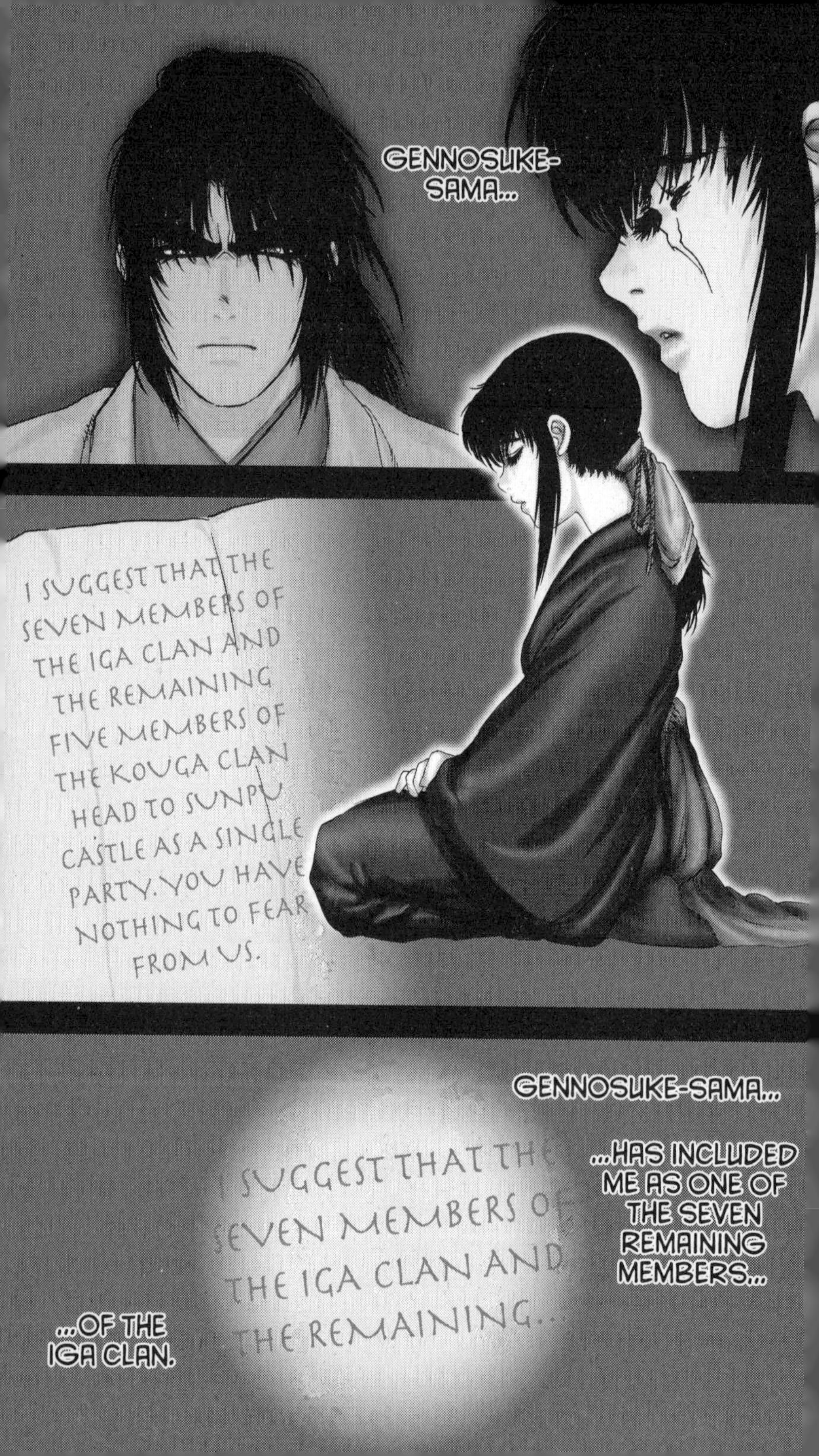
GENNOSUKE-SAMA...
I SUGGEST THAT THE SEVEN MEMBERS OF THE IGA CLAN AND THE REMAINING FIVE MEMBERS OF THE KOUGA CLAN HEAD TO SUNPU CASTLE AS A SINGLE PARTY. YOU HAVE NOTHING TO FEAR FROM US.
GENNOSUKE-SAMA...
...HAS INCLUDED ME AS ONE OF THE SEVEN REMAINING MEMBERS...
SUGGEST THAT TH
SEVEN MEMBERS O
THE IGA CLAN AND
THE REMAINING...
...OF THE IGA CLAN.

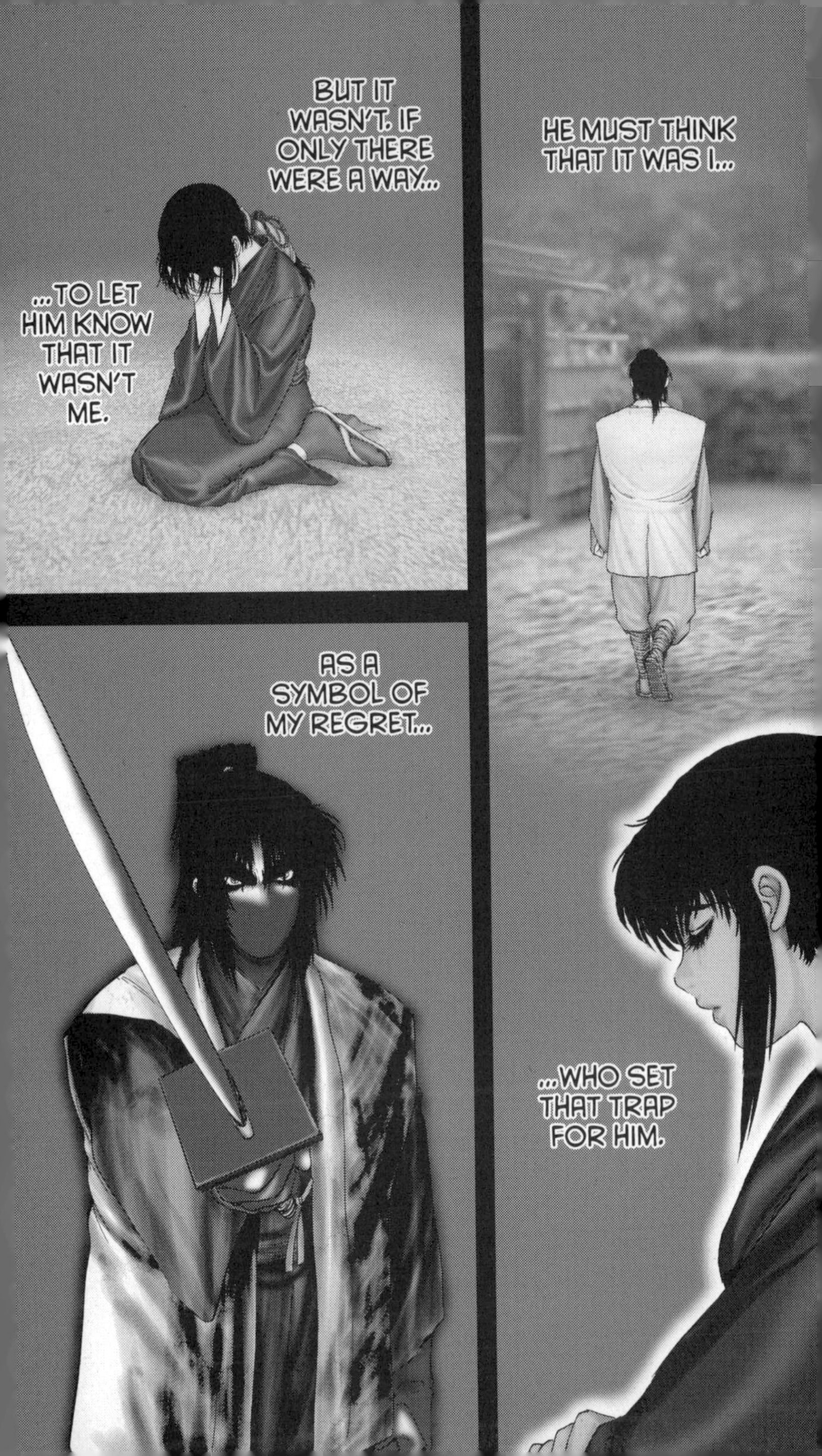
HE MUST THINK THAT IT WAS I...
...WHO SET THAT TRAP FOR HIM.
BUT IT WASN'T. IF ONLY THERE WERE A WAY...
...TO LET HIM KNOW THAT IT WASN'T ME.
AS A SYMBOL OF MY REGRET...

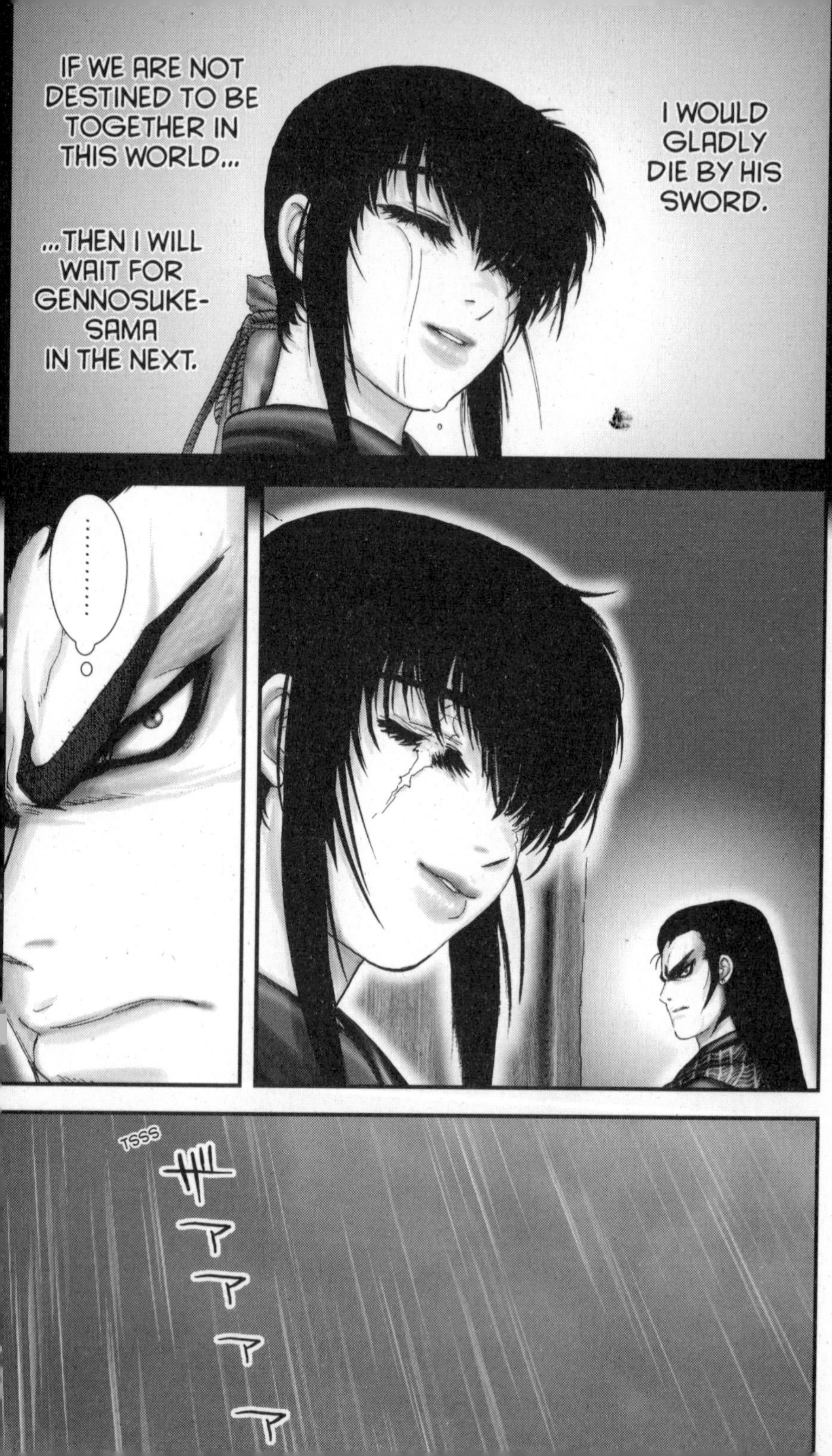
I WOULD GLADLY DIE BY HIS SWORD.
IF WE ARE NOT DESTINED TO BE TOGETHER IN THIS WORLD...
...THEN I WILL WAIT FOR GENNOSUKE-SAMA IN THE NEXT.
....
TSSS

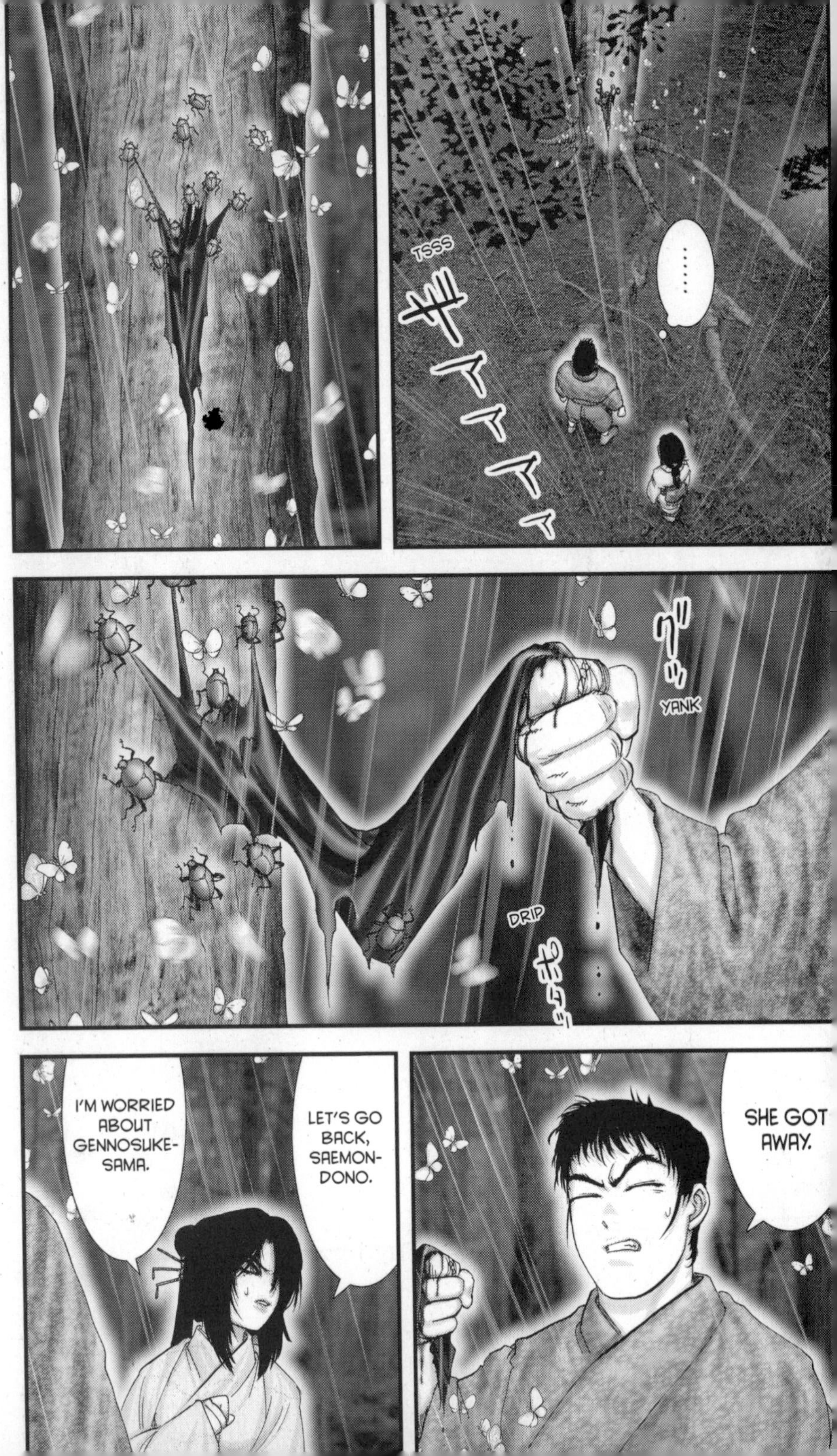

TSSS
......
YANK
DRIP
SHE GOT AWAY.
LET'S GO BACK, SAEMON-DONO.
I'M WORRIED ABOUT GENNOSUKE-SAMA.

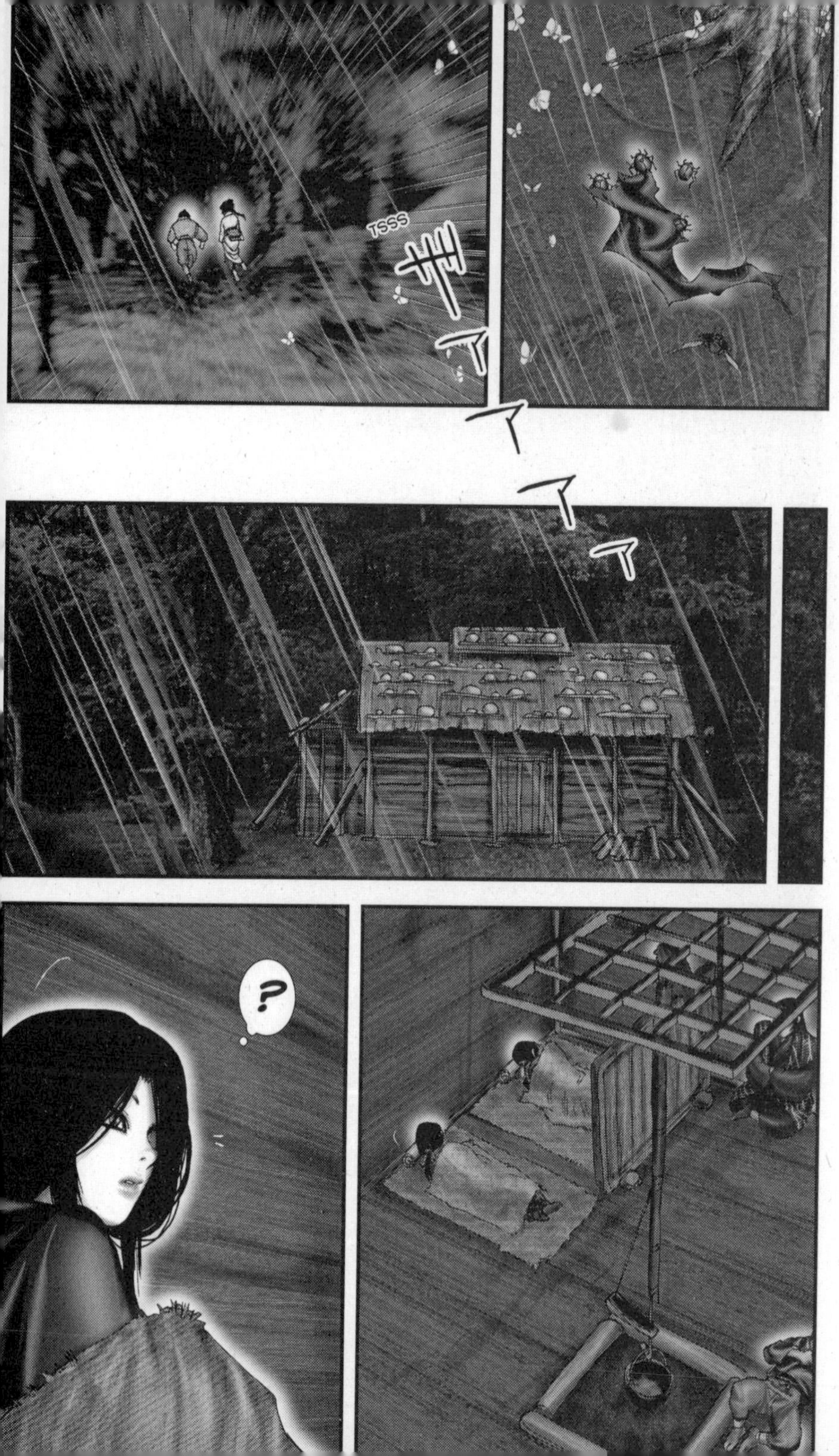
ザアアアア
TSSS
?

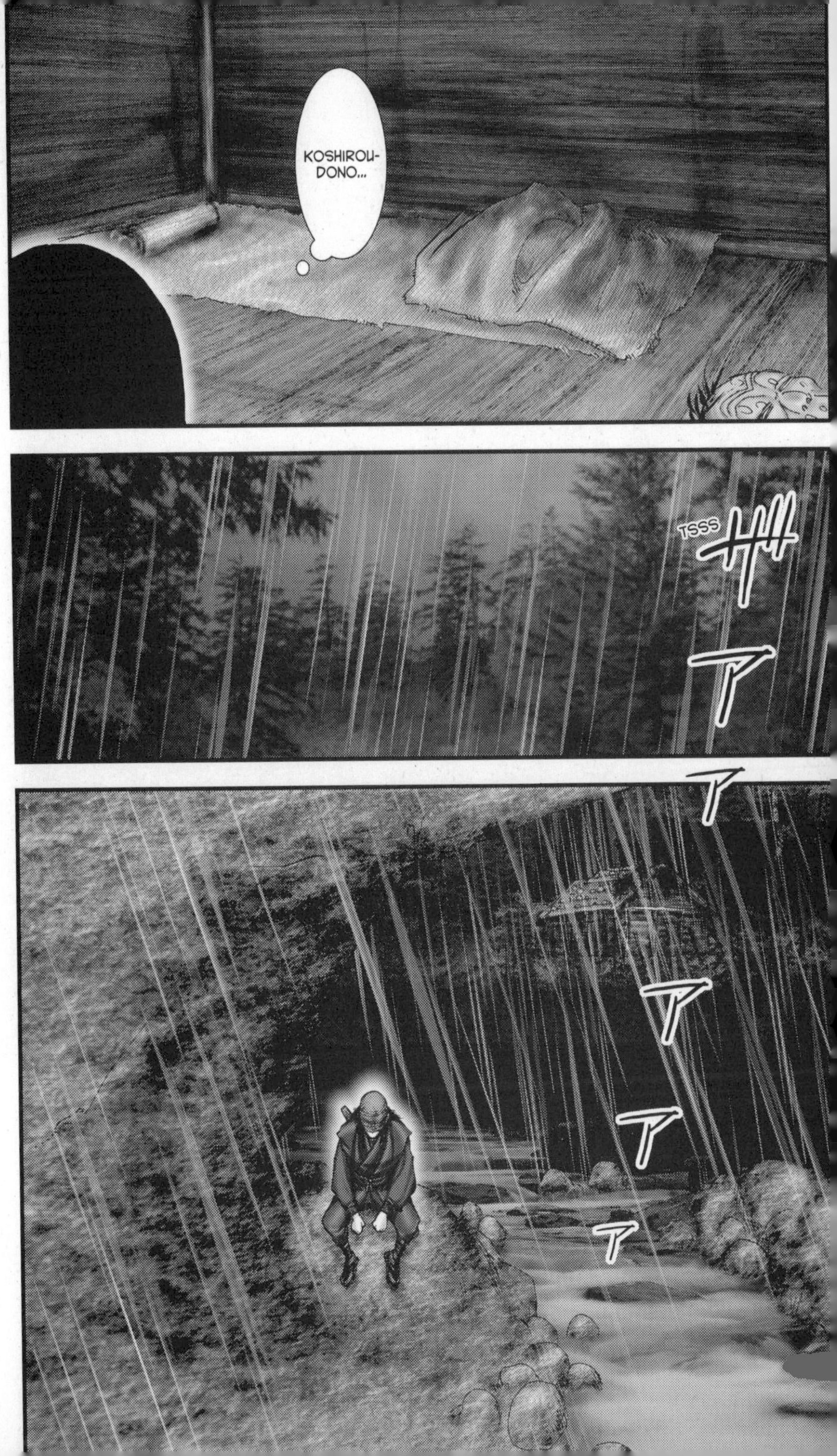
KOSHIROU-DONO...
TSSS

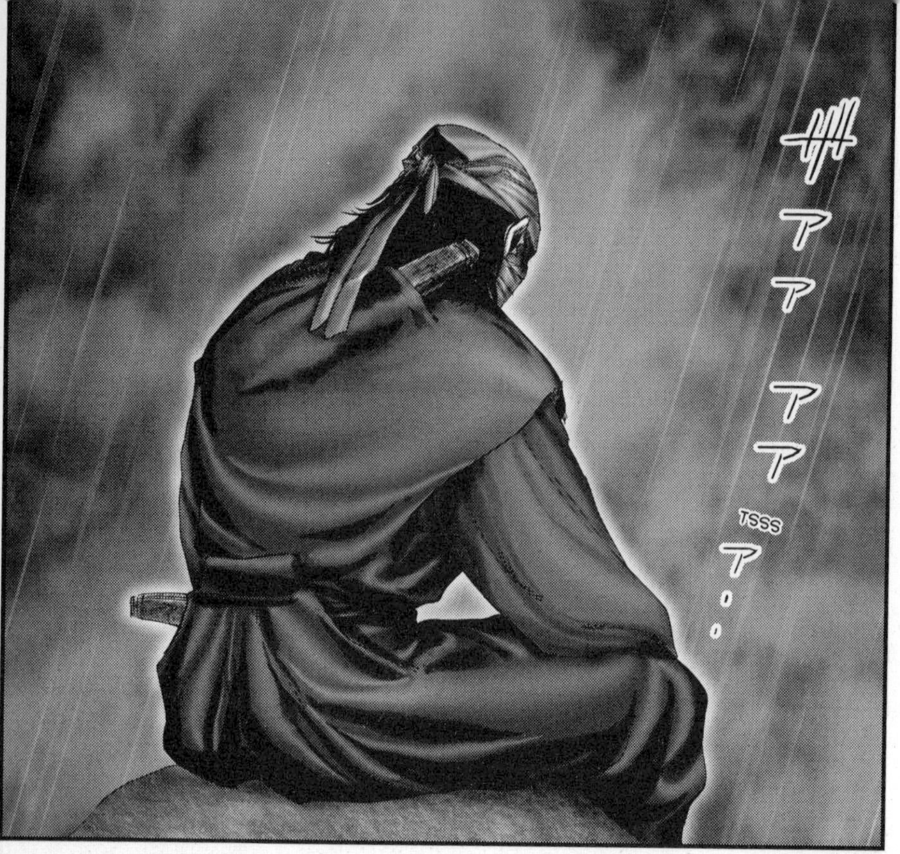
ザァァァァ..
TSSS
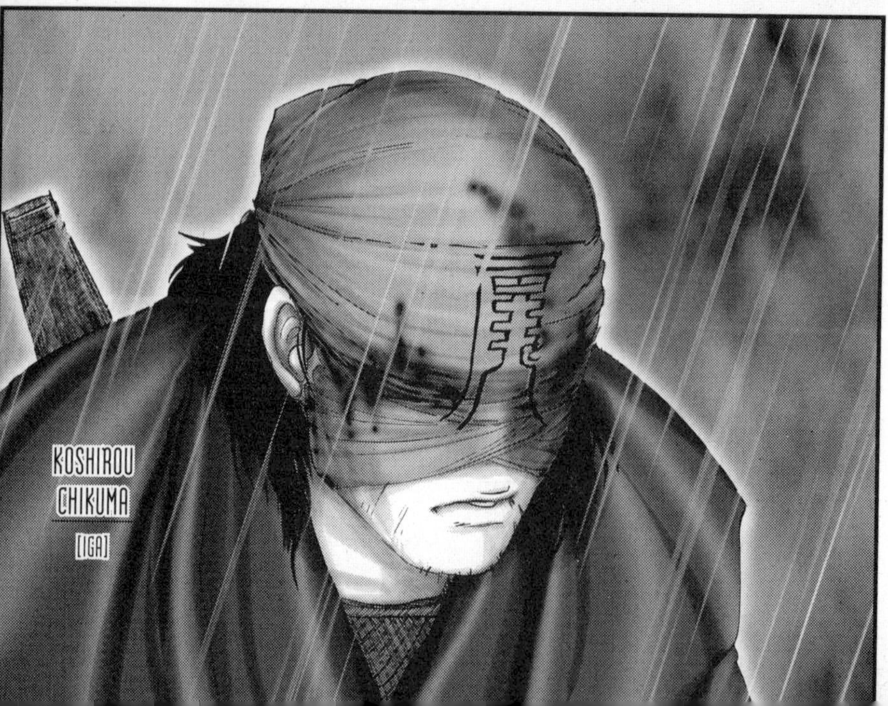
KOSHIROU
CHIKUMA
[IGA]

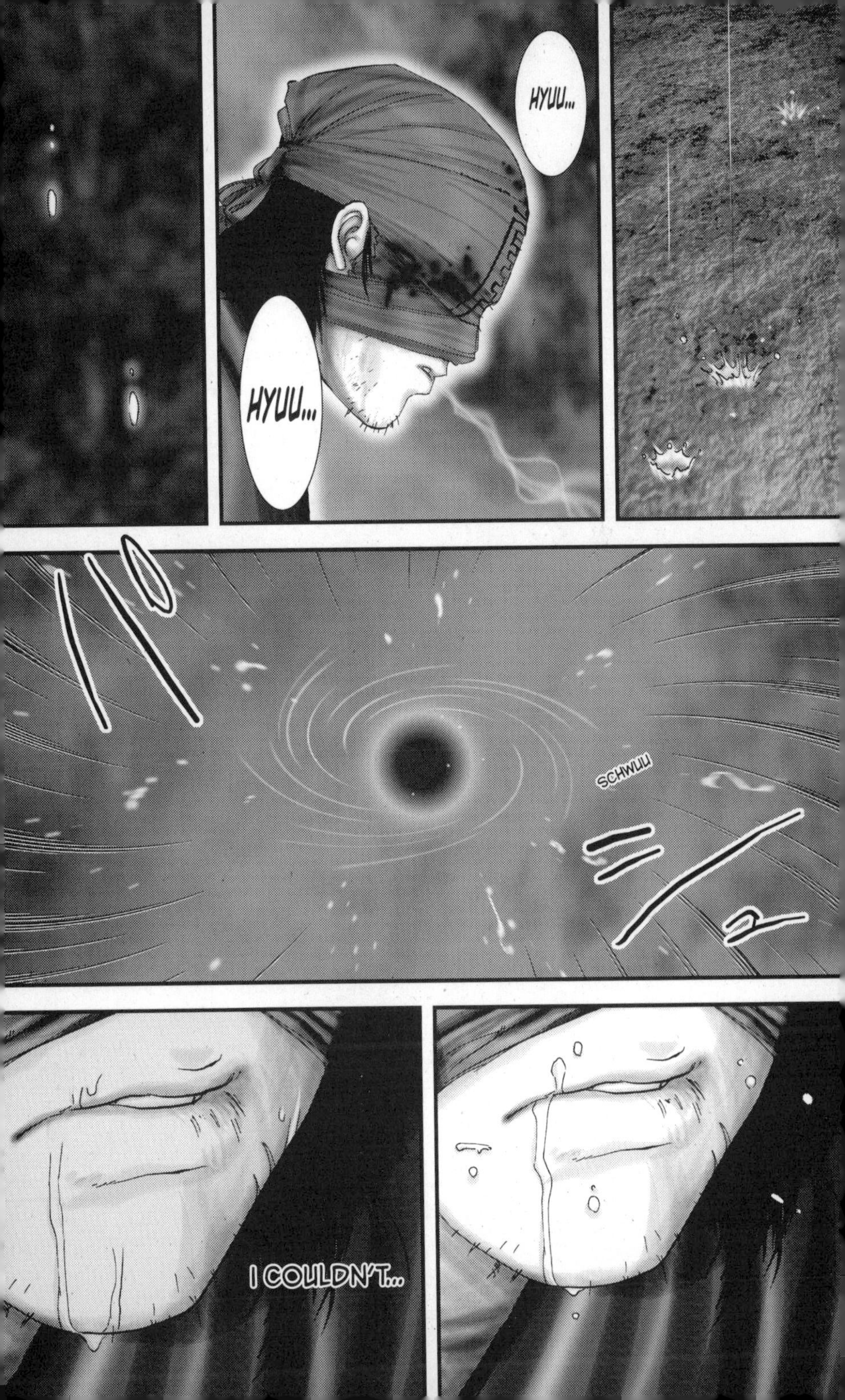
HYUU...
HYUU...
SCHWUU
I COULDN'T...

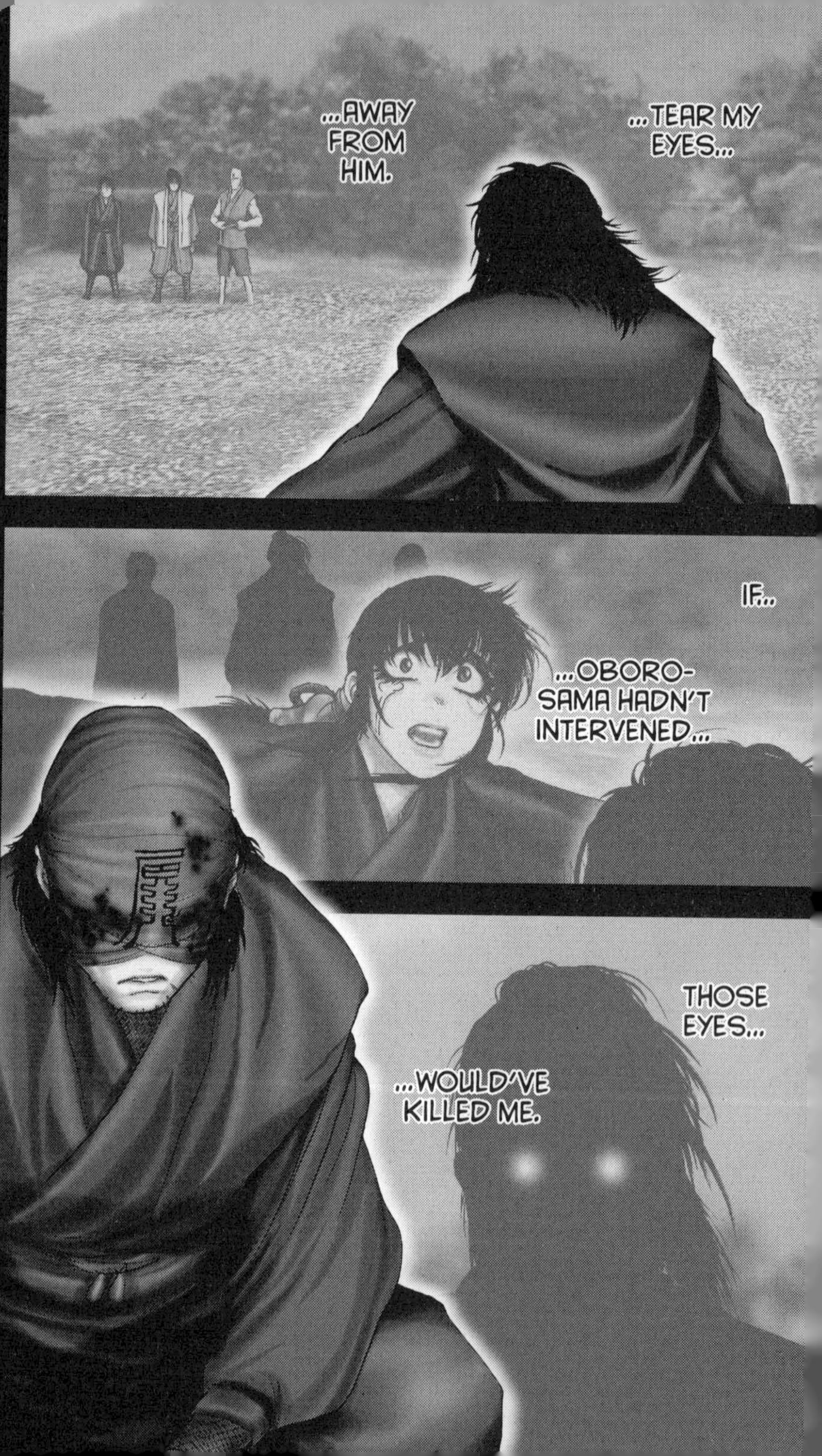
...TEAR MY EYES...
...AWAY FROM HIM.
IF...
...OBORO-SAMA HADN'T INTERVENED...
THOSE EYES...
...WOULD'VE KILLED ME.

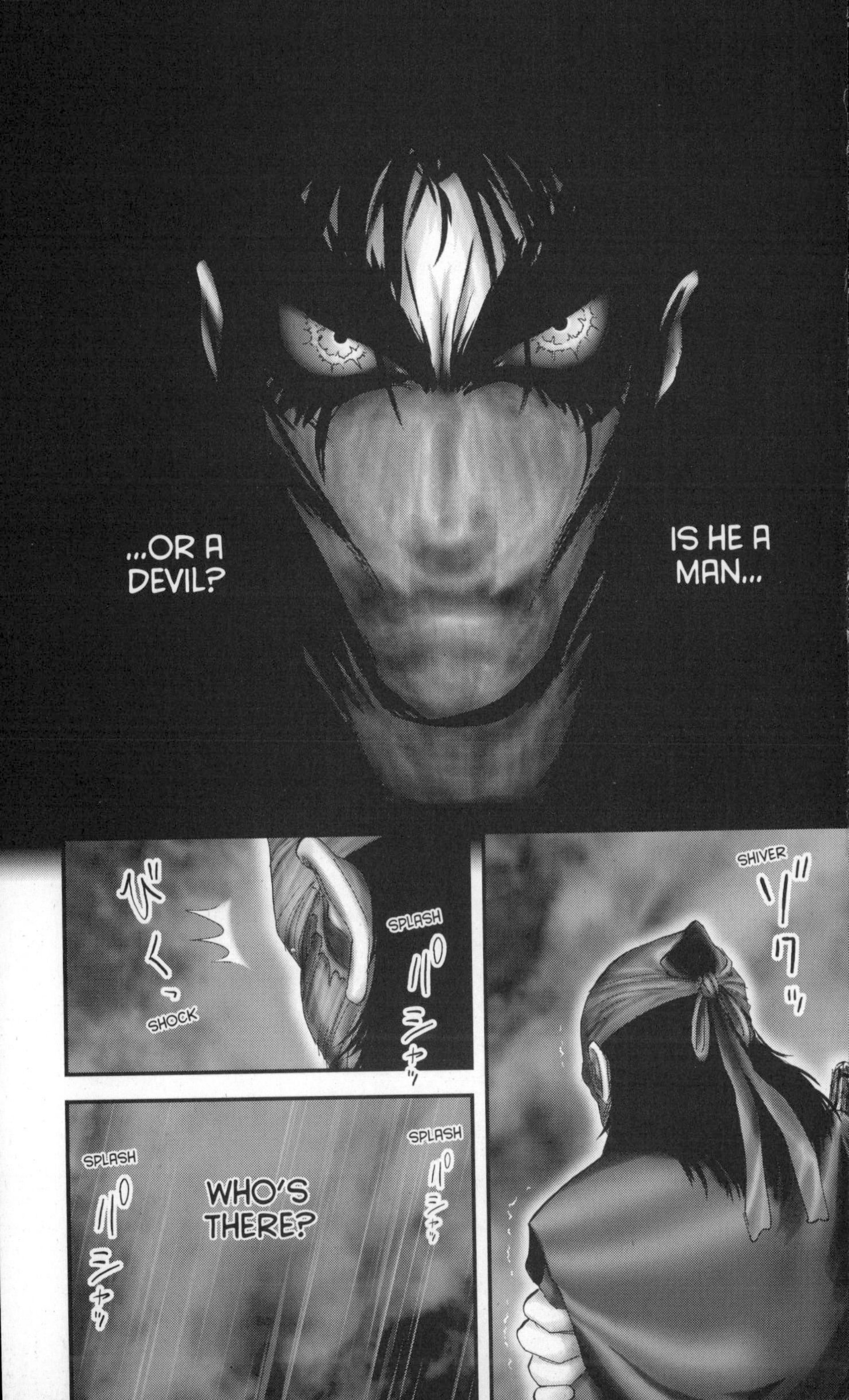

IS HE A MAN...
...OR A DEVIL?
SHIVER
SPLASH
SHOCK
SPLASH
WHO'S THERE?
SPLASH

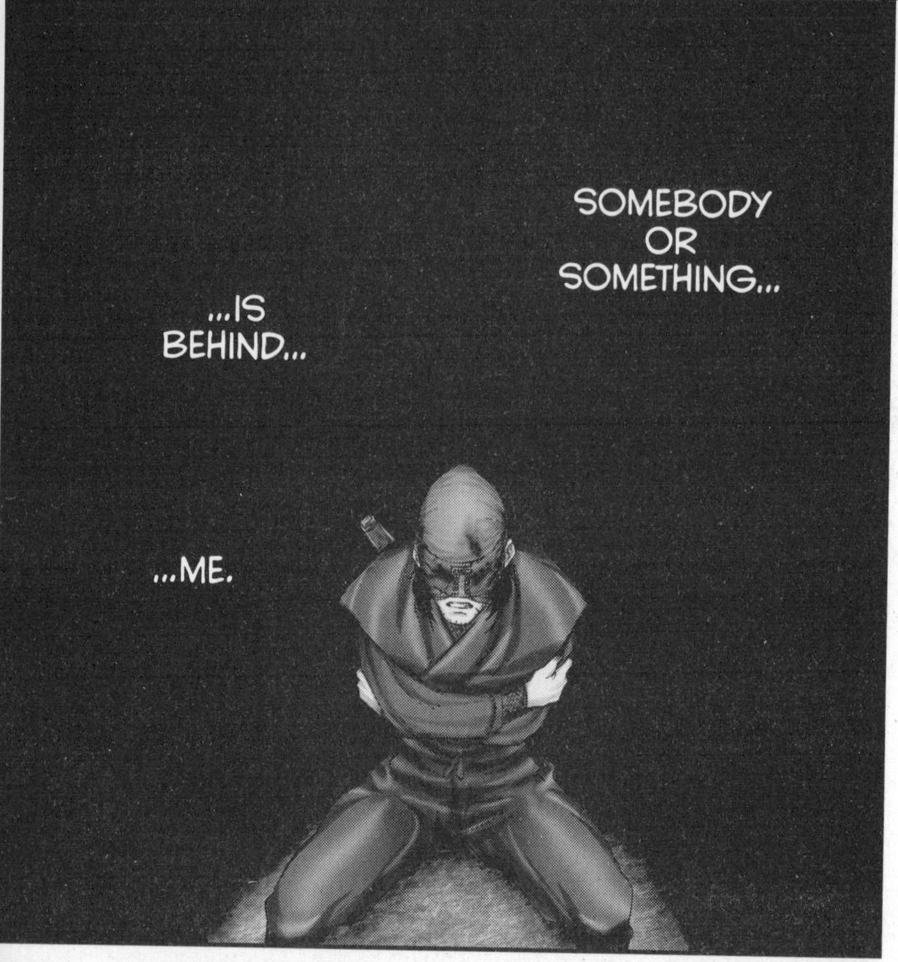
SOMEBODY OR SOMETHING...
...IS BEHIND...
...ME.
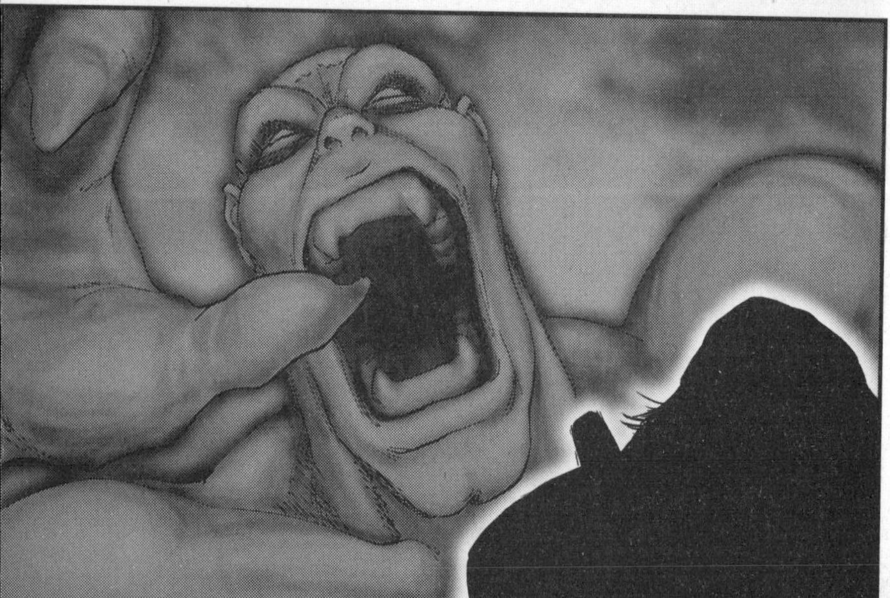

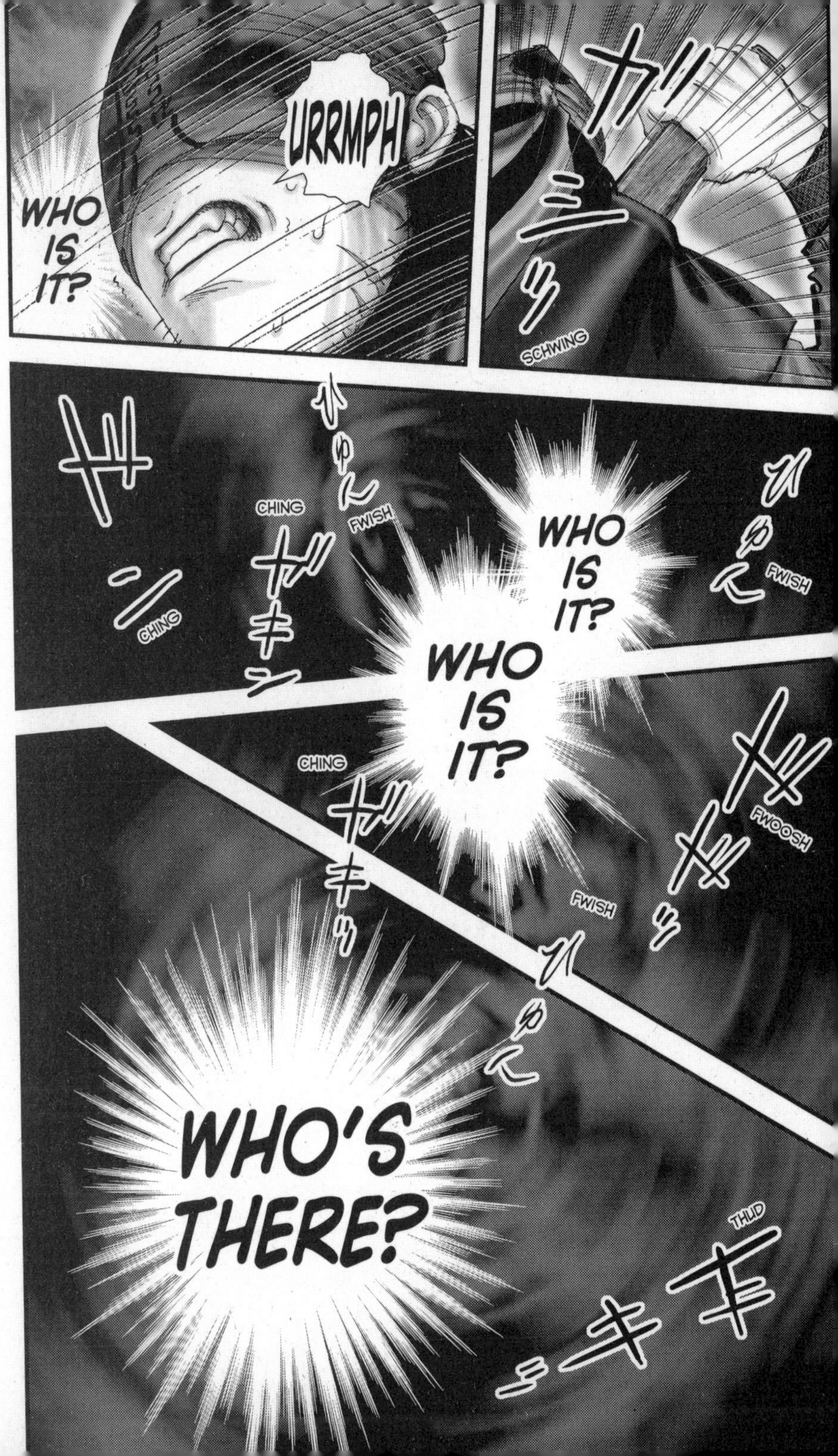
SCHWING
URRMPH
WHO IS IT?
FWISH
WHO IS IT?
FWISH
CHING
CHING
FWOOSH
WHO IS IT?
FWISH
CHING
THUD
WHO'S THERE?

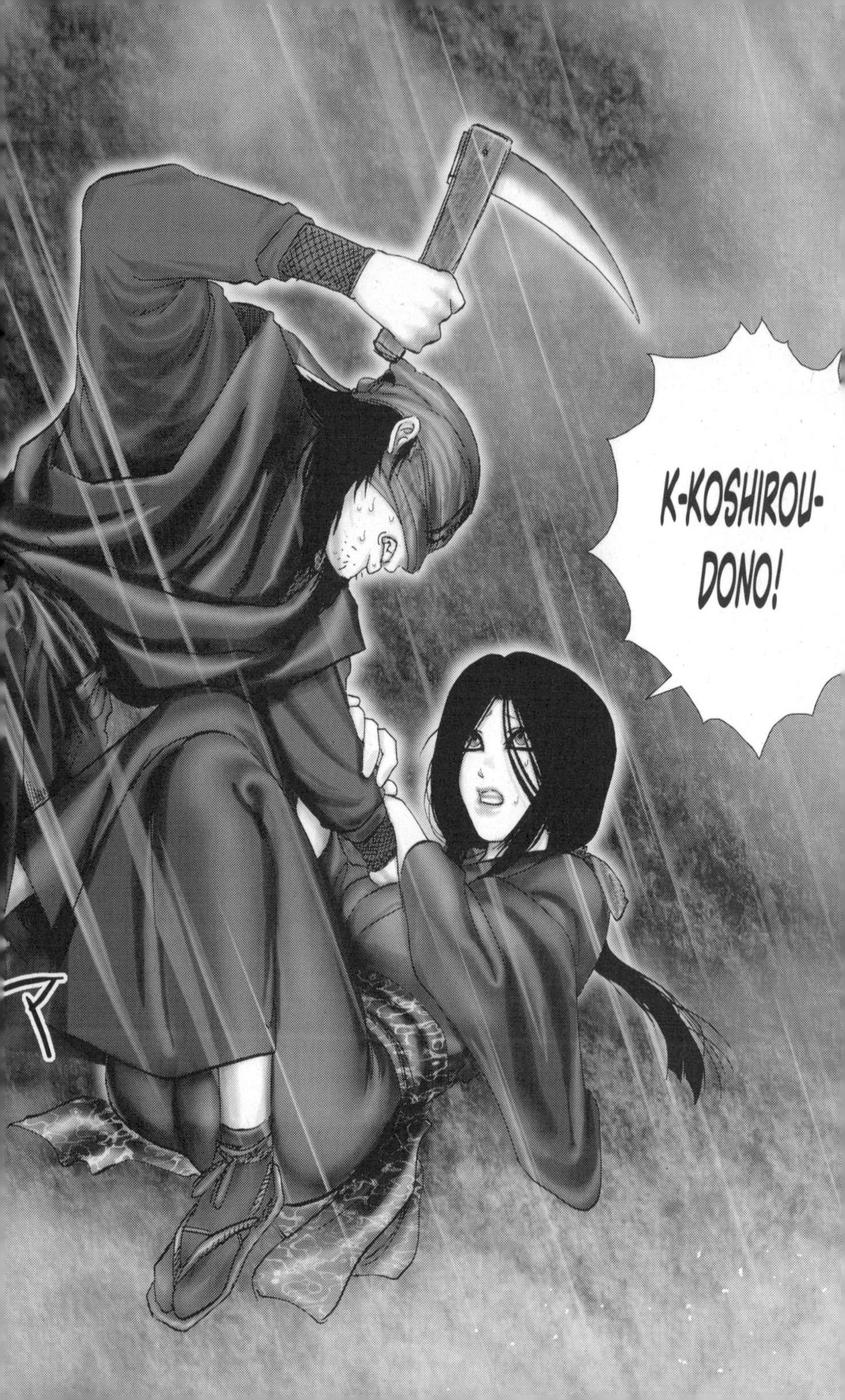
K-KOSHIROU-DONO!

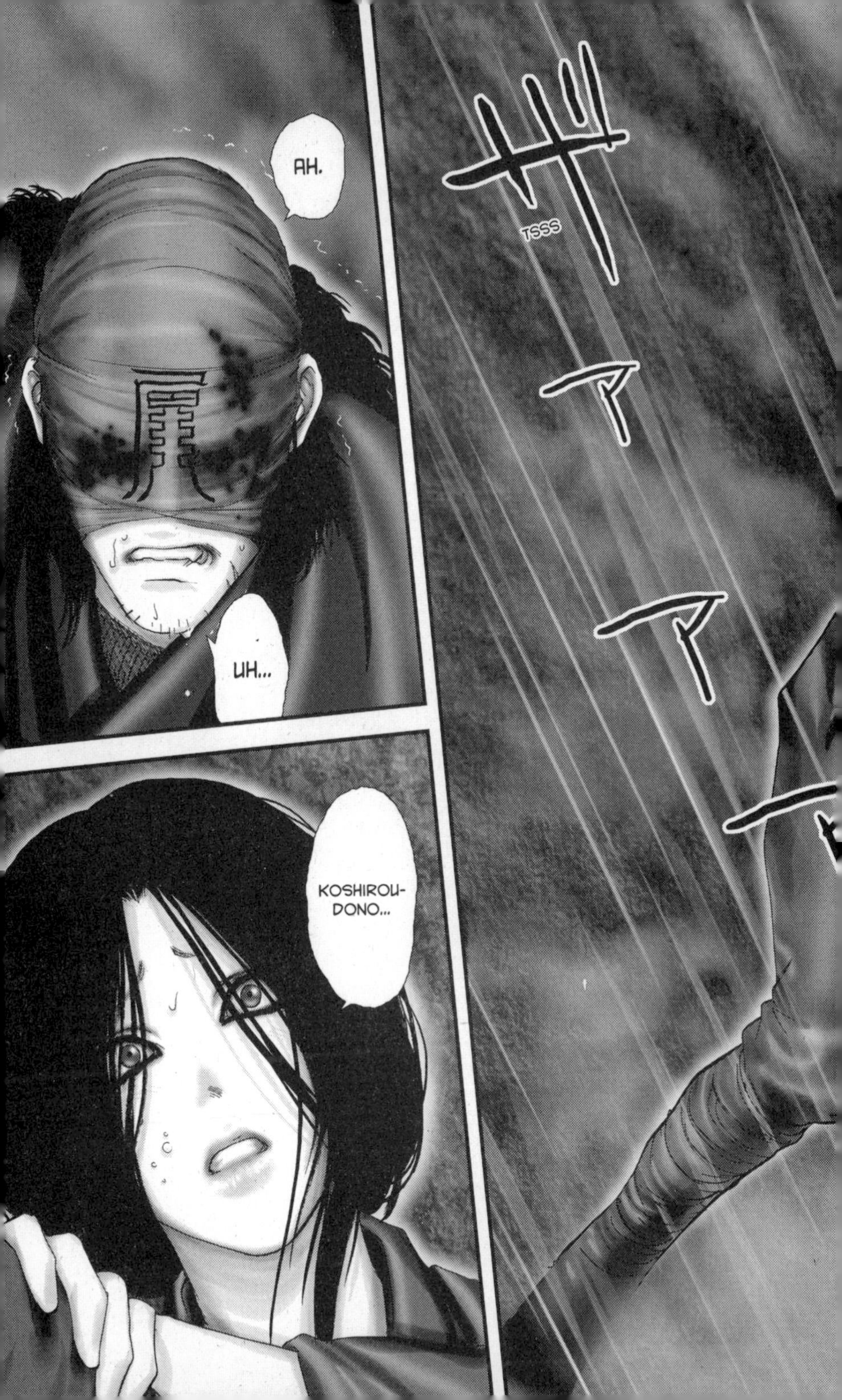
ザァァー
TSSS
AH.
UH...
KOSHIROU-
DONO...

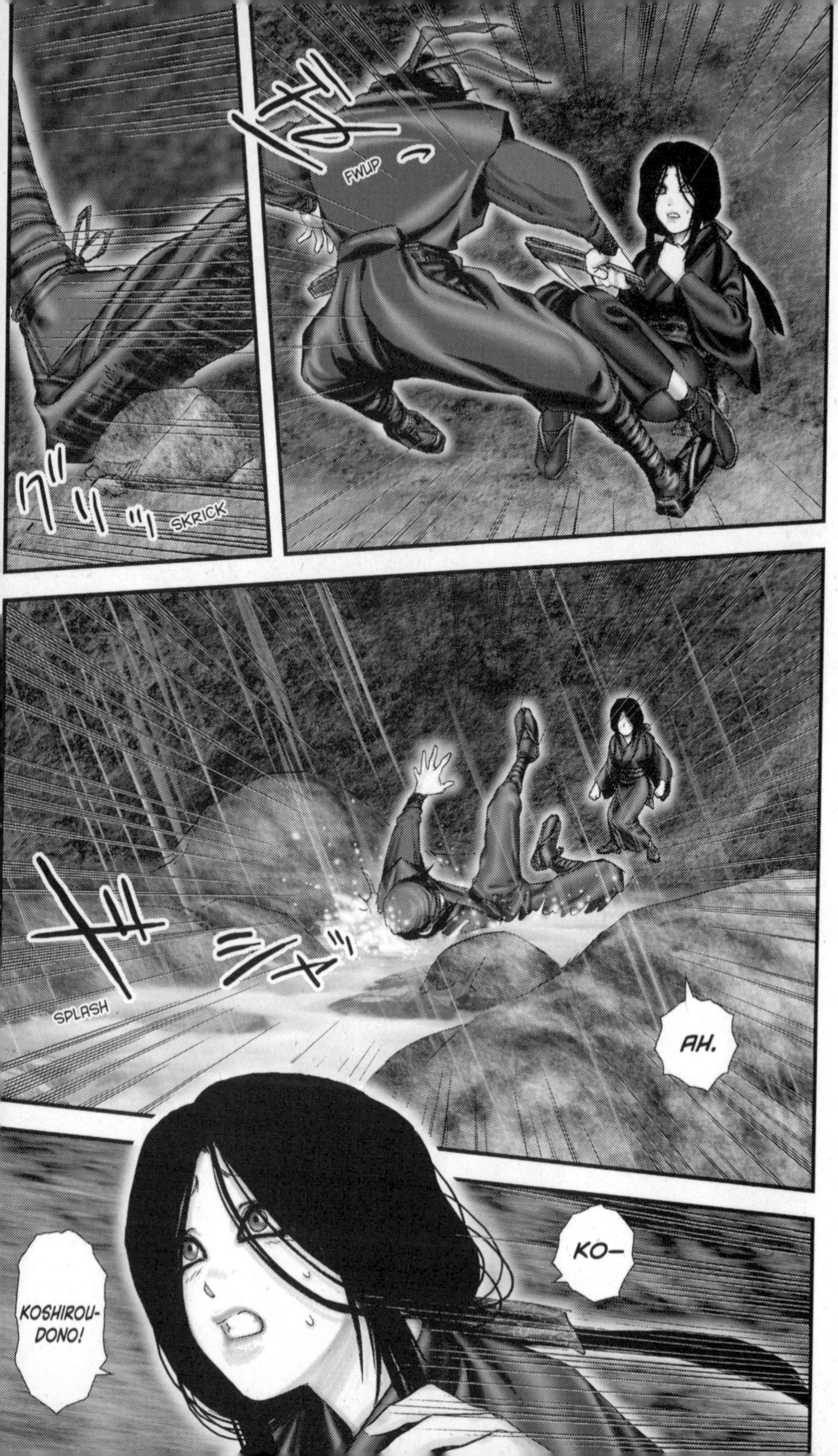
FWUP
SKRICK
SPLASH
AH.
KO–
KOSHIROU-DONO!

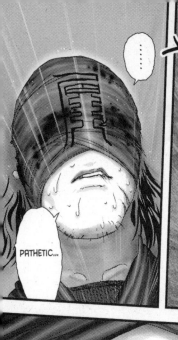

......

PATHETIC...

TSSS

HOW COULD I BE...

KOSHIROU-DONO.

...SO PATHETIC?

KRINCH

......

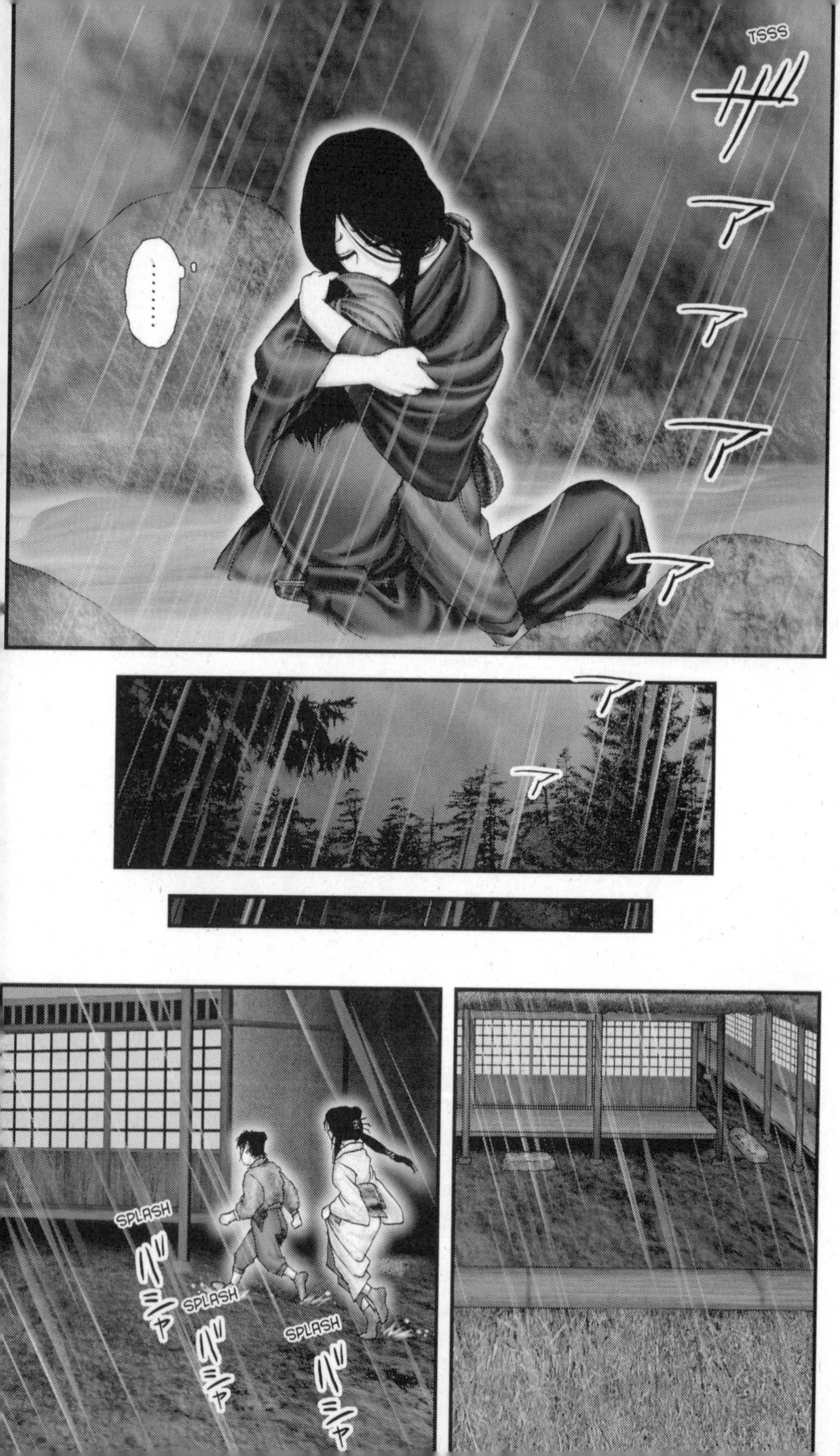
TSSS
ザァァァァァァ
……
SPLASH
バシャ
SPLASH
バシャ
SPLASH
バシャ

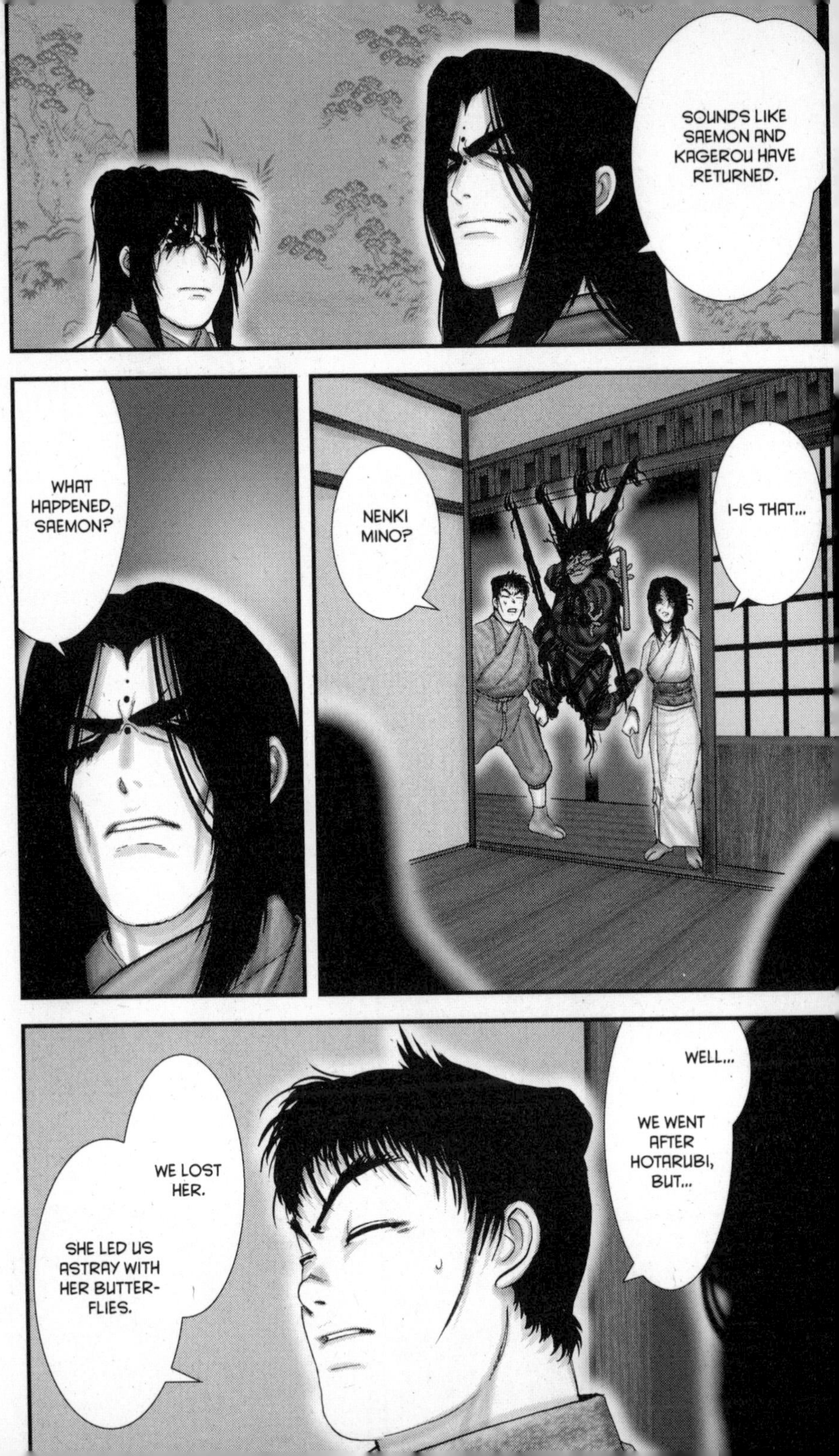
SOUNDS LIKE SAEMON AND KAGEROU HAVE RETURNED.
I-IS THAT...
NENKI MINO?
WHAT HAPPENED, SAEMON?
WELL...
WE WENT AFTER HOTARUBI, BUT...
WE LOST HER.
SHE LED US ASTRAY WITH HER BUTTER-FLIES.

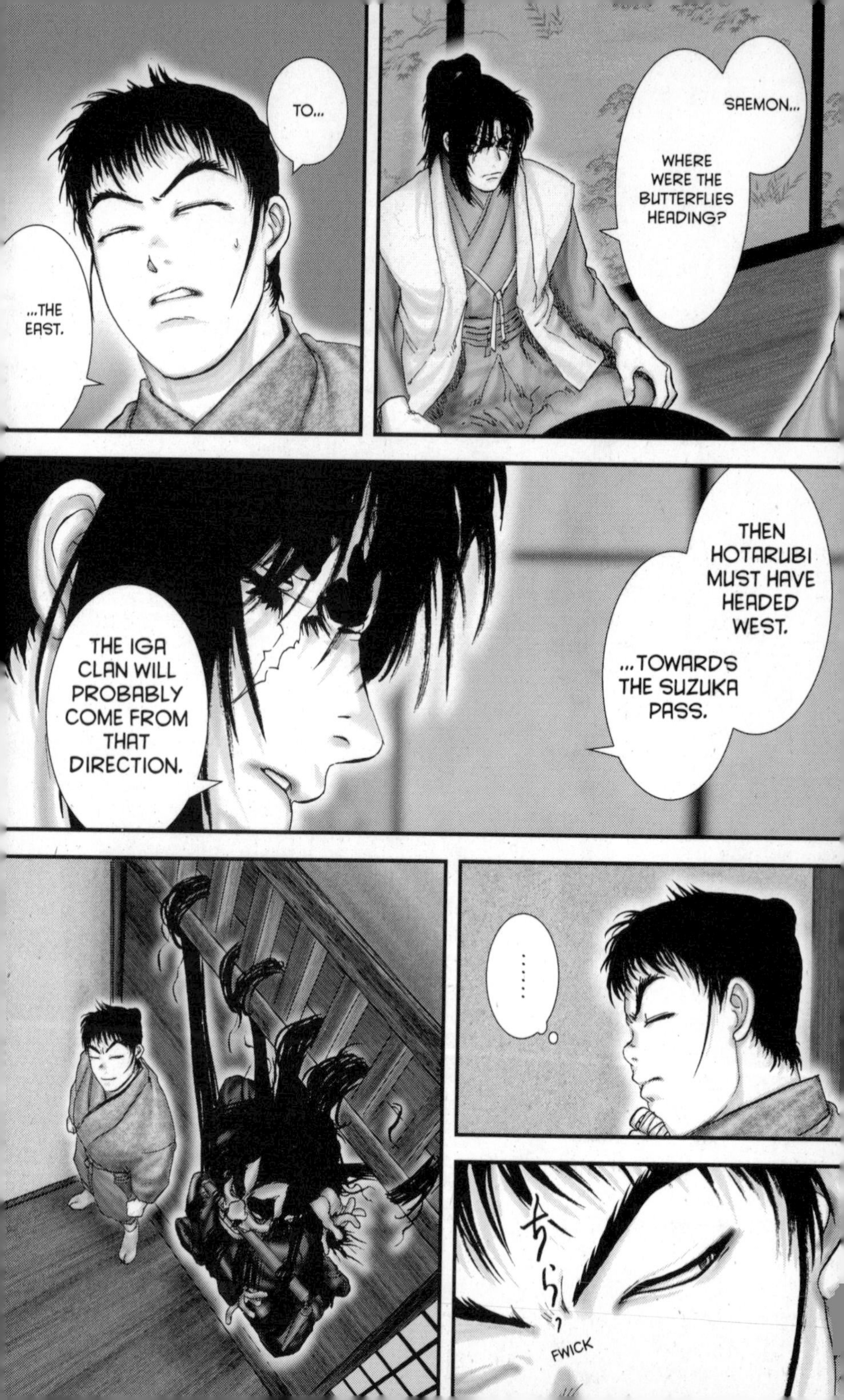
SAEMON...
WHERE WERE THE BUTTERFLIES HEADING?
TO...
...THE EAST.
THEN HOTARUBI MUST HAVE HEADED WEST.
...TOWARDS THE SUZUKA PASS.
THE IGA CLAN WILL PROBABLY COME FROM THAT DIRECTION.
......
FWICK

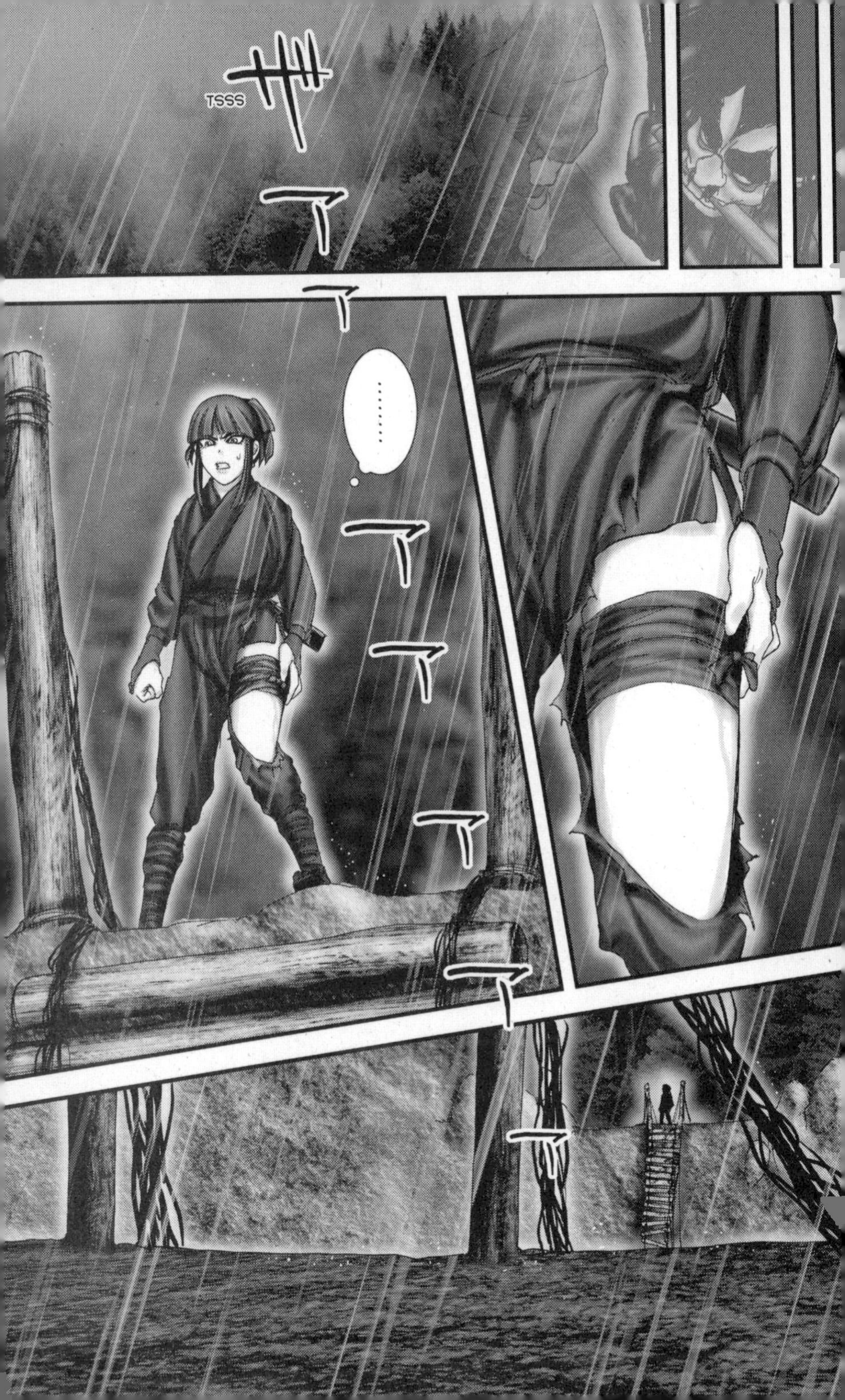
TSSS
......

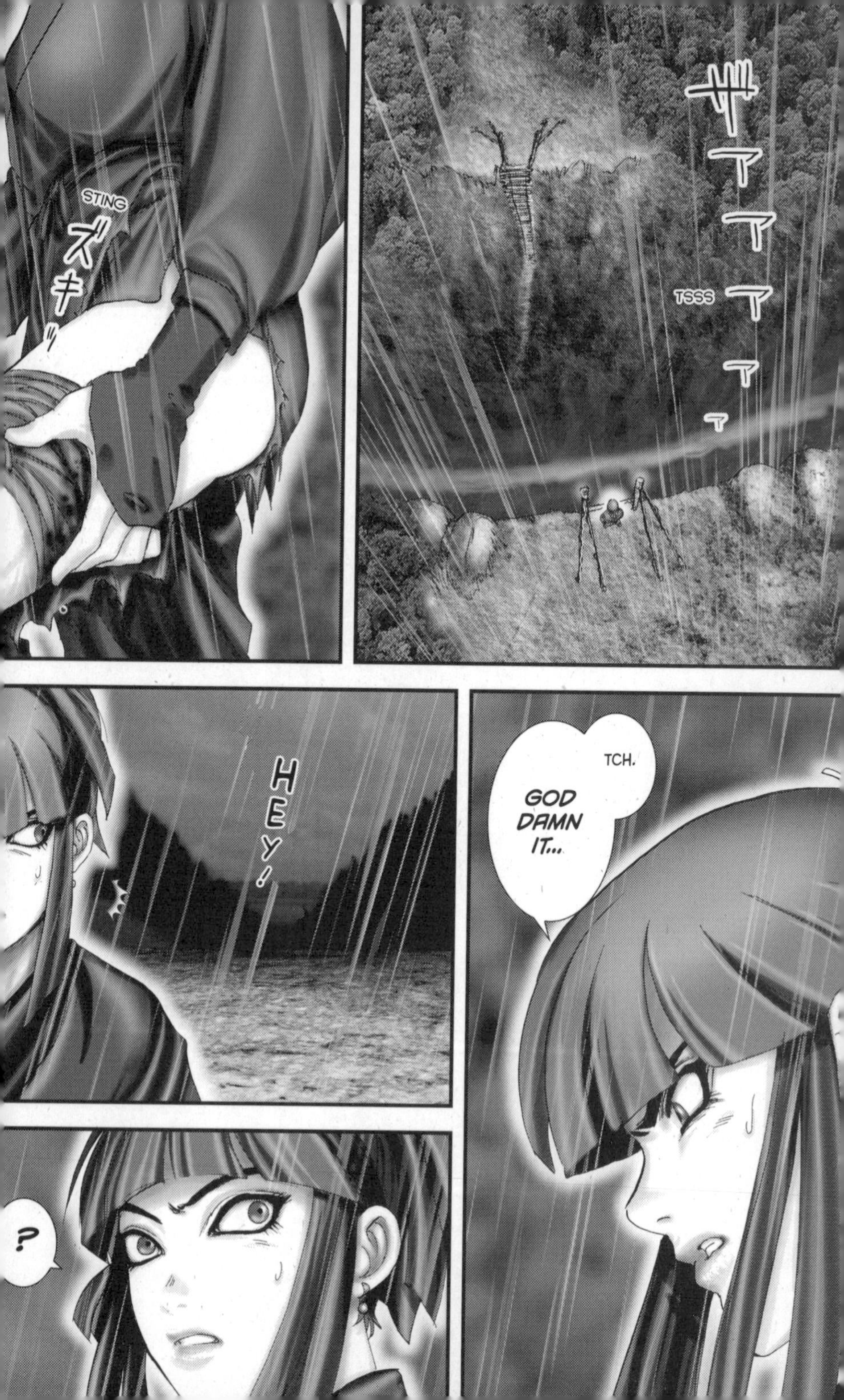
ザァァァァァ
TSSS
STING
ズキッ
TCH.
GOD DAMN IT...
HEY!
?

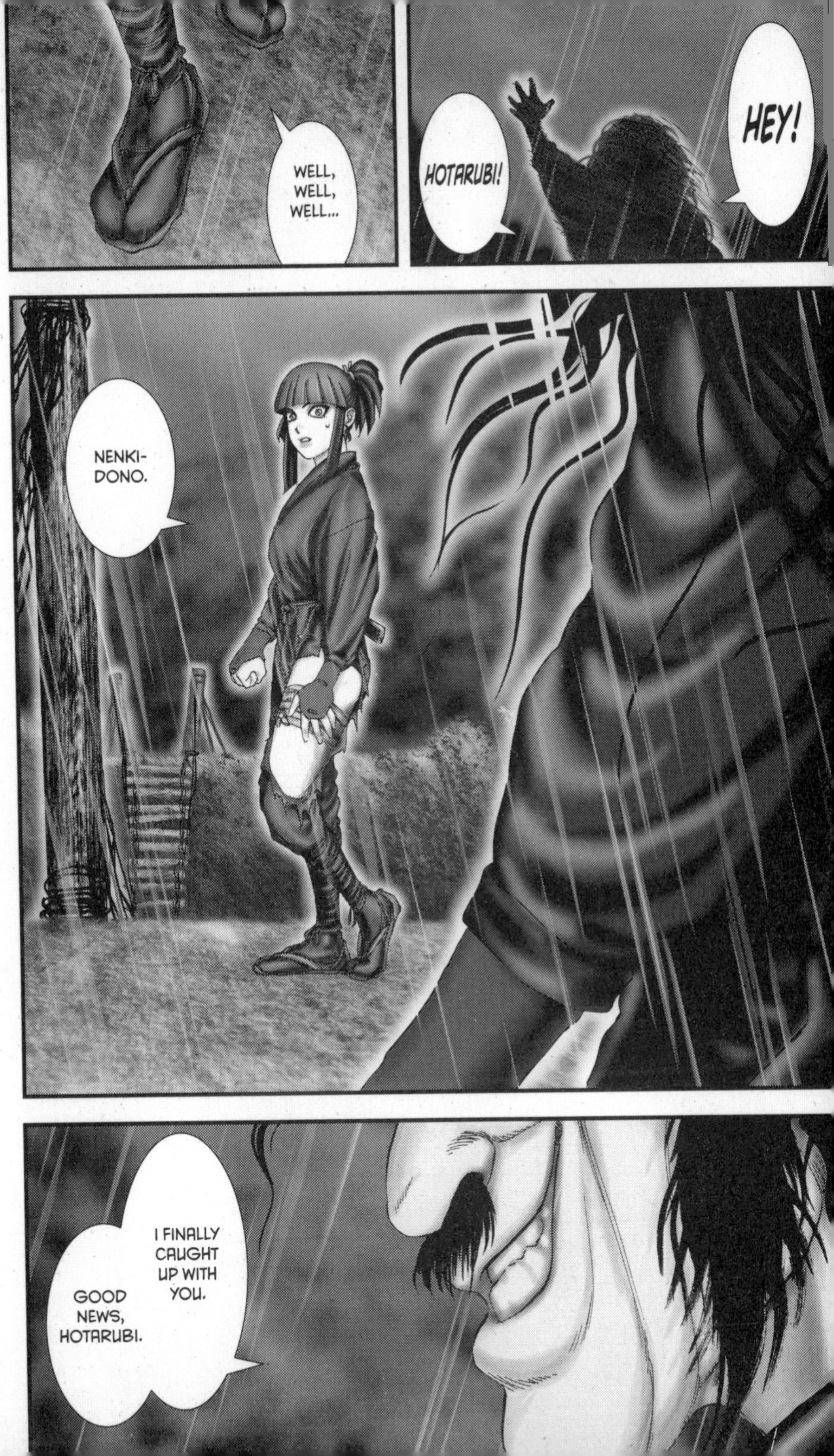
HEY!
HOTARUBI!
WELL, WELL, WELL...
NENKI-DONO.
I FINALLY CAUGHT UP WITH YOU.
GOOD NEWS, HOTARUBI.

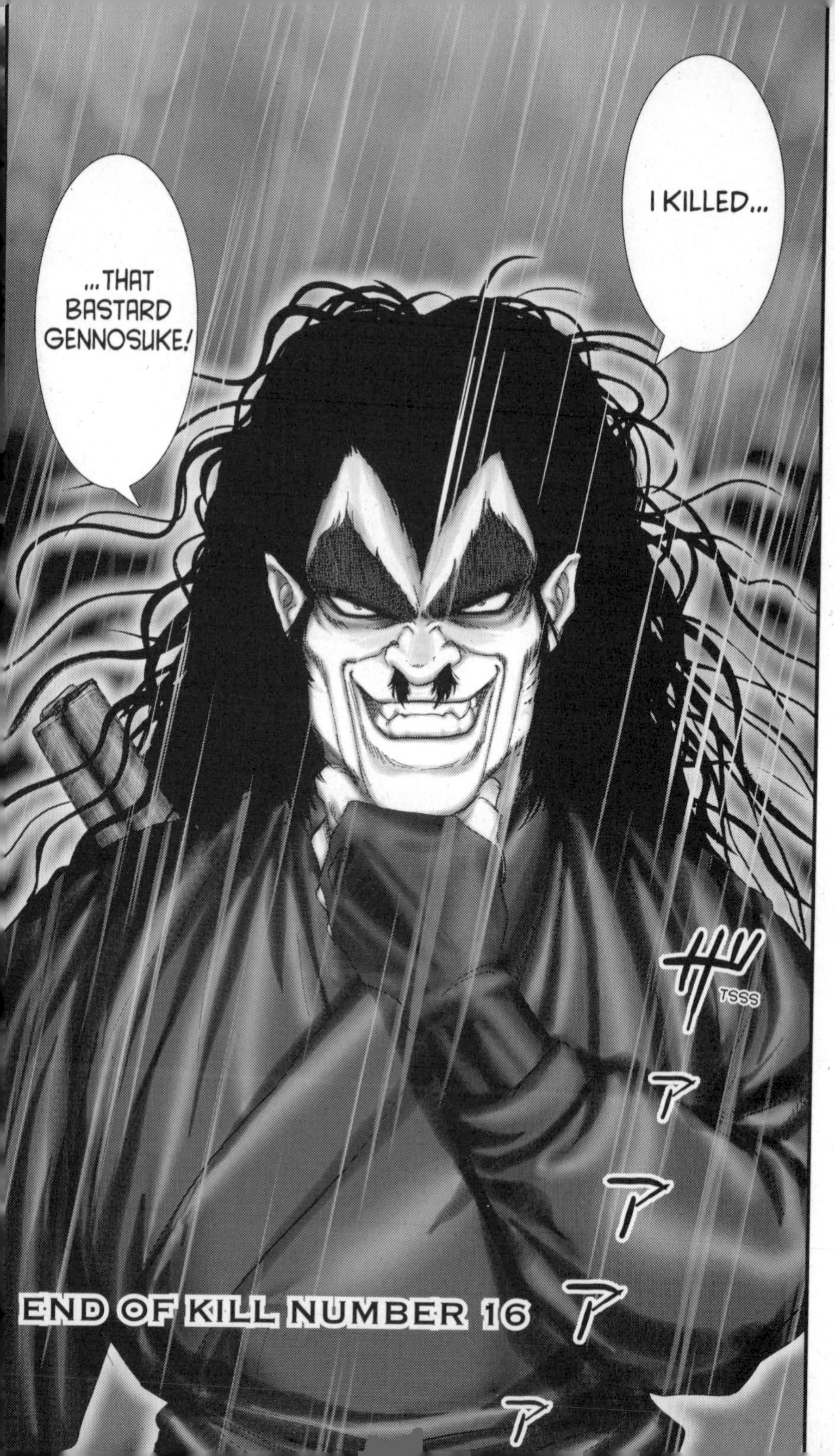
I KILLED...
...THAT BASTARD GENNOSUKE!
TSSS
END OF KILL NUMBER 16

駿府城へむかり　い聞いて殺すべし　解かれてんぬ　霞刑部

撮たば一族

雨夜陣五郎

筑摩小四郎

義念鬼

蛍火

朱絹

伊賀組十人衆

伊賀弾正

甲賀弦之介

地虫十兵衛

風待将監

栄禄かりん

徳川家

鵜殿丈助

如月左衛門

室賀豹馬

陽炎

出ずべきことその数々さを賭らうとなし勝たぐ

の秘巻をたずさえ五月廿日駿

の一代るもの、この

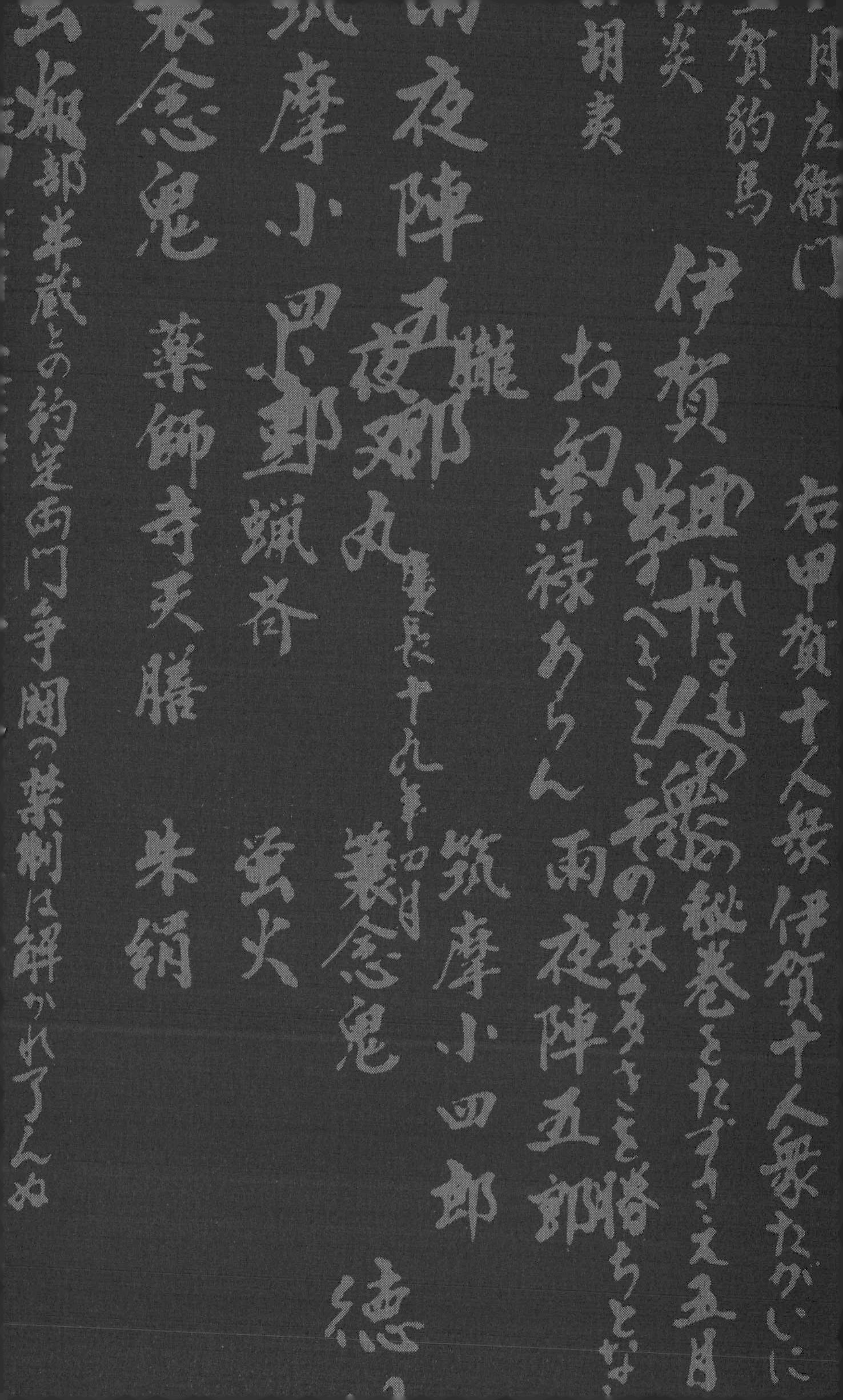

右甲賀十人衆　伊賀十人衆たがいに

伊賀

螺仏るもの薬へきこととその数々をたずさえ五月

お幻薬禄あらん　雨夜陣五郎

筑摩小四郎

兼念鬼

螢火

徳

夜陣五郎

夜叉丸

蠍斎

朧

南夜陣五郎

袋念鬼

薬師寺天膳

朱絹

筑摩小四郎

一賀釣馬

胡夷

英

月左衛門

又瀬部半蔵との釣道両門争闘の禁制は解かれてうんぬ

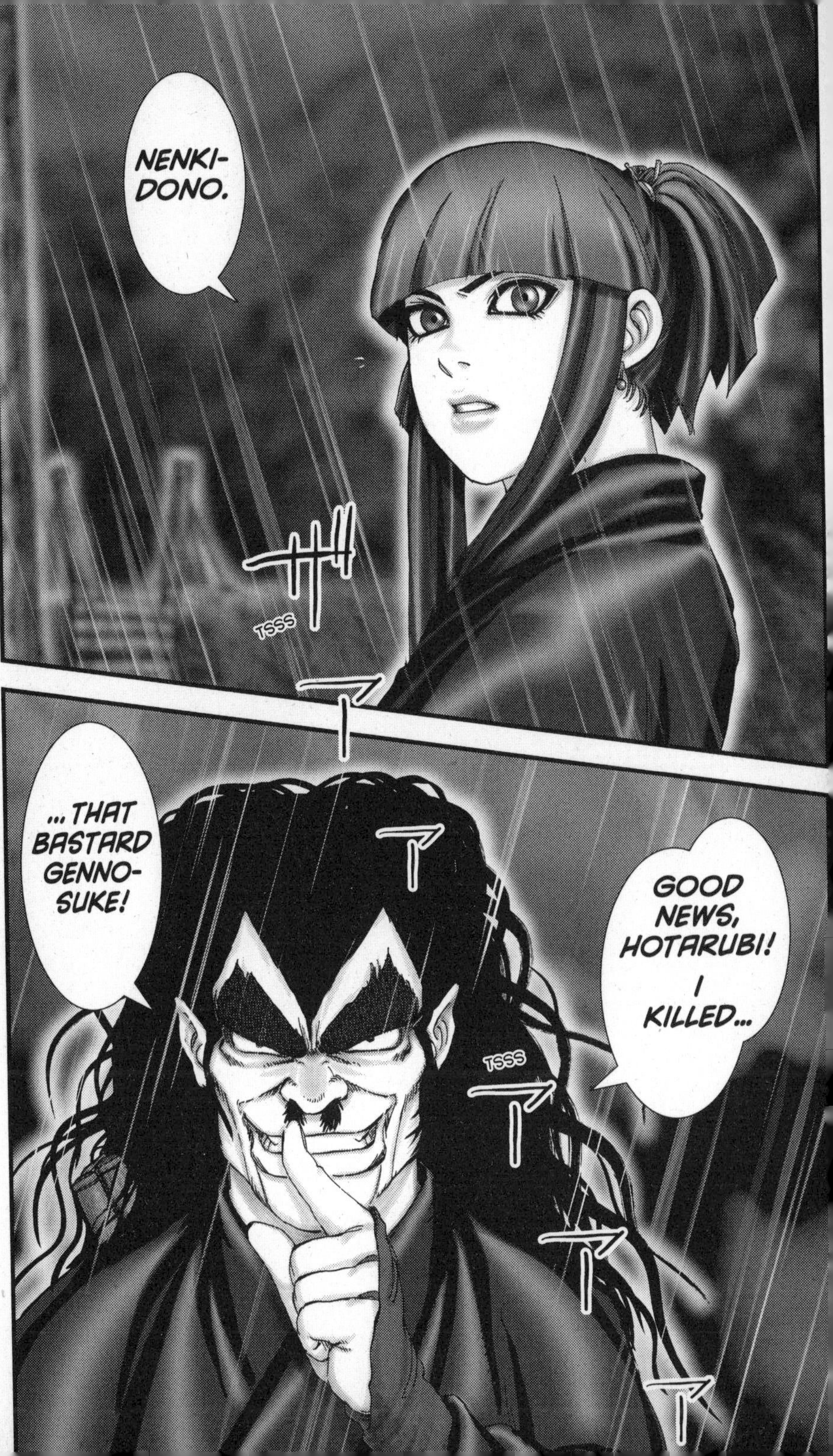
NENKI-DONO.
TSSS
GOOD NEWS, HOTARUBI! I KILLED...
...THAT BASTARD GENNO-SUKE!
TSSS

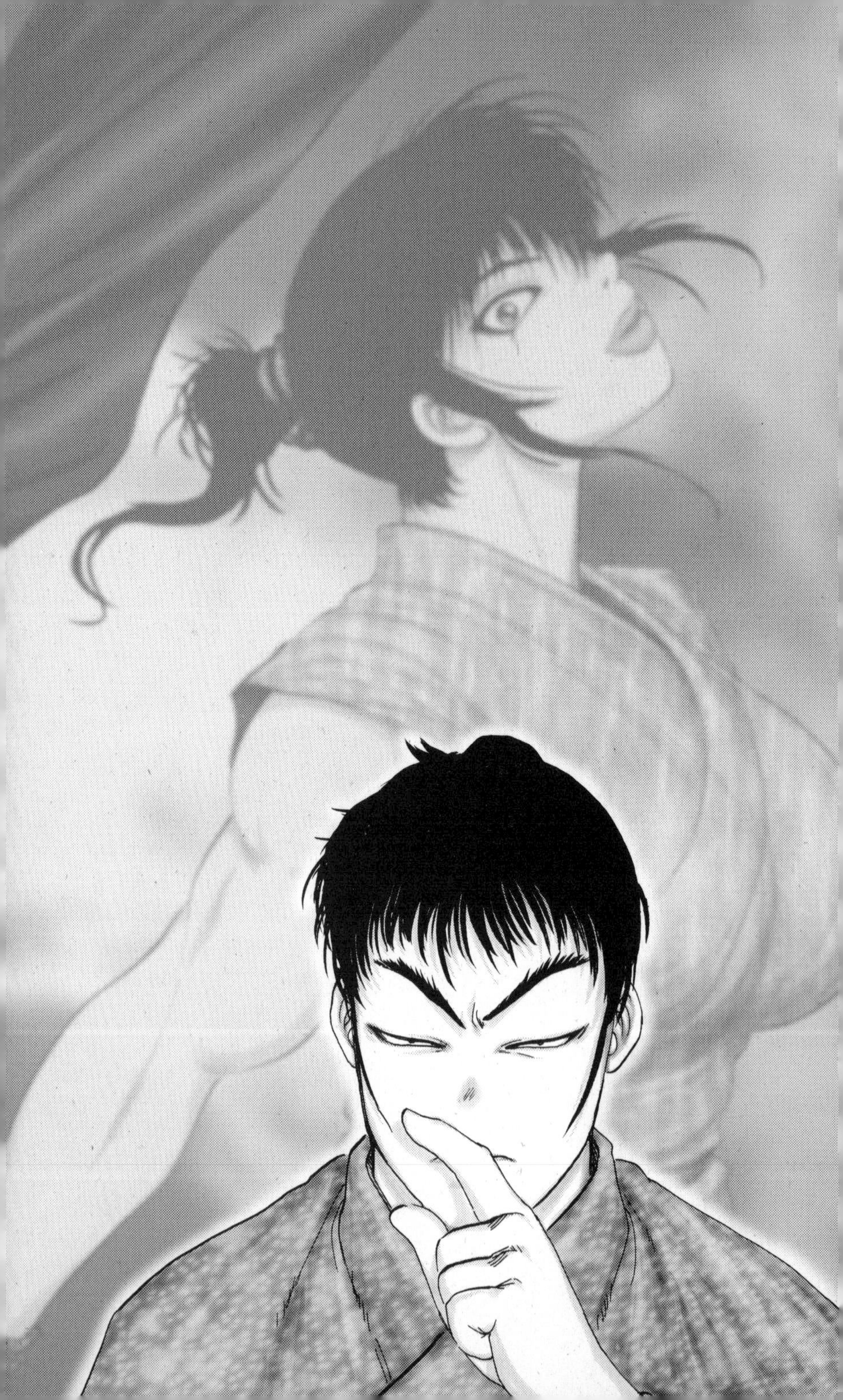

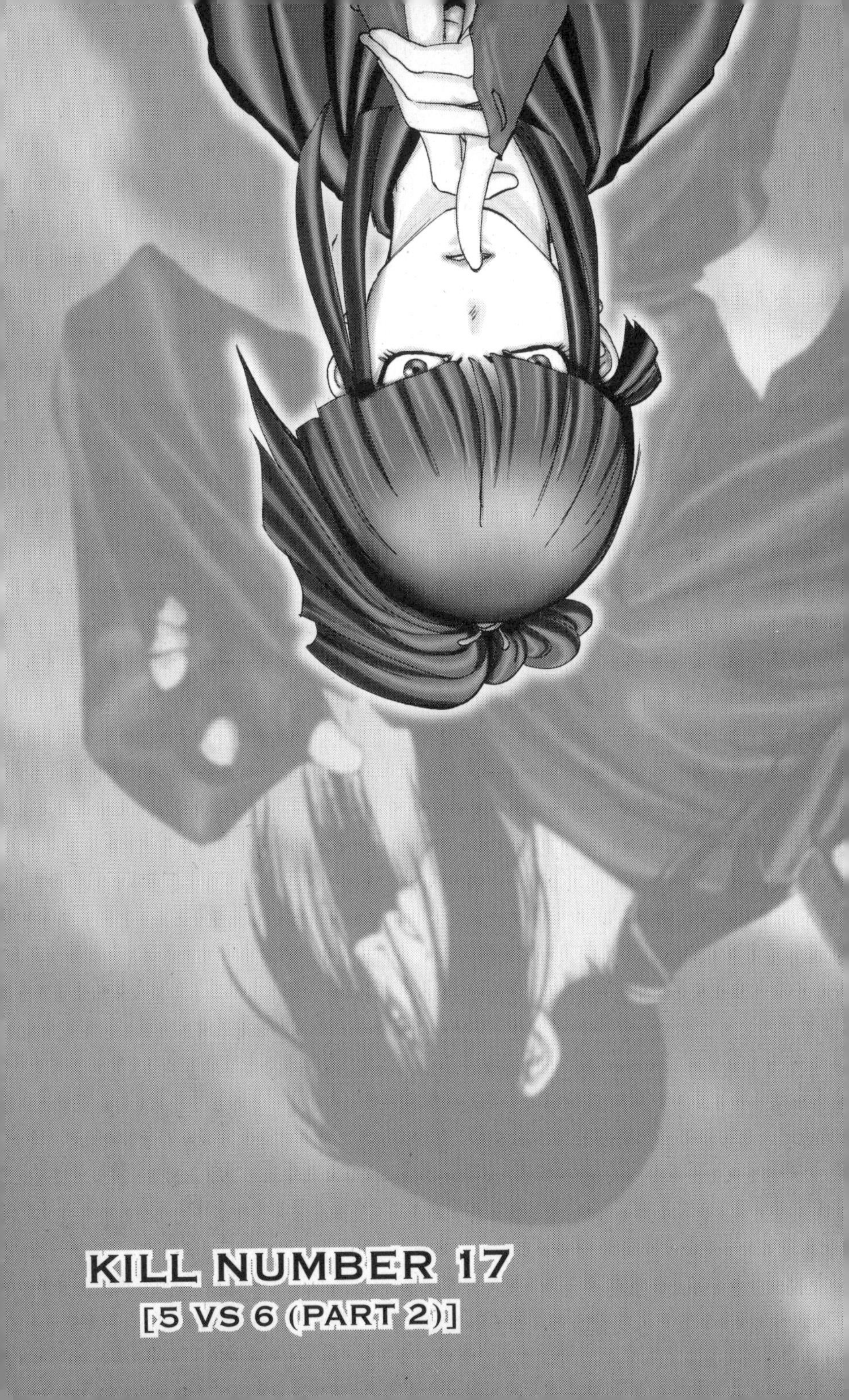

KILL NUMBER 17

[5 VS 6 (PART 2)]

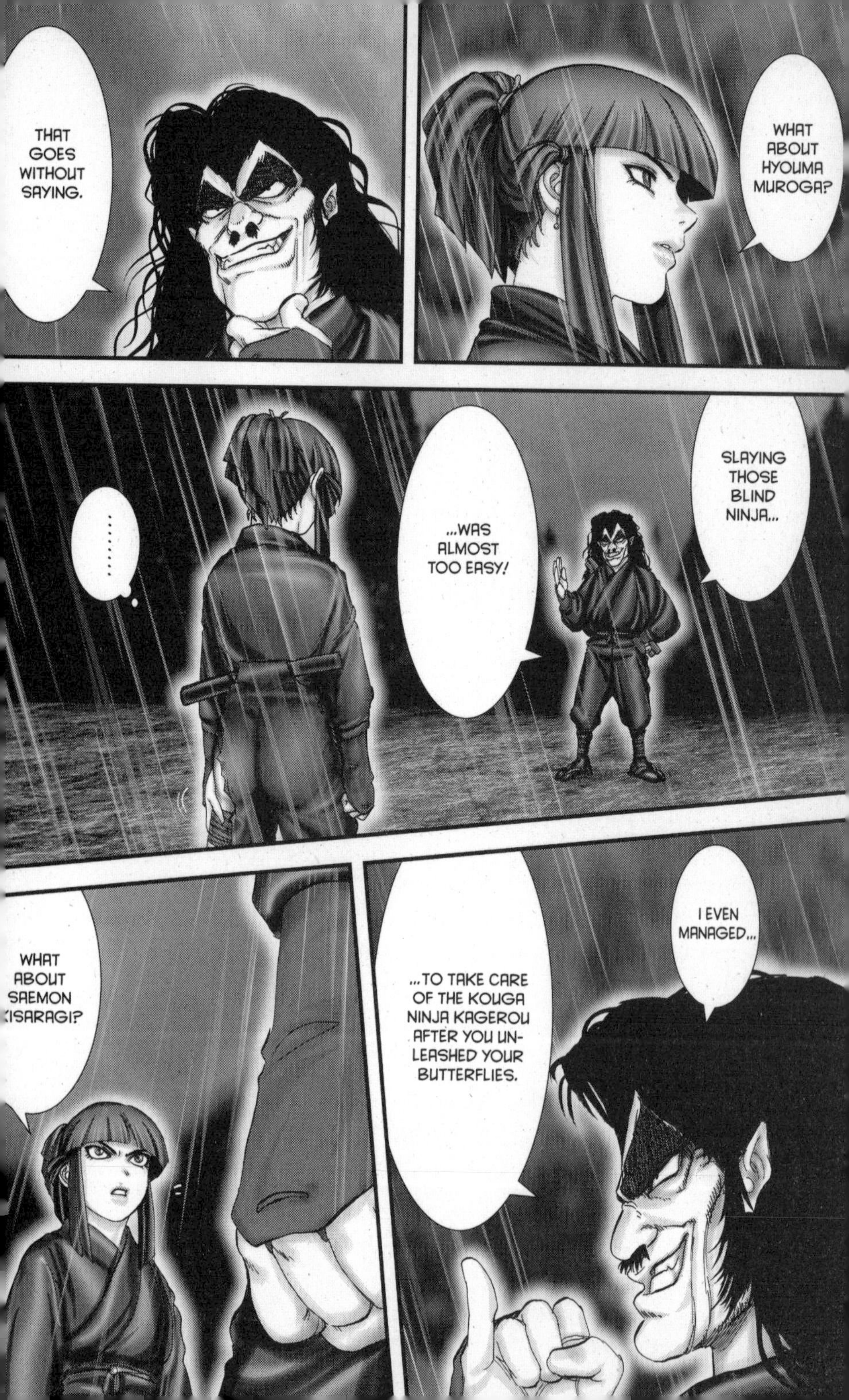
WHAT ABOUT HYOUMA MUROGA?
THAT GOES WITHOUT SAYING.
SLAYING THOSE BLIND NINJA...
...WAS ALMOST TOO EASY!
......
I EVEN MANAGED...
...TO TAKE CARE OF THE KOUGA NINJA KAGEROU AFTER YOU UN-LEASHED YOUR BUTTERFLIES.
WHAT ABOUT SAEMON KISARAGI?

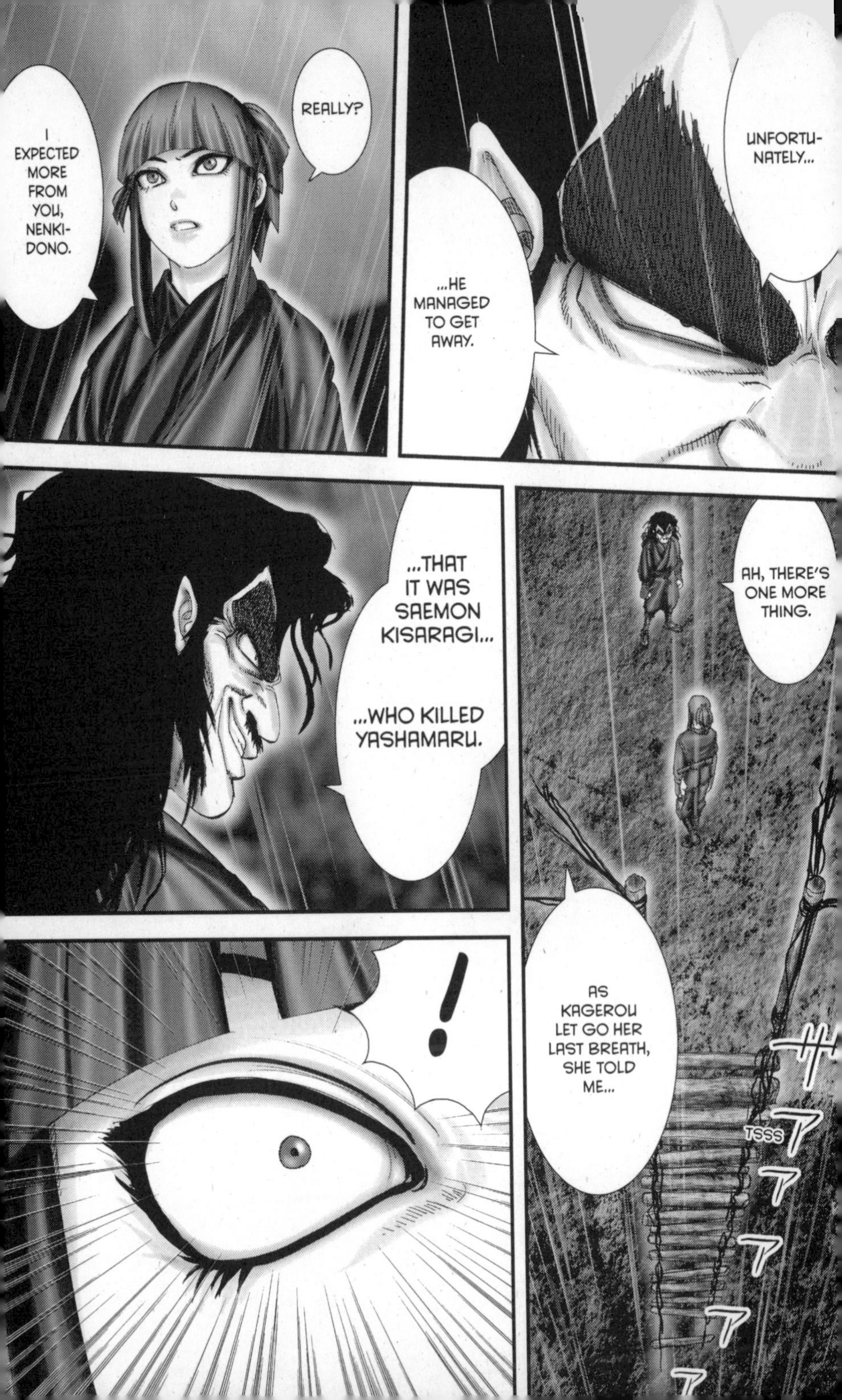
UNFORTU-NATELY...
...HE MANAGED TO GET AWAY.
REALLY?
I EXPECTED MORE FROM YOU, NENKI-DONO.
AH, THERE'S ONE MORE THING.
AS KAGEROU LET GO HER LAST BREATH, SHE TOLD ME...
TSSS
...THAT IT WAS SAEMON KISARAGI...
...WHO KILLED YASHAMARU.
!

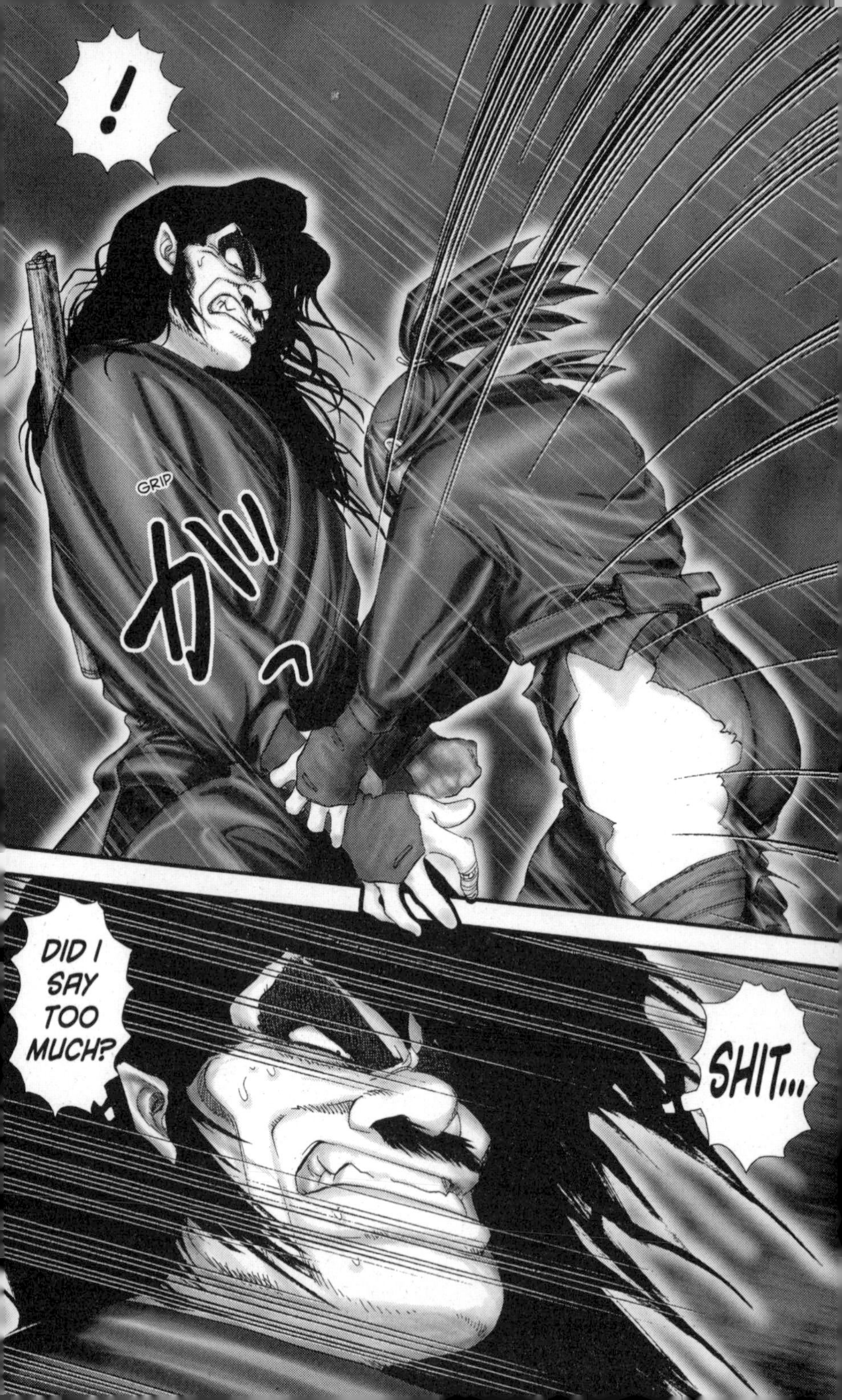
!
GRIP
ガッ
SHIT...
DID I SAY TOO MUCH?

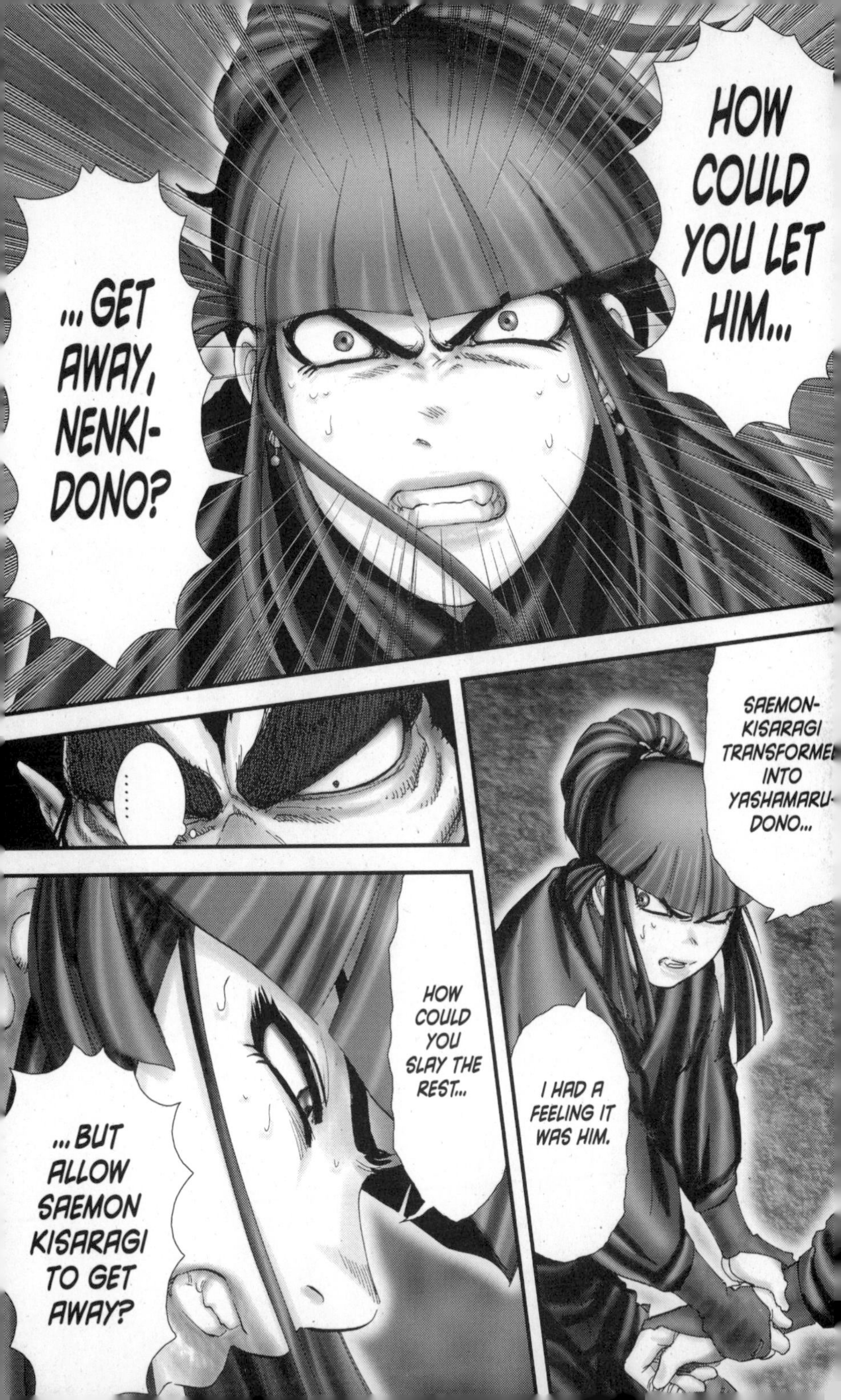
HOW COULD YOU LET HIM...
...GET AWAY, NENKI-DONO?
SAEMON-KISARAGI TRANSFORME INTO YASHAMARU-DONO...
I HAD A FEELING IT WAS HIM.
......
HOW COULD YOU SLAY THE REST...
...BUT ALLOW SAEMON KISARAGI TO GET AWAY?

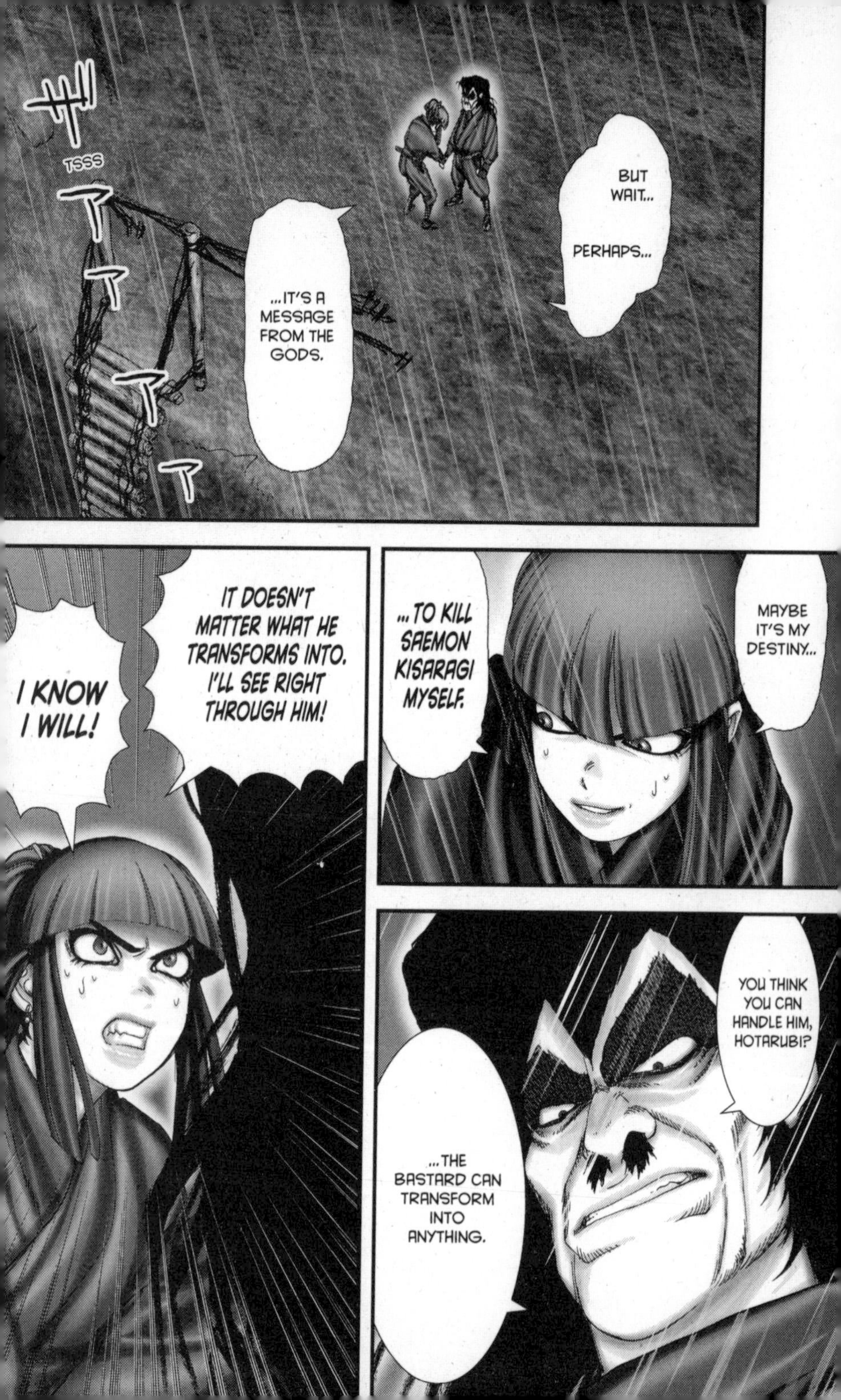
BUT WAIT...
PERHAPS...
...IT'S A MESSAGE FROM THE GODS.
TSSS
MAYBE IT'S MY DESTINY...
...TO KILL SAEMON KISARAGI MYSELF.
YOU THINK YOU CAN HANDLE HIM, HOTARUBI?
...THE BASTARD CAN TRANSFORM INTO ANYTHING.
IT DOESN'T MATTER WHAT HE TRANSFORMS INTO. I'LL SEE RIGHT THROUGH HIM!
I KNOW I WILL!

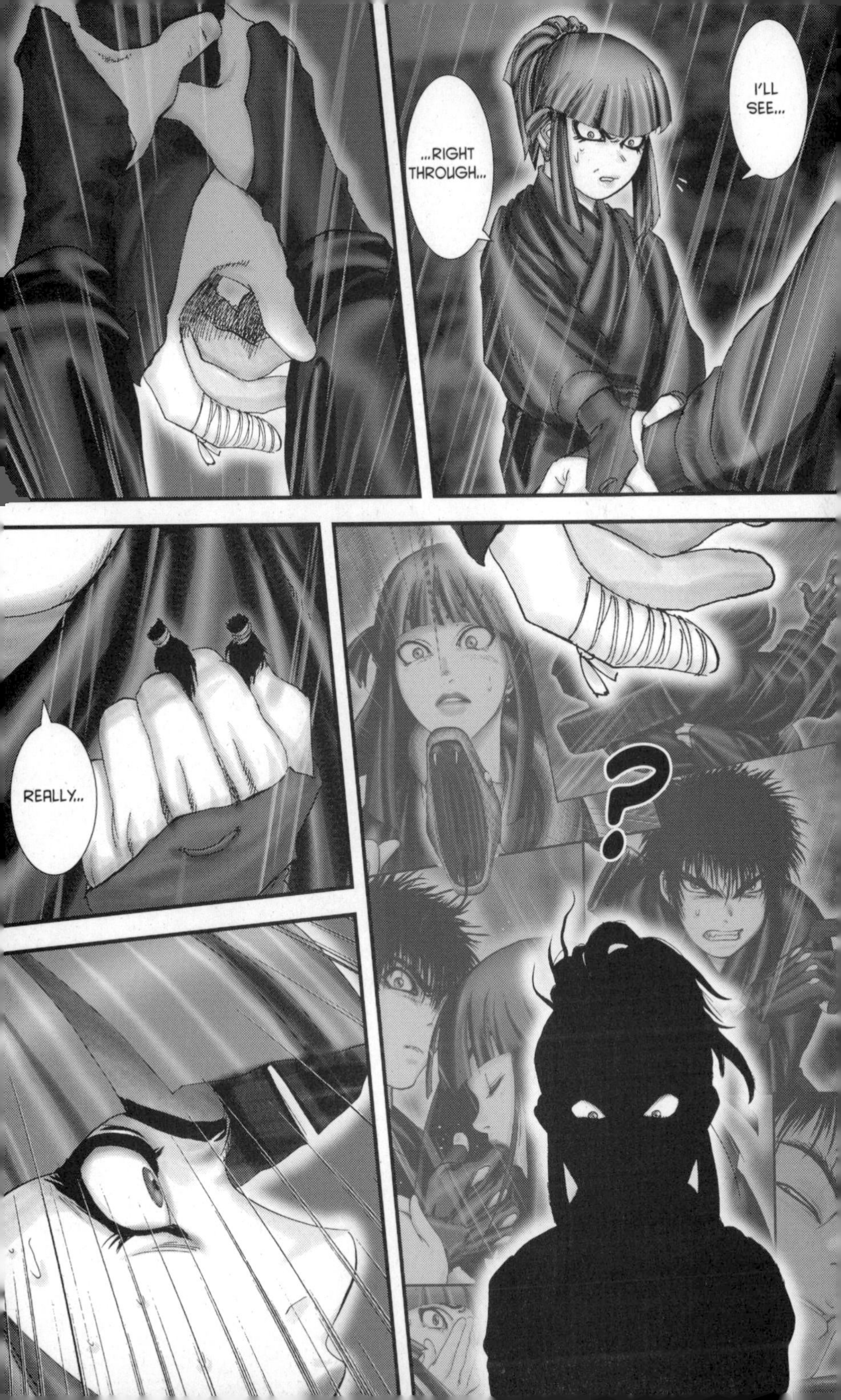
I'LL SEE...
...RIGHT THROUGH...
REALLY...
?

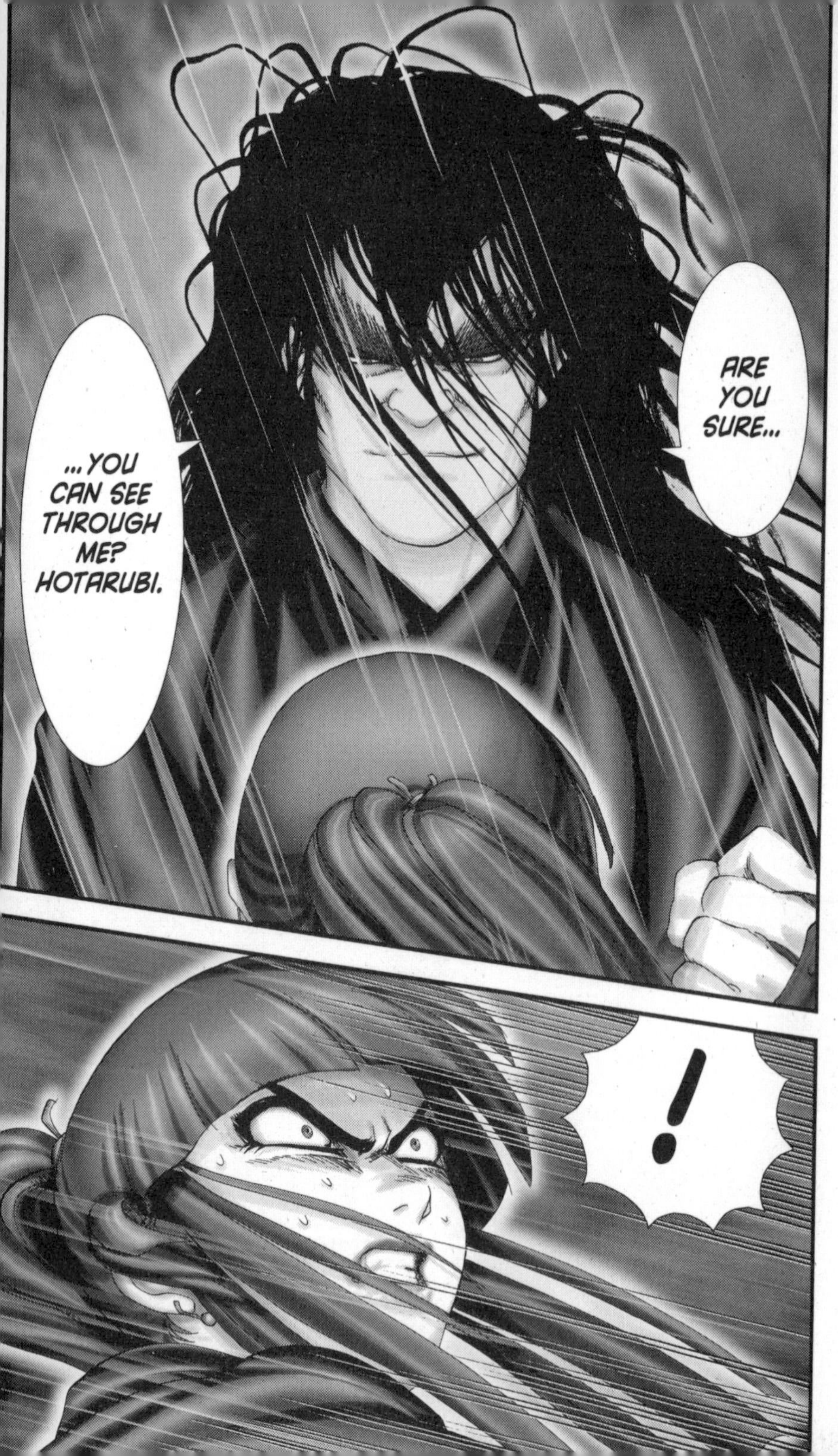
ARE YOU SURE...
...YOU CAN SEE THROUGH ME? HOTARUBI.
!

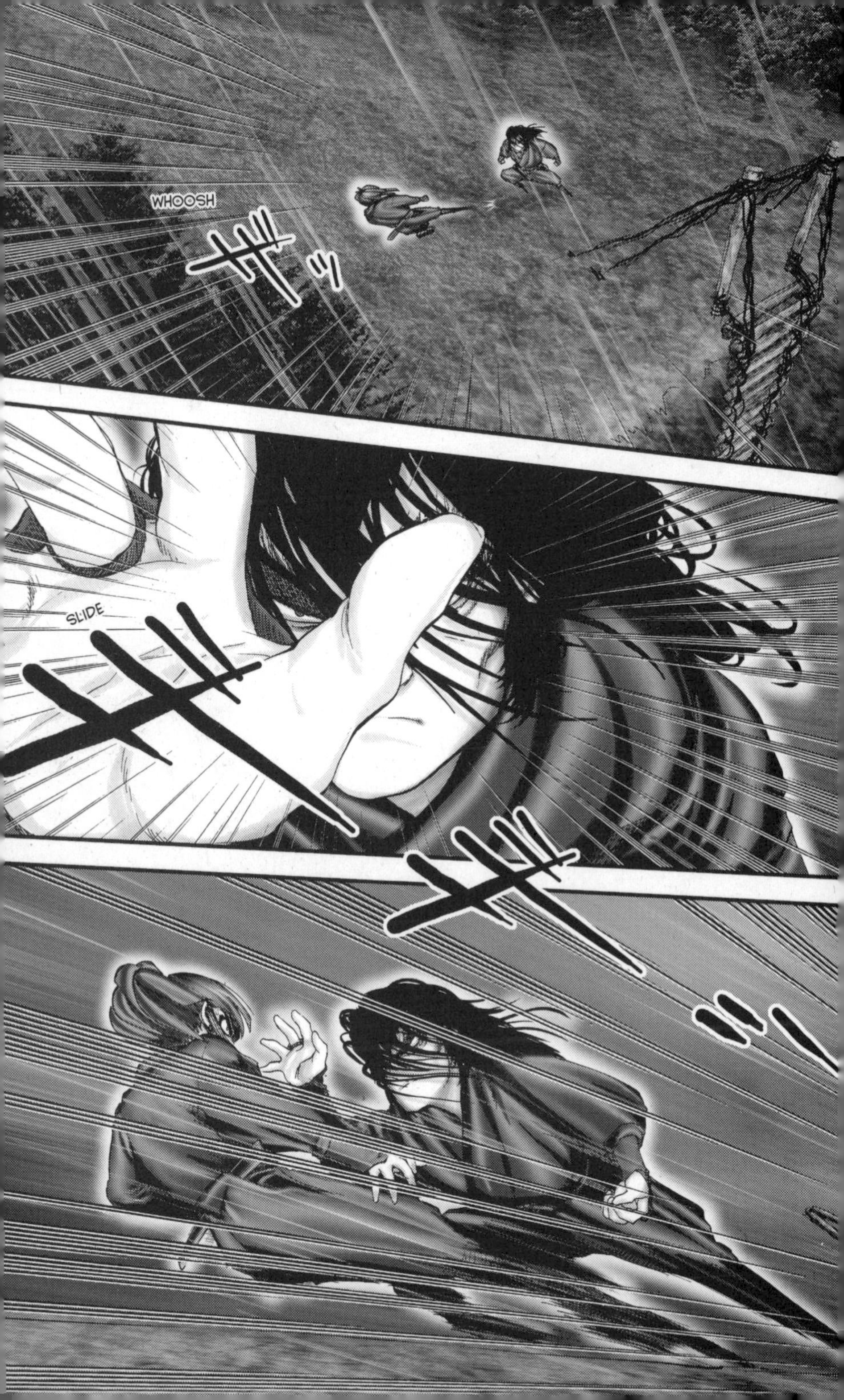
WHOOSH
SLIDE

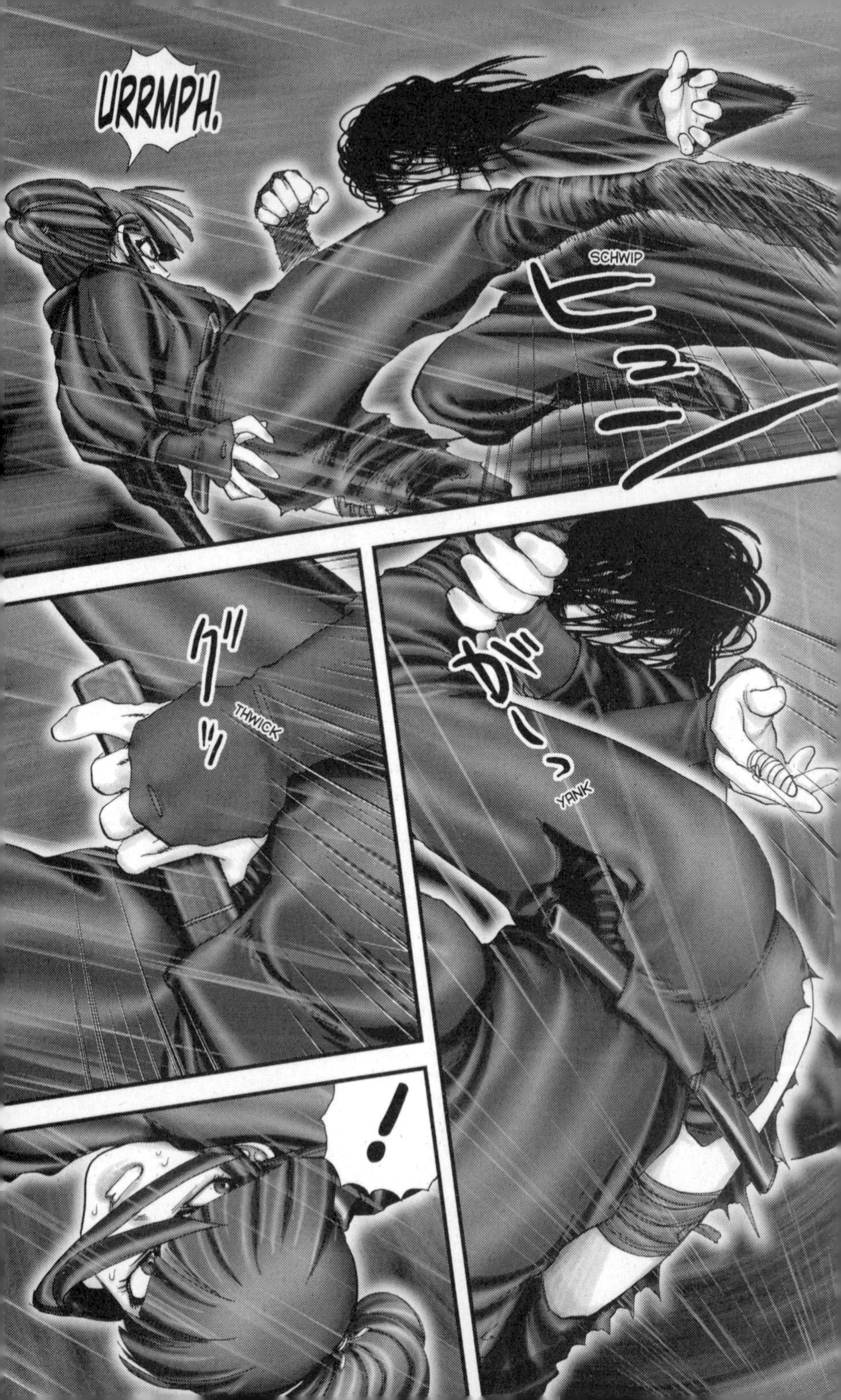

URRMPH.
SCHWIP
YANK
THWICK
!

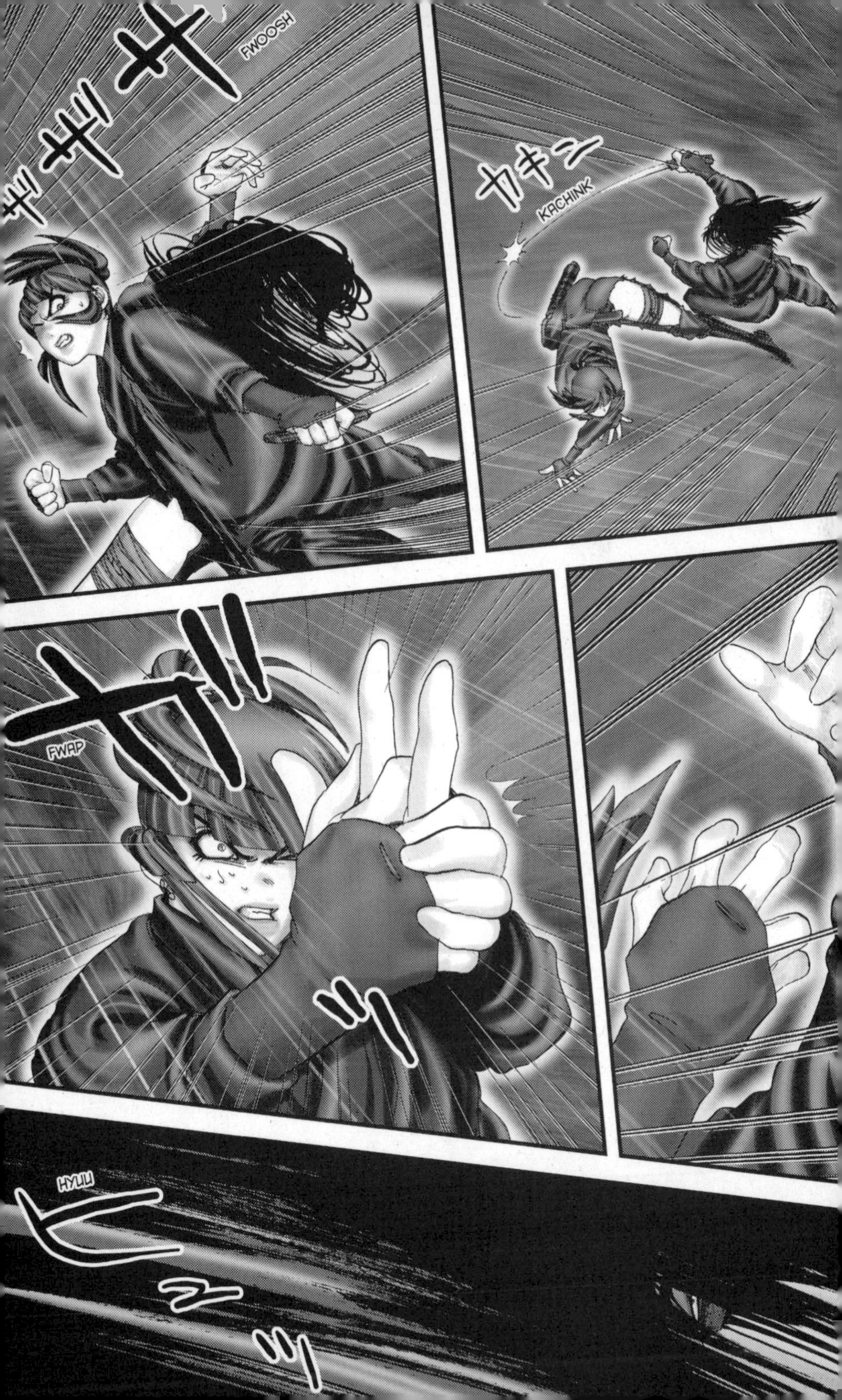
KACHINK
FWOOSH
FWAP
HYUU

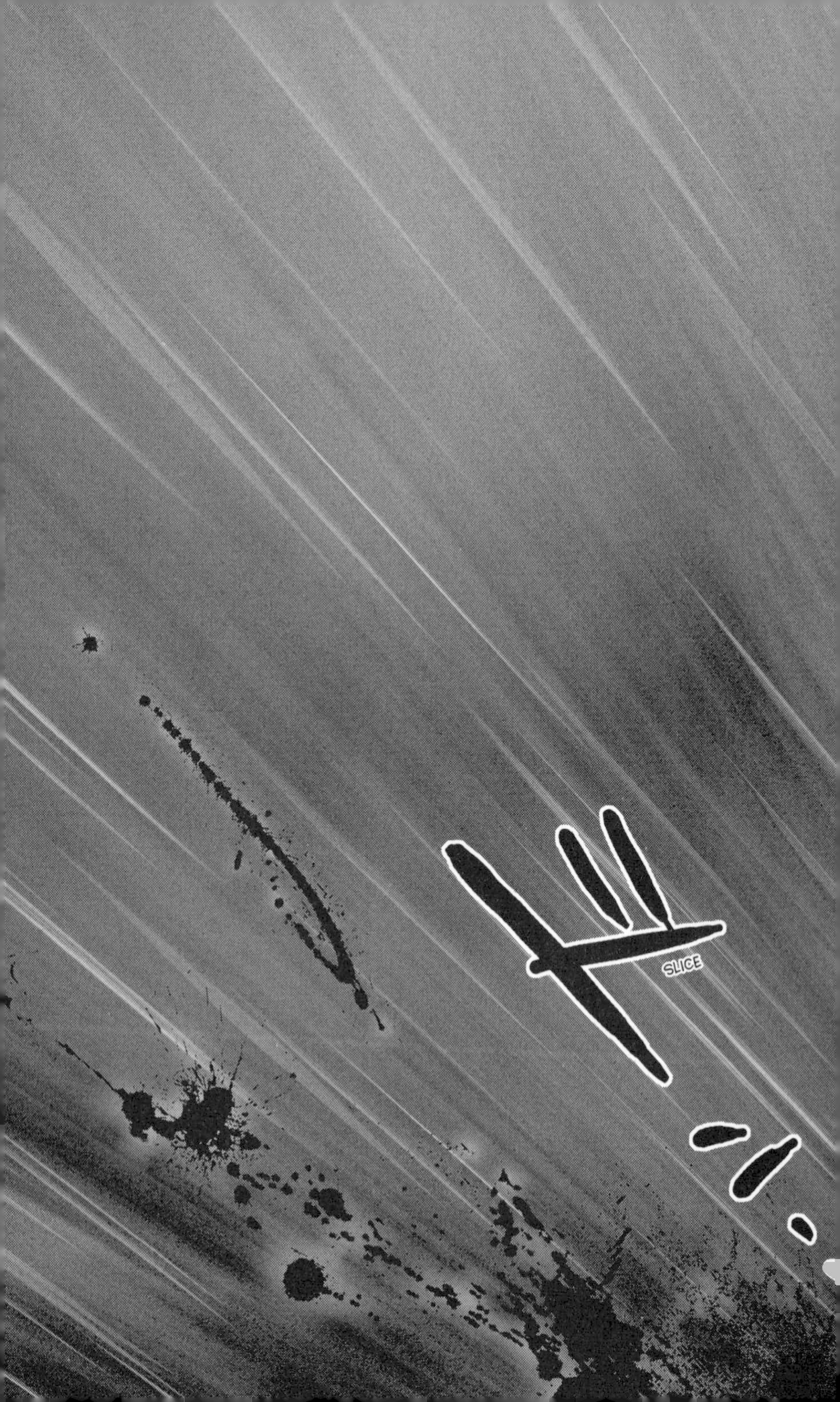
SLICE

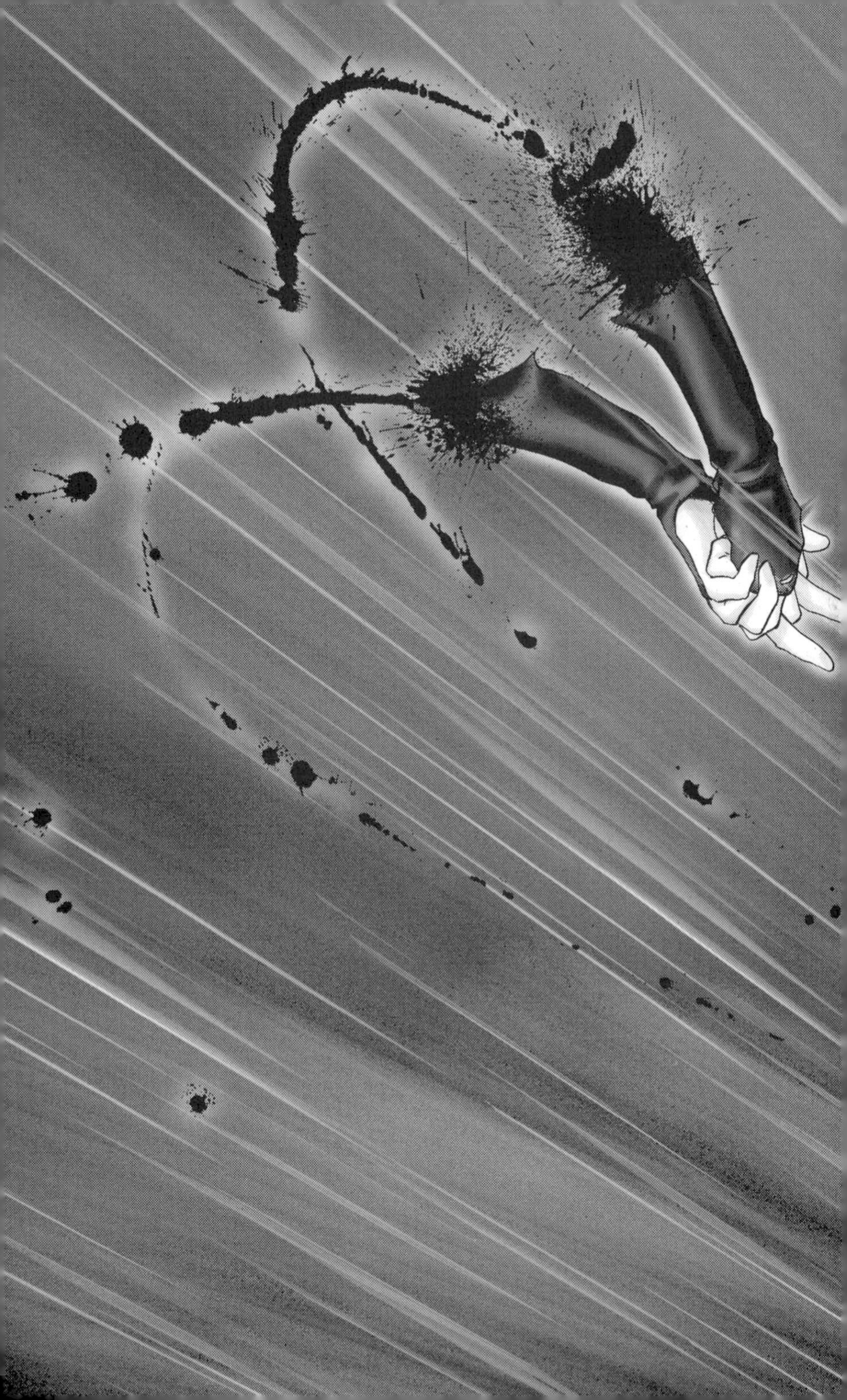

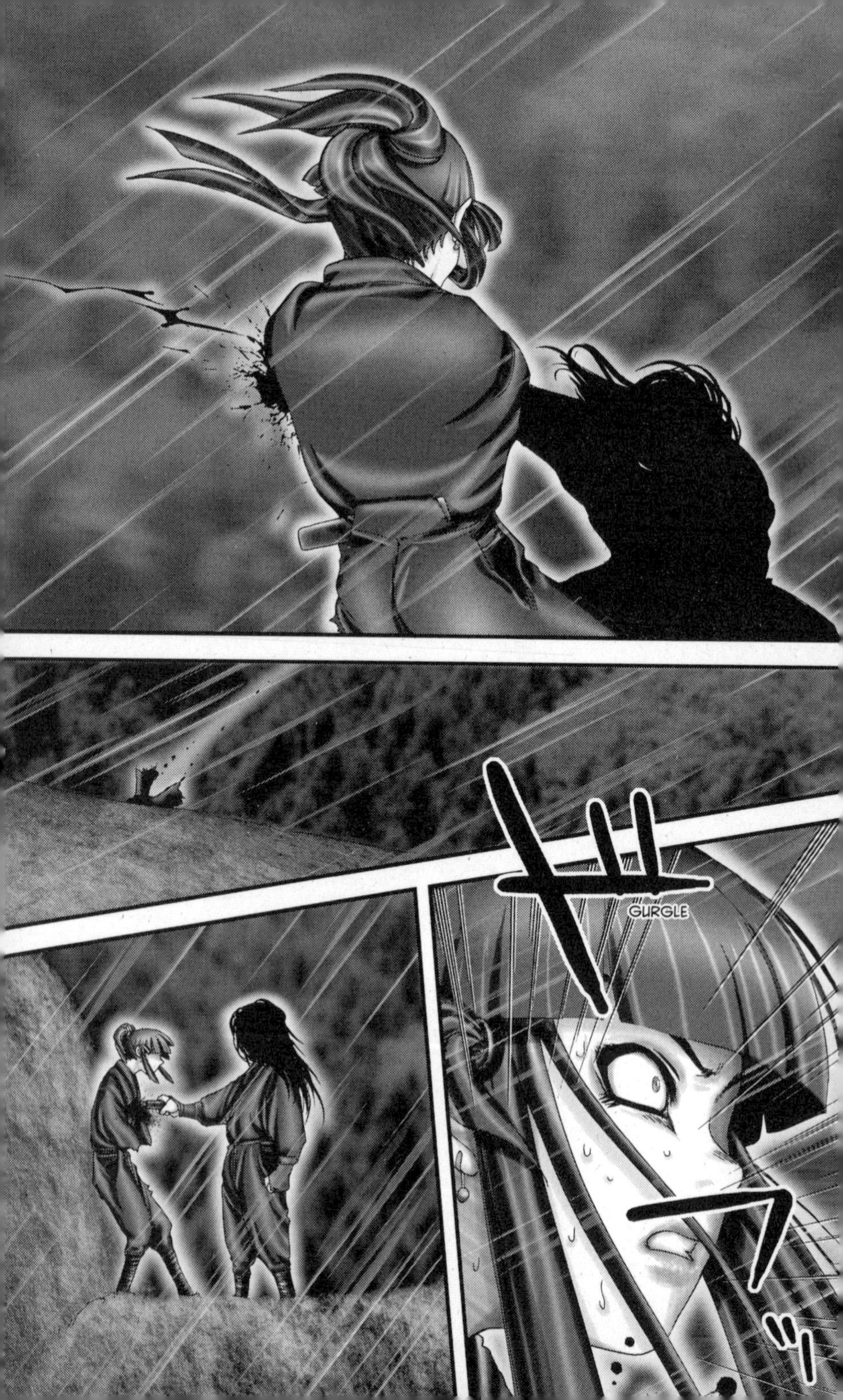
GURGLE

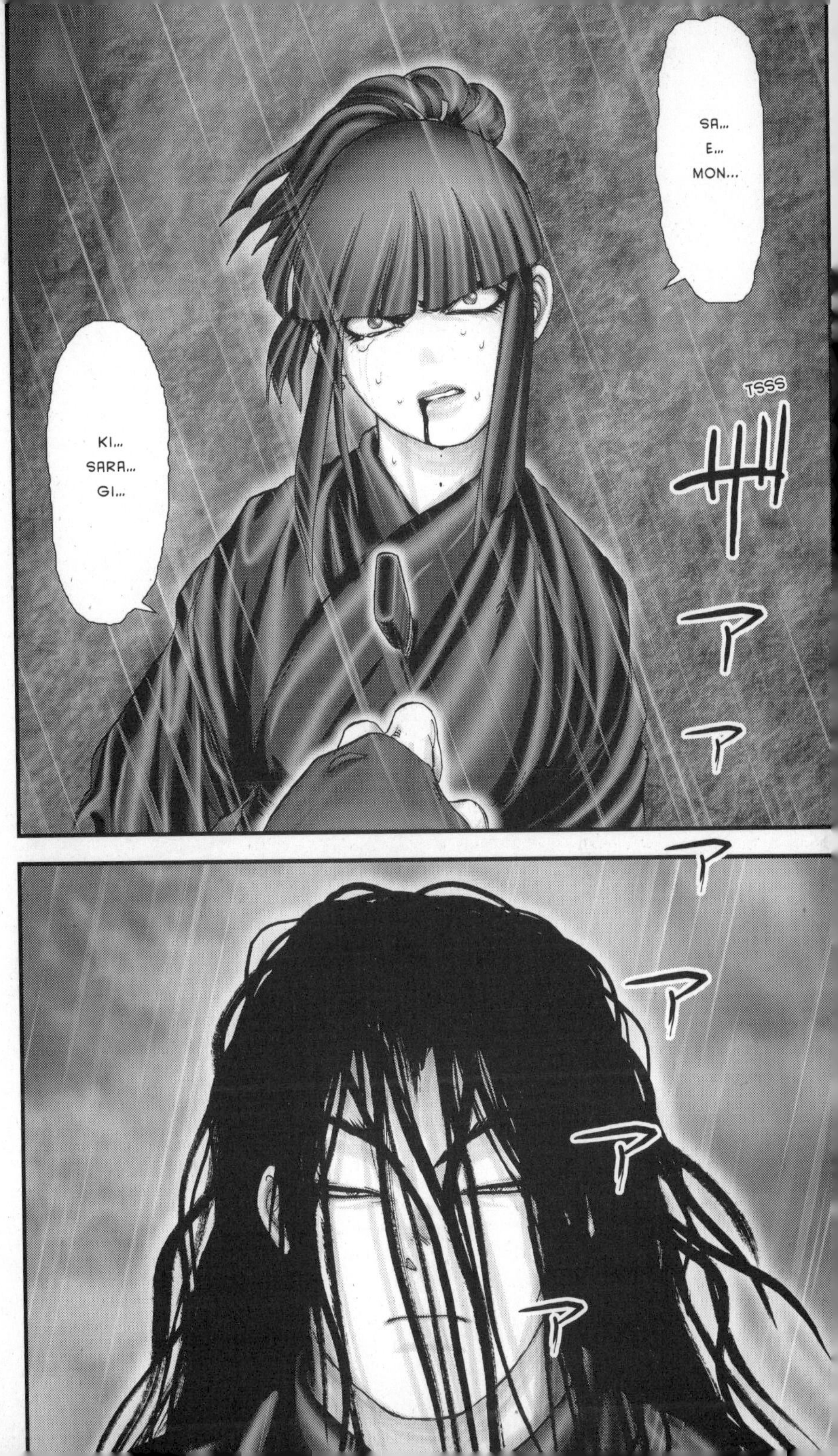
SA... E... MON...
KI... SARA... GI...
TSSS

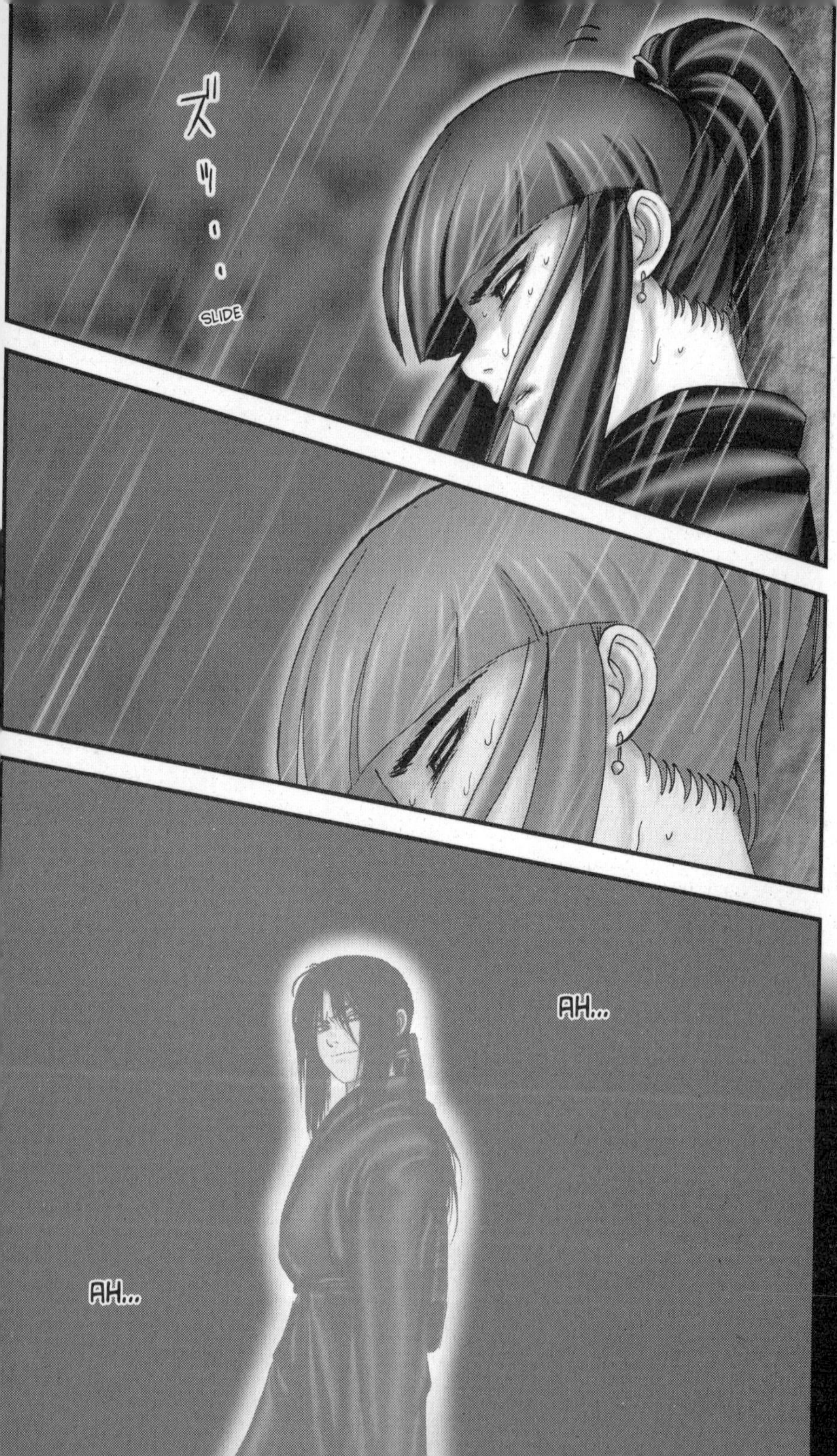
ズッ...
SLIDE
AH...
AH...

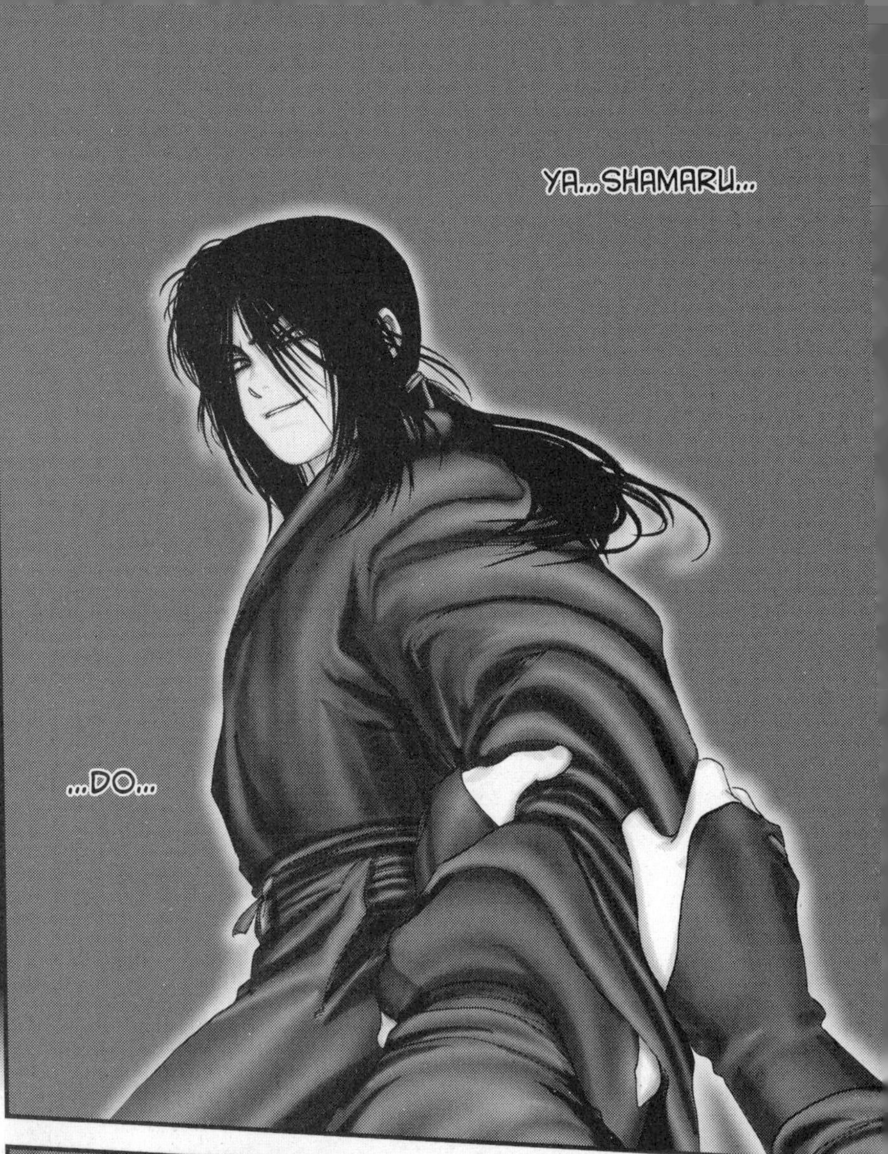
YA... SHAMARU...
...DO...
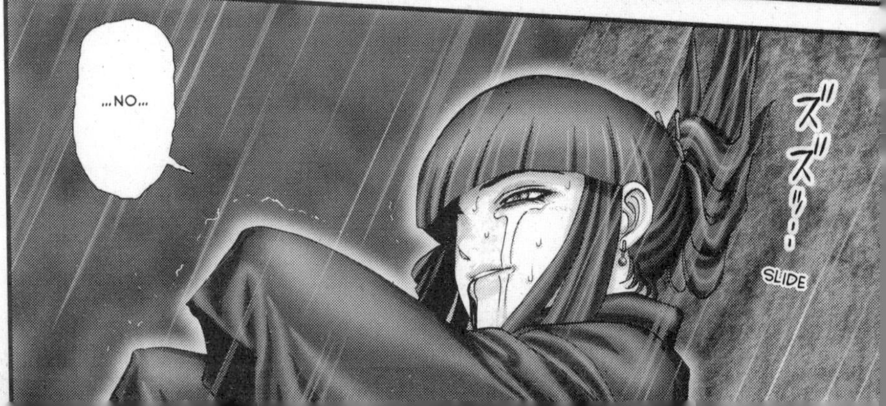
ズズズッ・・
SLIDE
...NO...

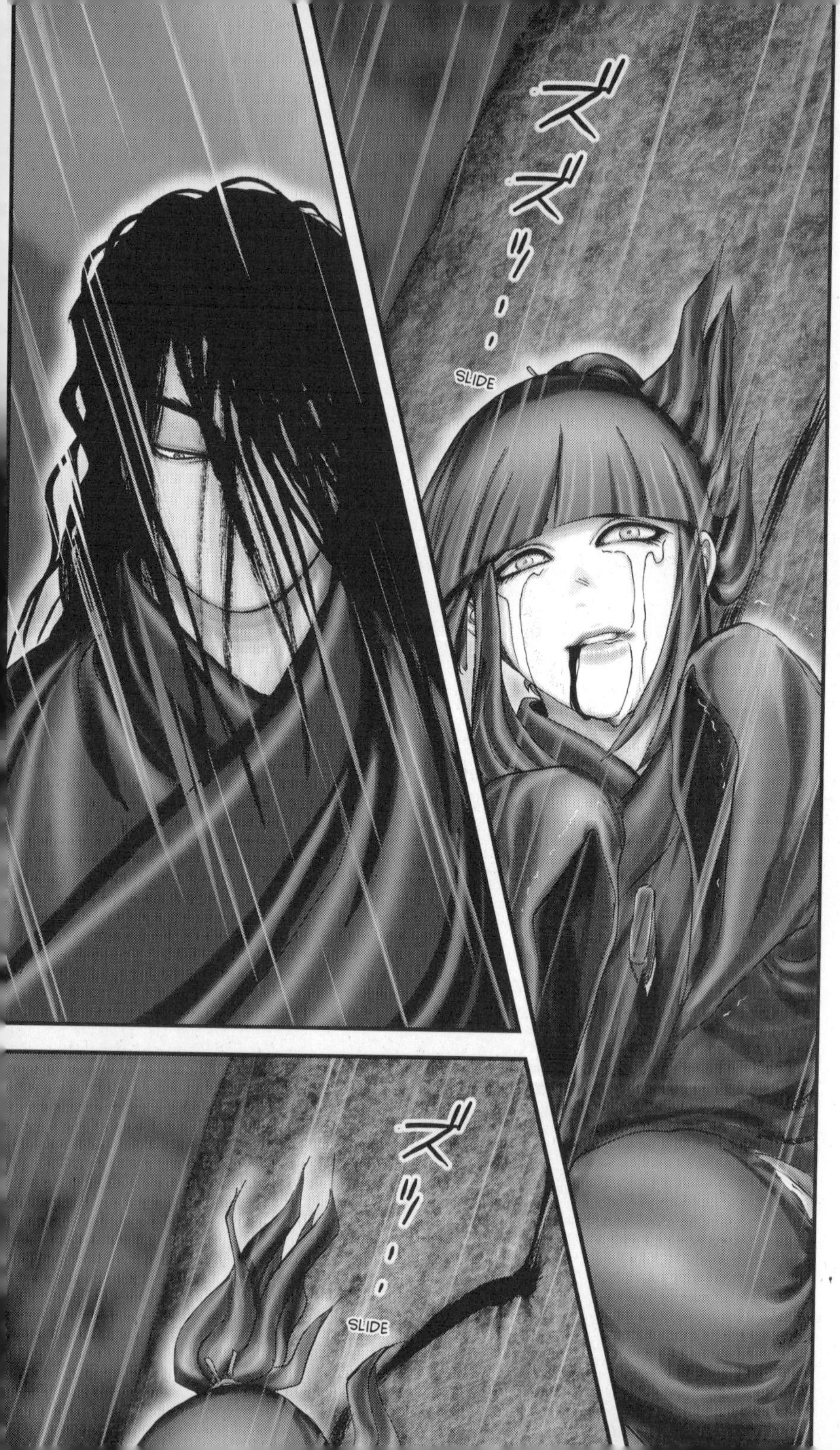
ズズッ...
SLIDE
ズッ...
SLIDE

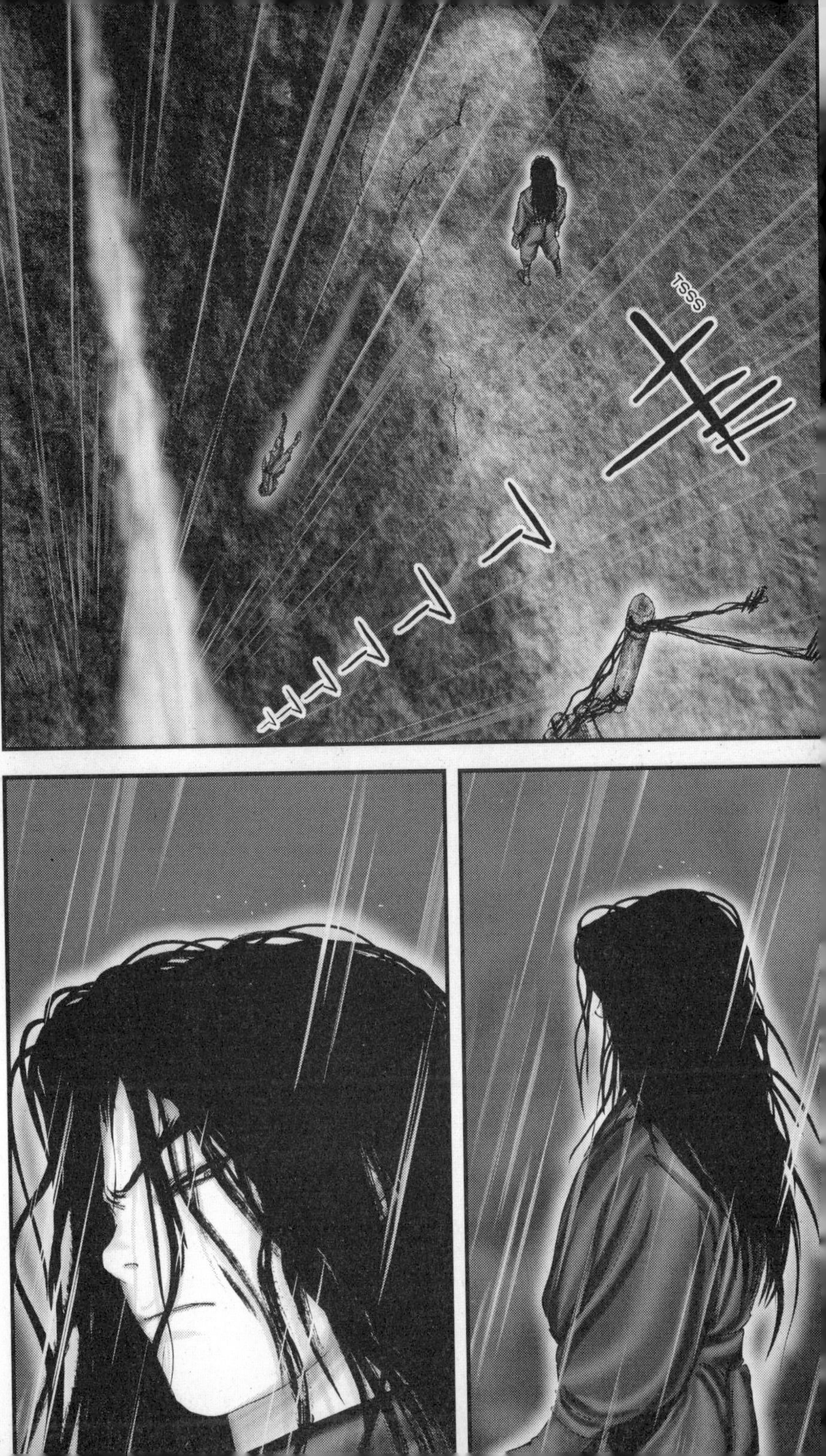
TSSS

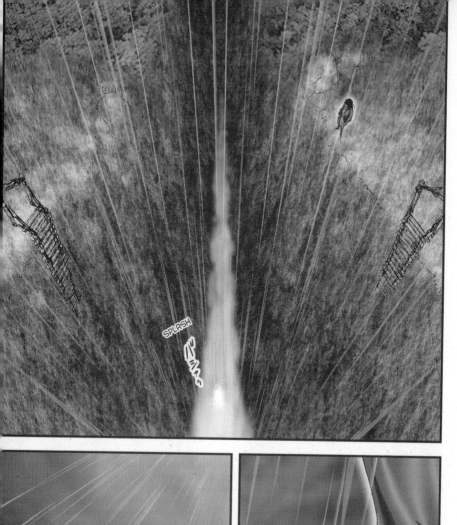

SPLASH

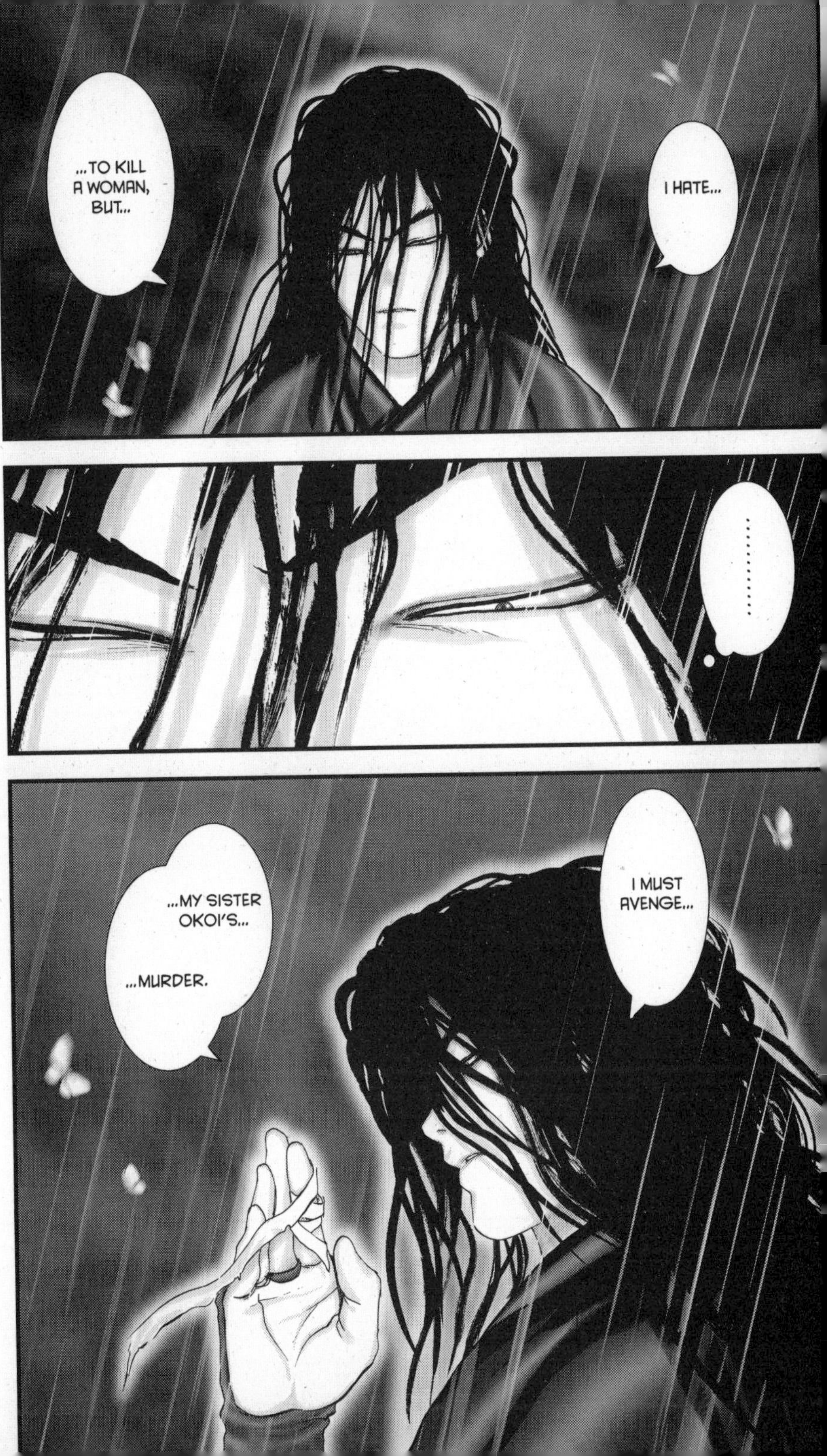
I HATE...
...TO KILL A WOMAN, BUT...
......
I MUST AVENGE...
...MY SISTER OKOI'S... ...MURDER.

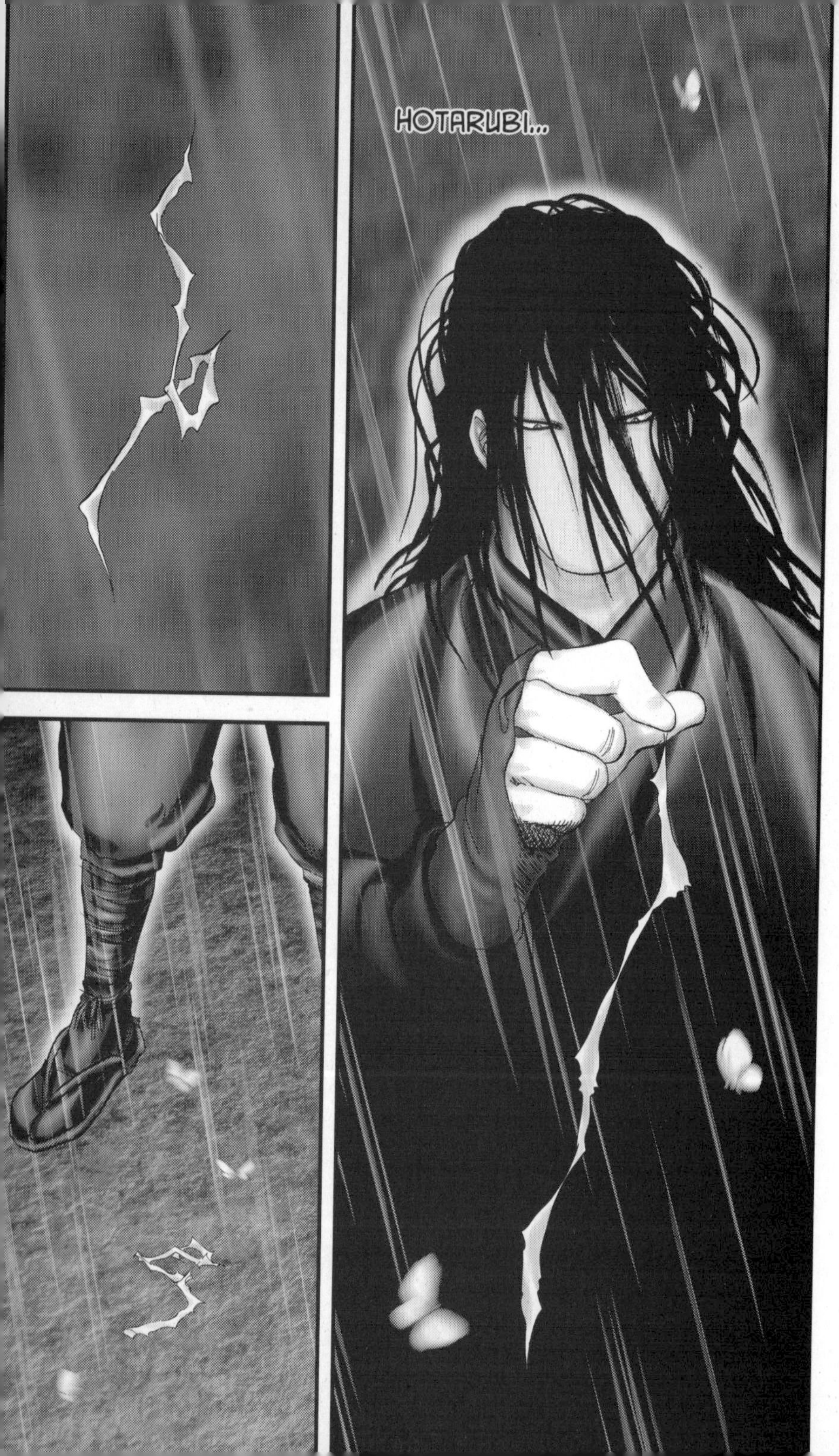
HOTARUBI...

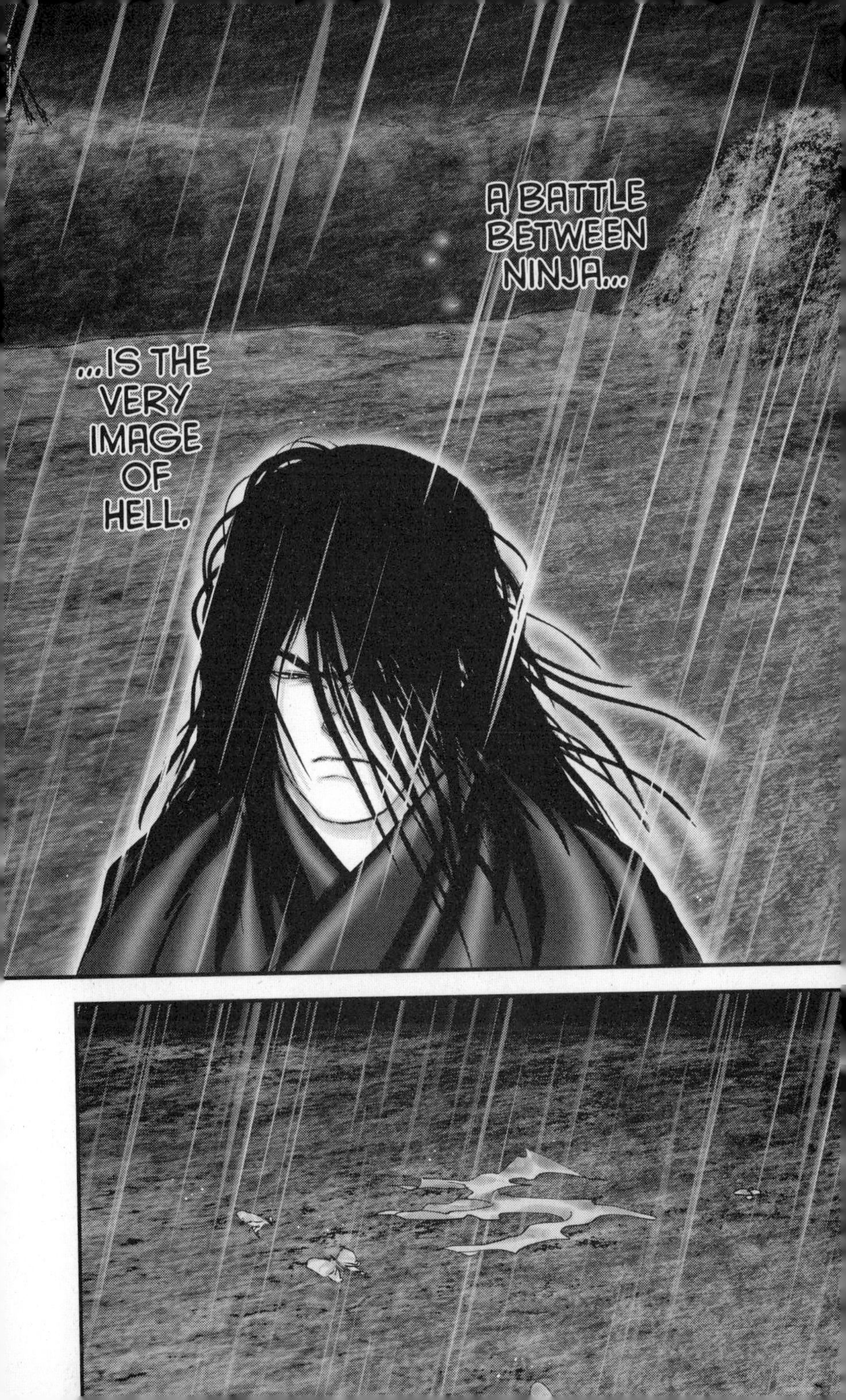
A BATTLE BETWEEN NINJA...
...IS THE VERY IMAGE OF HELL.

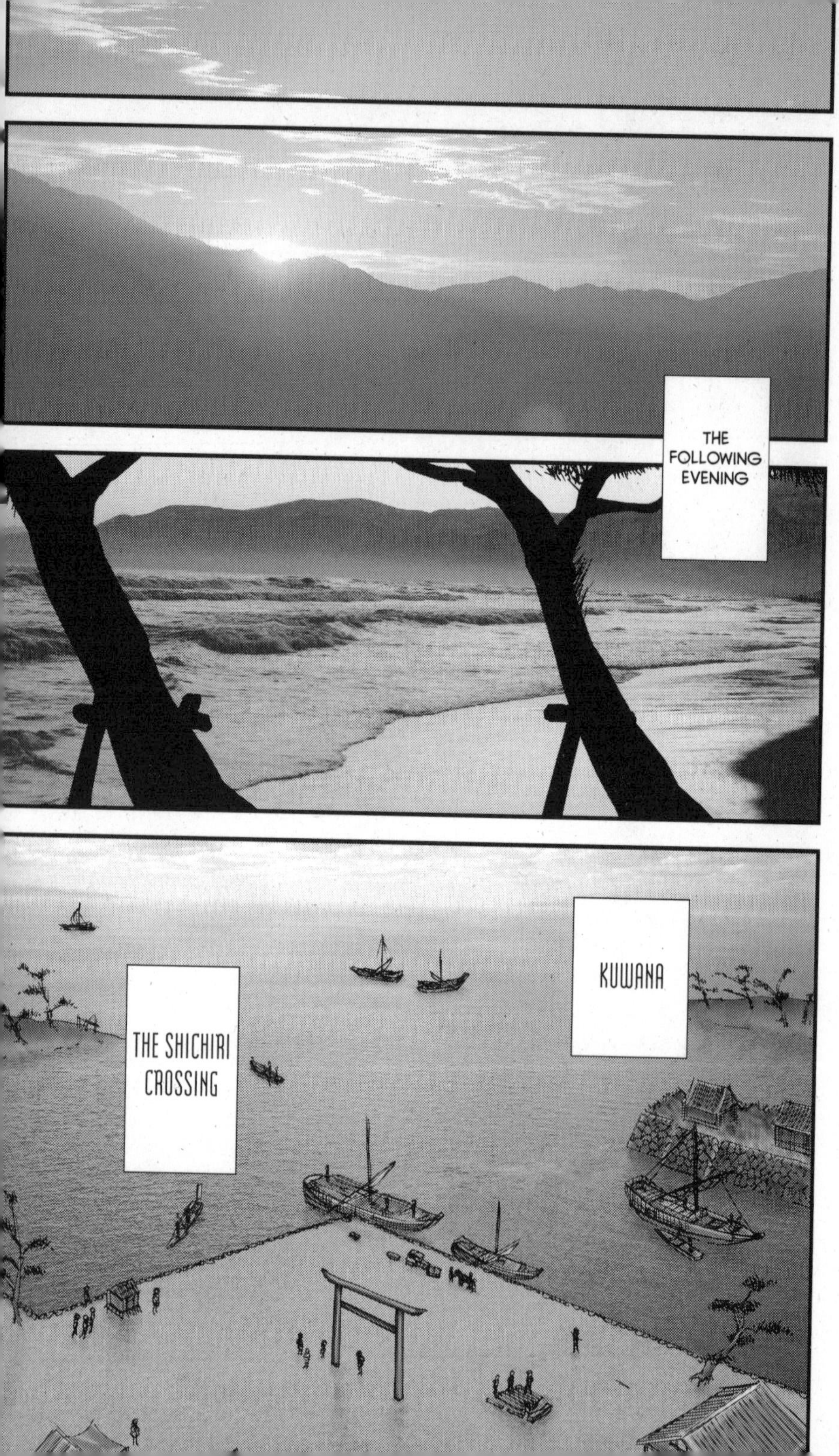
THE FOLLOWING EVENING
KUWANA
THE SHICHIRI CROSSING

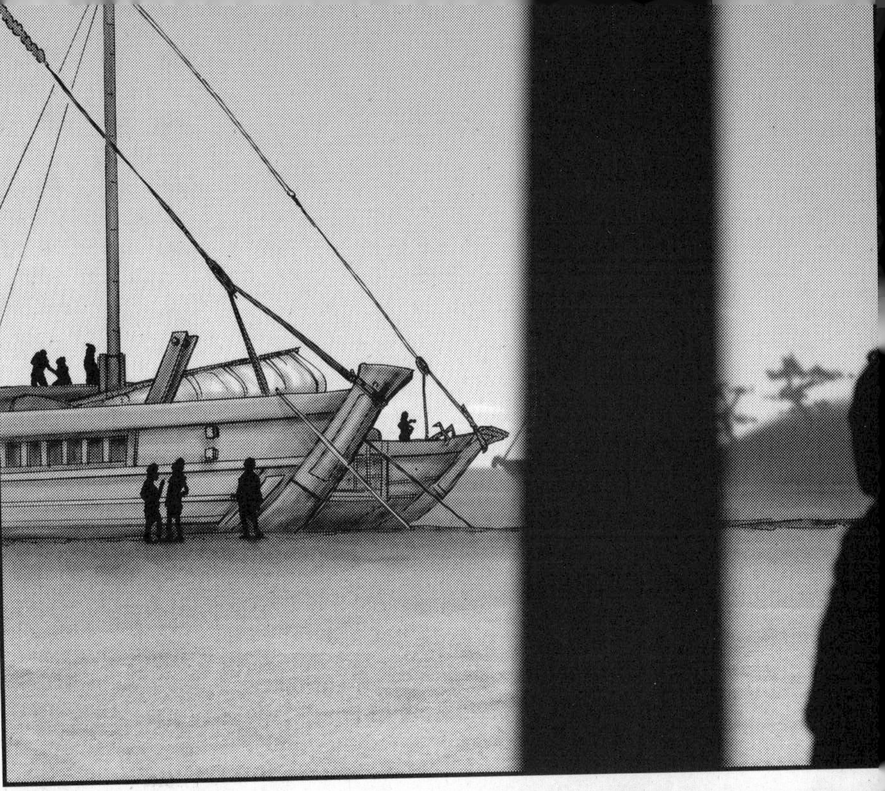

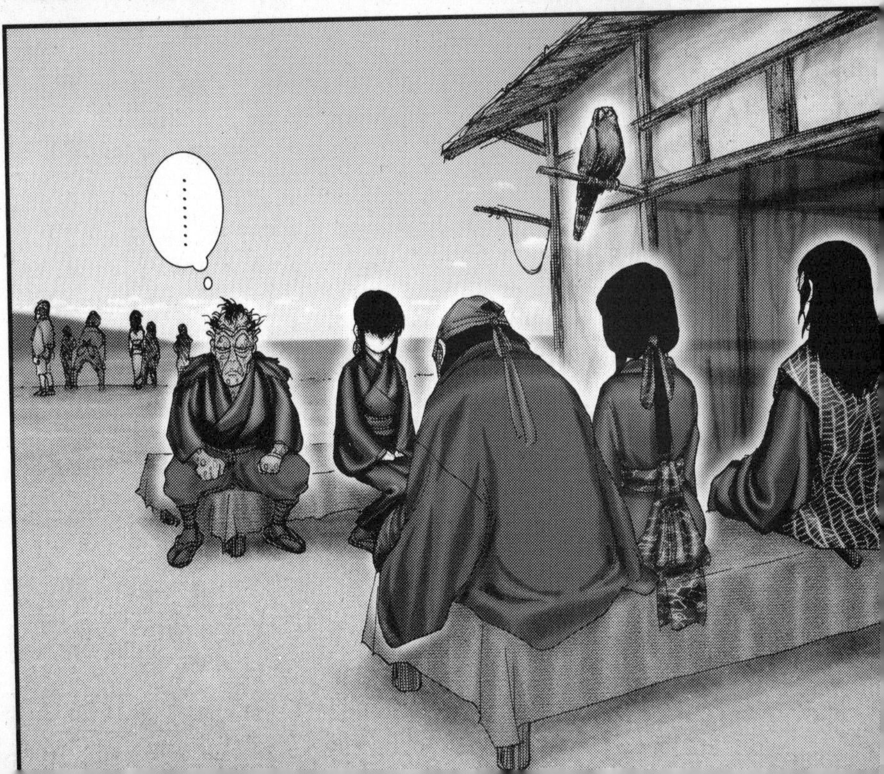
....

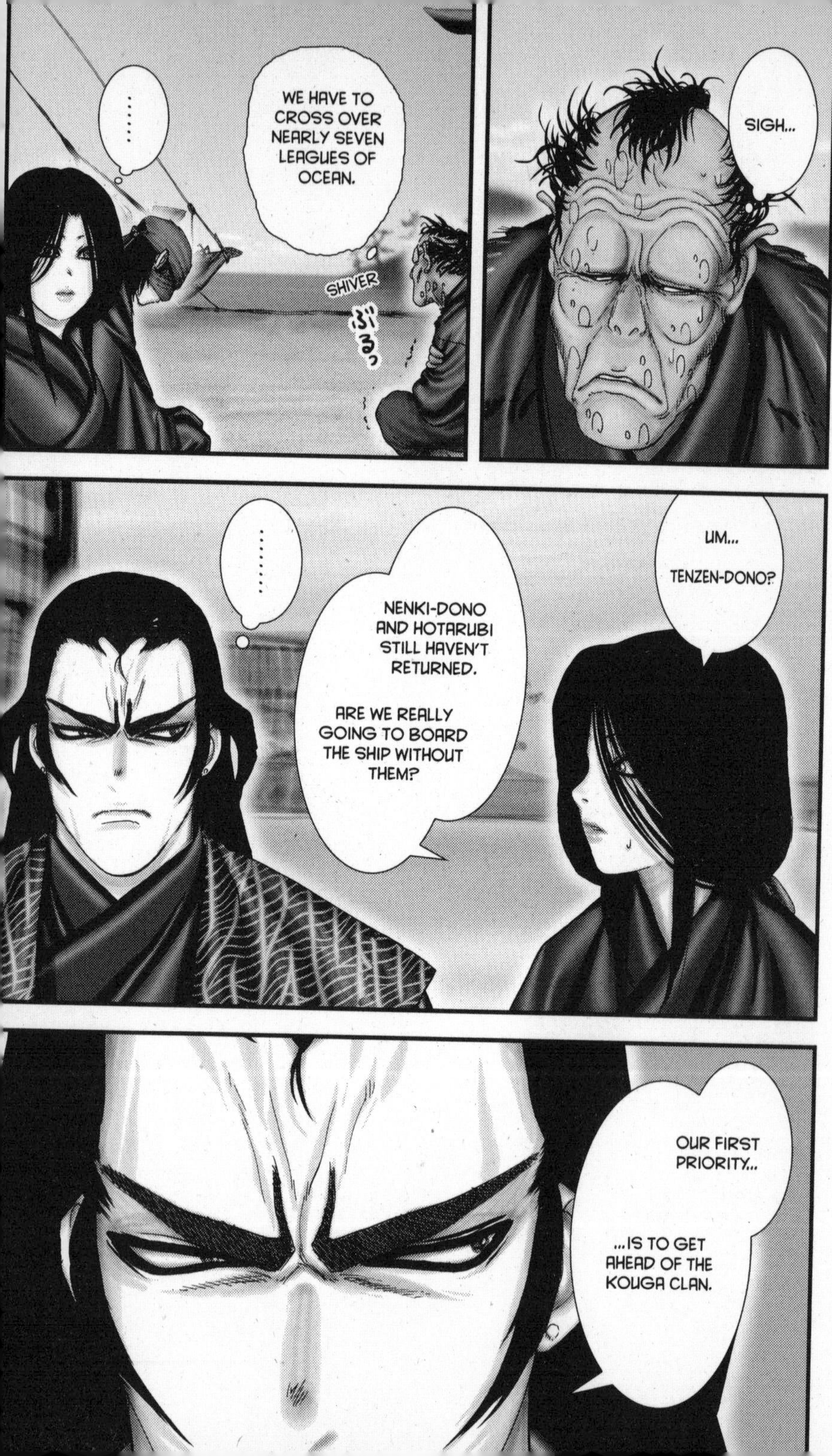
SIGH...
WE HAVE TO CROSS OVER NEARLY SEVEN LEAGUES OF OCEAN.
......
SHIVER
ぶるっ
UM...
TENZEN-DONO?
NENKI-DONO AND HOTARUBI STILL HAVEN'T RETURNED.
ARE WE REALLY GOING TO BOARD THE SHIP WITHOUT THEM?
......
OUR FIRST PRIORITY...
...IS TO GET AHEAD OF THE KOUGA CLAN.

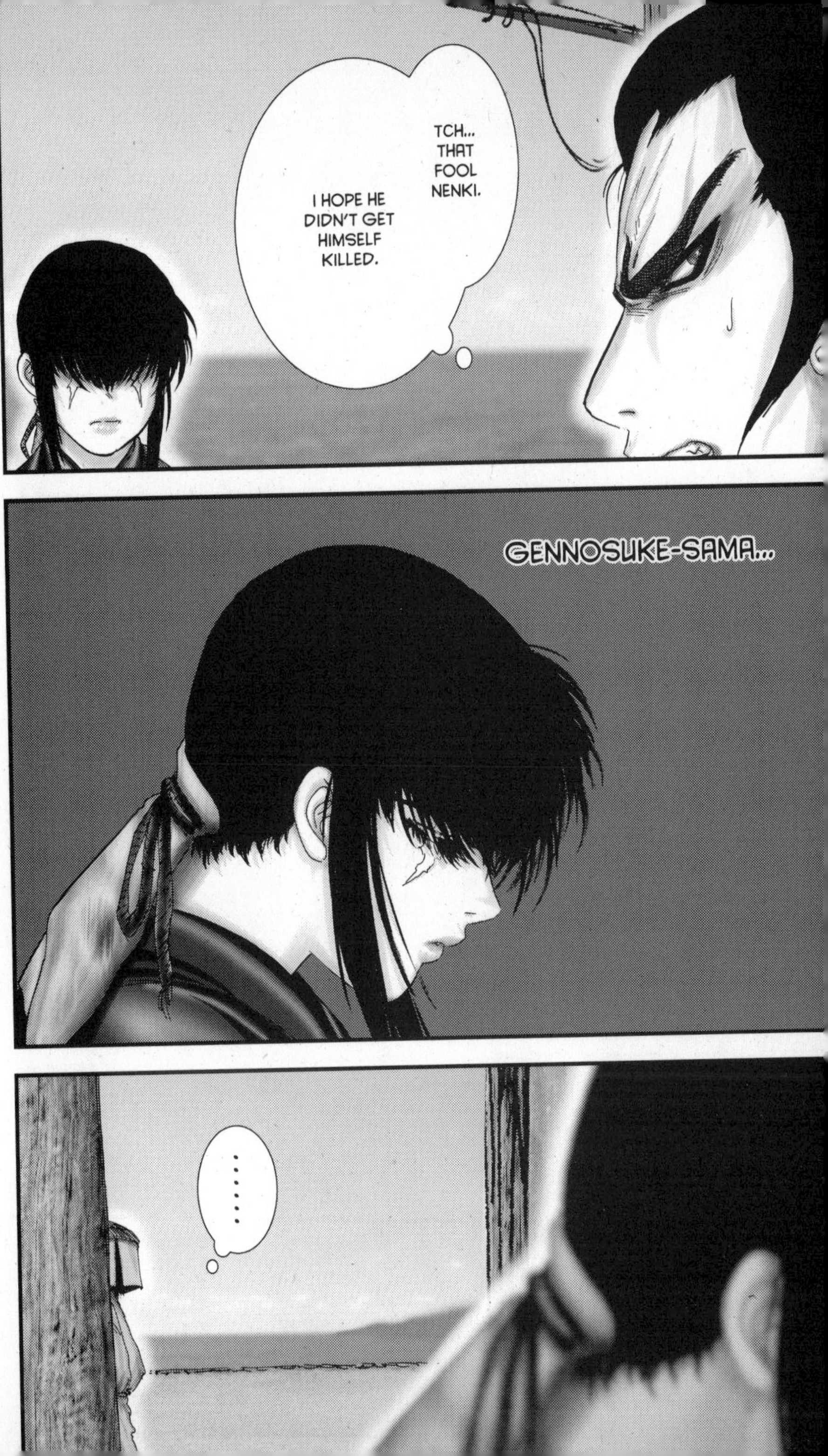
TCH... THAT FOOL NENKI.
I HOPE HE DIDN'T GET HIMSELF KILLED.
GENNOSUKE-SAMA...
....

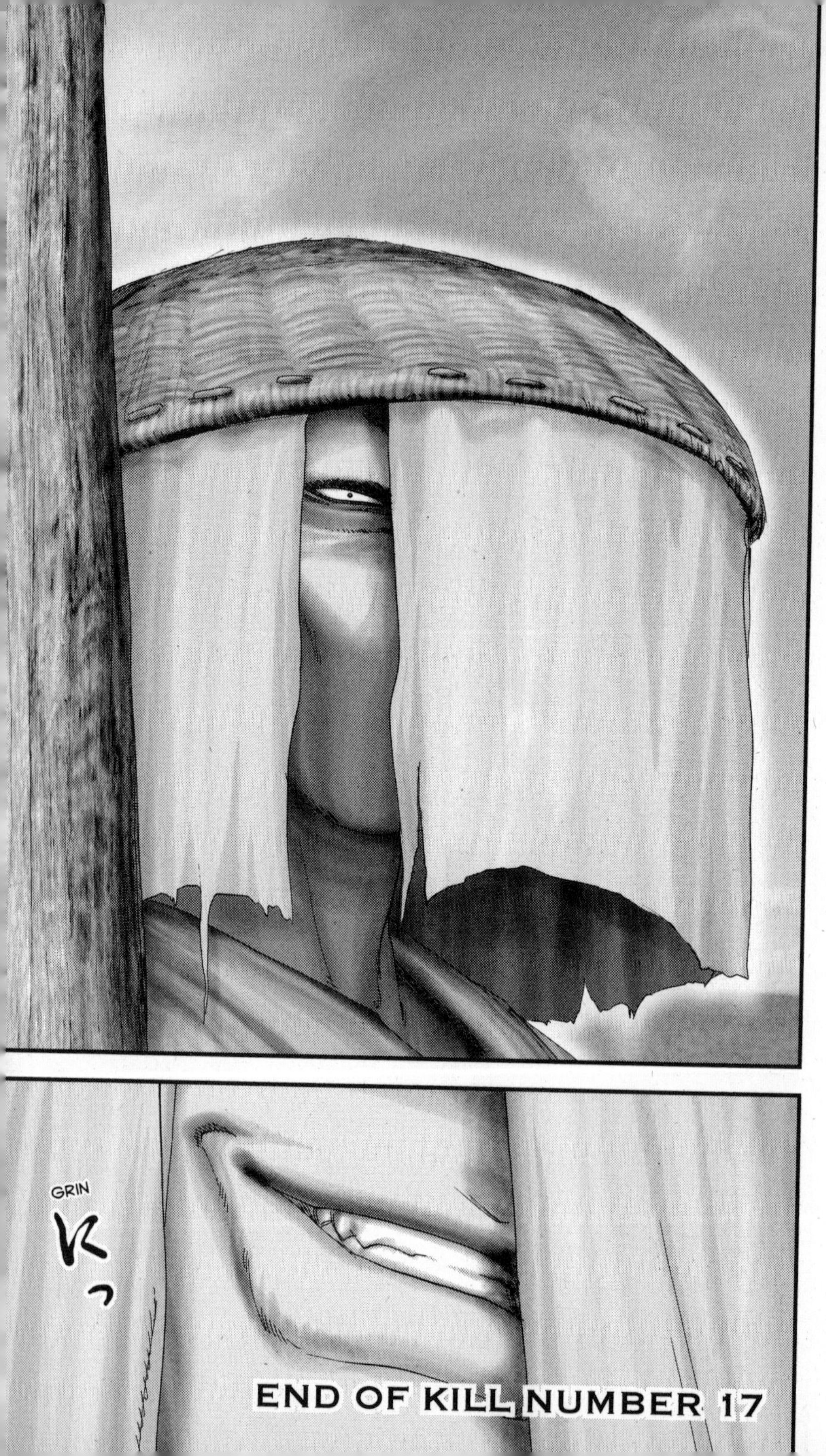
GRIN
ニッ
END OF KILL NUMBER 17

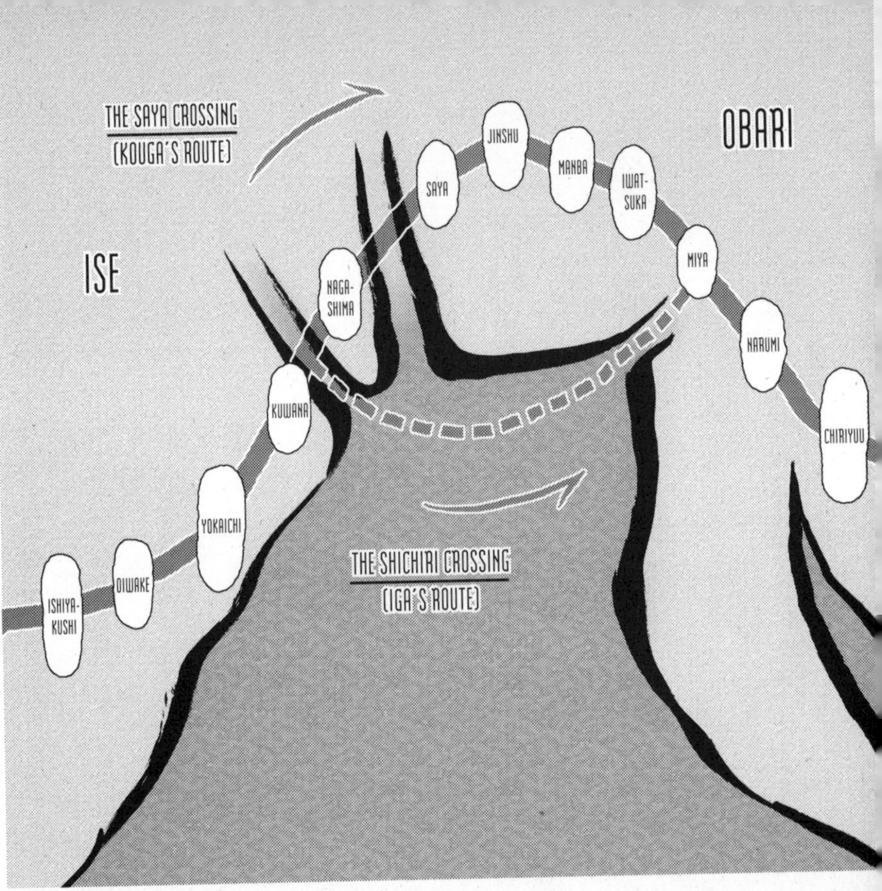
OBARI
THE SAYA CROSSING
(KOUGA'S ROUTE)
ISE
JINSHU
MANBA
IWAT-
SUKA
SAYA
NAGA-
SHIMA
MIYA
NARUMI
KUWANA
CHIRIYUU
YOKAICHI
OIWAKE
ISHIYA-
KUSHI
THE SHICHIRI CROSSING
(IGA'S ROUTE)

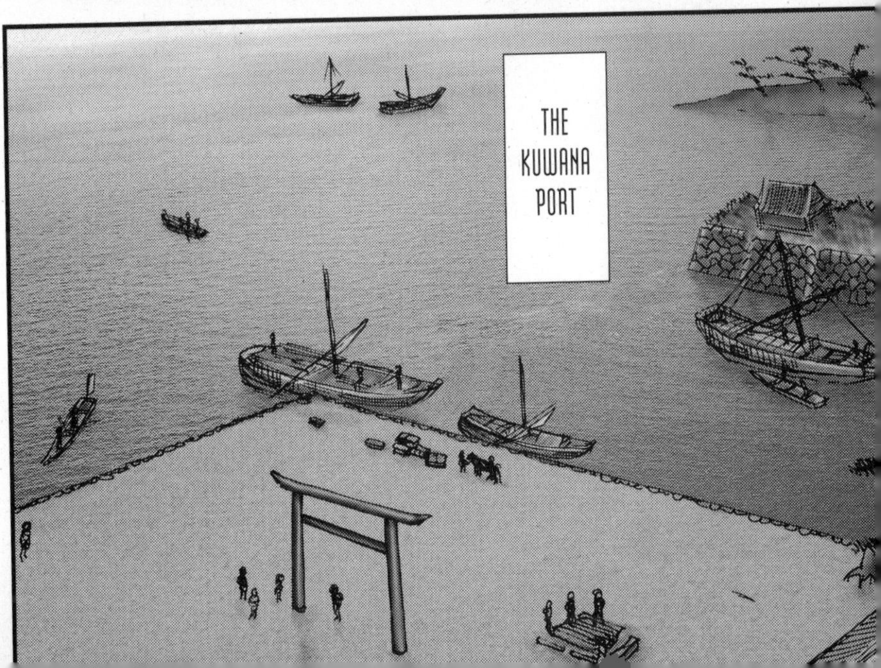
THE KUWANA PORT

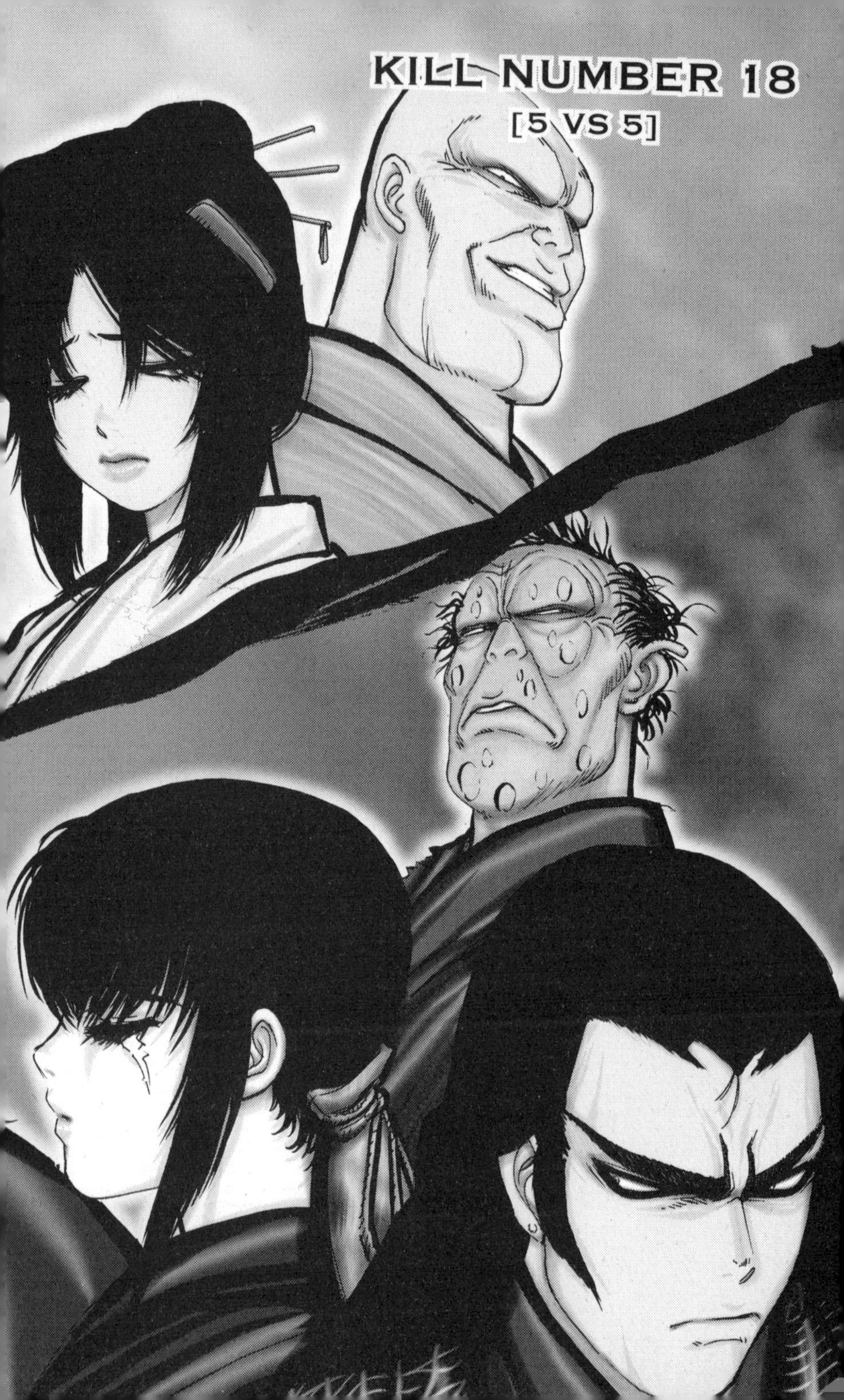
KILL NUMBER 18
[5 VS 5]

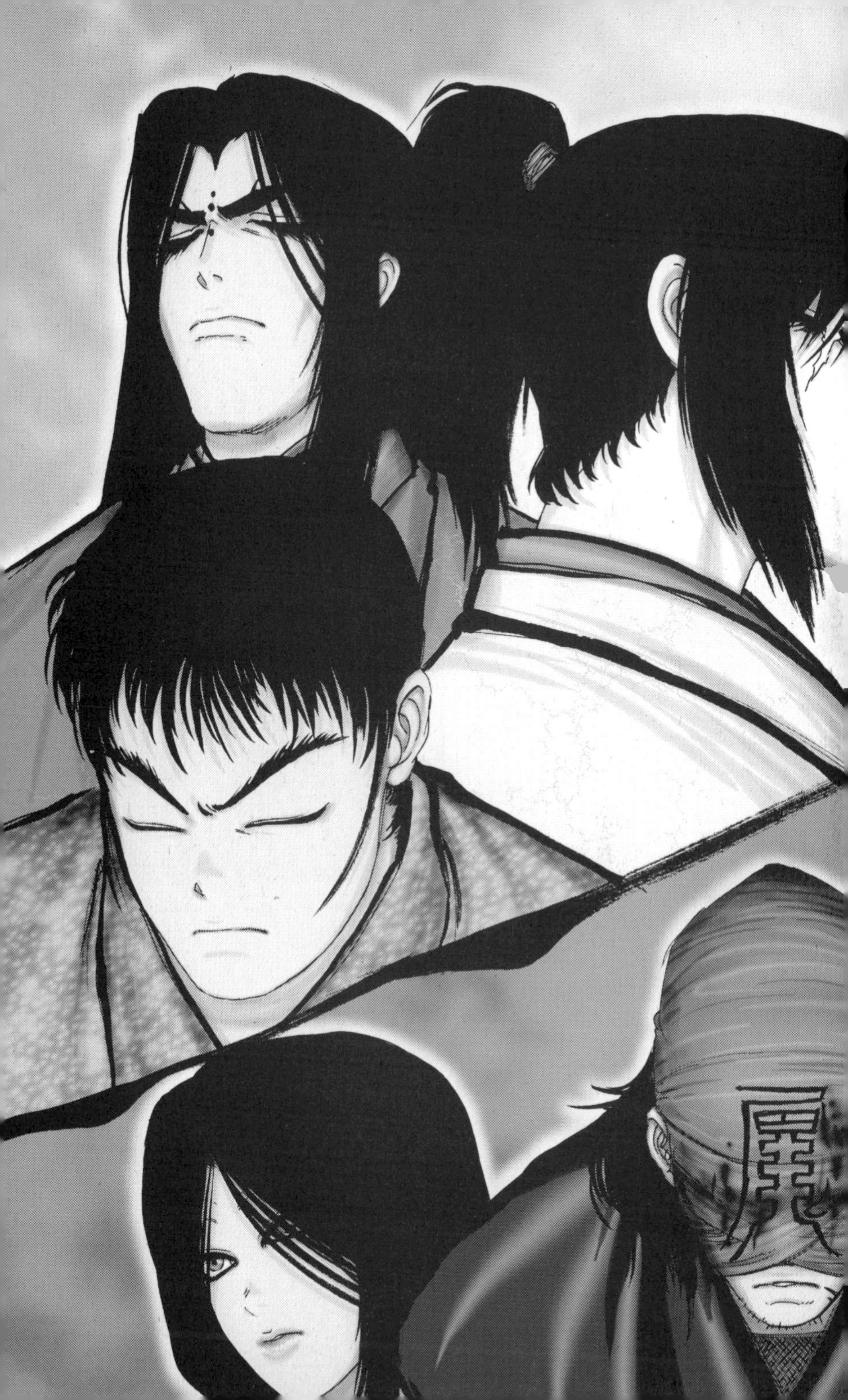

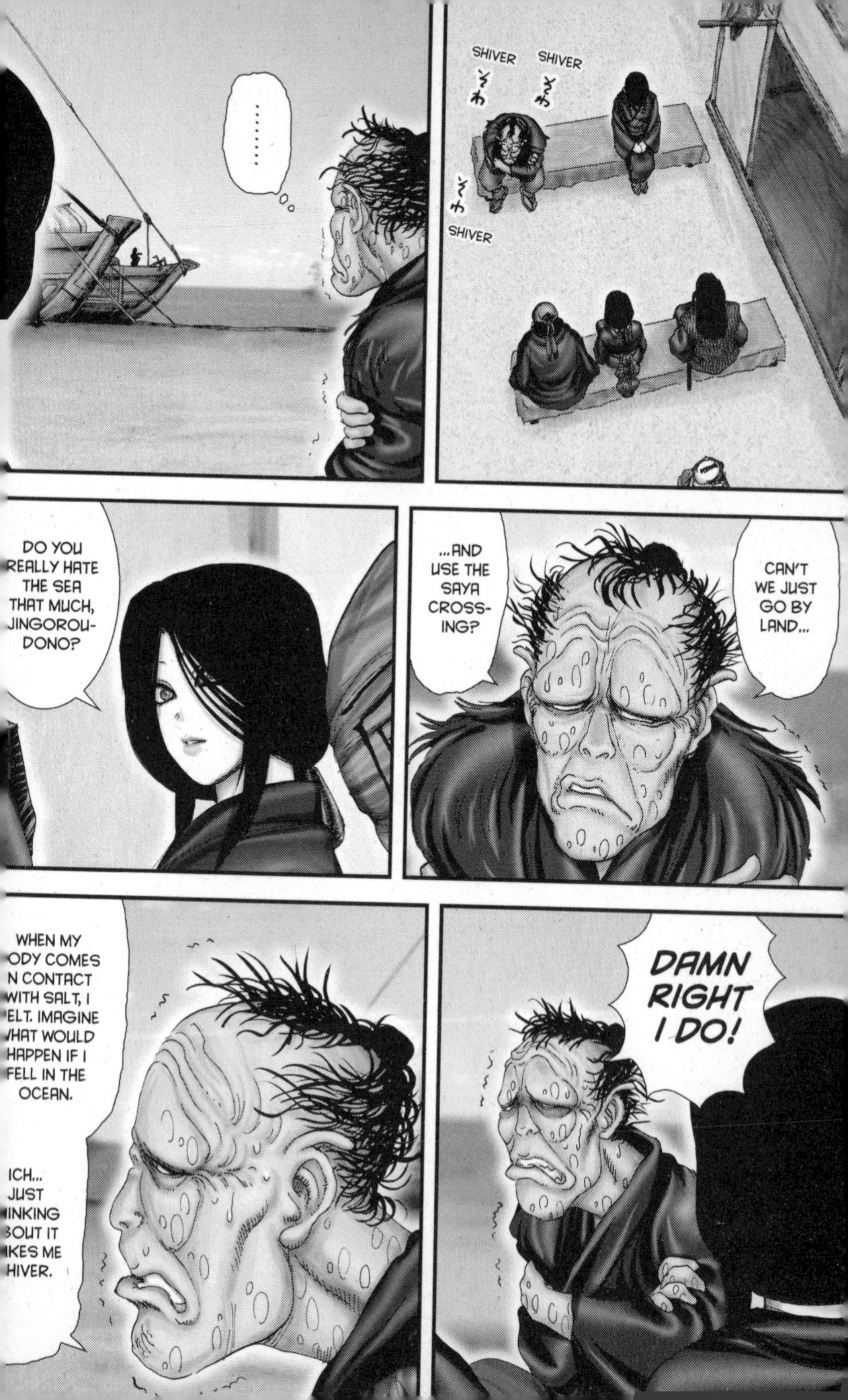

SHIVER
ぞわ
SHIVER
ぞわ
ぞわ
SHIVER
......
CAN'T WE JUST GO BY LAND...
...AND USE THE SAYA CROSSING?
DO YOU REALLY HATE THE SEA THAT MUCH, JINGOROU-DONO?
DAMN RIGHT I DO!
WHEN MY ODY COMES N CONTACT WITH SALT, I ELT. IMAGINE VHAT WOULD HAPPEN IF I FELL IN THE OCEAN.
ICH... JUST INKING BOUT IT IKES ME HIVER.

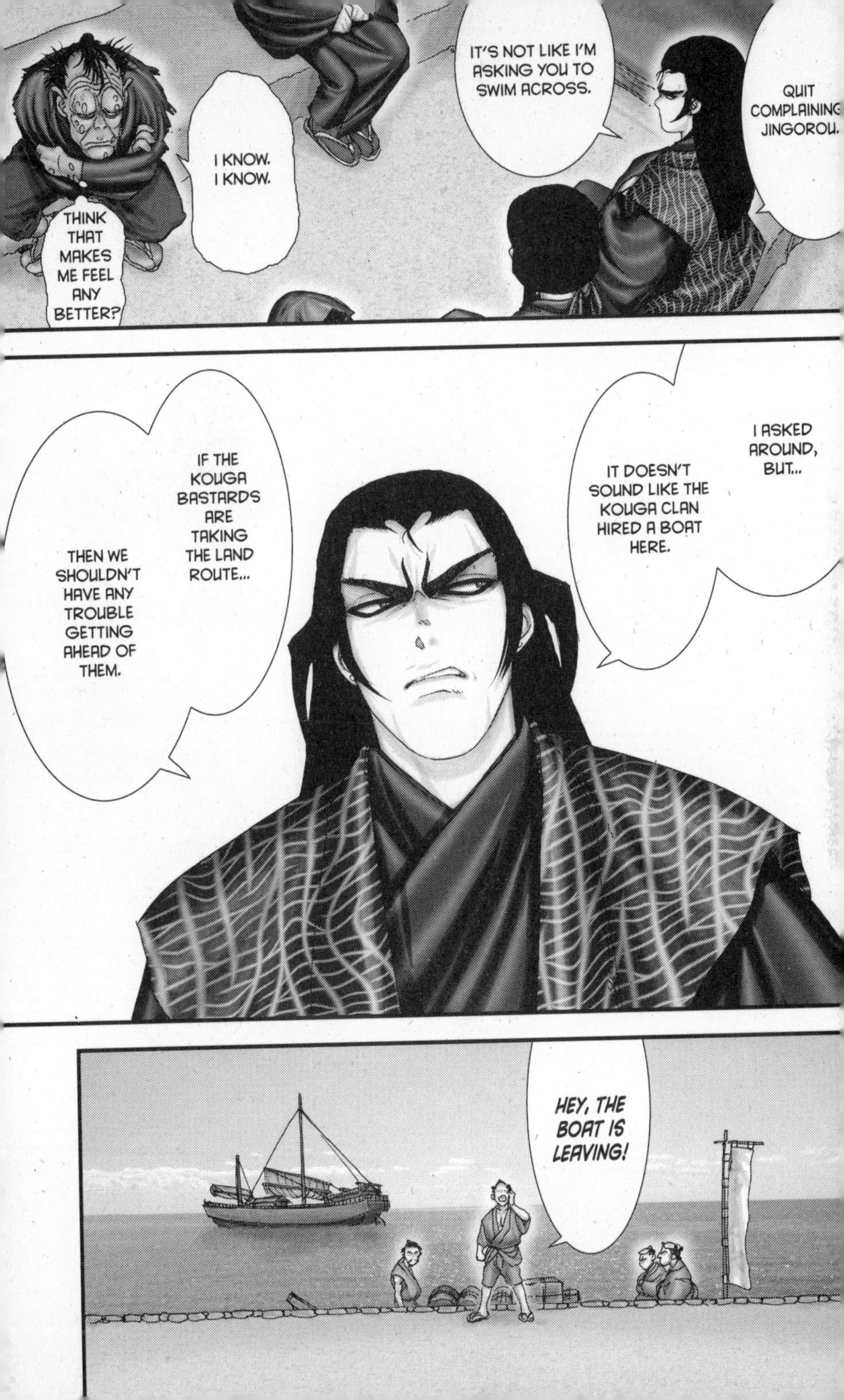
QUIT COMPLAINING JINGOROU.
IT'S NOT LIKE I'M ASKING YOU TO SWIM ACROSS.
I KNOW. I KNOW.
THINK THAT MAKES ME FEEL ANY BETTER?
I ASKED AROUND, BUT...
IT DOESN'T SOUND LIKE THE KOUGA CLAN HIRED A BOAT HERE.
IF THE KOUGA BASTARDS ARE TAKING THE LAND ROUTE...
THEN WE SHOULDN'T HAVE ANY TROUBLE GETTING AHEAD OF THEM.
HEY, THE BOAT IS LEAVING!

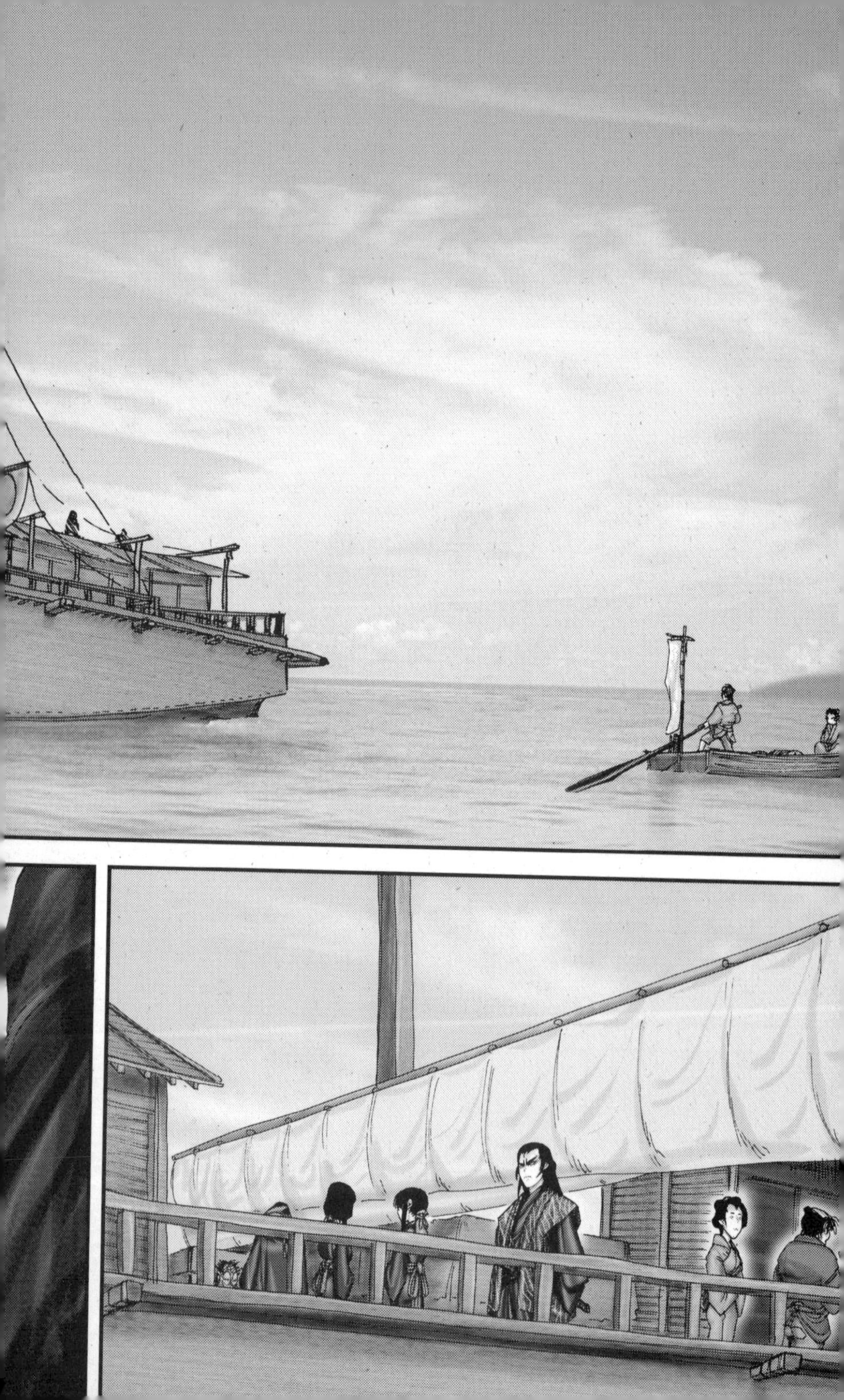

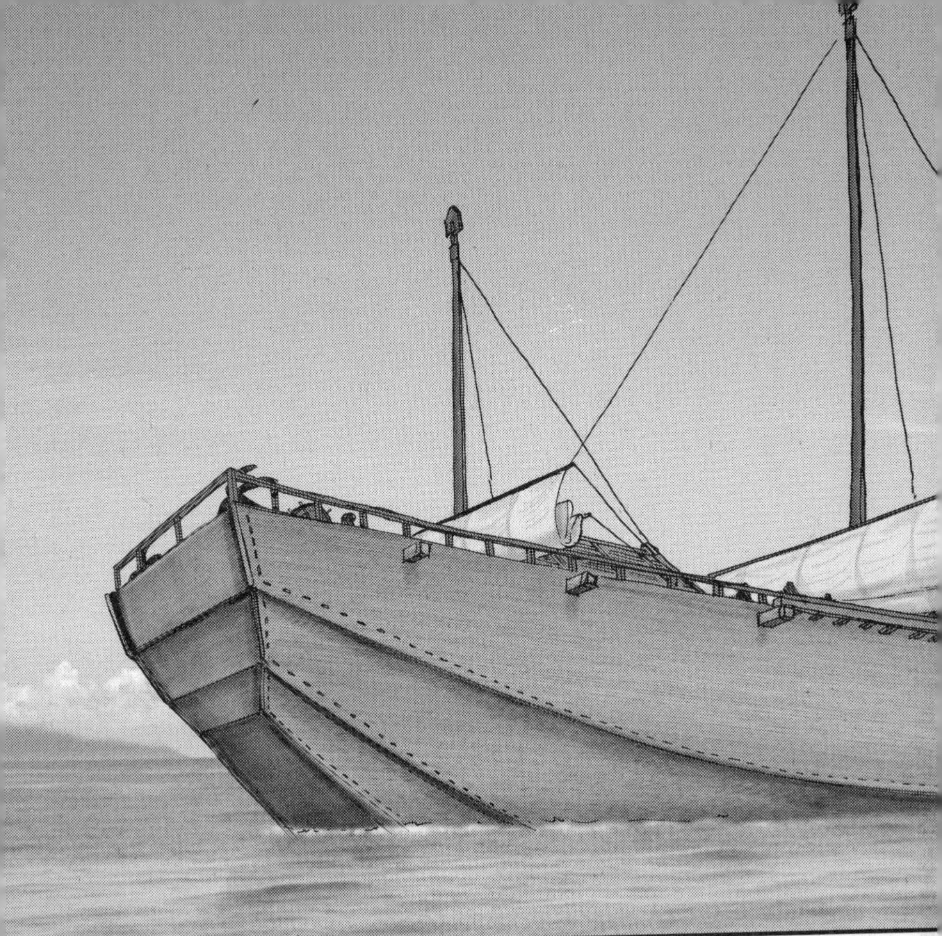

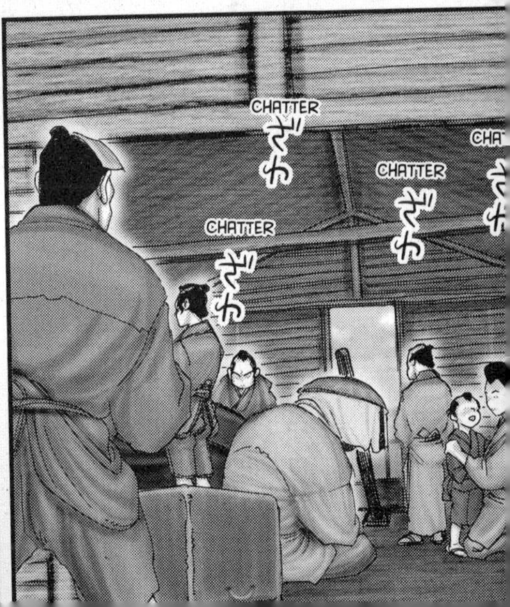
CHATTER
ざわ
CHATTER
ざわ
CHATTER
ざわ

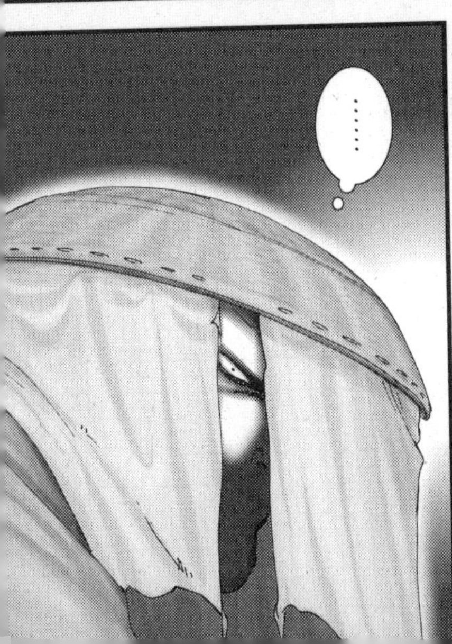
......

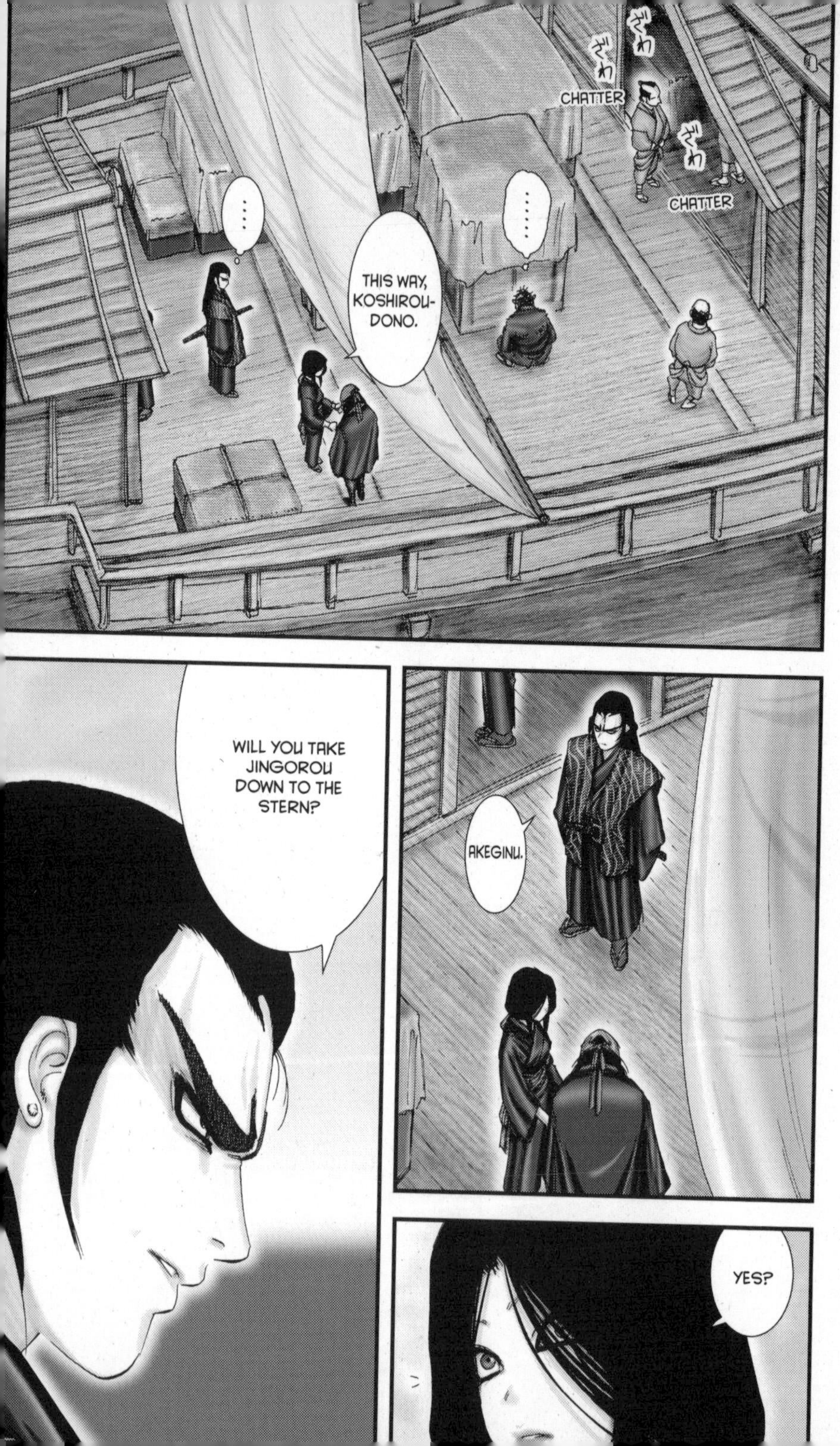
ざわ
ざわ
CHATTER
ざわ
CHATTER
......
THIS WAY, KOSHIROU-DONO.
......
AKEGINU.
YES?
WILL YOU TAKE JINGOROU DOWN TO THE STERN?

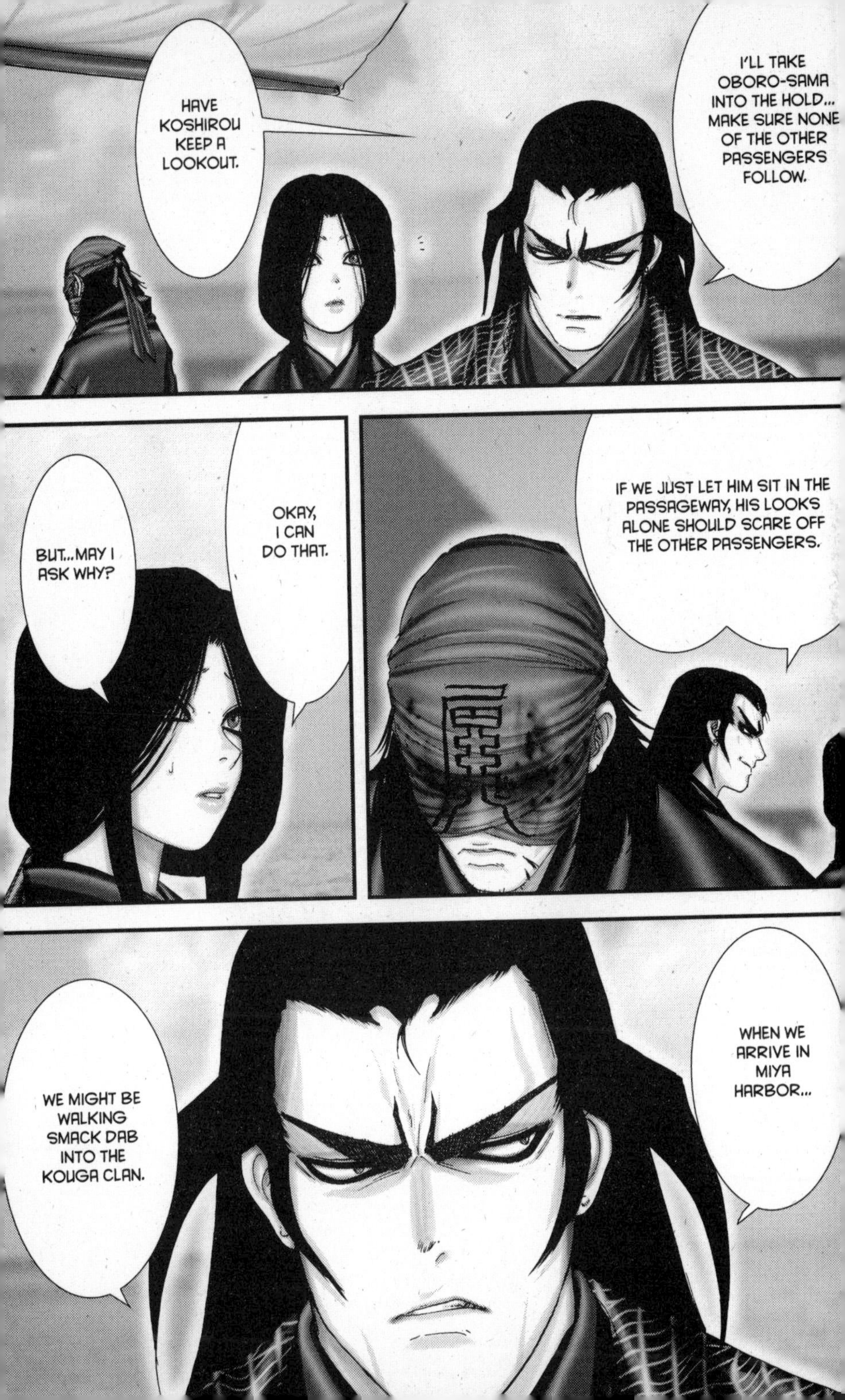
I'LL TAKE OBORO-SAMA INTO THE HOLD... MAKE SURE NONE OF THE OTHER PASSENGERS FOLLOW.
HAVE KOSHIROU KEEP A LOOKOUT.
IF WE JUST LET HIM SIT IN THE PASSAGEWAY, HIS LOOKS ALONE SHOULD SCARE OFF THE OTHER PASSENGERS.
OKAY, I CAN DO THAT.
BUT...MAY I ASK WHY?
WHEN WE ARRIVE IN MIYA HARBOR...
WE MIGHT BE WALKING SMACK DAB INTO THE KOUGA CLAN.

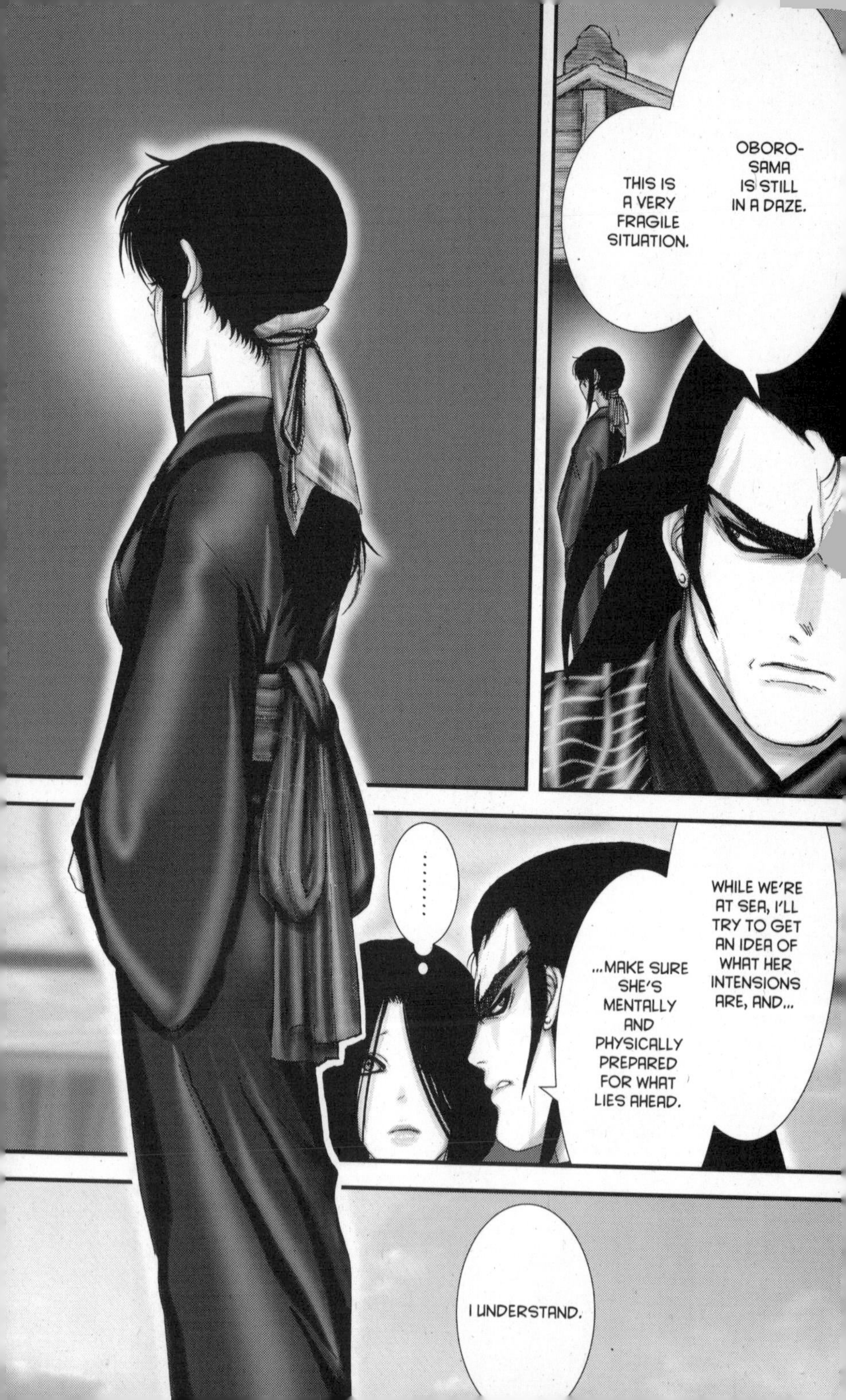
OBORO-SAMA IS STILL IN A DAZE.
THIS IS A VERY FRAGILE SITUATION.
WHILE WE'RE AT SEA, I'LL TRY TO GET AN IDEA OF WHAT HER INTENSIONS ARE, AND...
...MAKE SURE SHE'S MENTALLY AND PHYSICALLY PREPARED FOR WHAT LIES AHEAD.
....
I UNDERSTAND.

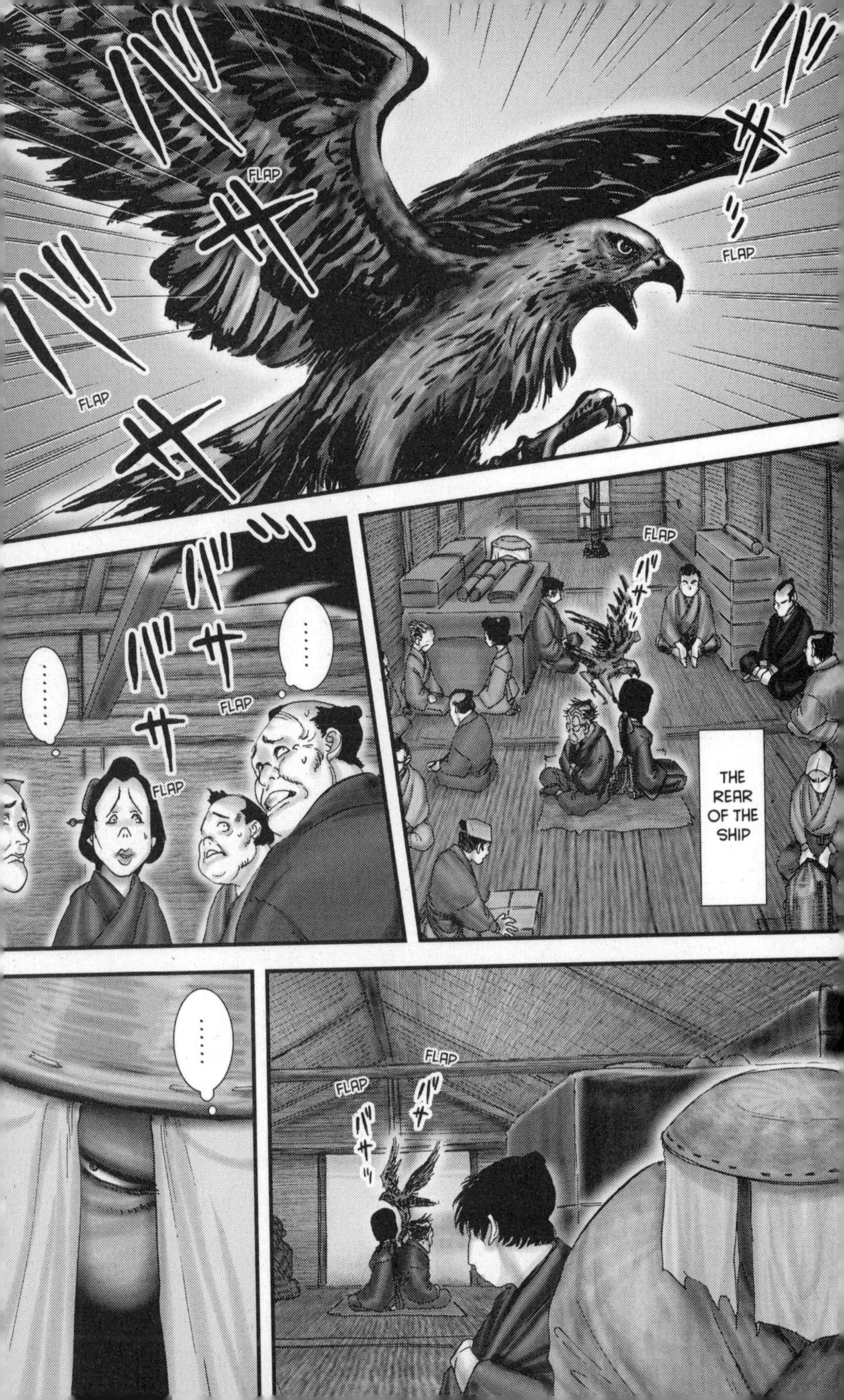
FLAP
FLAP
FLAP
FLAP
THE REAR OF THE SHIP
......
FLAP
FLAP
......
FLAP
FLAP
......

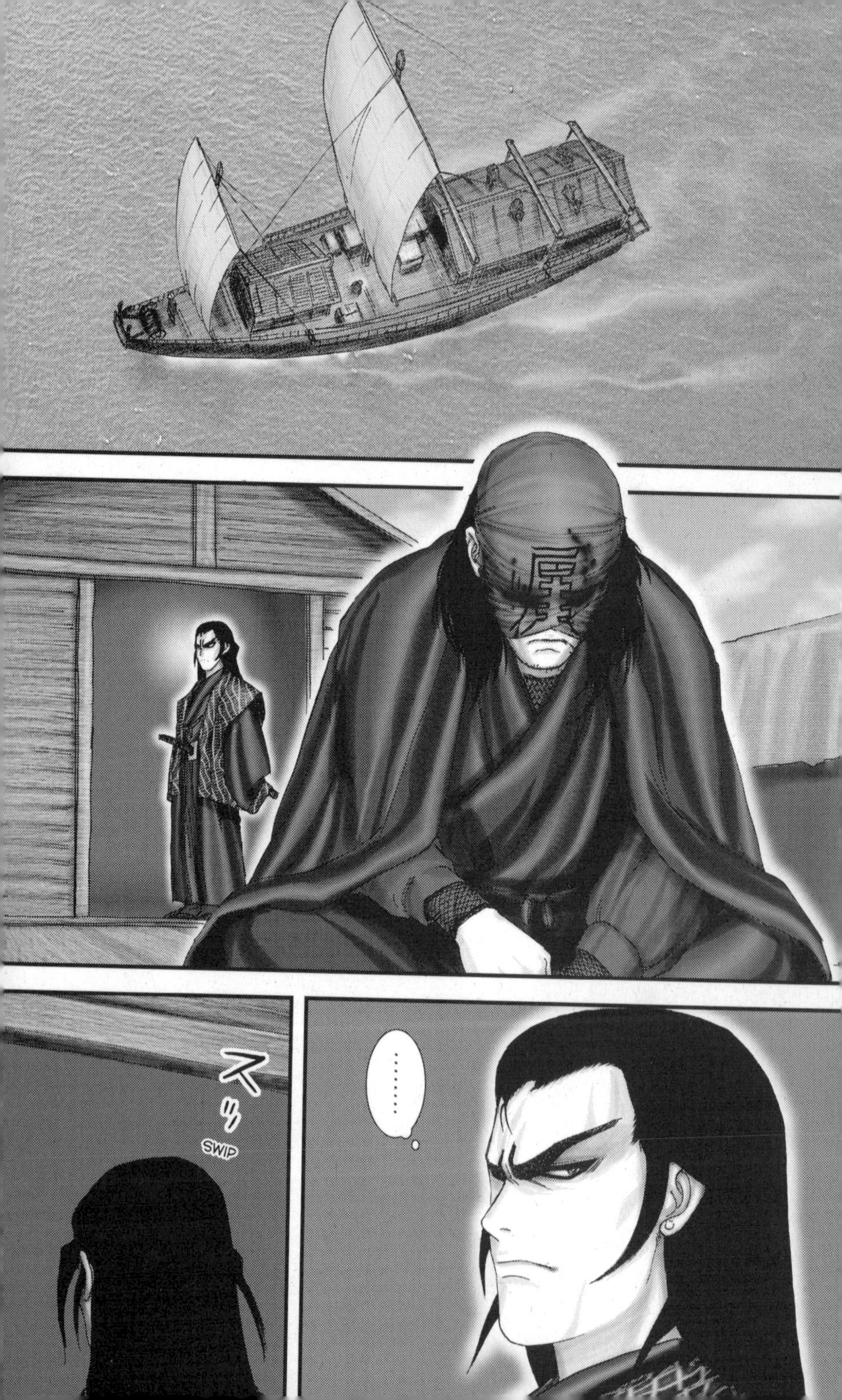
....
スッ
SWIP

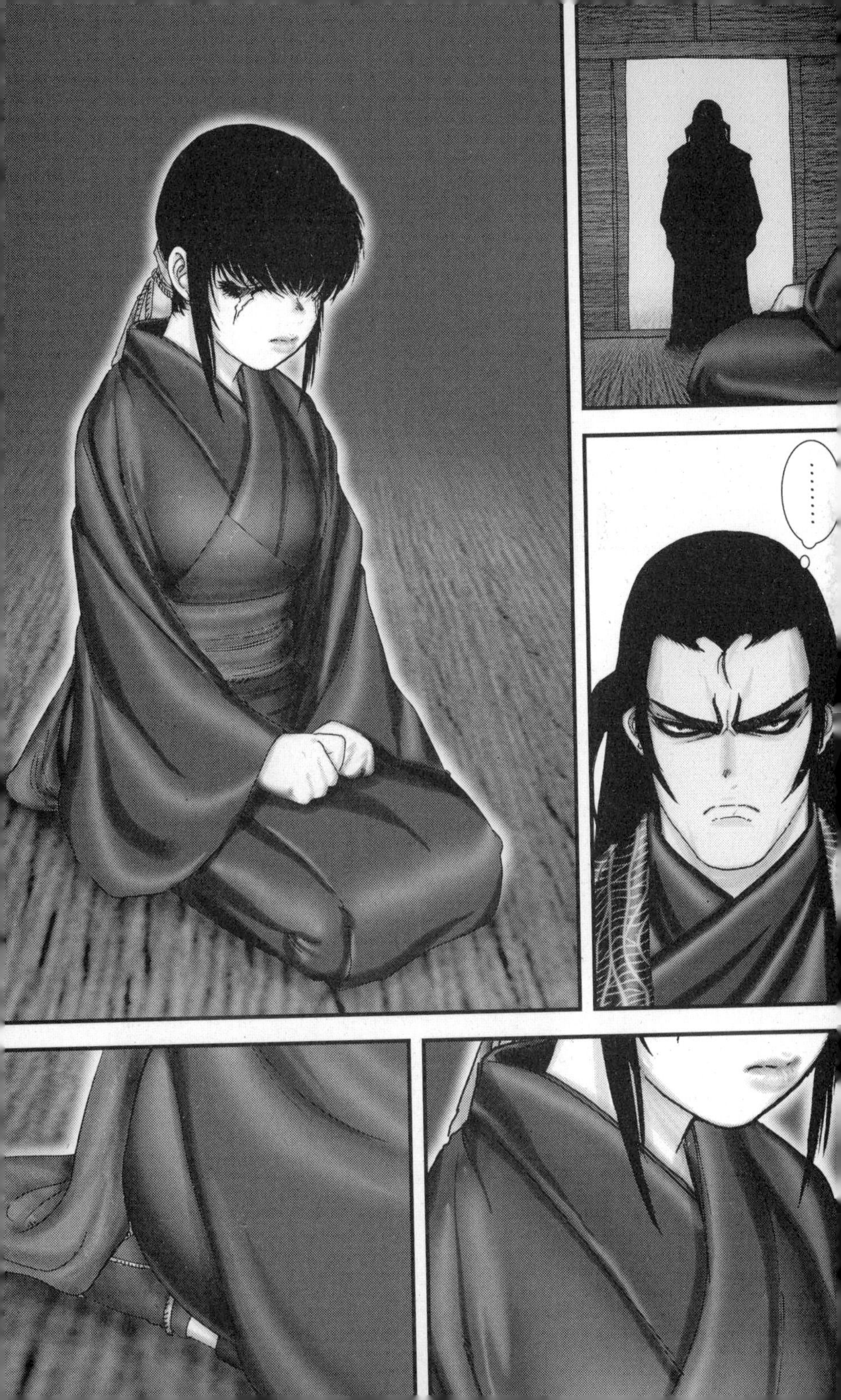
……

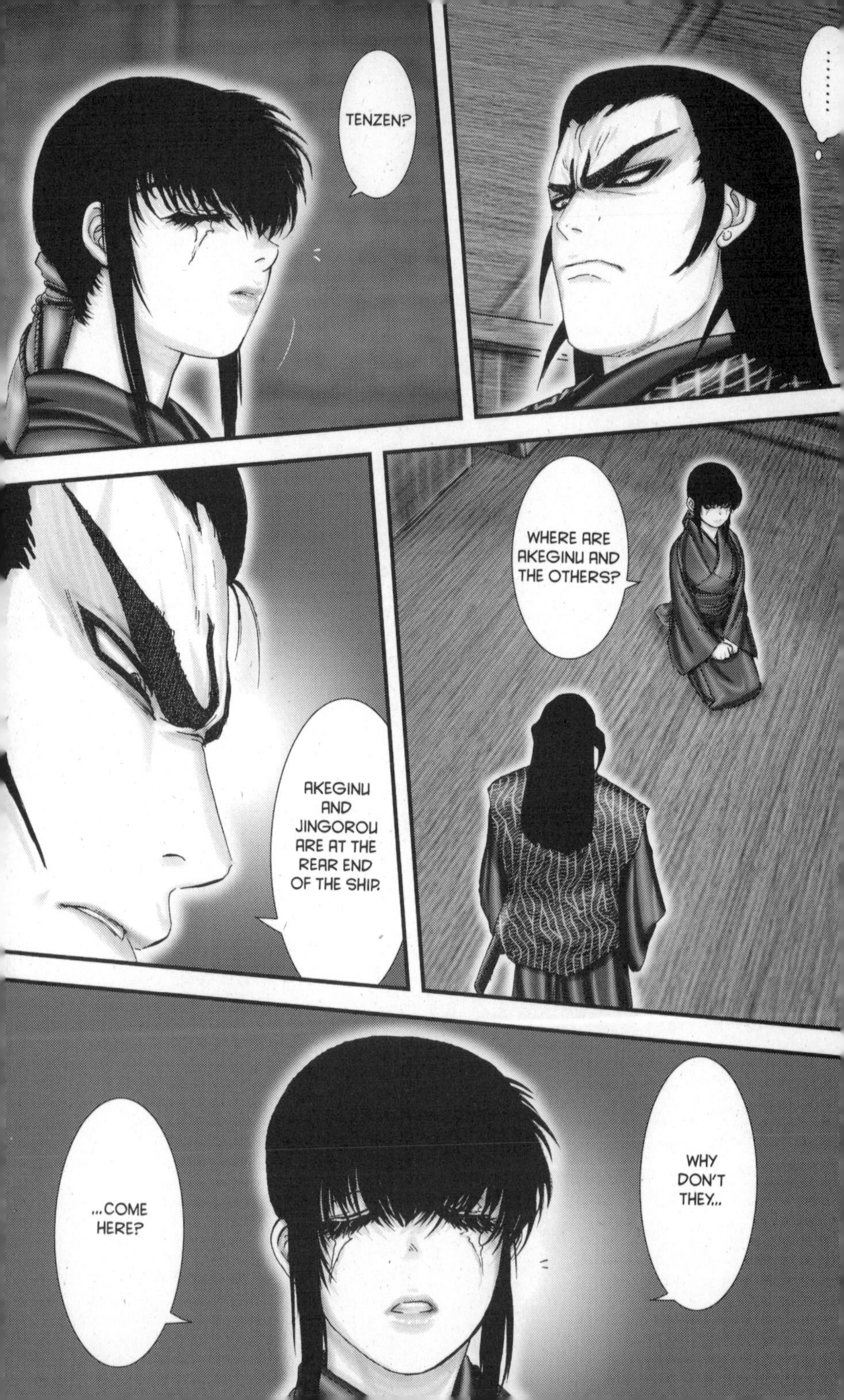
......
TENZEN?
WHERE ARE AKEGINU AND THE OTHERS?
AKEGINU AND JINGOROU ARE AT THE REAR END OF THE SHIP.
WHY DON'T THEY...
...COME HERE?

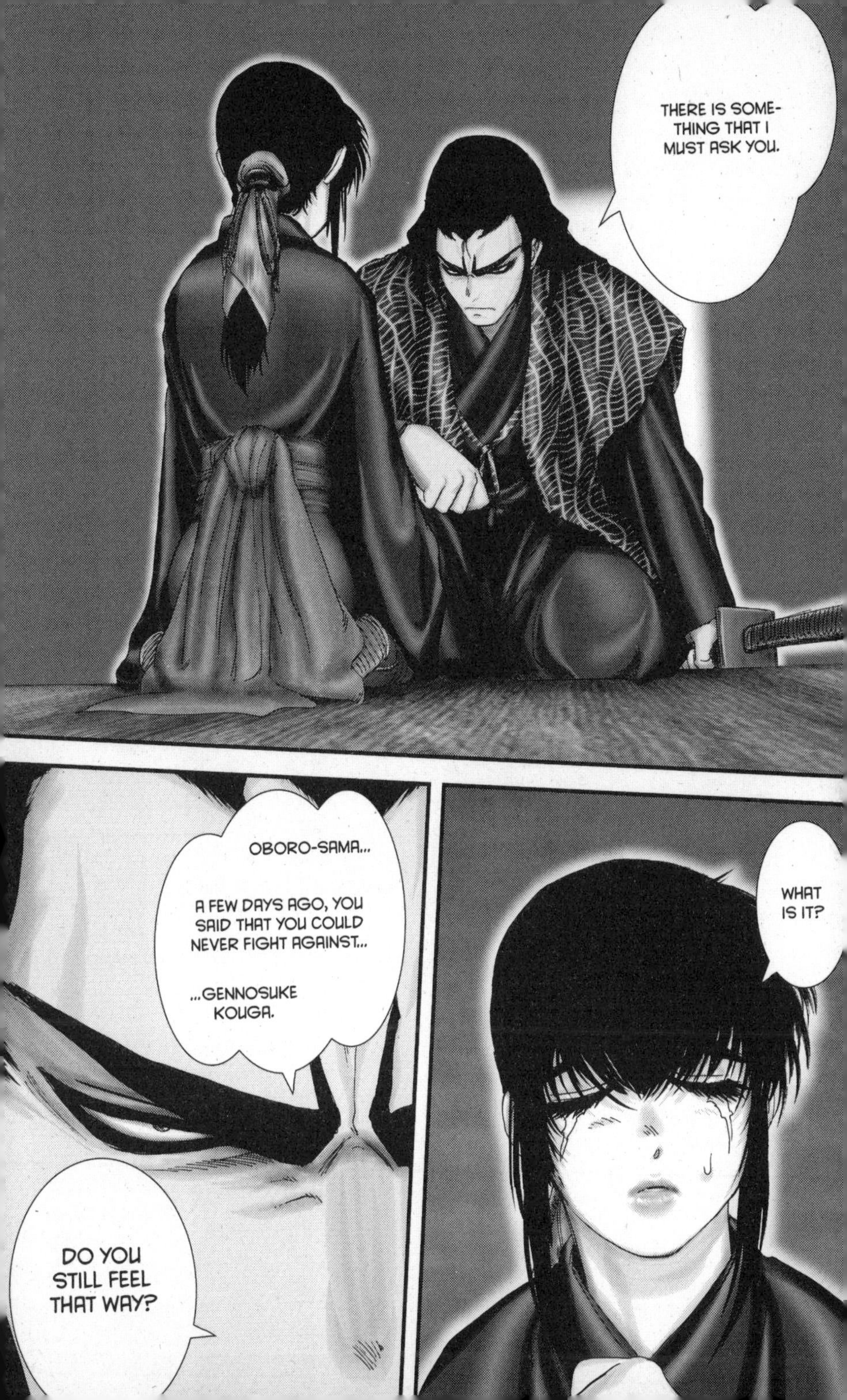
THERE IS SOMETHING THAT I MUST ASK YOU.
WHAT IS IT?
OBORO-SAMA...
A FEW DAYS AGO, YOU SAID THAT YOU COULD NEVER FIGHT AGAINST...
...GENNOSUKE KOUGA.
DO YOU STILL FEEL THAT WAY?

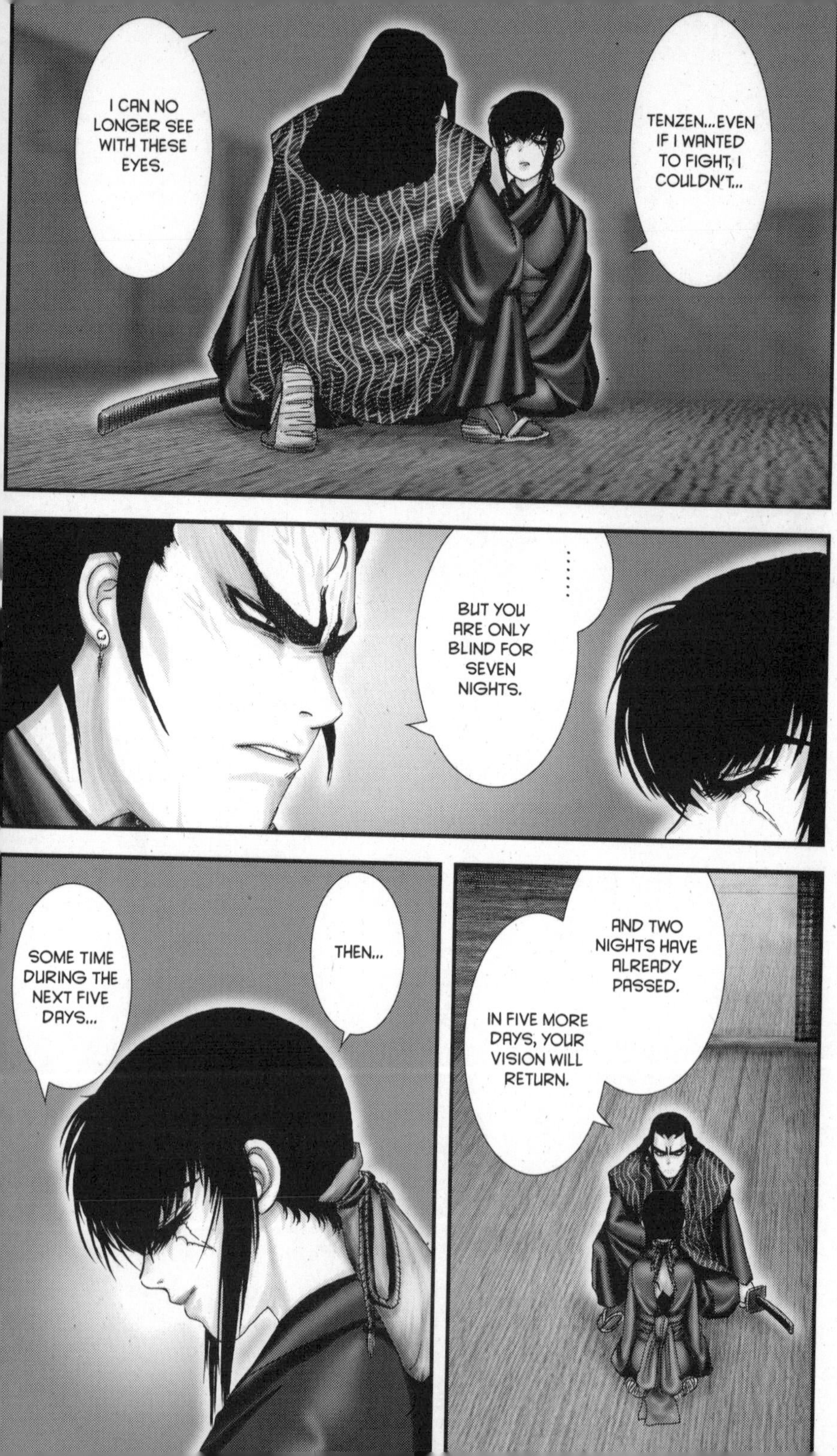
TENZEN...EVEN IF I WANTED TO FIGHT, I COULDN'T...
I CAN NO LONGER SEE WITH THESE EYES.
......
BUT YOU ARE ONLY BLIND FOR SEVEN NIGHTS.
AND TWO NIGHTS HAVE ALREADY PASSED.
IN FIVE MORE DAYS, YOUR VISION WILL RETURN.
THEN...
SOME TIME DURING THE NEXT FIVE DAYS...

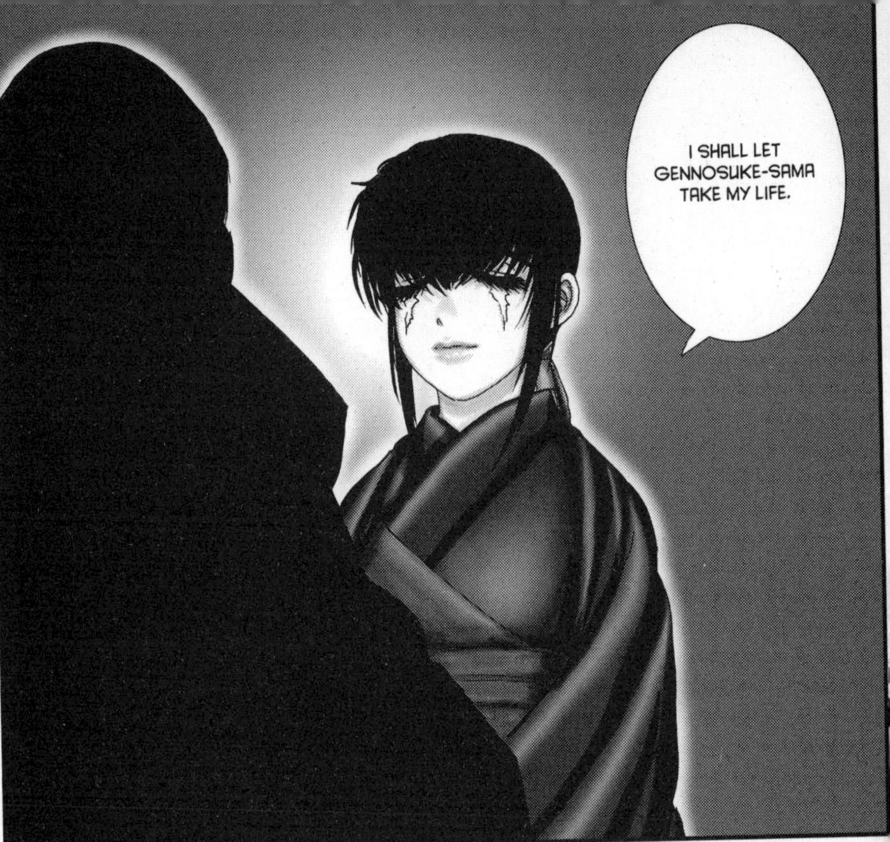
I SHALL LET GENNOSUKE-SAMA TAKE MY LIFE.

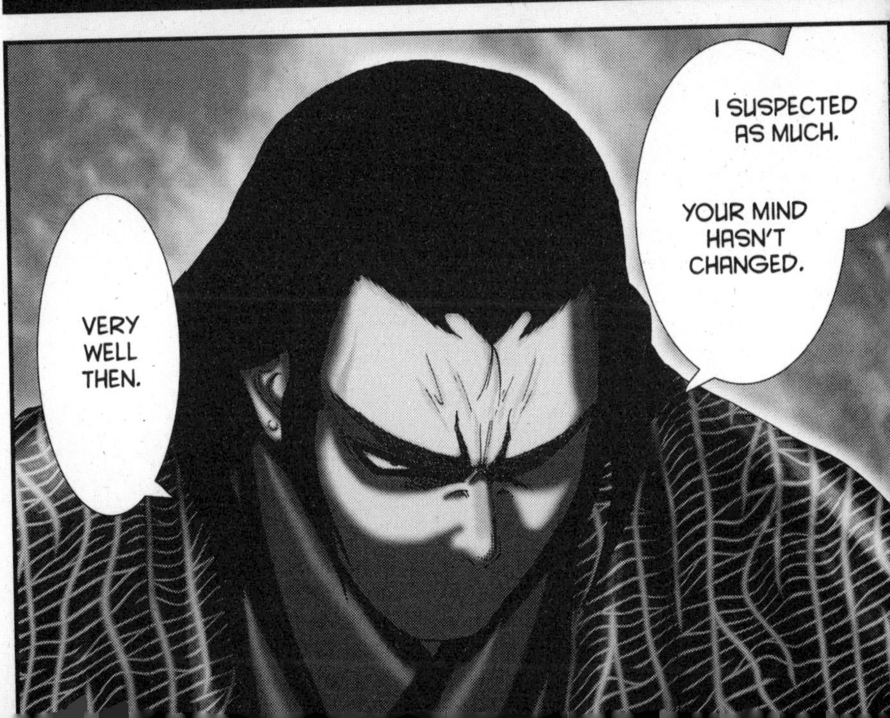
I SUSPECTED AS MUCH.
YOUR MIND HASN'T CHANGED.
VERY WELL THEN.

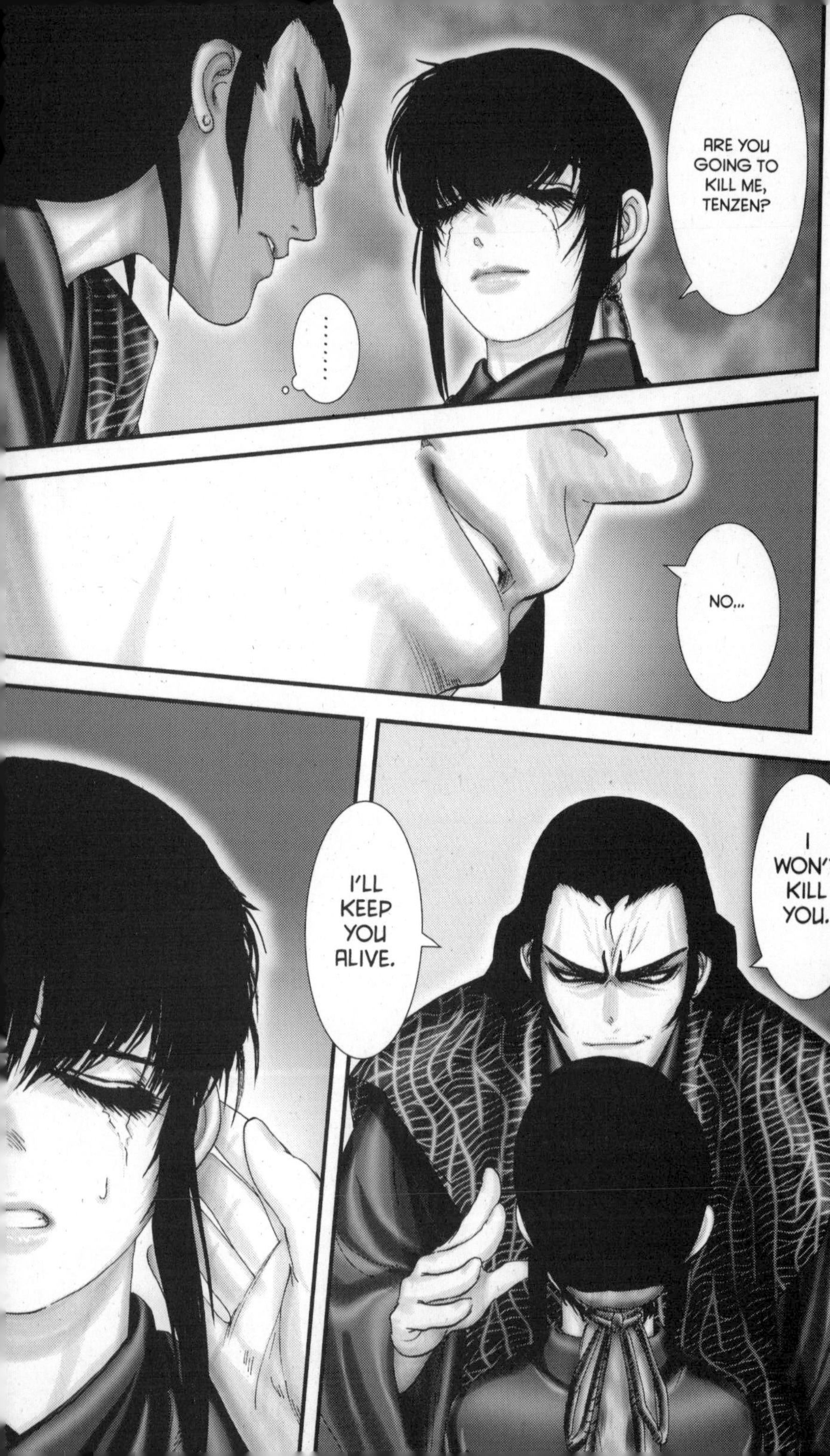
ARE YOU GOING TO KILL ME, TENZEN?
....
NO...
I WON'T KILL YOU.
I'LL KEEP YOU ALIVE.

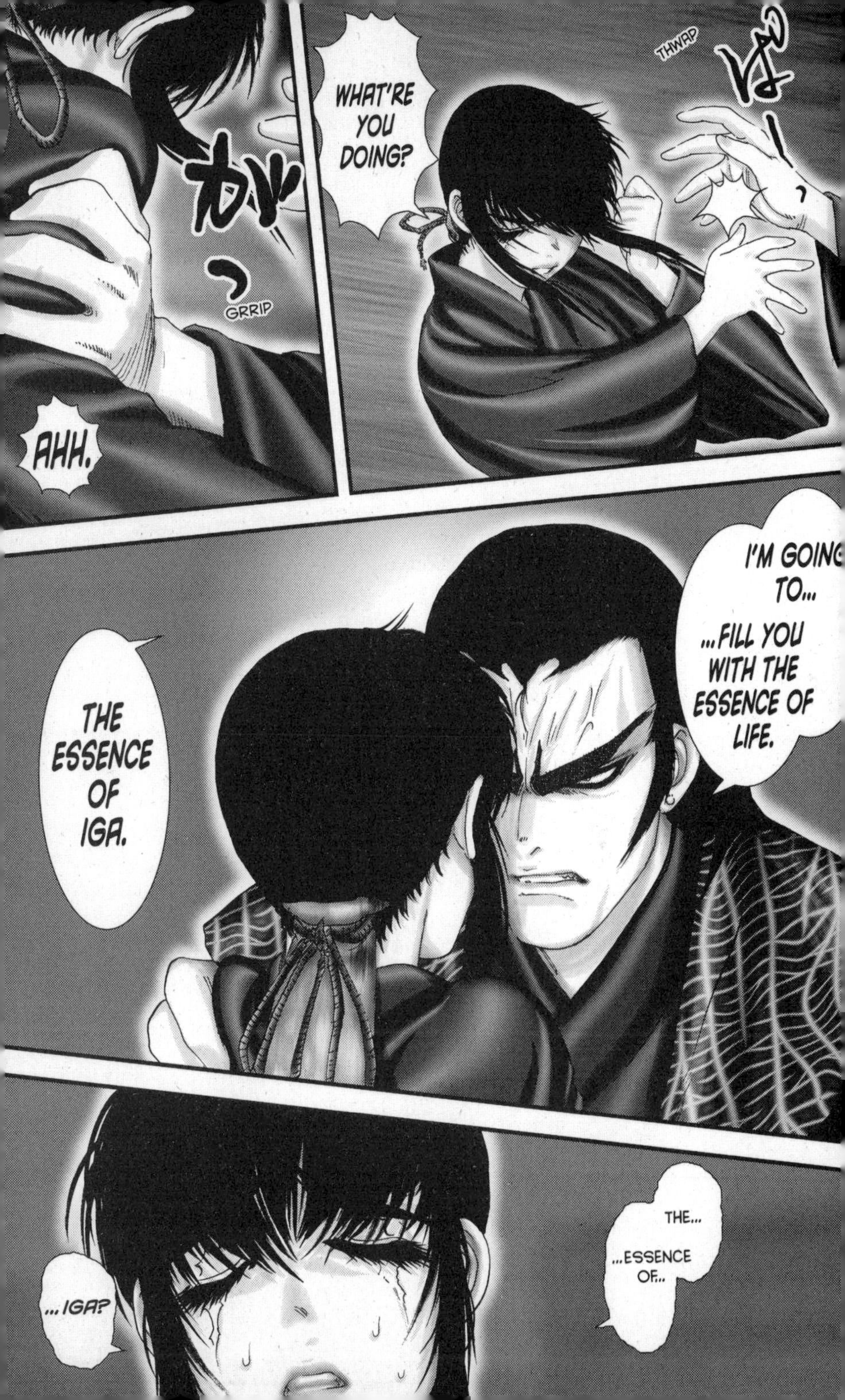
WHAT'RE YOU DOING?
THWAP
GRRIP
AHH.
I'M GOING TO...
...FILL YOU WITH THE ESSENCE OF LIFE.
THE ESSENCE OF IGA.
THE...
...ESSENCE OF...
...IGA?

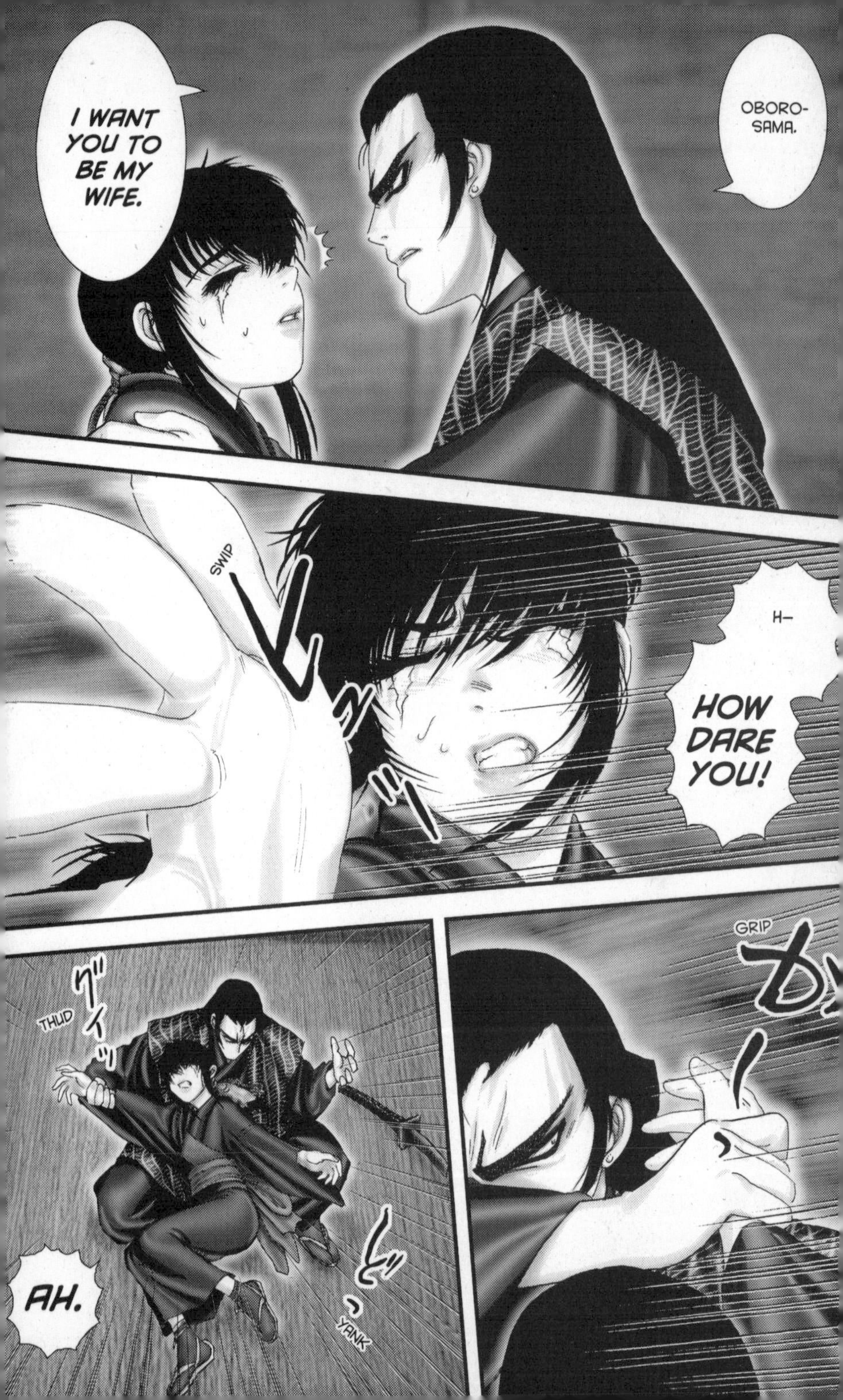
OBORO-SAMA.
I WANT YOU TO BE MY WIFE.
H—
HOW DARE YOU!
SWIP
GRIP
THUD
YANK
AH.

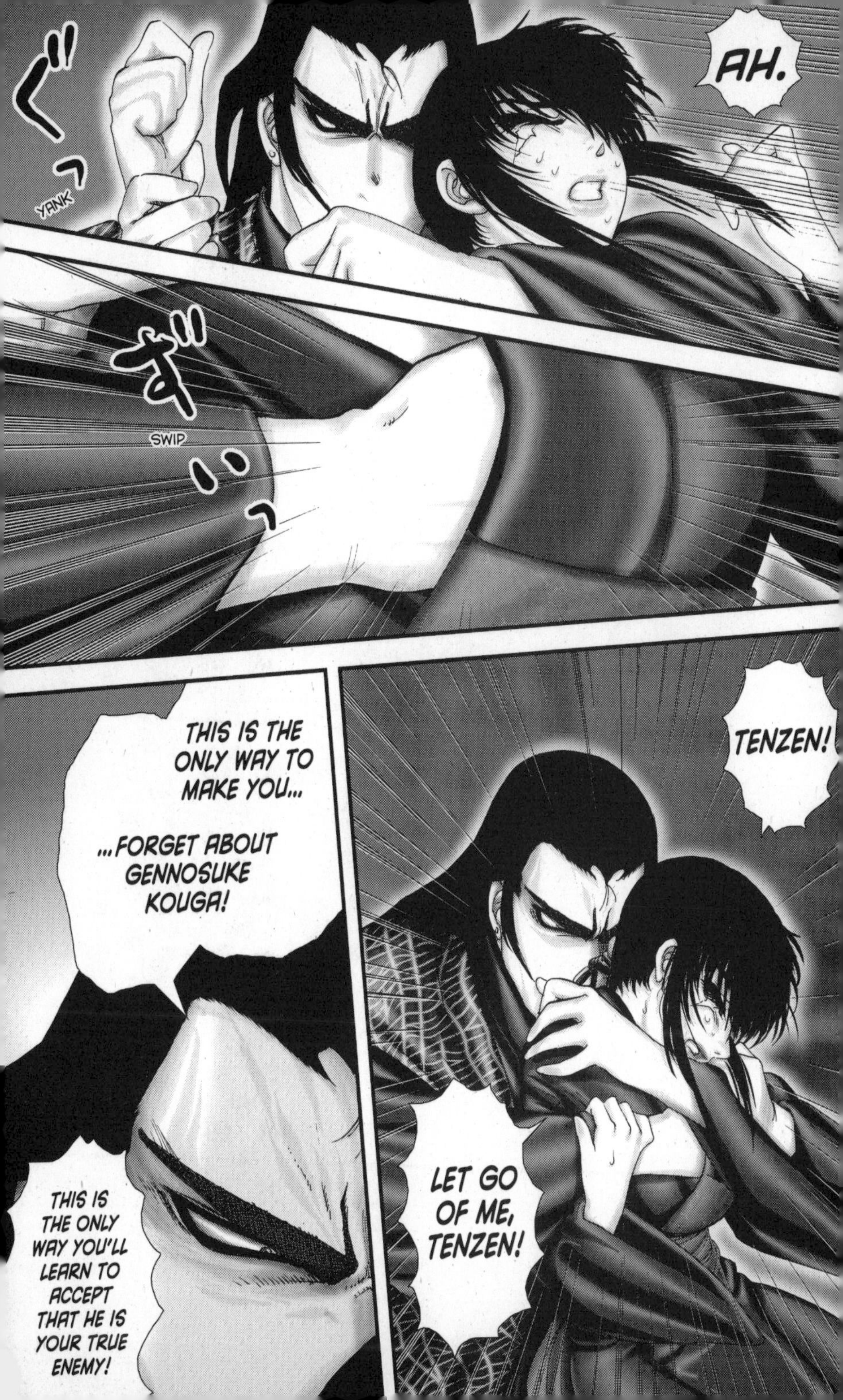
AH.
ぐっ
YANK
ずいっ
SWIP
TENZEN!
LET GO OF ME, TENZEN!
THIS IS THE ONLY WAY TO MAKE YOU...
...FORGET ABOUT GENNOSUKE KOUGA!
THIS IS THE ONLY WAY YOU'LL LEARN TO ACCEPT THAT HE IS YOUR TRUE ENEMY!

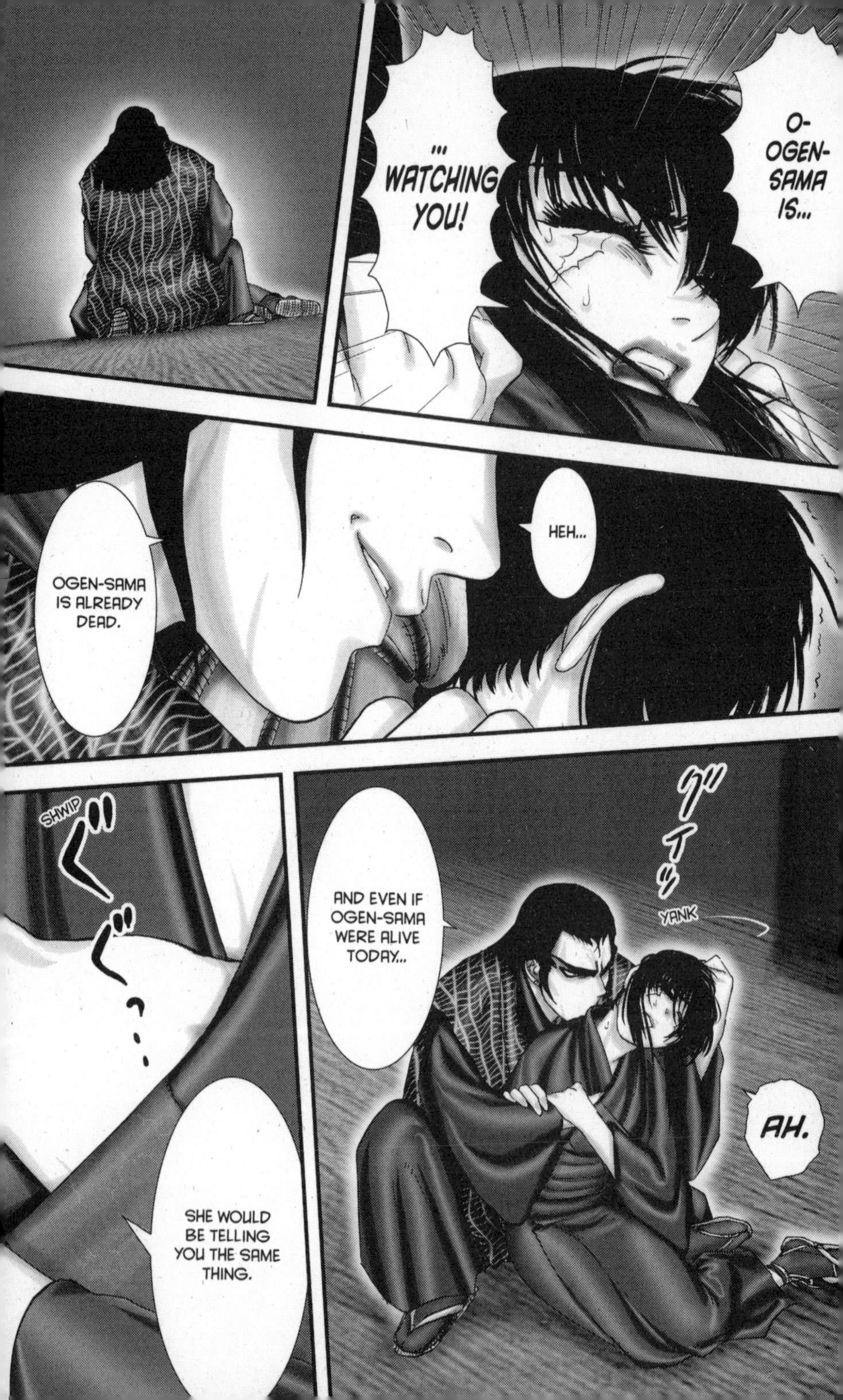

O- OGEN-SAMA IS...
...WATCHING YOU!
HEH...
OGEN-SAMA IS ALREADY DEAD.
グイッ
YANK
AND EVEN IF OGEN-SAMA WERE ALIVE TODAY...
AH.
SHWIP
SHE WOULD BE TELLING YOU THE SAME THING.

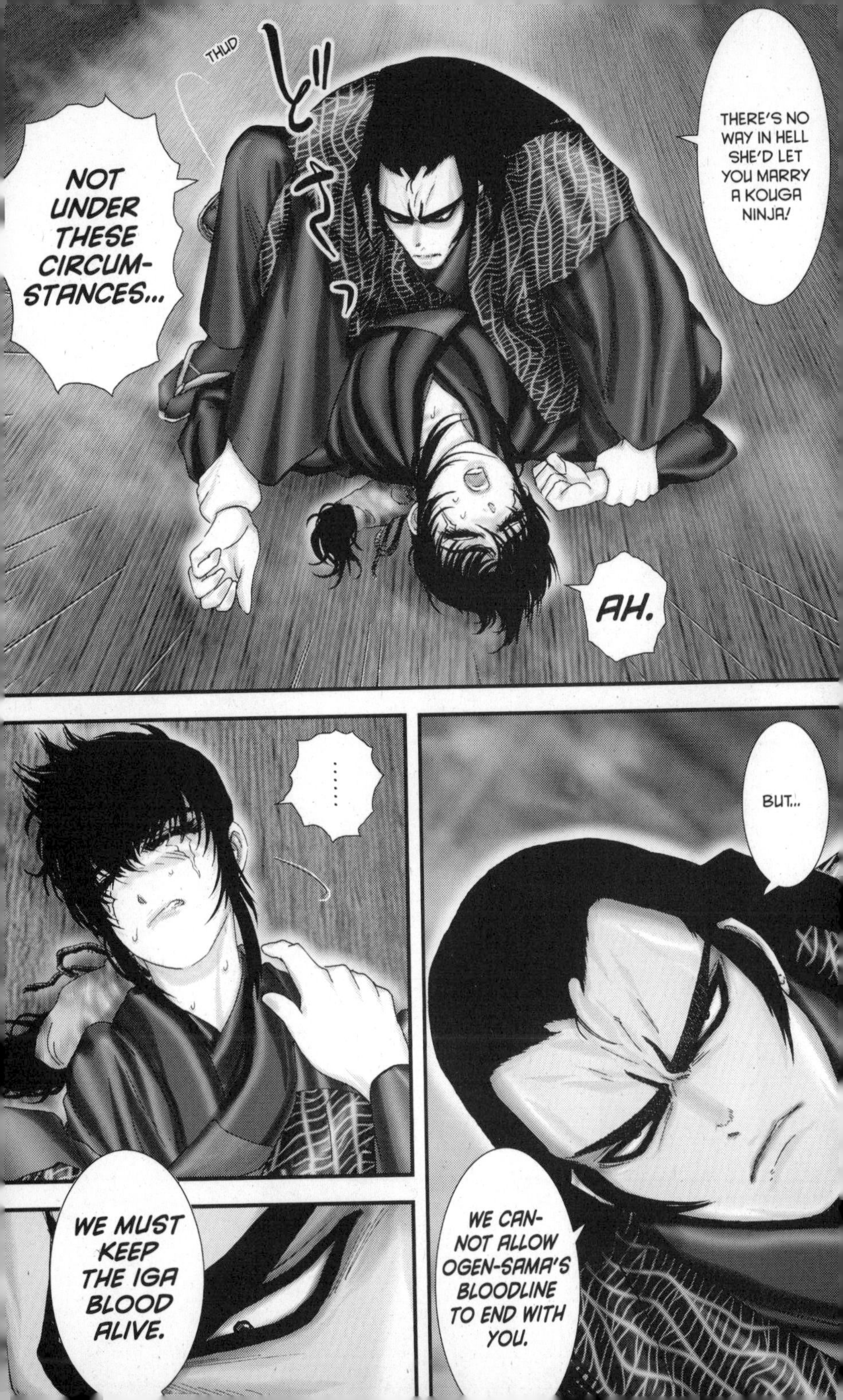
THERE'S NO WAY IN HELL SHE'D LET YOU MARRY A KOUGA NINJA!
THUD
NOT UNDER THESE CIRCUM-STANCES...
AH.
BUT...
WE CAN-NOT ALLOW OGEN-SAMA'S BLOODLINE TO END WITH YOU.
......
WE MUST KEEP THE IGA BLOOD ALIVE.

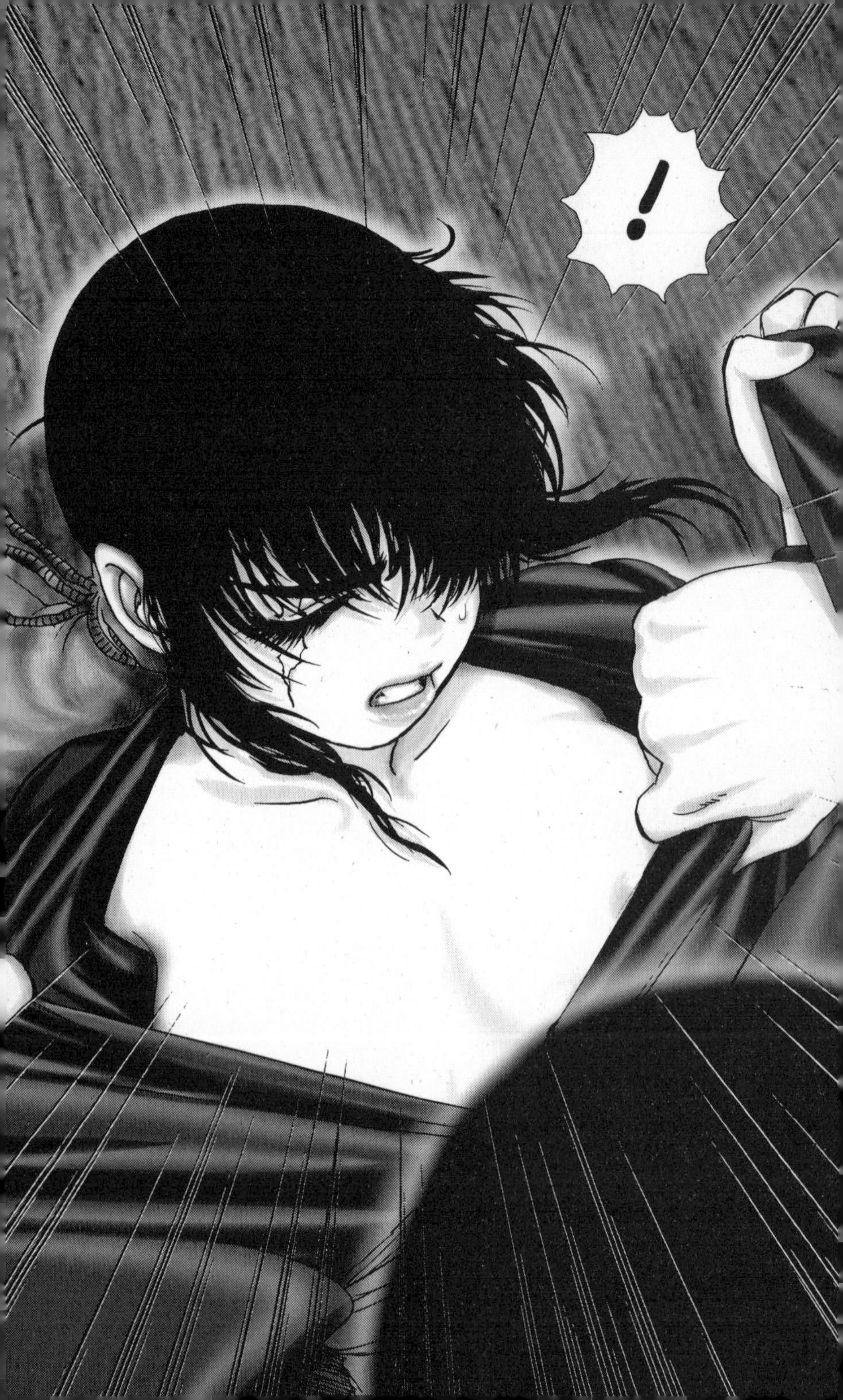
!

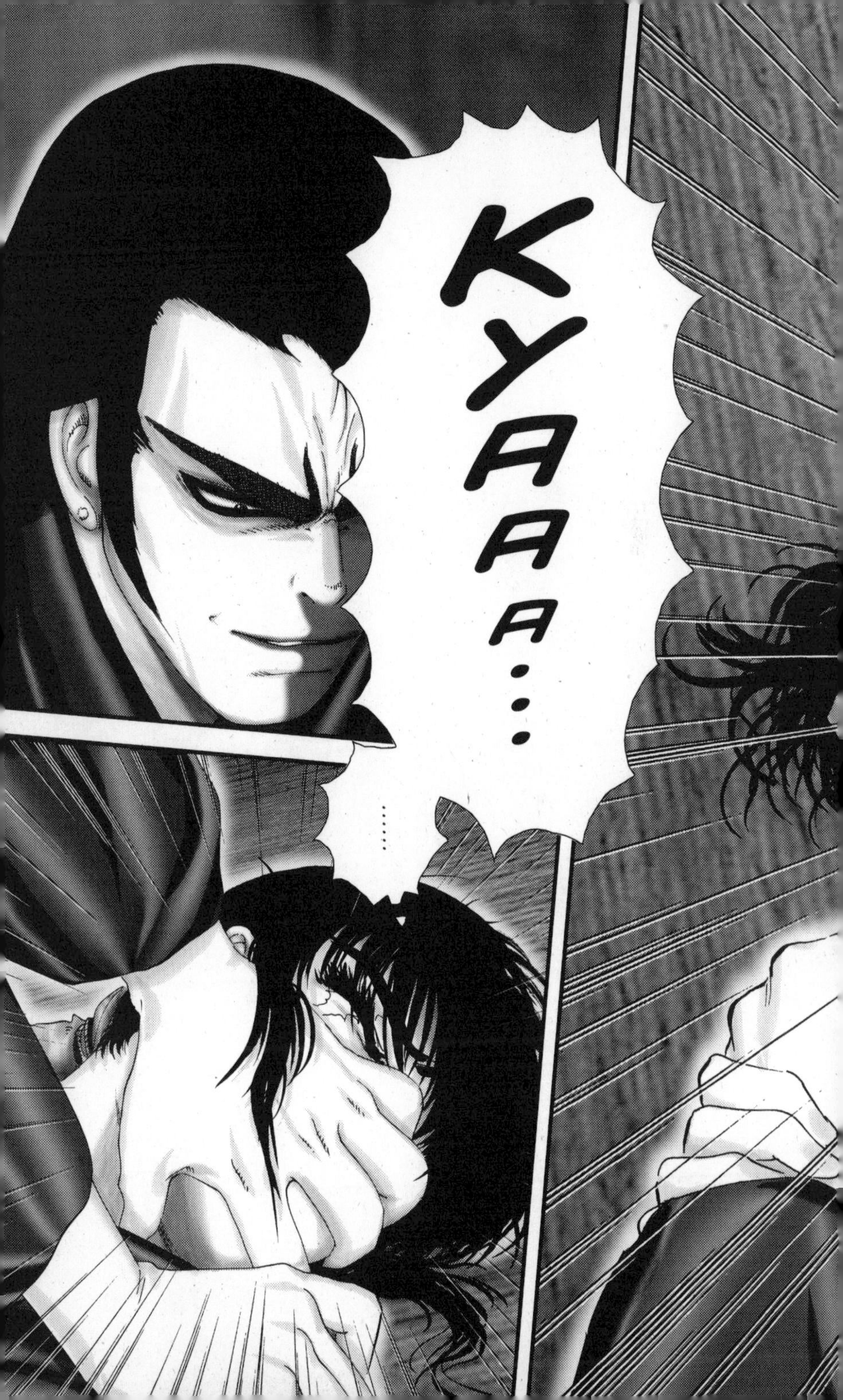
KYAAAA...
......

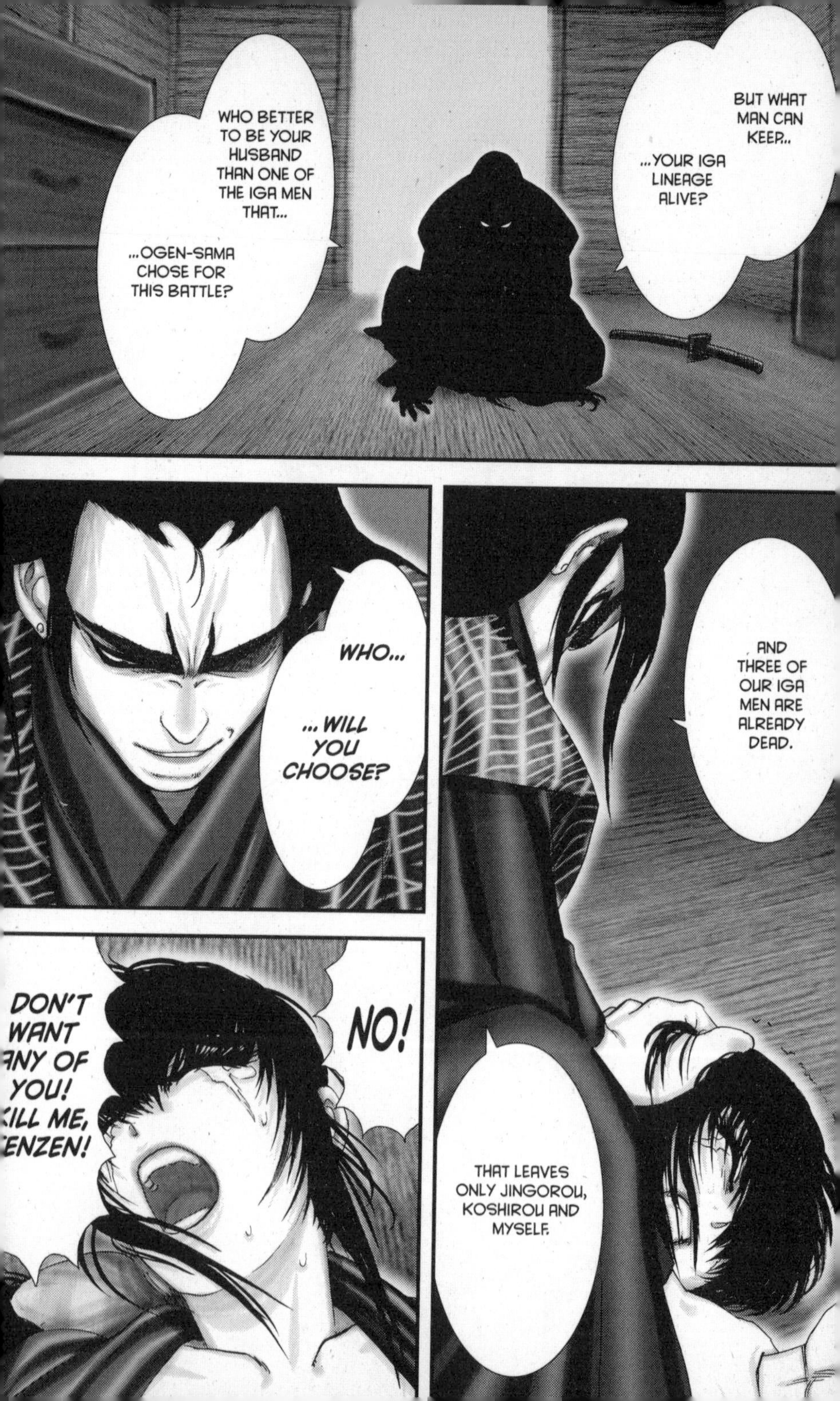
BUT WHAT MAN CAN KEEP...
...YOUR IGA LINEAGE ALIVE?
WHO BETTER TO BE YOUR HUSBAND THAN ONE OF THE IGA MEN THAT...
...OGEN-SAMA CHOSE FOR THIS BATTLE?
AND THREE OF OUR IGA MEN ARE ALREADY DEAD.
THAT LEAVES ONLY JINGOROU, KOSHIROU AND MYSELF.
WHO...
...WILL YOU CHOOSE?
NO!
DON'T WANT ANY OF YOU! KILL ME, ENZEN!

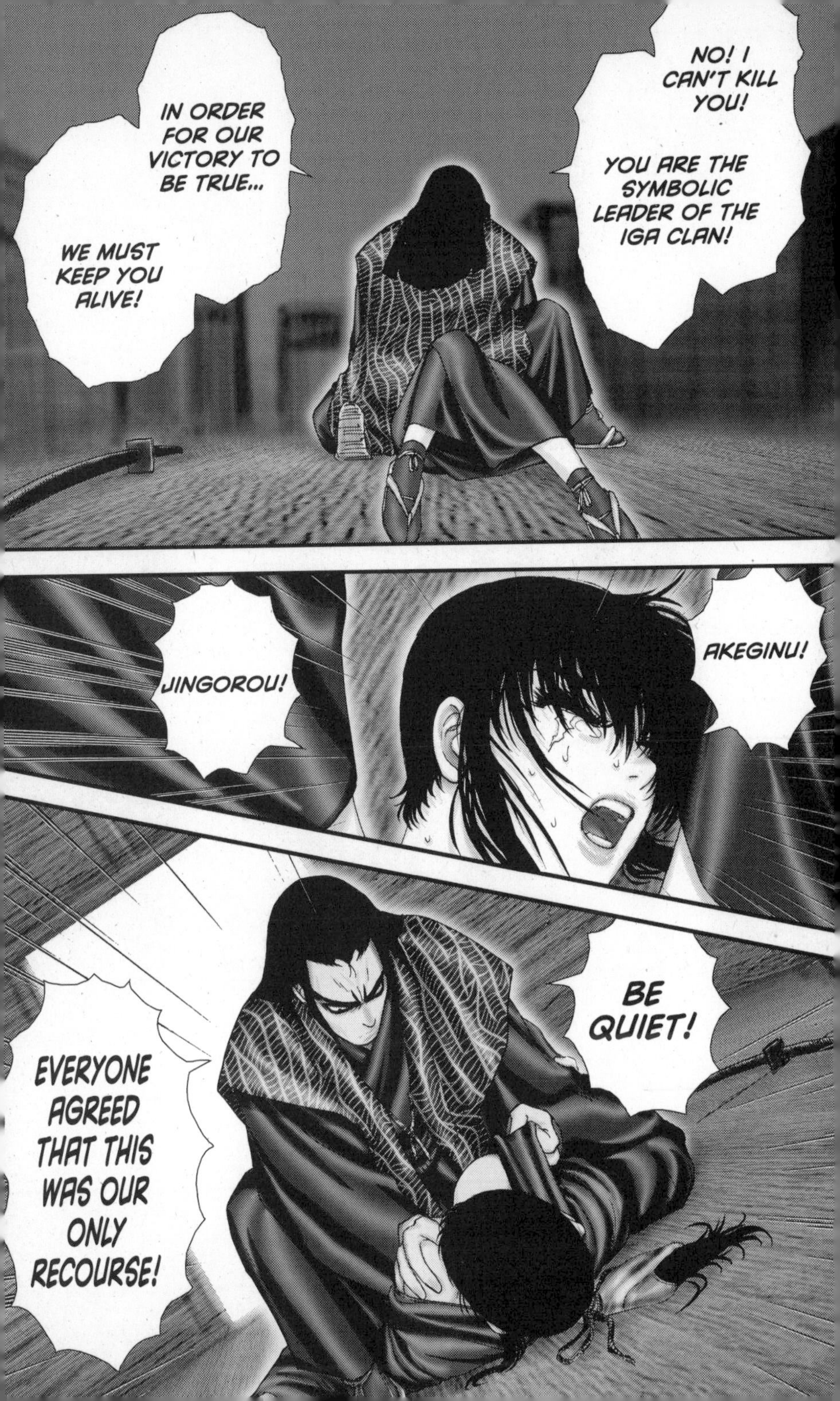
NO! I CAN'T KILL YOU!
YOU ARE THE SYMBOLIC LEADER OF THE IGA CLAN!
IN ORDER FOR OUR VICTORY TO BE TRUE...
WE MUST KEEP YOU ALIVE!
AKEGINU!
JINGOROU!
BE QUIET!
EVERYONE AGREED THAT THIS WAS OUR ONLY RECOURSE!

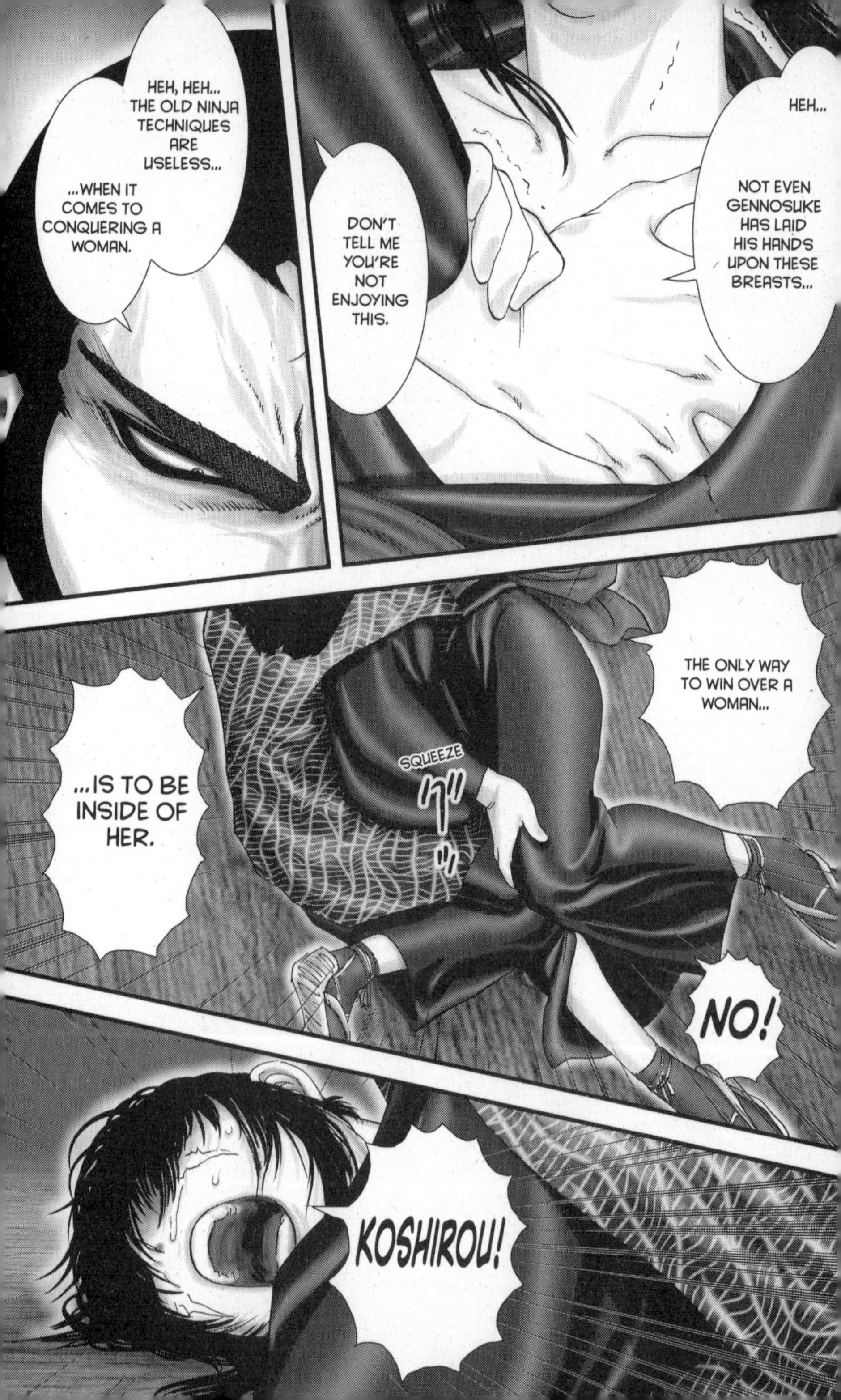
HEH...
NOT EVEN GENNOSUKE HAS LAID HIS HANDS UPON THESE BREASTS...
DON'T TELL ME YOU'RE NOT ENJOYING THIS.
HEH, HEH... THE OLD NINJA TECHNIQUES ARE USELESS...
...WHEN IT COMES TO CONQUERING A WOMAN.
THE ONLY WAY TO WIN OVER A WOMAN...
SQUEEZE
...IS TO BE INSIDE OF HER.
NO!
KOSHIROU!

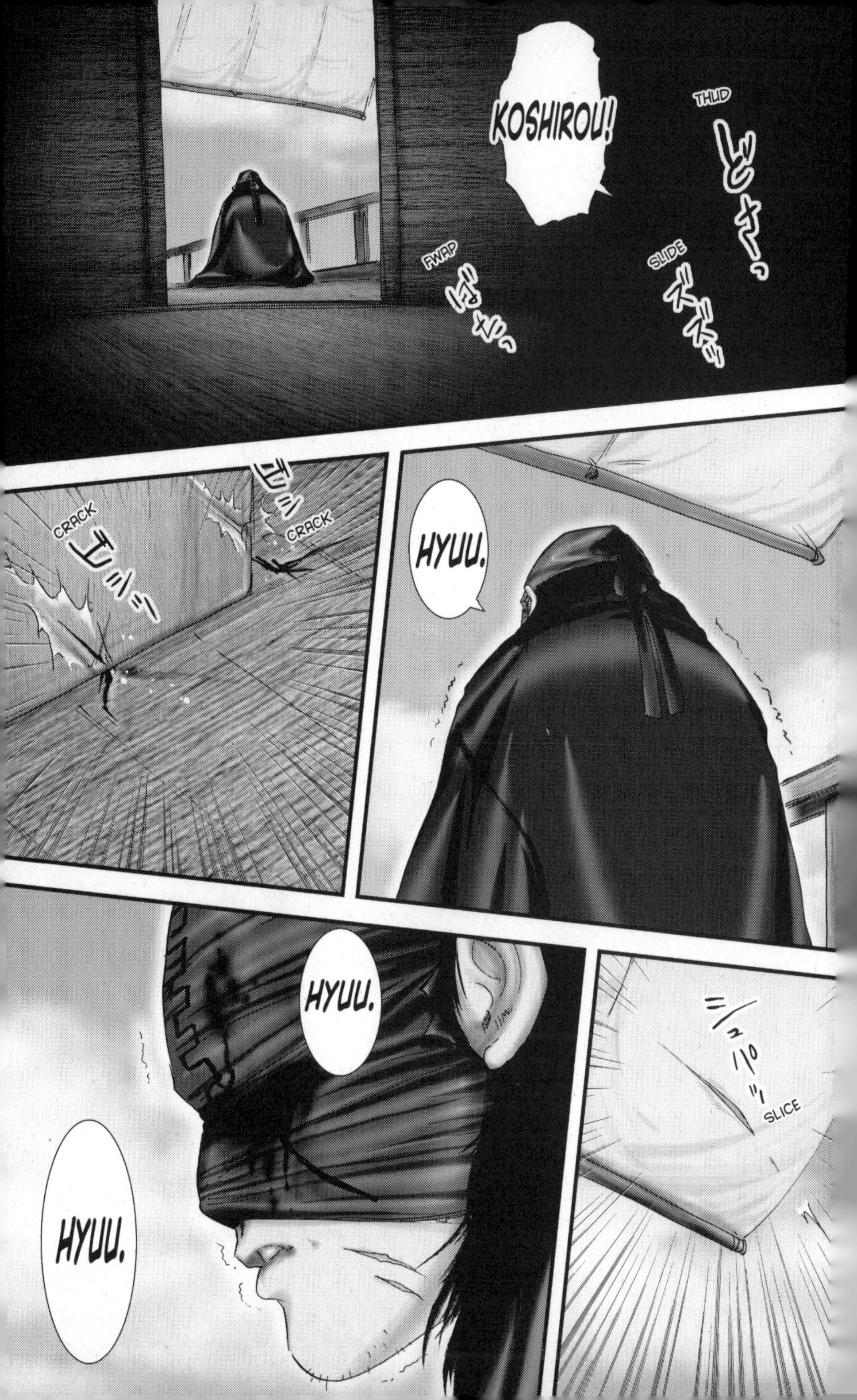
THUD
KOSHIROU!
SLIDE
FWAP
HYUU.
CRACK
CRACK
SLICE
HYUU.
HYUU.

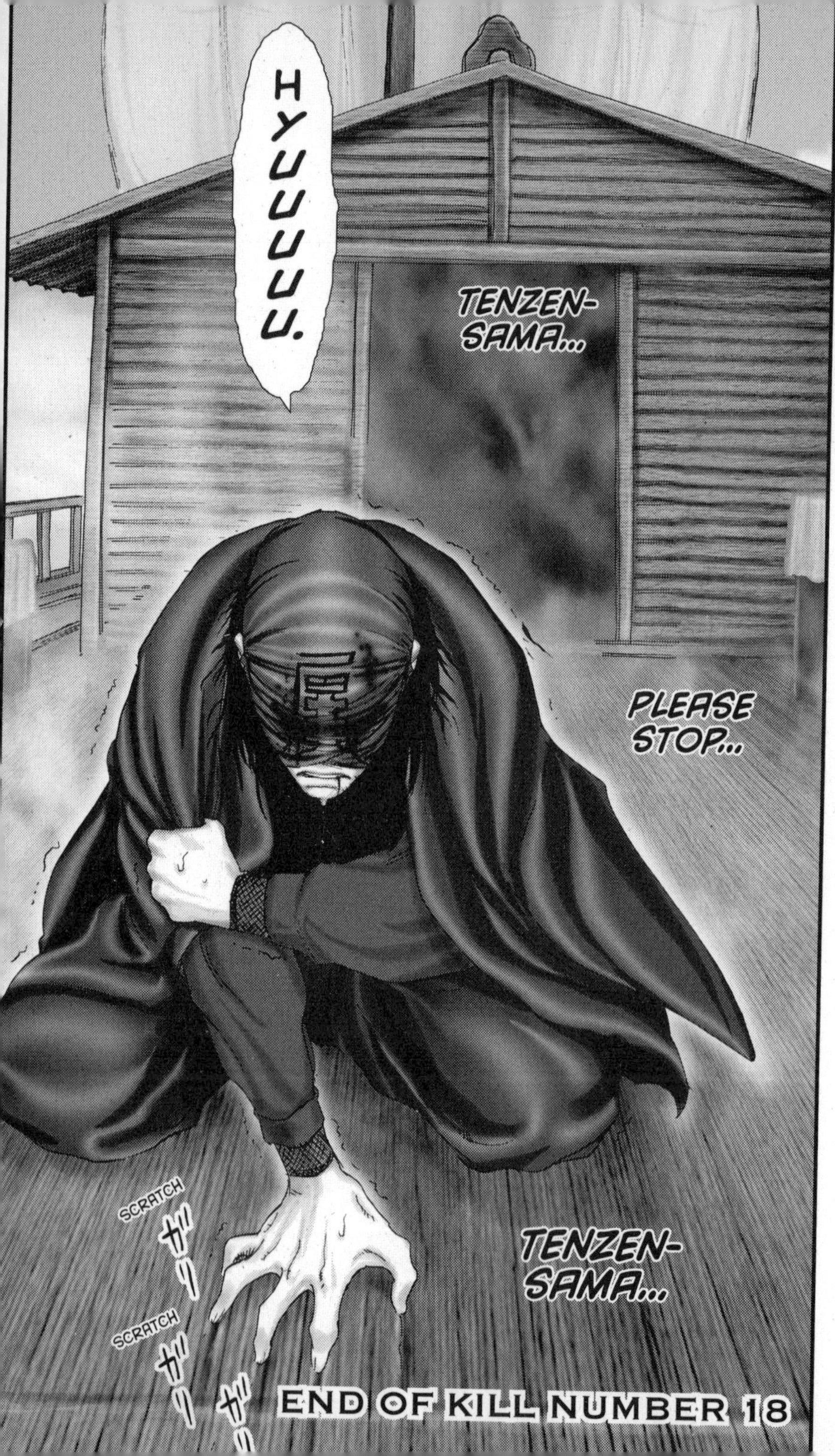
HYUUUUUU.
TENZEN-SAMA...
PLEASE STOP...
TENZEN-SAMA...
SCRATCH
SCRATCH
END OF KILL NUMBER 18

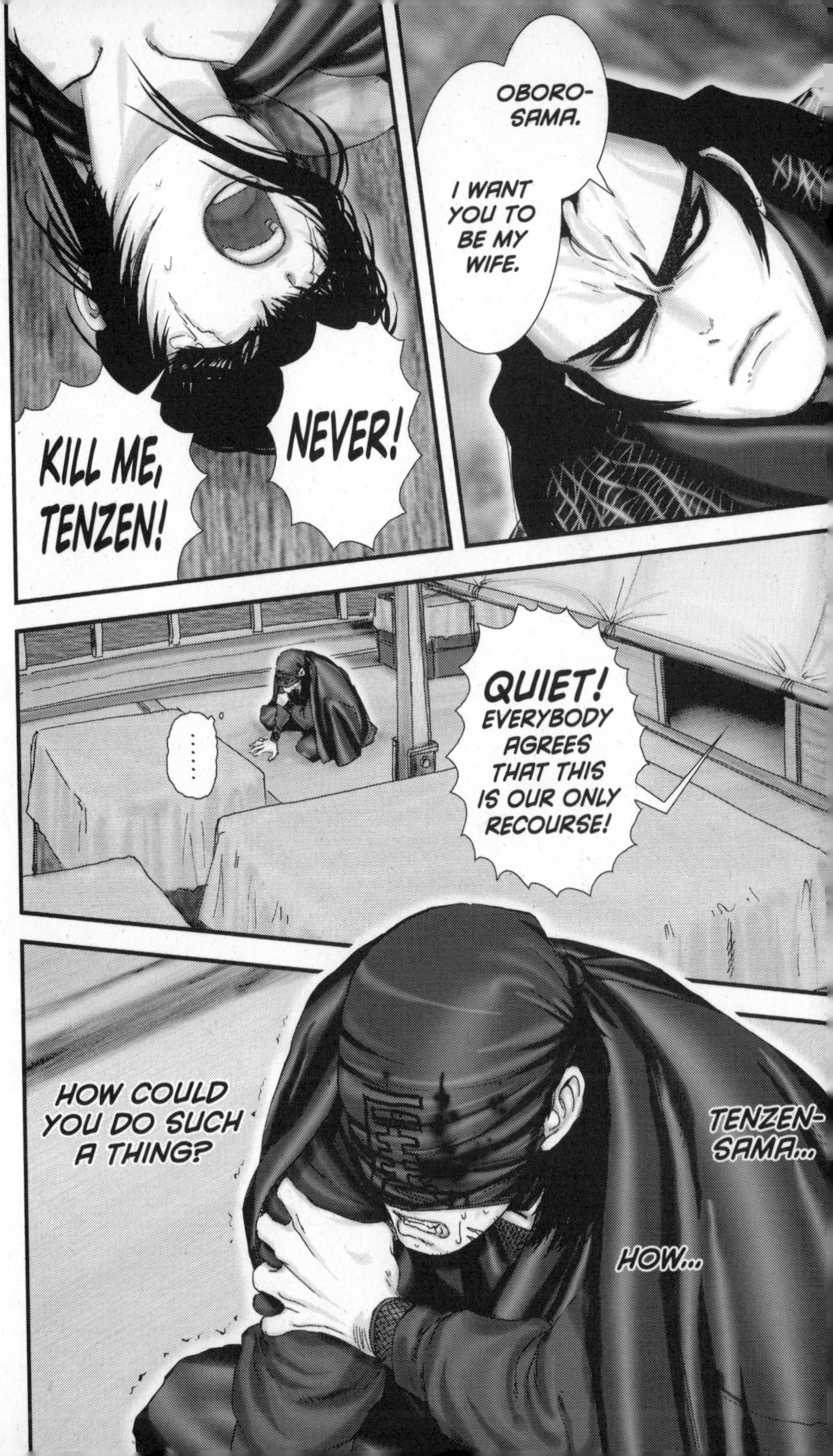
OBORO-SAMA.
I WANT YOU TO BE MY WIFE.
NEVER!
KILL ME, TENZEN!
QUIET! EVERYBODY AGREES THAT THIS IS OUR ONLY RECOURSE!
......
TENZEN-SAMA...
HOW...
HOW COULD YOU DO SUCH A THING?

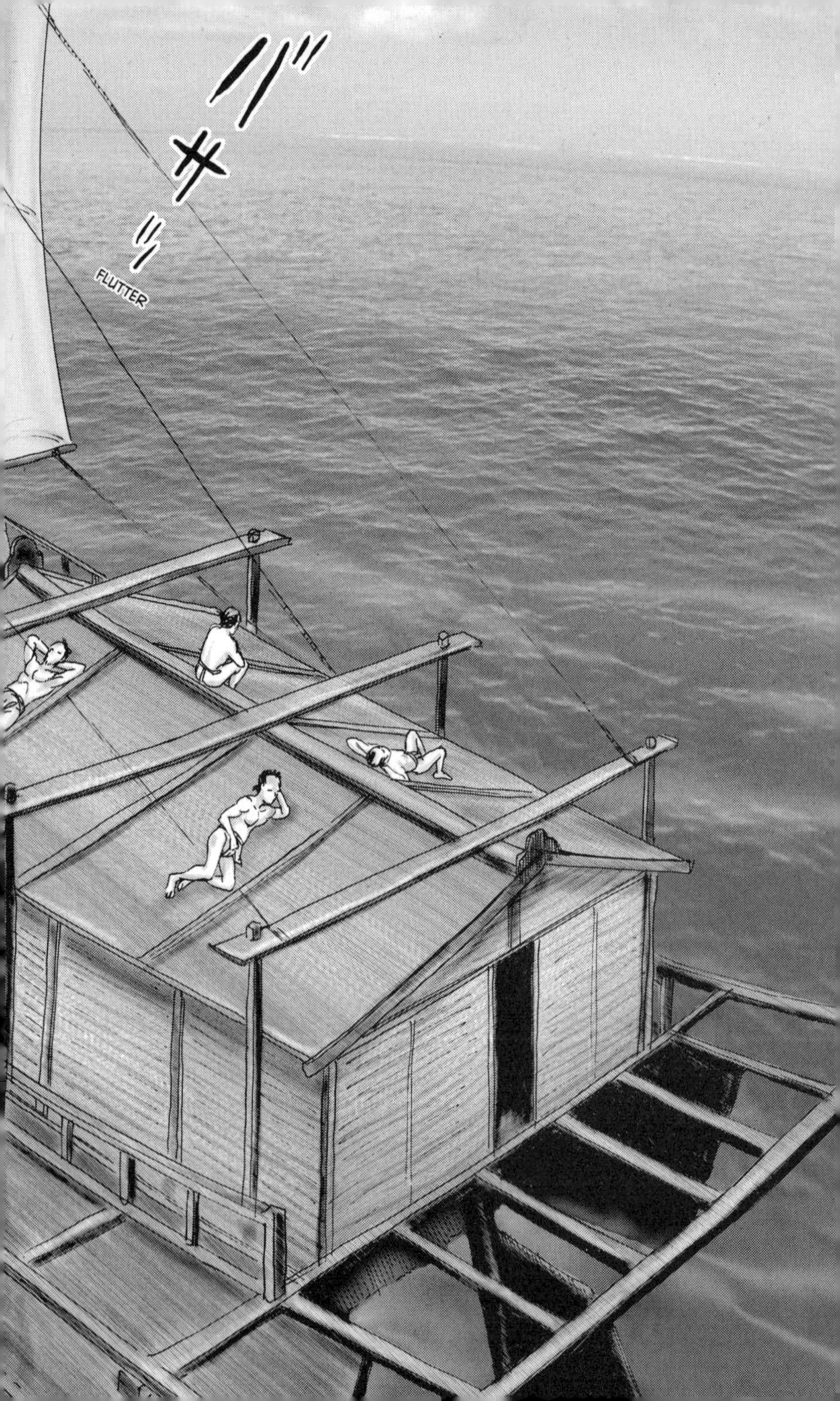
バサッ
FLUTTER

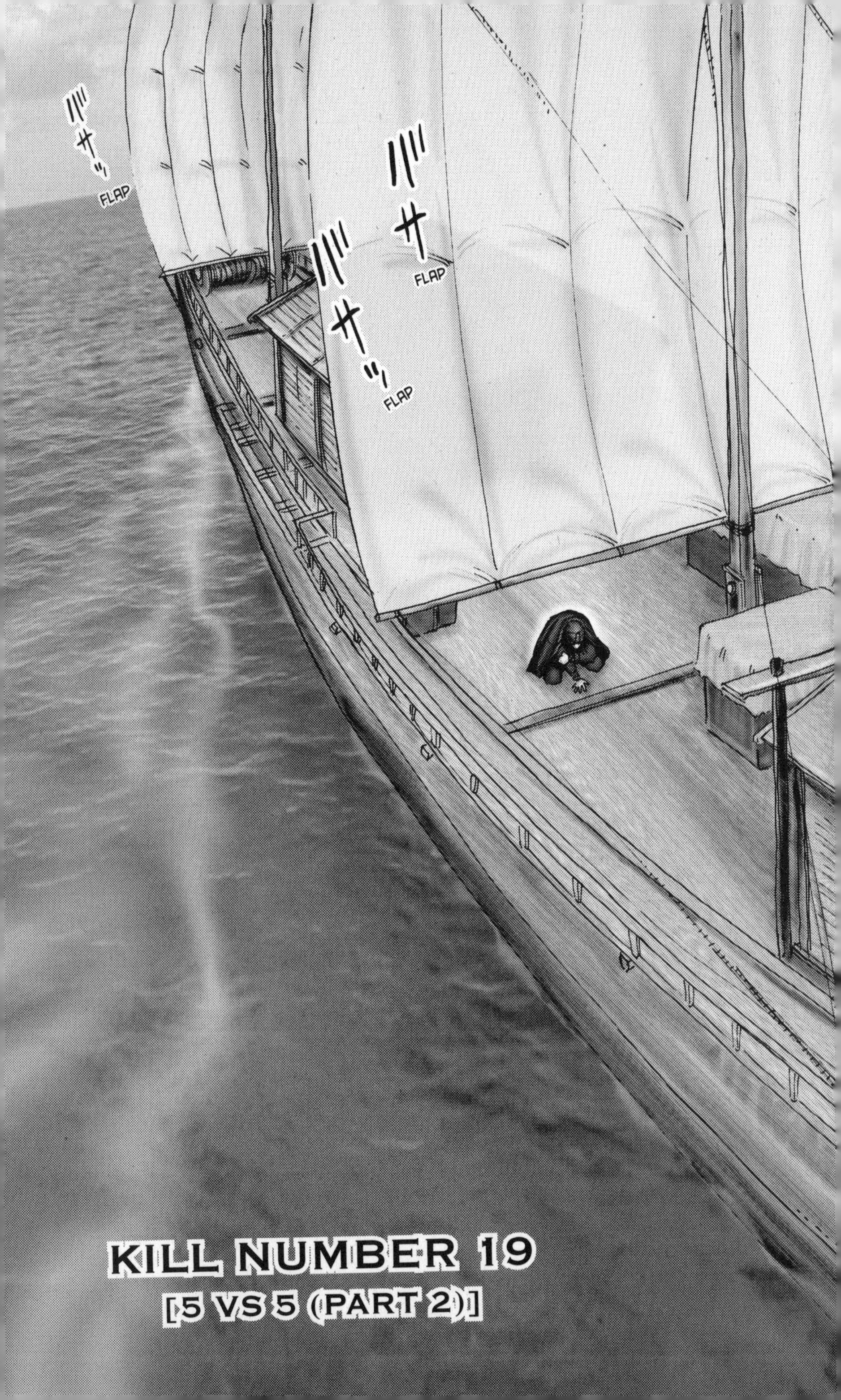
バサ
FLAP
バサッ
FLAP
バサッ
FLAP

KILL NUMBER 19

[5 VS 5 (PART 2)]

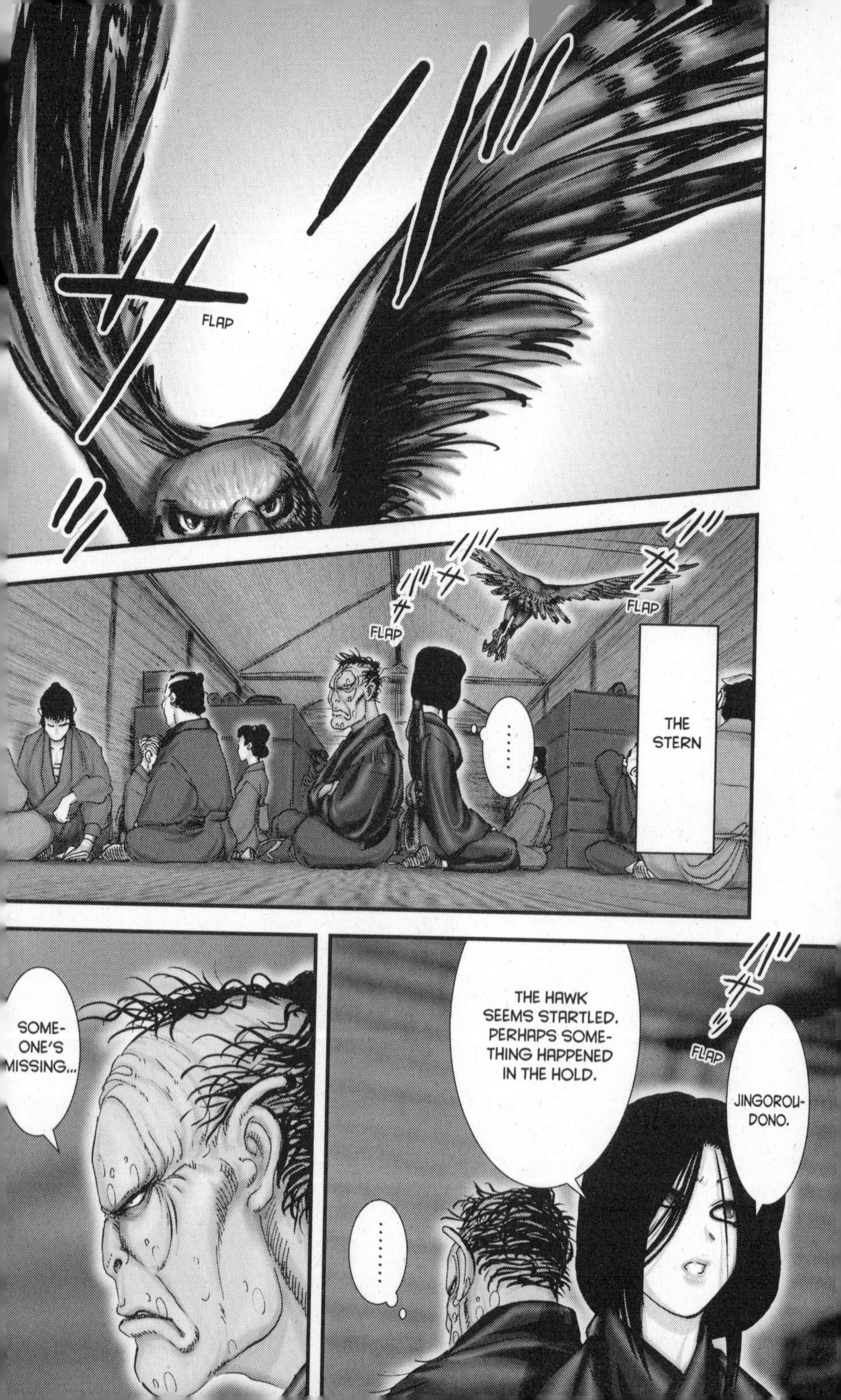
FLAP
THE STERN
FLAP
......
FLAP
FLAP
JINGOROU-DONO.
THE HAWK SEEMS STARTLED. PERHAPS SOMETHING HAPPENED IN THE HOLD.
......
SOMEONE'S MISSING...

ONE OF THE PASSENGERS...

...IS MISSING.

HUH?

FLAP

FLAP

SWIP

YOU'RE RIGHT...

WHEN WE BOARDED, THERE WAS A LARGE MAN WEARING A WOVEN KASA HAT. I DON'T SEE HIM ANYWHERE.

THE FRONT OF THE SHIP

URRMPH...

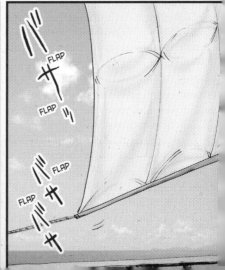

FLAP

FLAP

FLAP

FLAP

TE...
TENZEN-SAMA... WANTS OUR LEADER...
OBORO-SAMA... TO BECOME...
...HIS WIFE.
I HAVE NO OBJECTIONS...
E-EVEN IF I DID... I COULD NEVER SPEAK OUT...
CRINCH
...AGAINST TENZEN-SAMA.
KYAAAA!
SHIVER

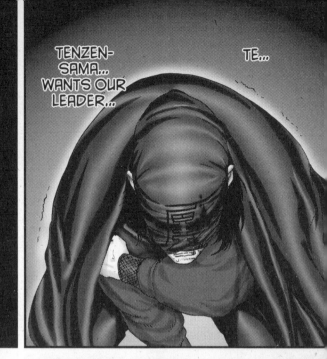

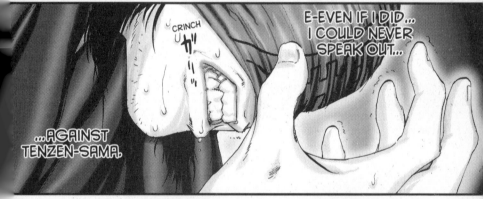

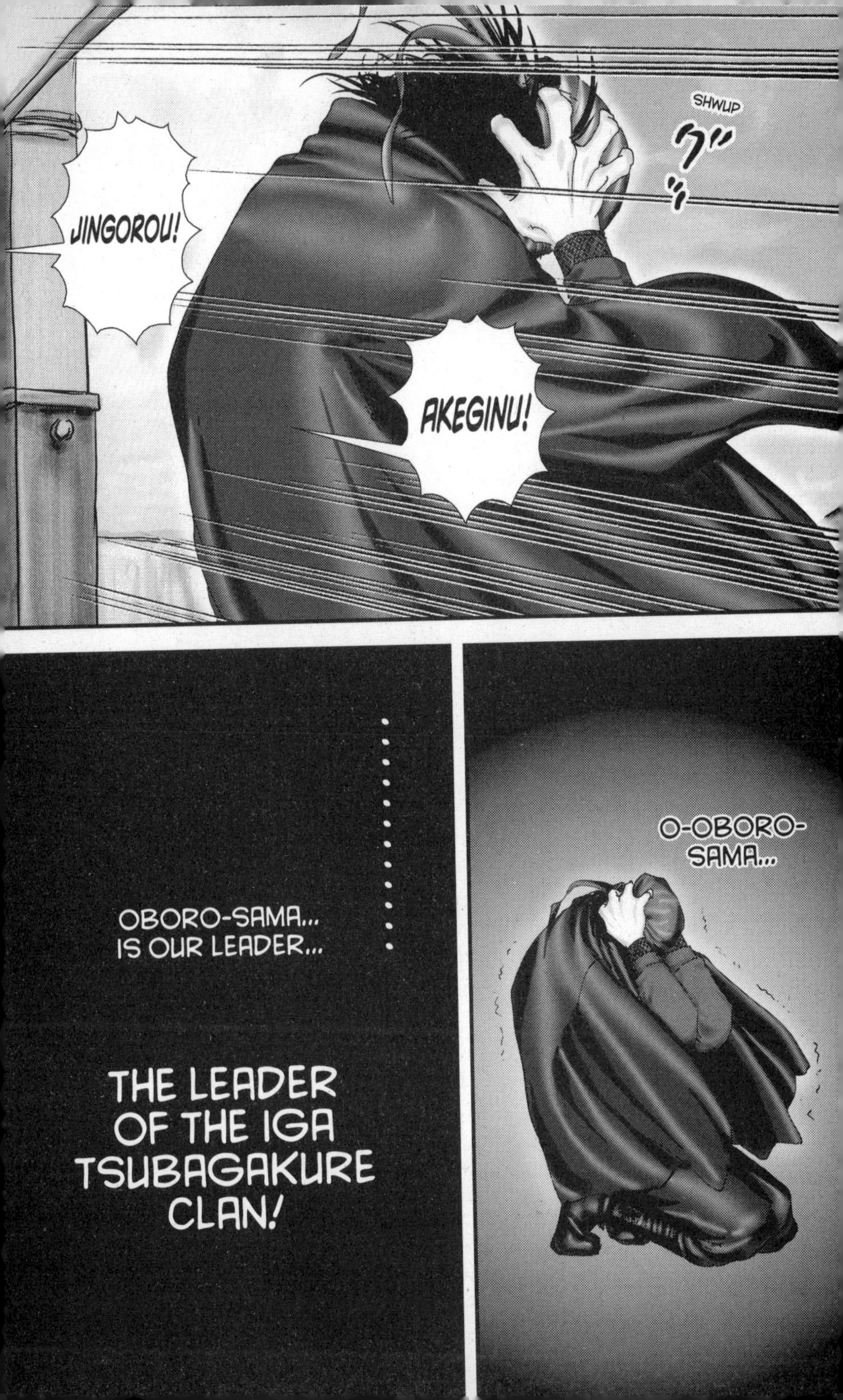
SHWUP
AKEGINU!
JINGOROU!
O-OBORO-SAMA...
....
OBORO-SAMA... IS OUR LEADER...
THE LEADER OF THE IGA TSUBAGAKURE CLAN!

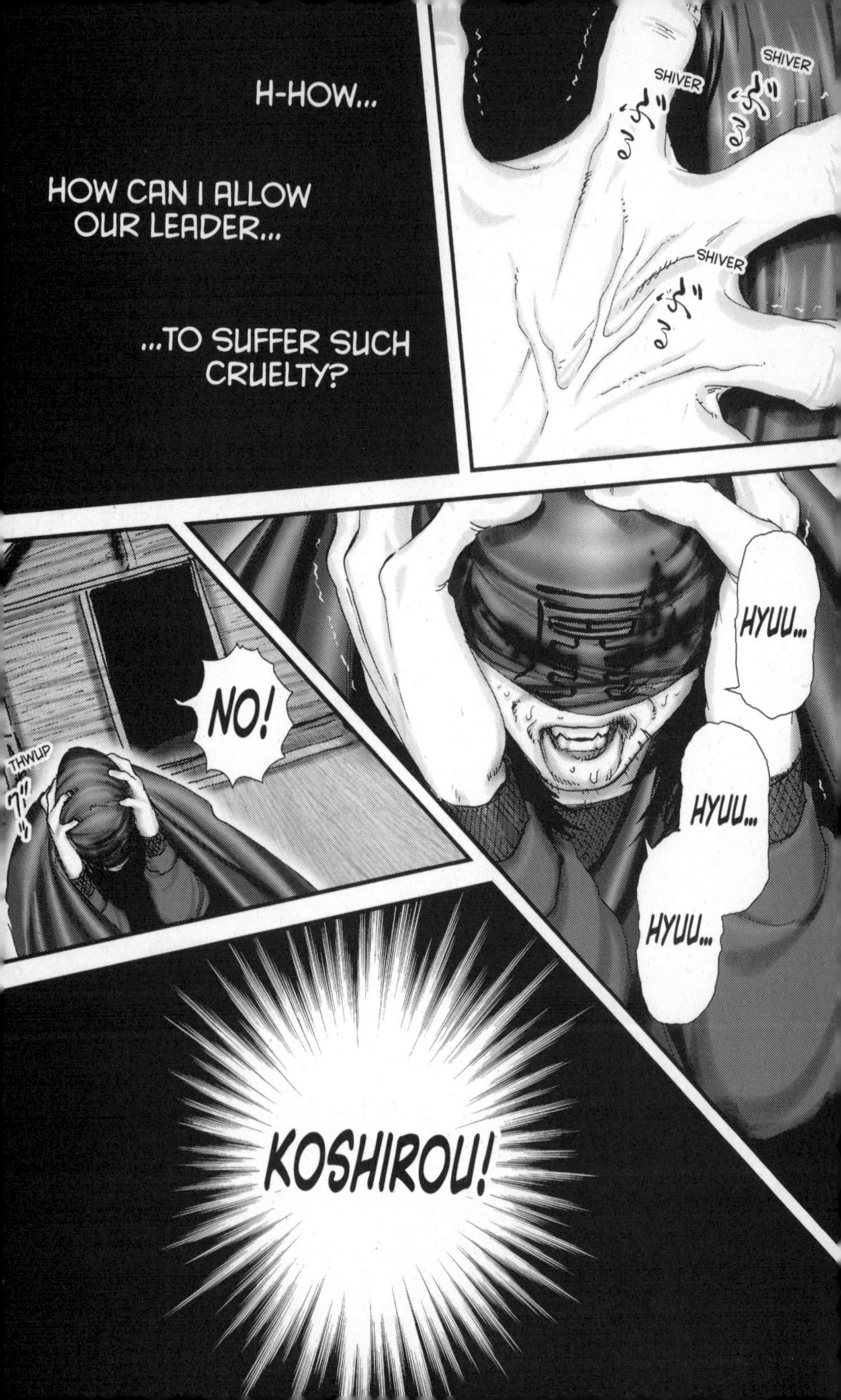
SHIVER
SHIVER
SHIVER
H-HOW...
HOW CAN I ALLOW OUR LEADER...
...TO SUFFER SUCH CRUELTY?
HYUU...
HYUU...
HYUU...
NO!
THWUP
KOSHIROU!

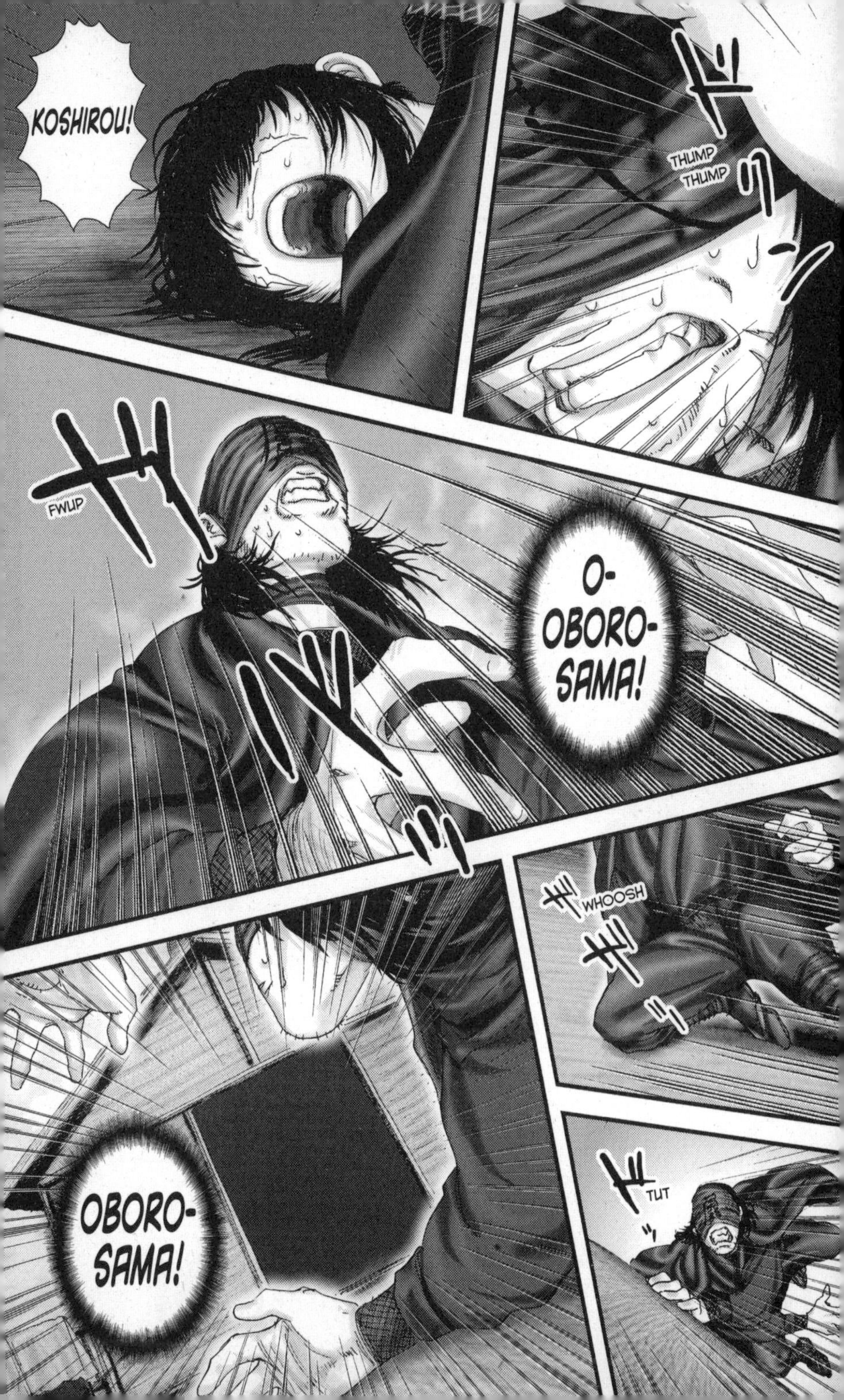
THUMP THUMP
KOSHIROU!
O-OBORO-SAMA!
FWUP
WHOOSH
TUT
OBORO-SAMA!

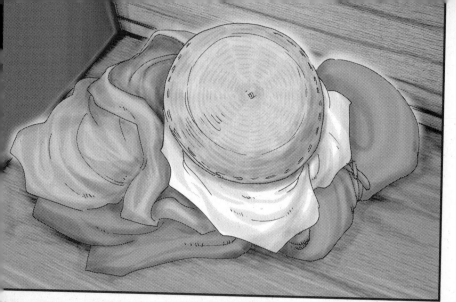

HE DISAP-
PEARED?

IT CAN'T
BE...

WH-WHAT
THE—

DAMN
IT!

!

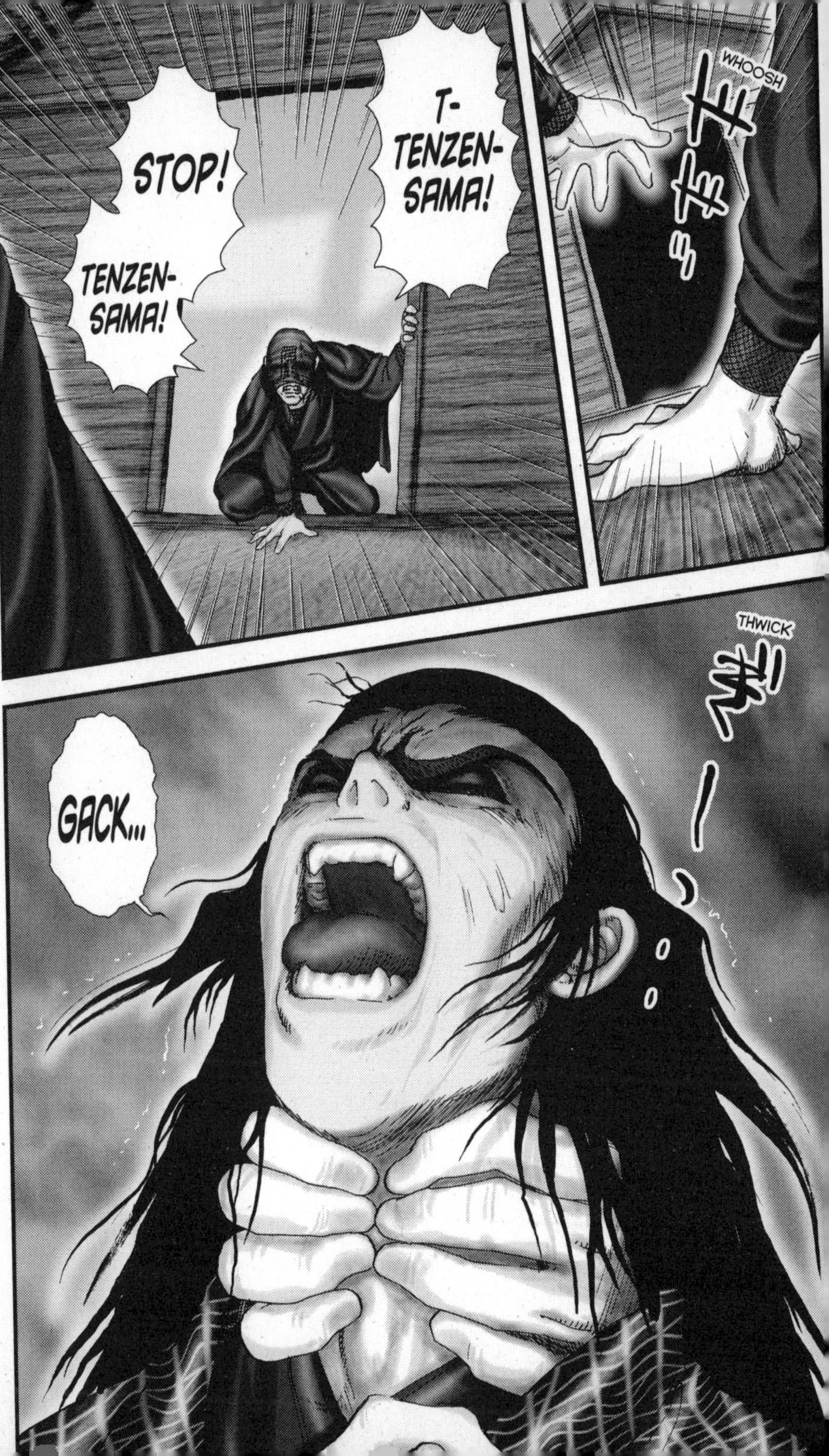
WHOOSH
T-TENZEN-SAMA!
STOP!
TENZEN-SAMA!
THWICK
GACK...

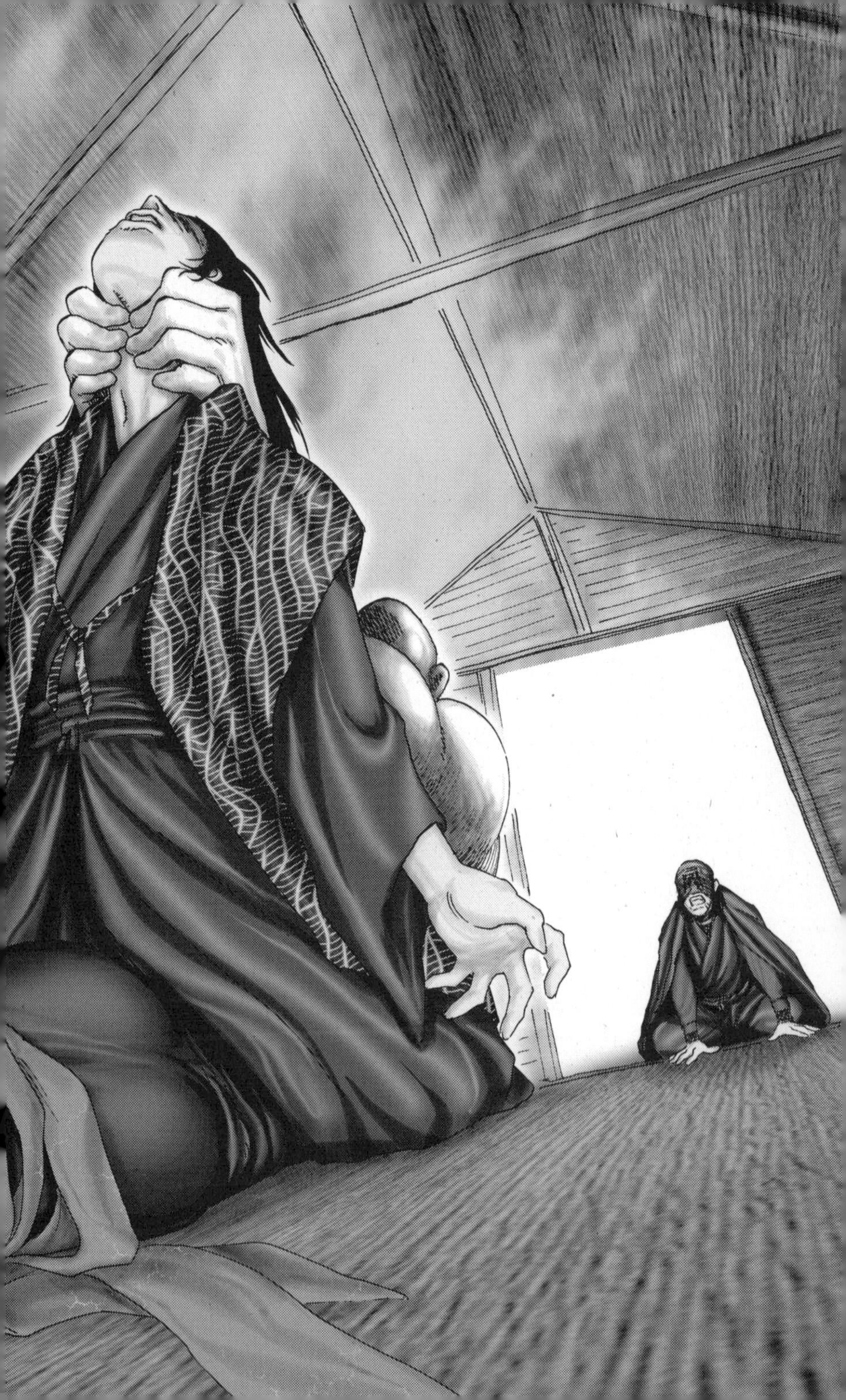

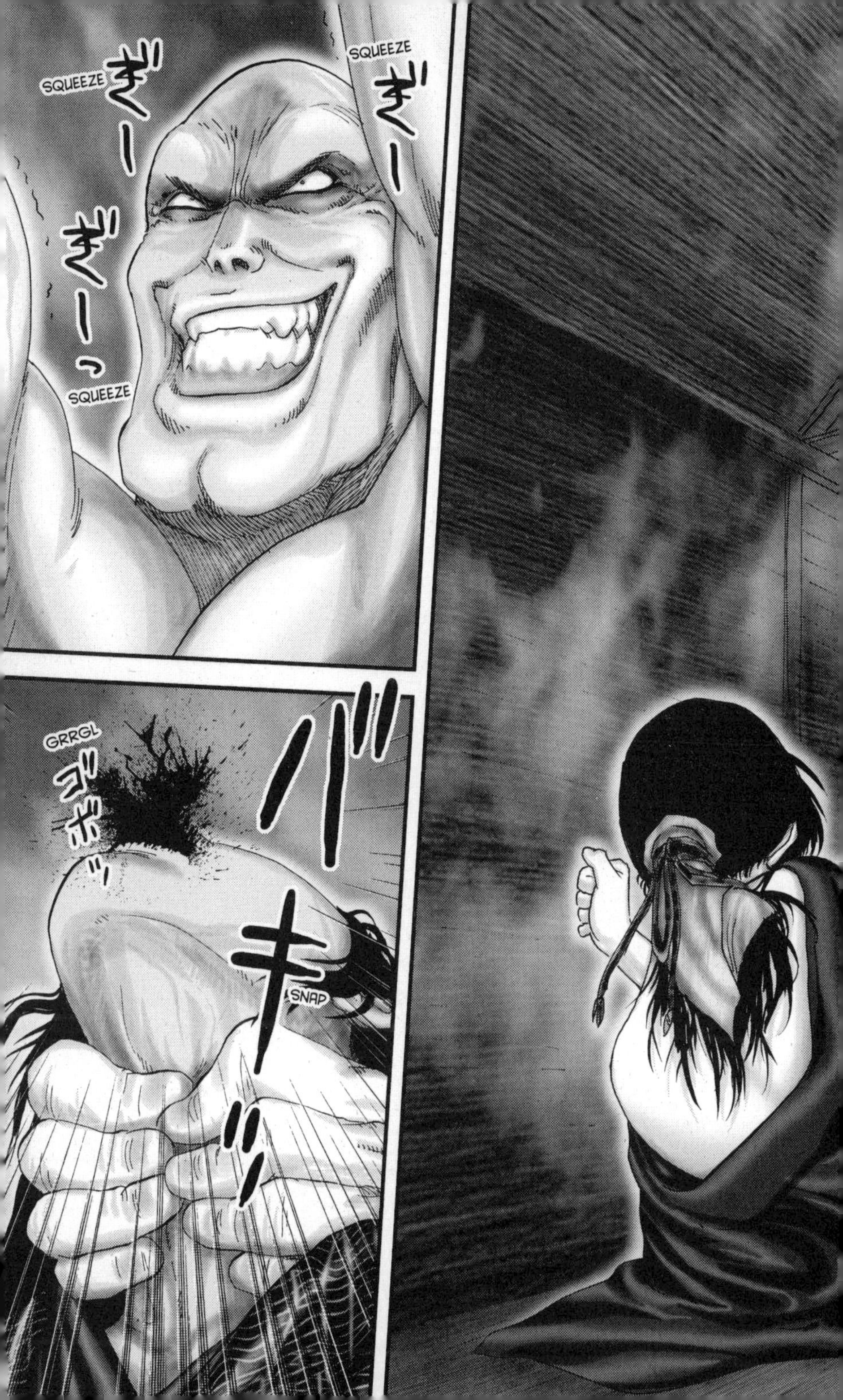

SQUEEZE
ぎー
SQUEEZE
ぎー
ぎーっ
SQUEEZE
バキッ
SNAP
GRRGL
ゴボッ

TCH.

TENZEN-
SAMA?

T—

FWAH

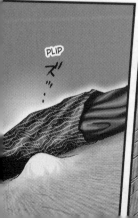

PLIP

THUD

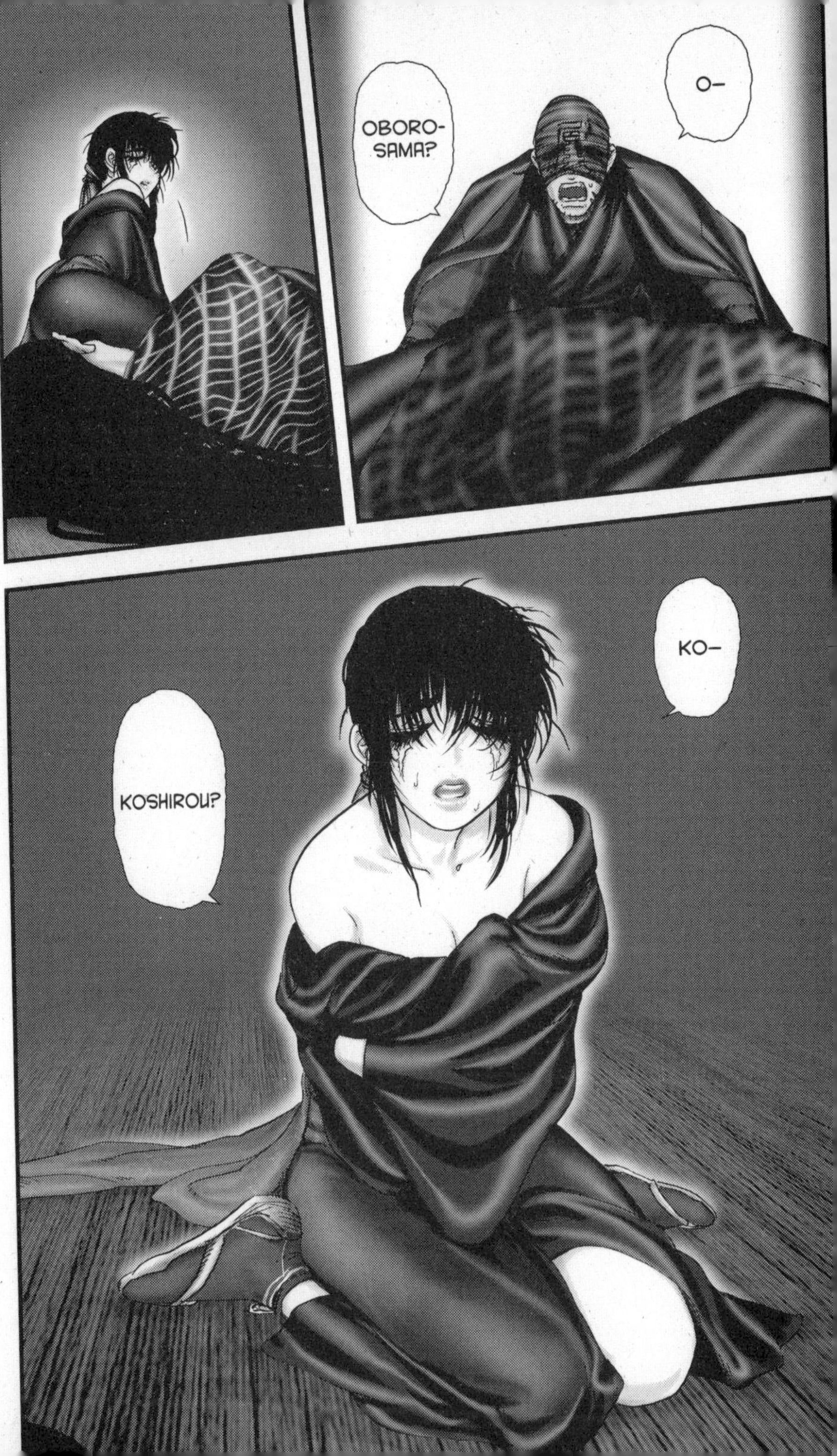
O–
OBORO-SAMA?
KO–
KOSHIROU?

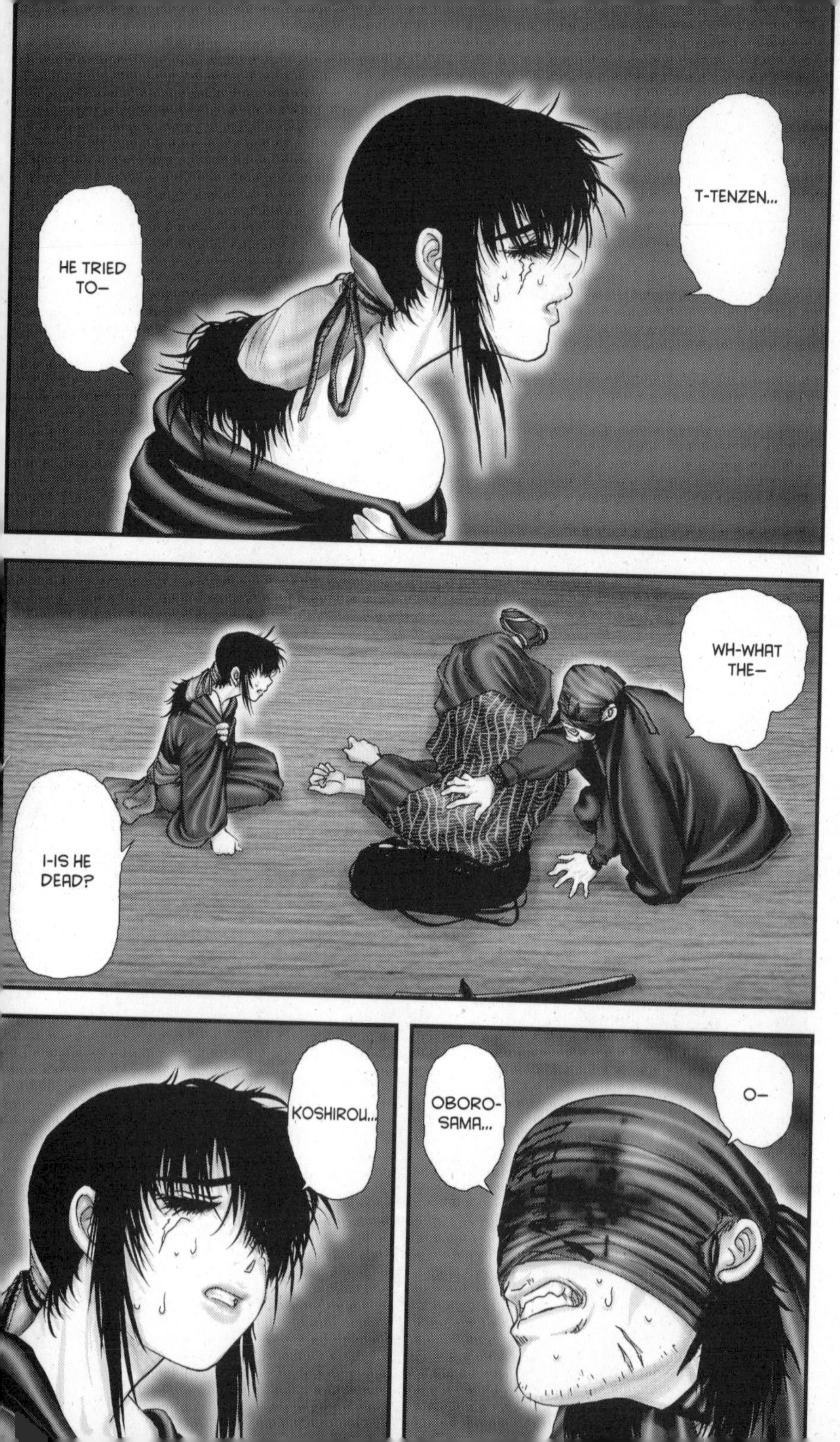
T-TENZEN...
HE TRIED TO—
WH-WHAT THE—
I-IS HE DEAD?
O—
OBORO-SAMA...
KOSHIROU...

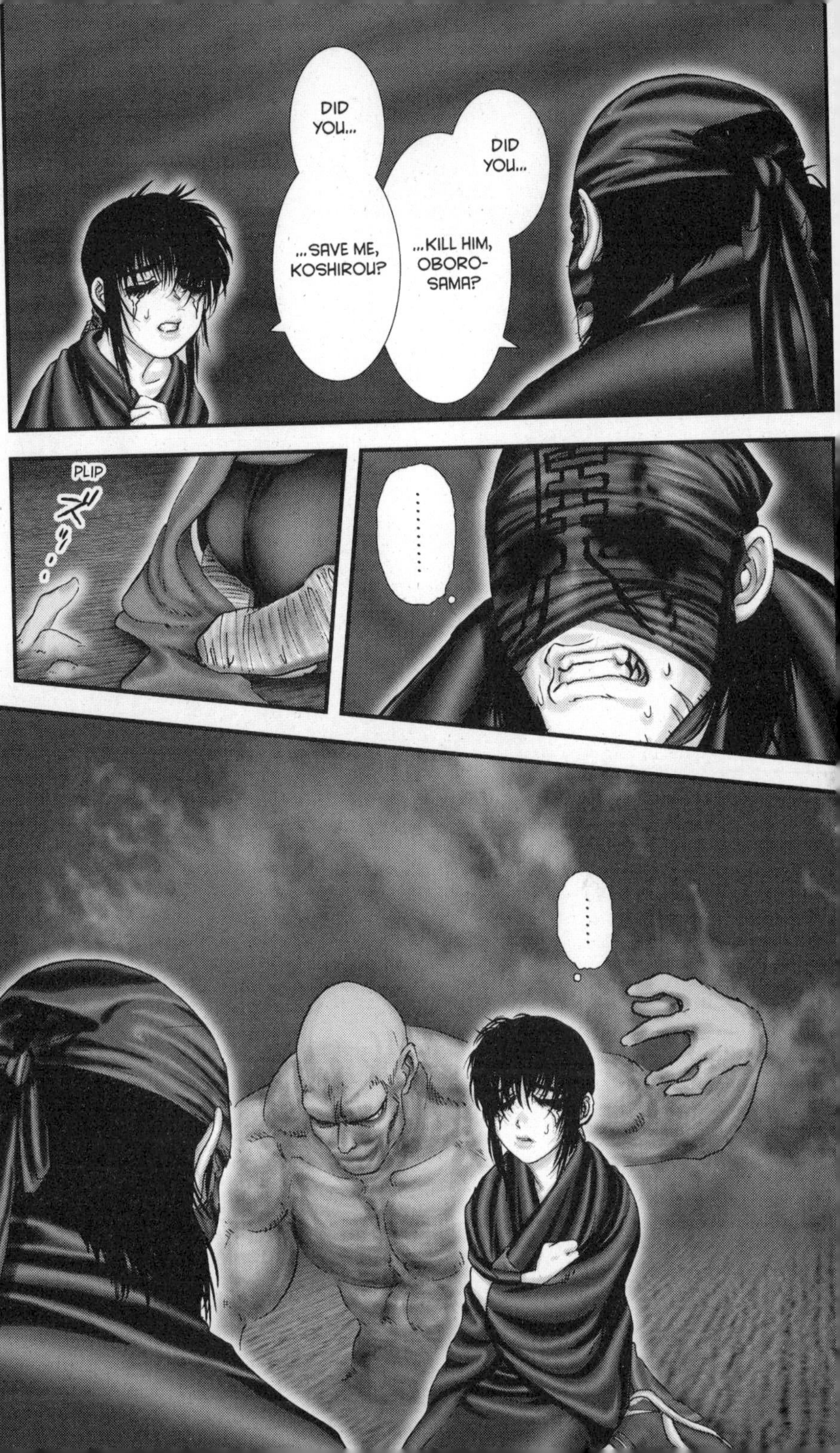
DID YOU...
...KILL HIM, OBORO-SAMA?
DID YOU...
...SAVE ME, KOSHIROU?
......
PLIP
......

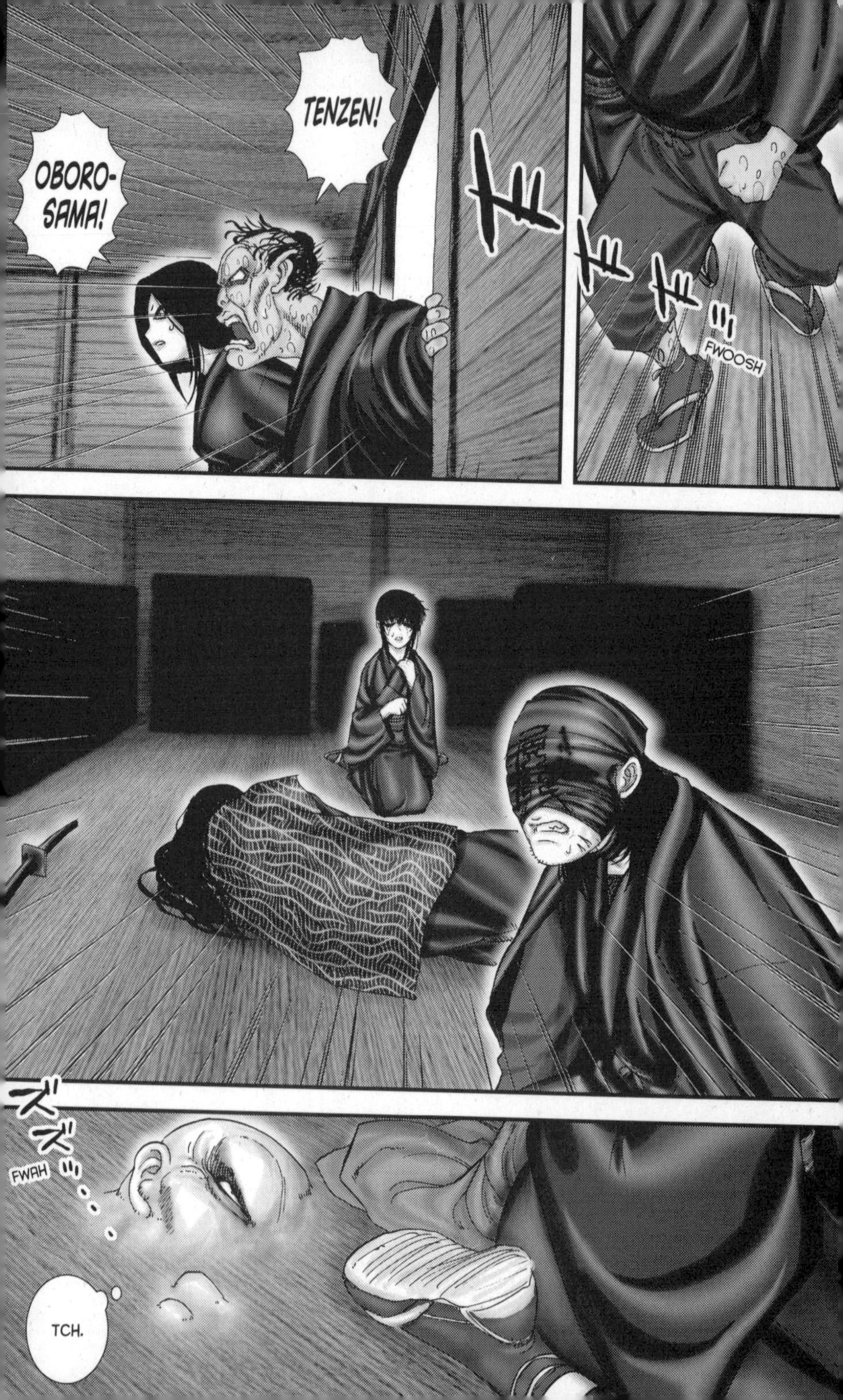
FWOOSH
TENZEN!
OBORO-SAMA!
FWAH
...
TCH.

DAMN IT...

THWIP

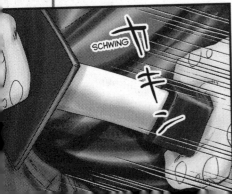

SCHWING

WAS IT HIM?

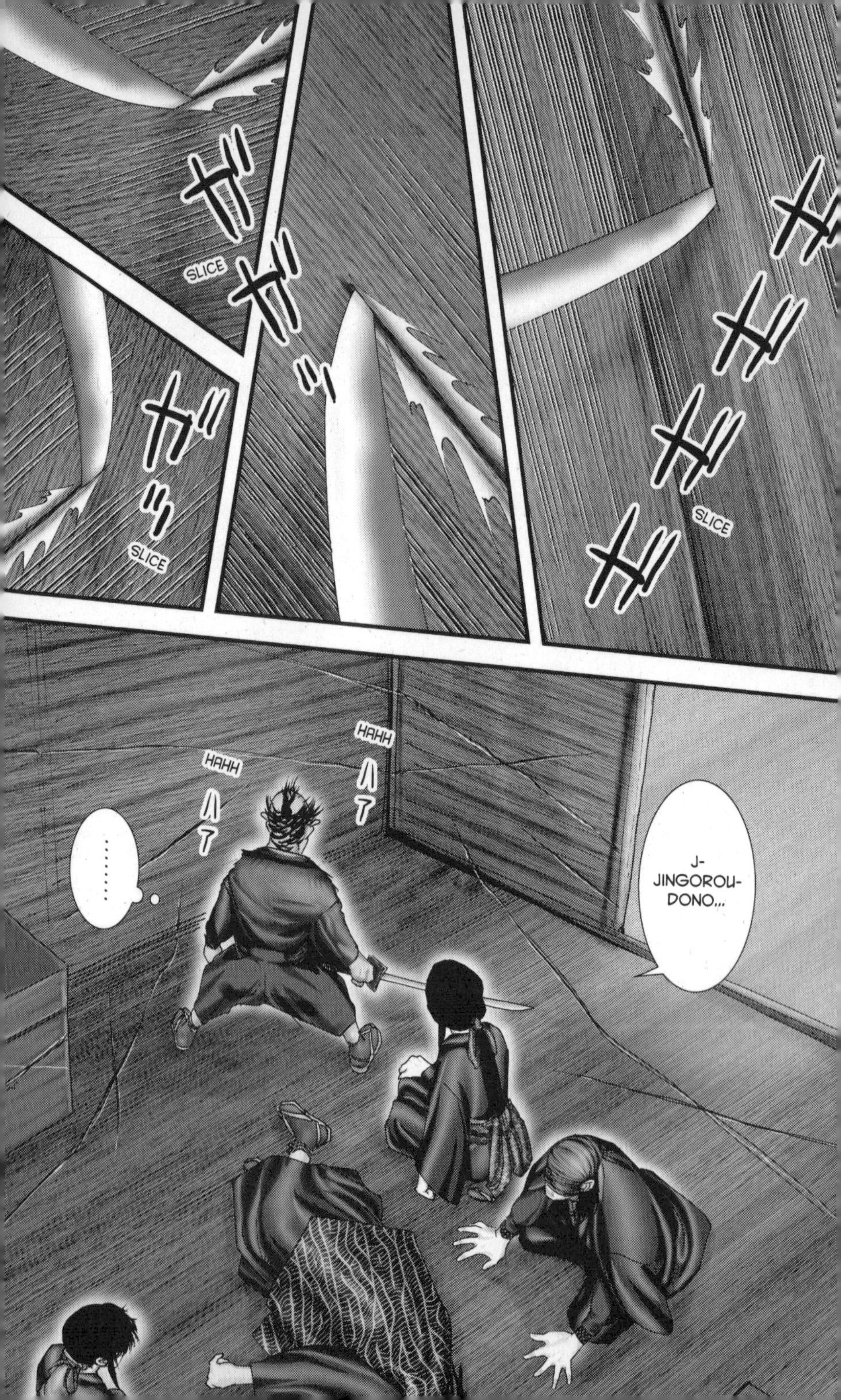
SLICE
SLICE
SLICE
J-
JINGOROU-
DONO...
HAHH
ハァ
HAHH
ハァ
......

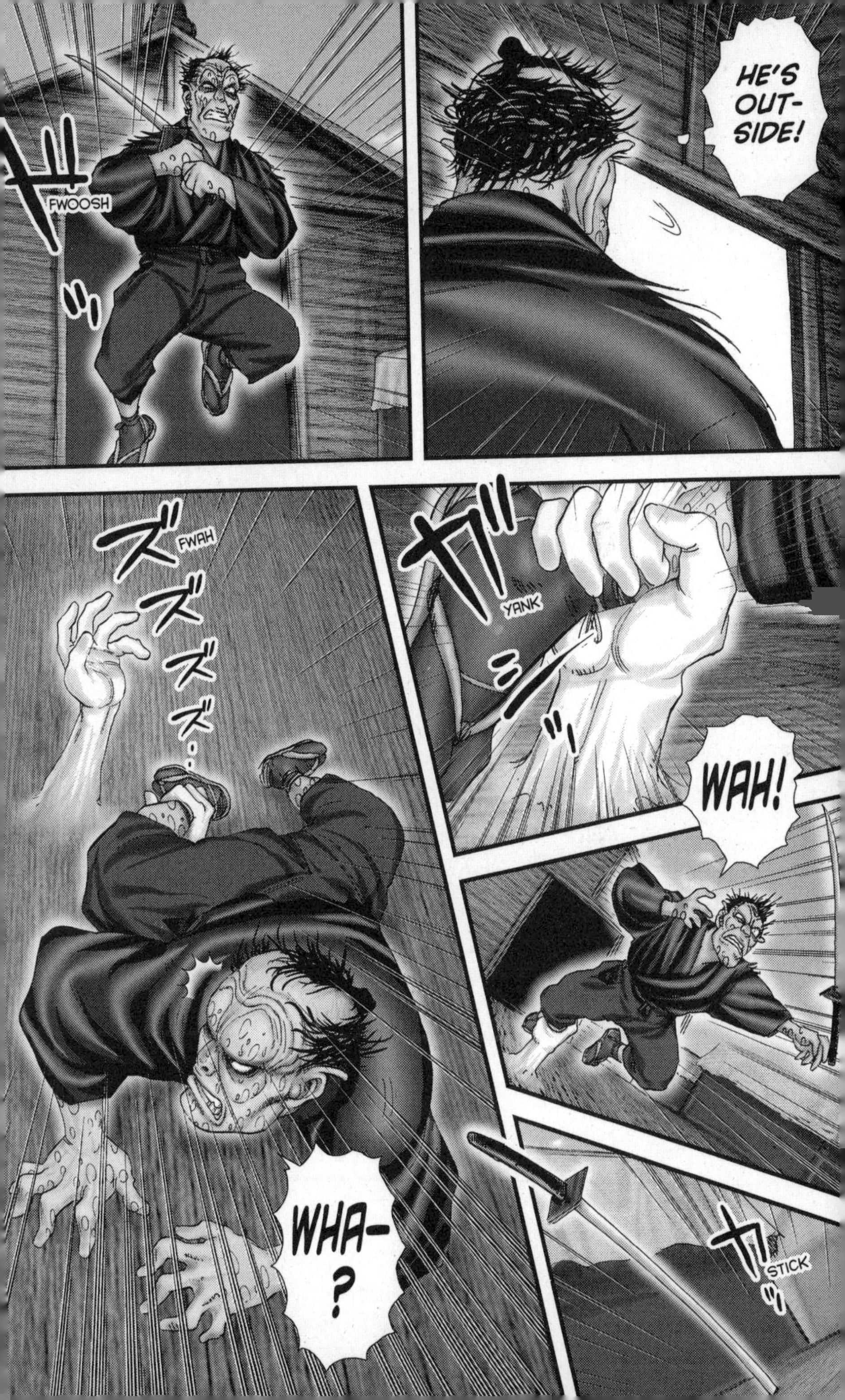
HE'S OUT-SIDE!
FWOOSH
YANK
WAH!
STICK
FWAH
WHA-?

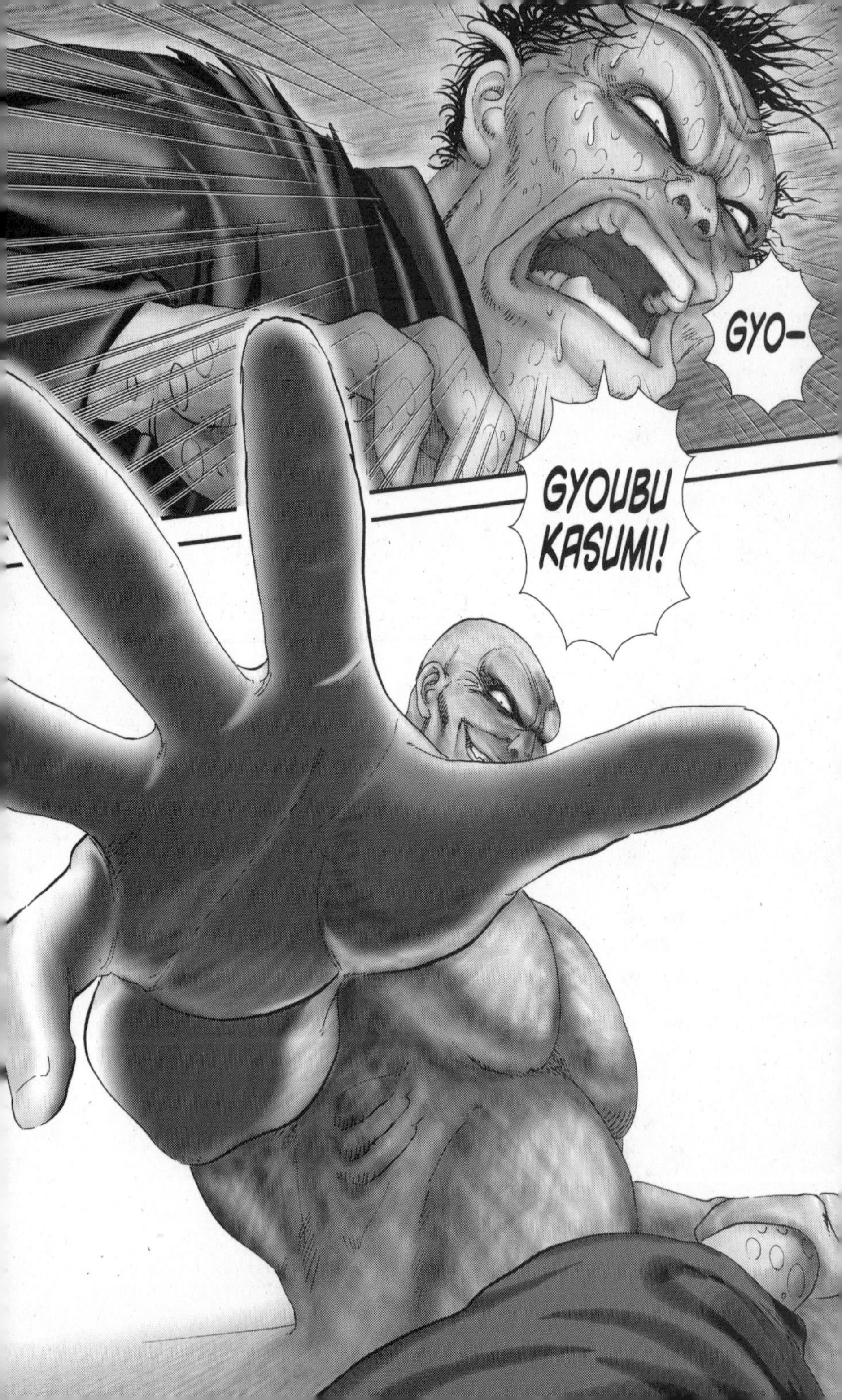
GYO-
GYOUBU KASUMI!

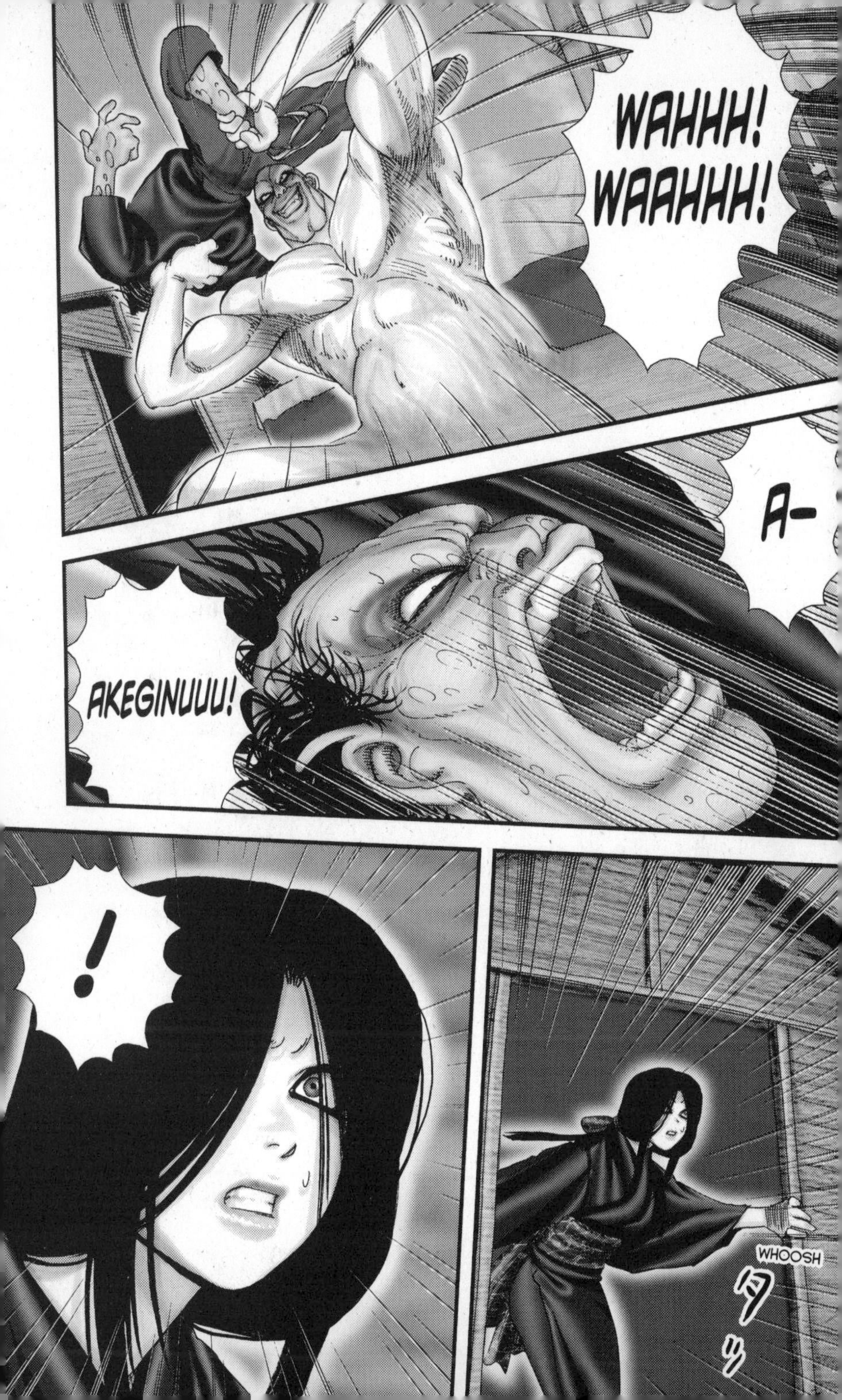
WAHHH!
WAAHHH!
A-
AKEGINUUU!
WHOOSH
!

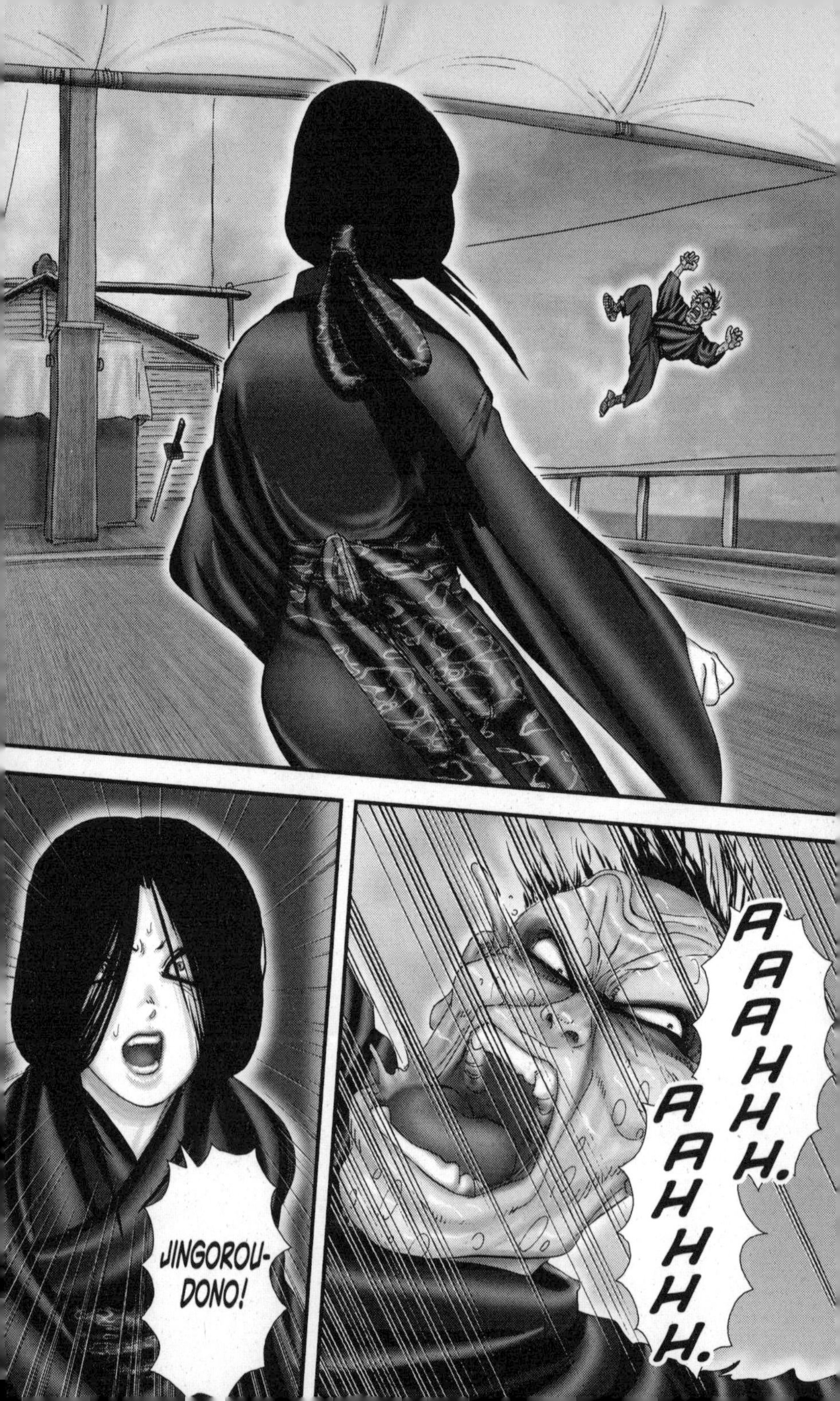
AAAHHH.
AAHHHHH.
JINGOROU-DONO!

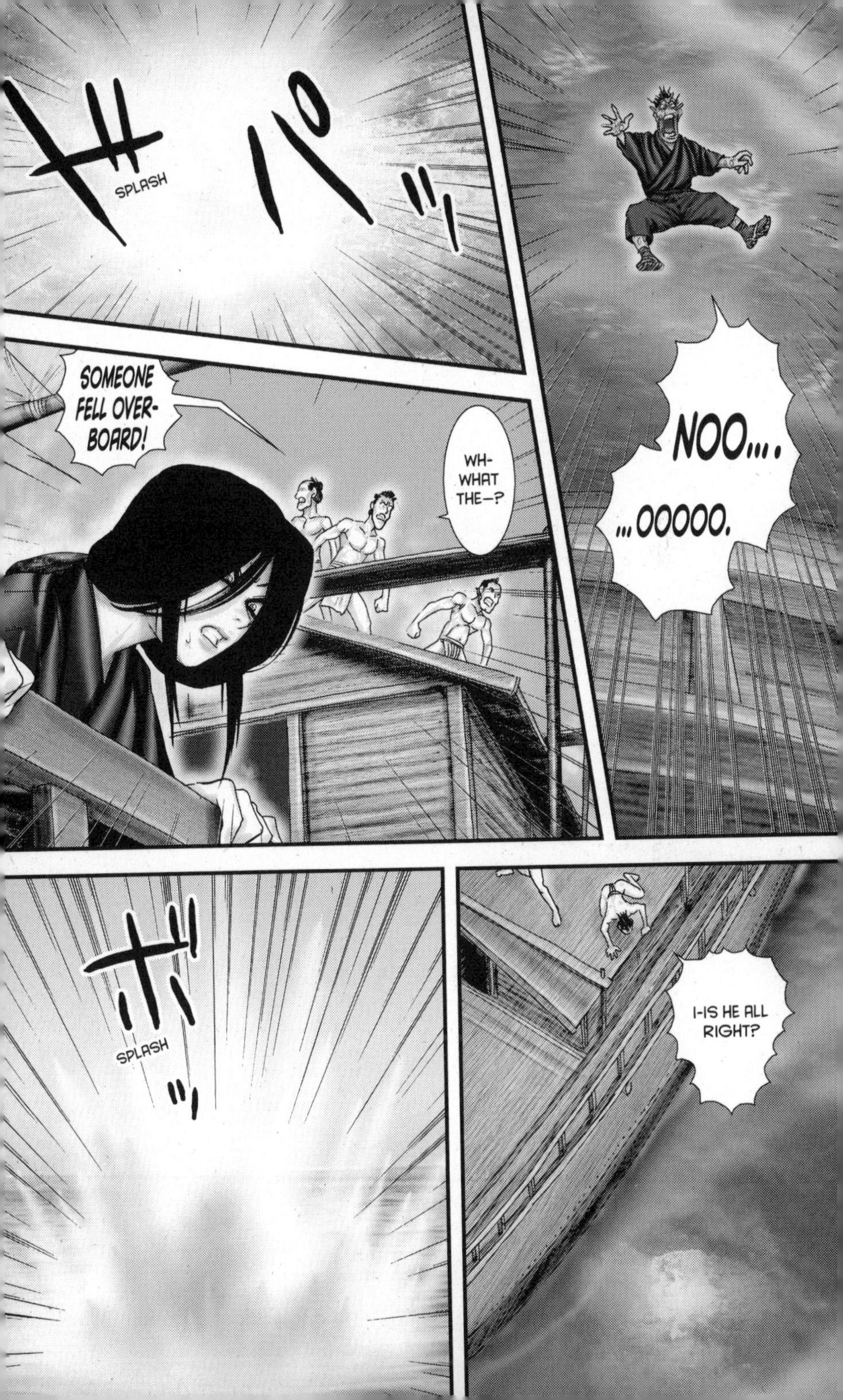
NOO....
...OOOOO.
SPLASH
WH- WHAT THE–?
SOMEONE FELL OVER-BOARD!
I-IS HE ALL RIGHT?
SPLASH

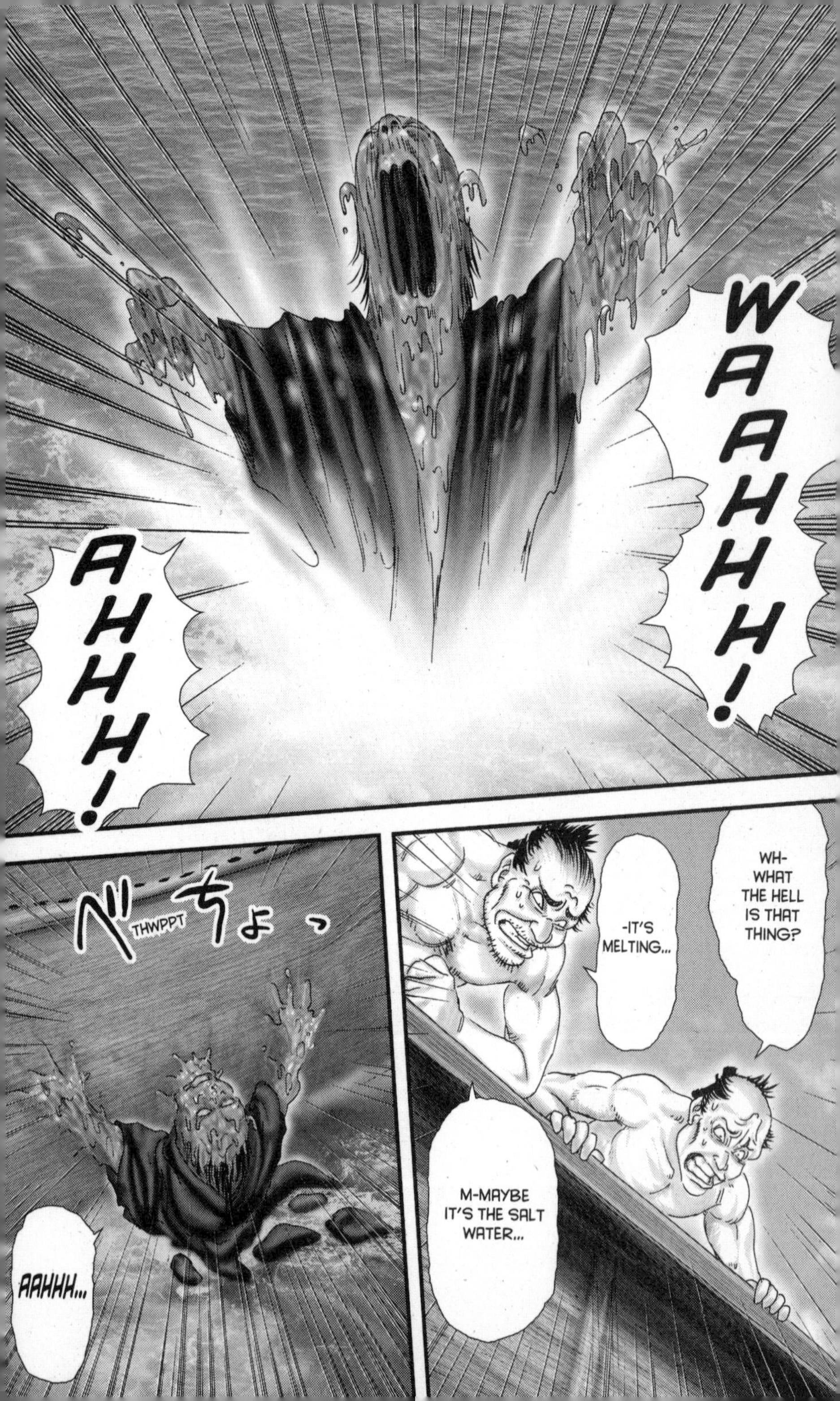
WAAHHH!
AHHH!
WH- WHAT THE HELL IS THAT THING?
-IT'S MELTING...
M-MAYBE IT'S THE SALT WATER...
べちょっ
THWPPT
AAHHH...

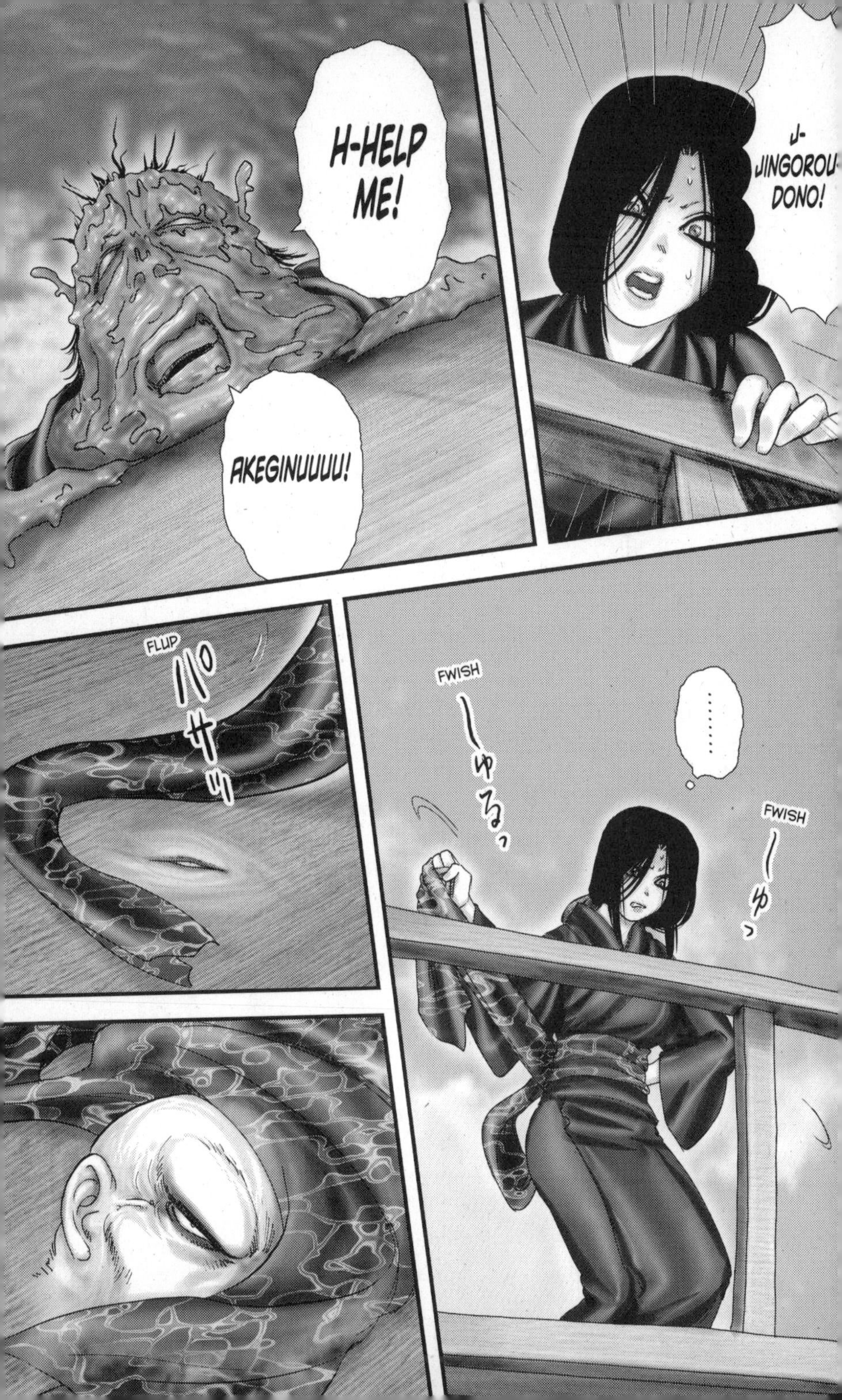
J-JINGOROU-DONO!
H-HELP ME!
AKEGINUUUU!
......
FWISH
しゅるっ
FWISH
しゅっ
FLUP
パサッ

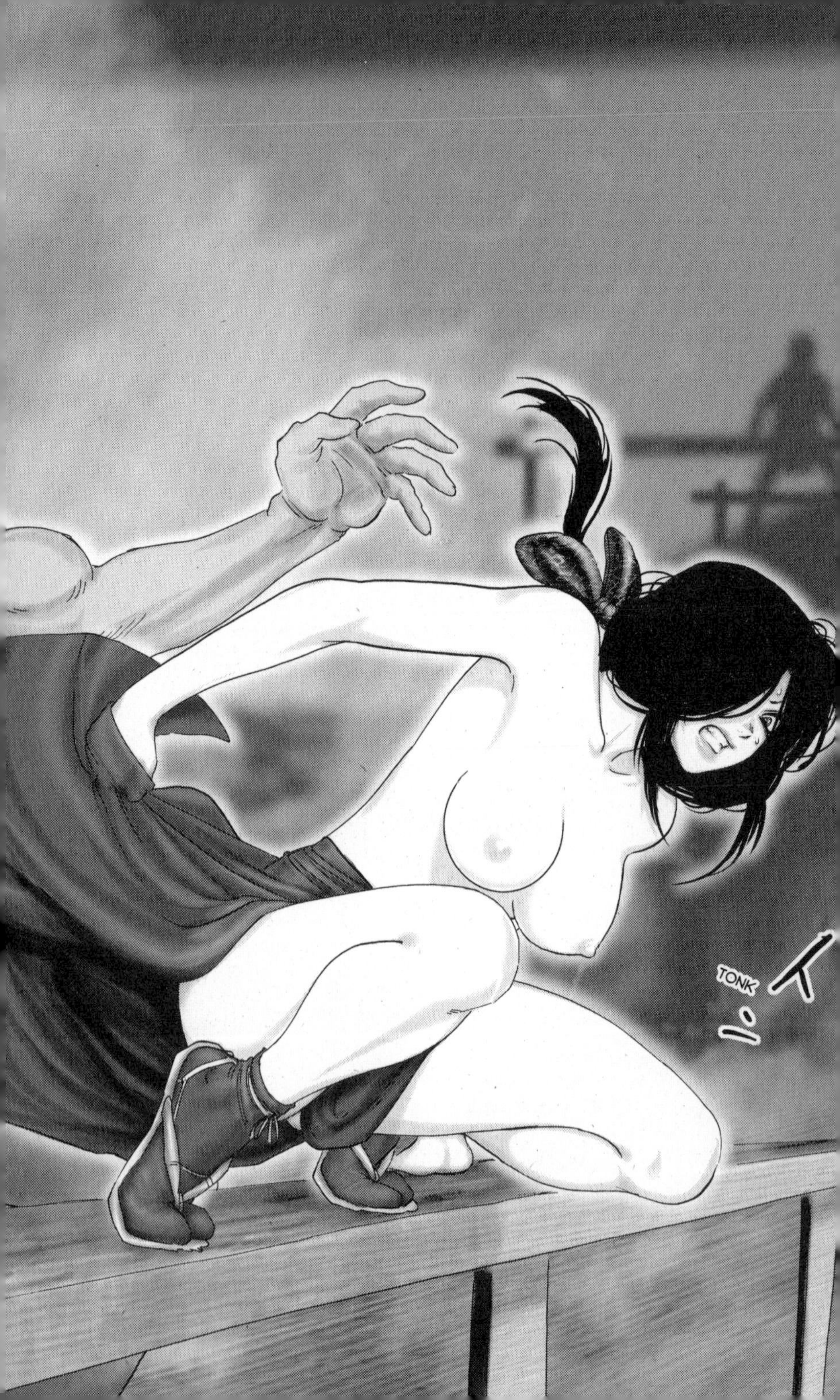
TONK

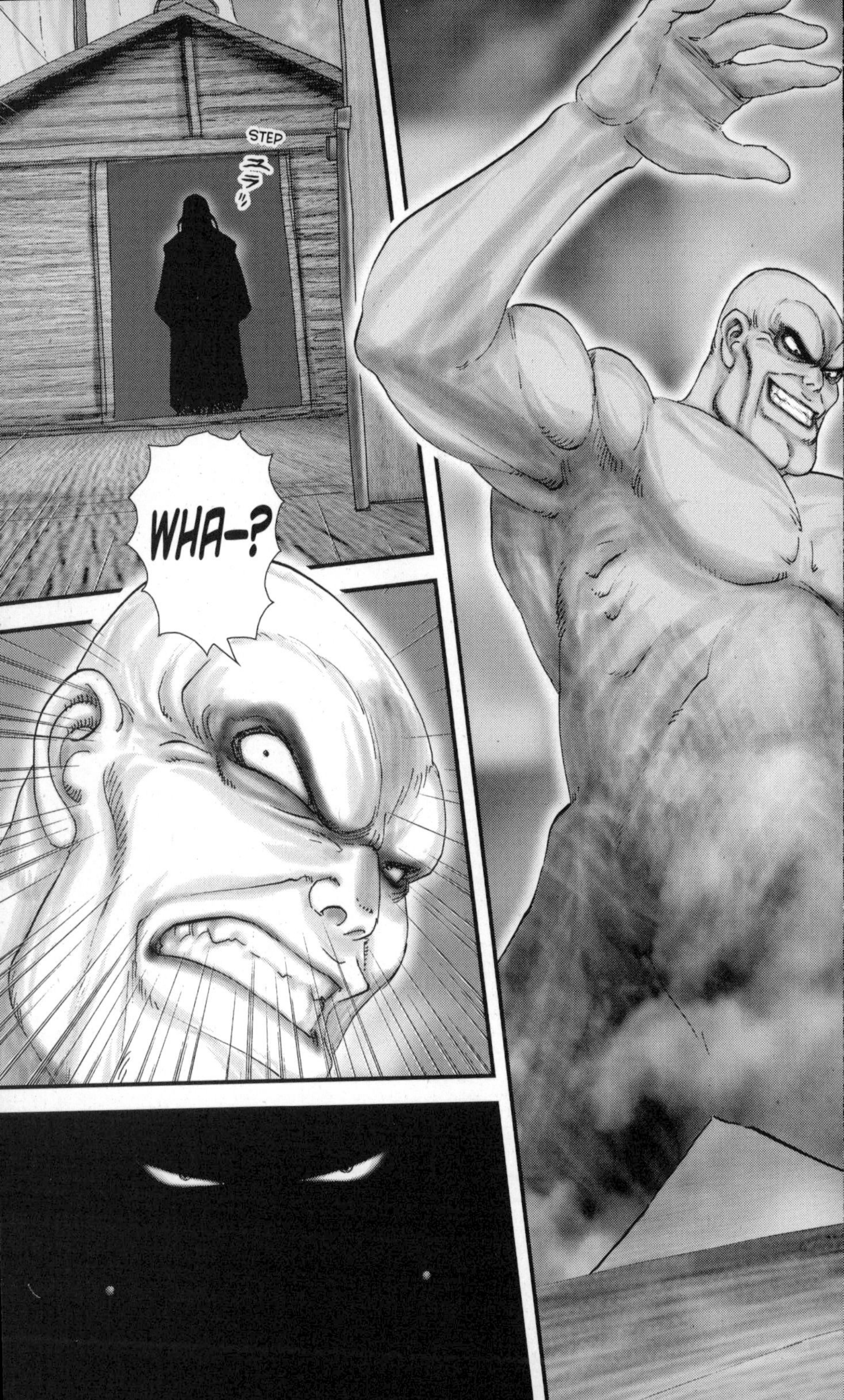
STEP
WHA-?

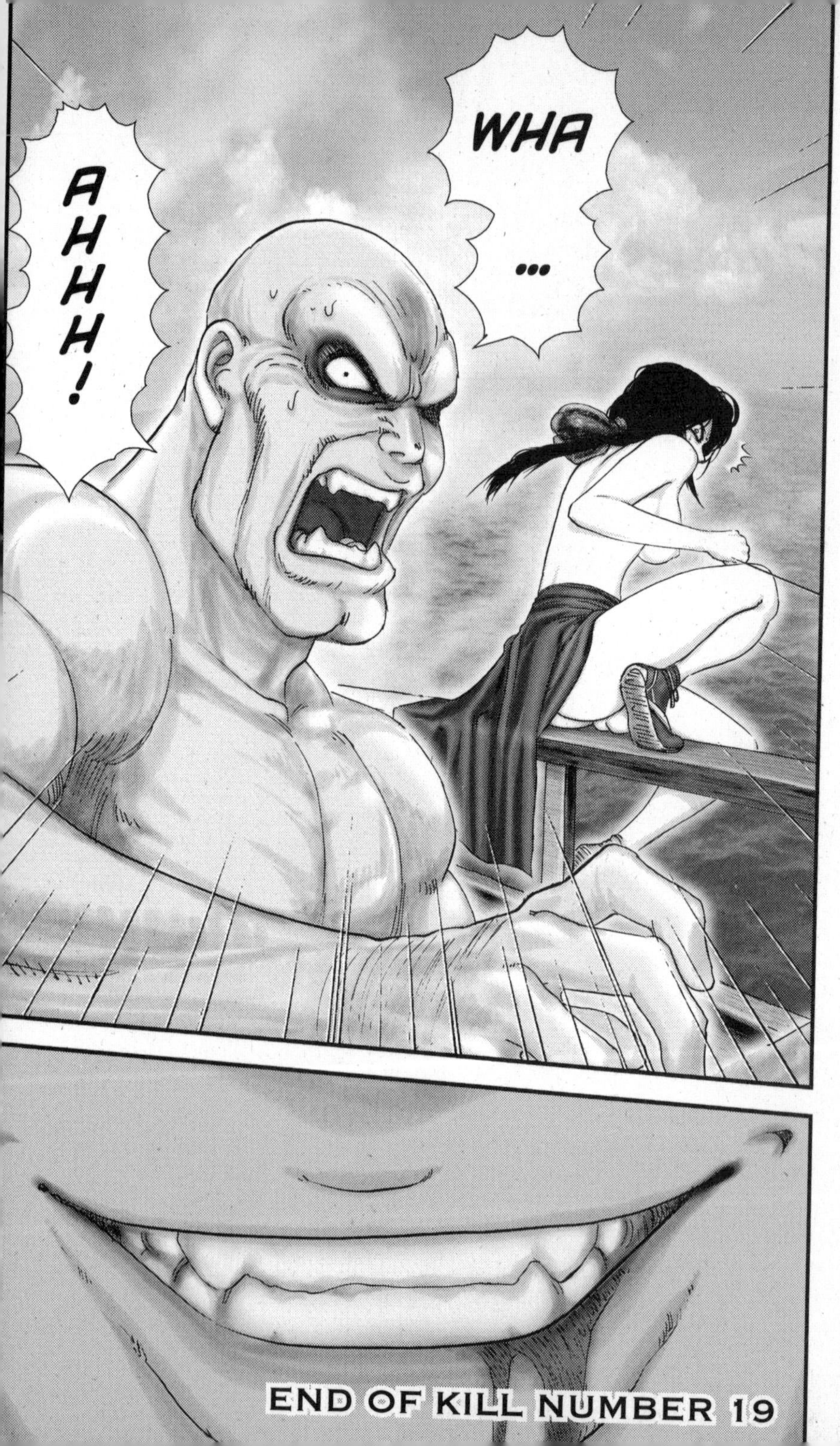
WHA ...
AHHHH!
END OF KILL NUMBER 19

賓刑部

解かれるんや

い間いて殺すべし

駿府城へまかり

勝たば一族

雨夜陣五郎

筑摩小

兼念鬼

弦火

朱絹

のこれるものこの秘巻をたずさえ五月晦日駿
出ずべきことその数多をに勝らとなし勝だ

禄禄わらん

徳川家

甲賀組十人衆

甲賀弾正

甲賀弦之介

地虫十兵衛

風待将監

鵜殿丈助

如月左衛門

室賀豹馬

陽炎

如月左衛門

室賀豹馬

陽炎

お胡夷

右甲賀十人衆 伊賀十人衆たがいに

伊賀鍔隠れ

[illegible]秘巻をたずさえ五月

[illegible]べきこと その数多きを勝ちとな

お幻 [illegible]

雨夜陣五郎

朧

筑摩小四郎

徳

雨夜陣五郎

夜叉丸

慶長十九年四月

蓑念鬼

筑摩小四郎

蝋斎

蛍火

蓑念鬼

薬師寺天膳

朱絹

服部半蔵との約定両門争闘の禁制は解かれ了んぬ

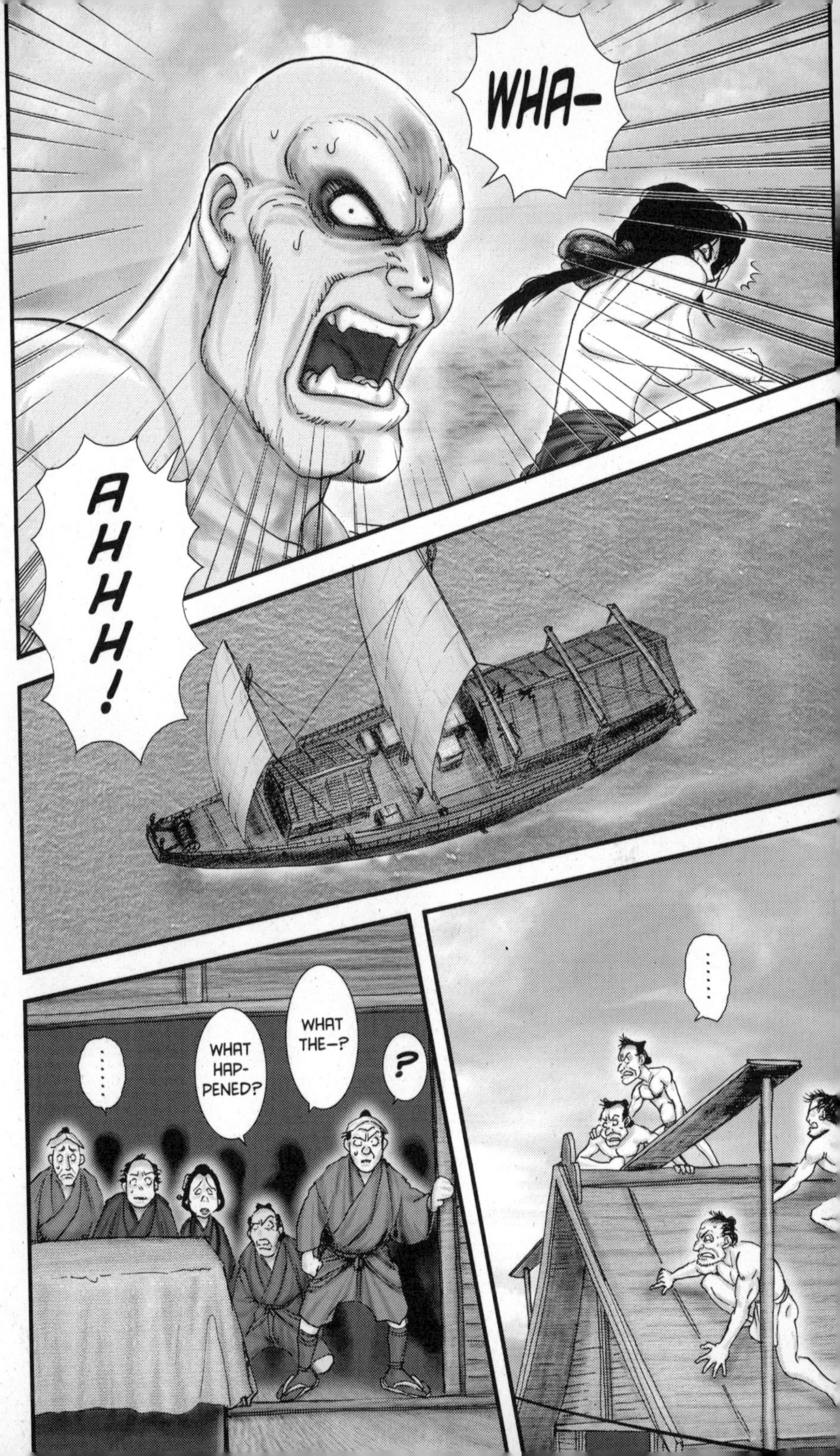
WHA-
AHHHH!
......
?
WHAT THE—?
WHAT HAP-PENED?
......

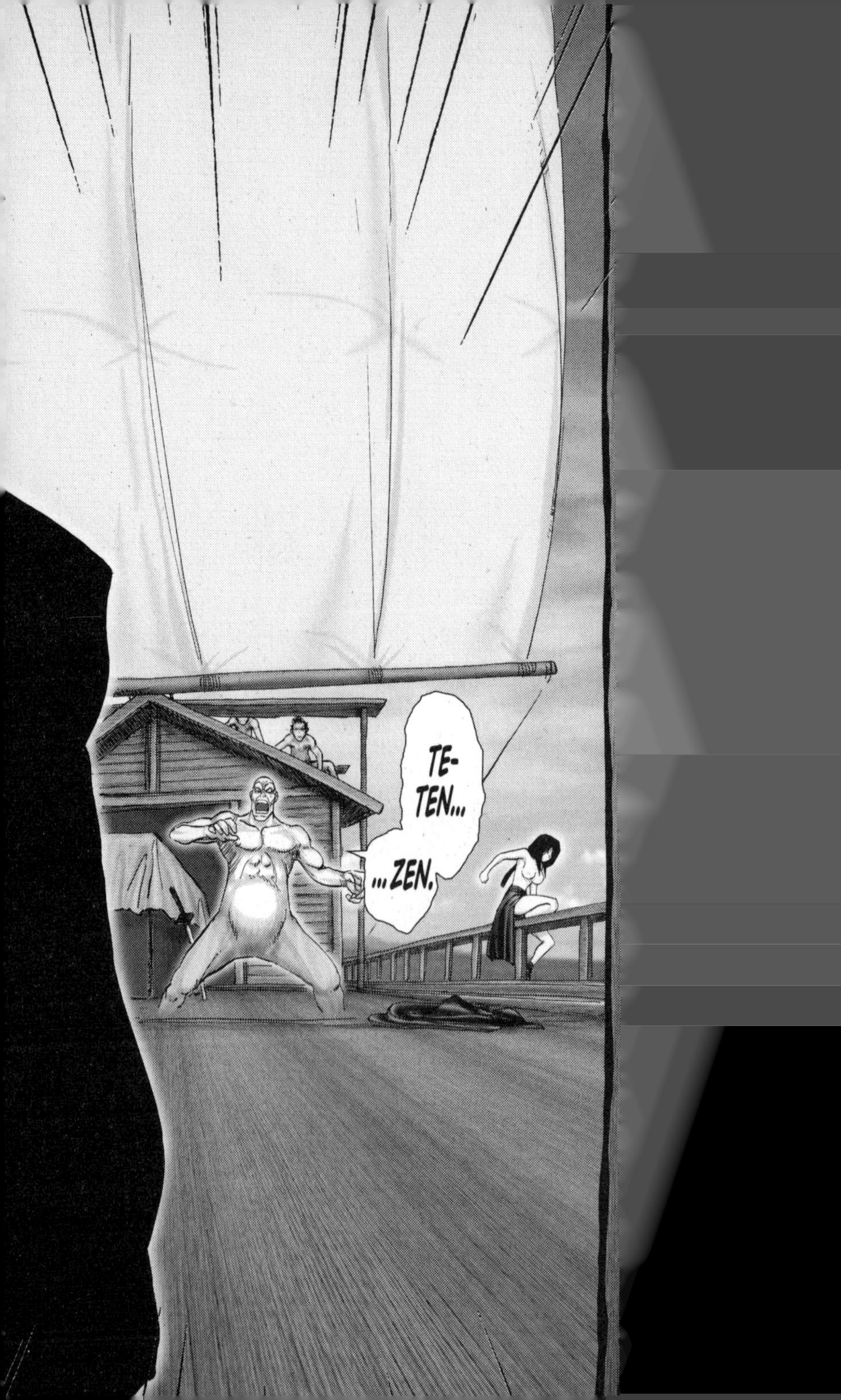

TE-
TEN...
...ZEN.

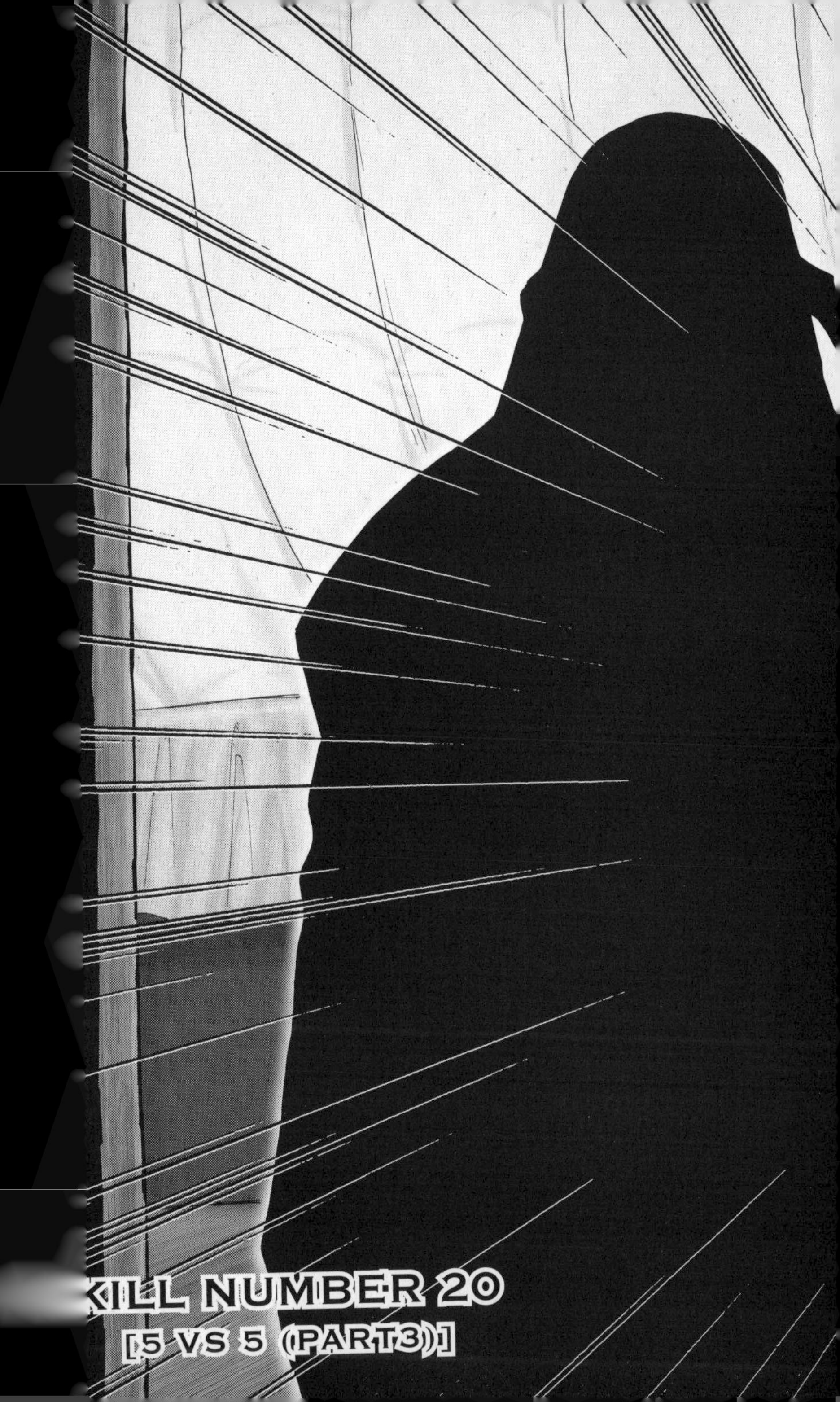
KILL NUMBER 20
[5 VS 5 (PART3)]

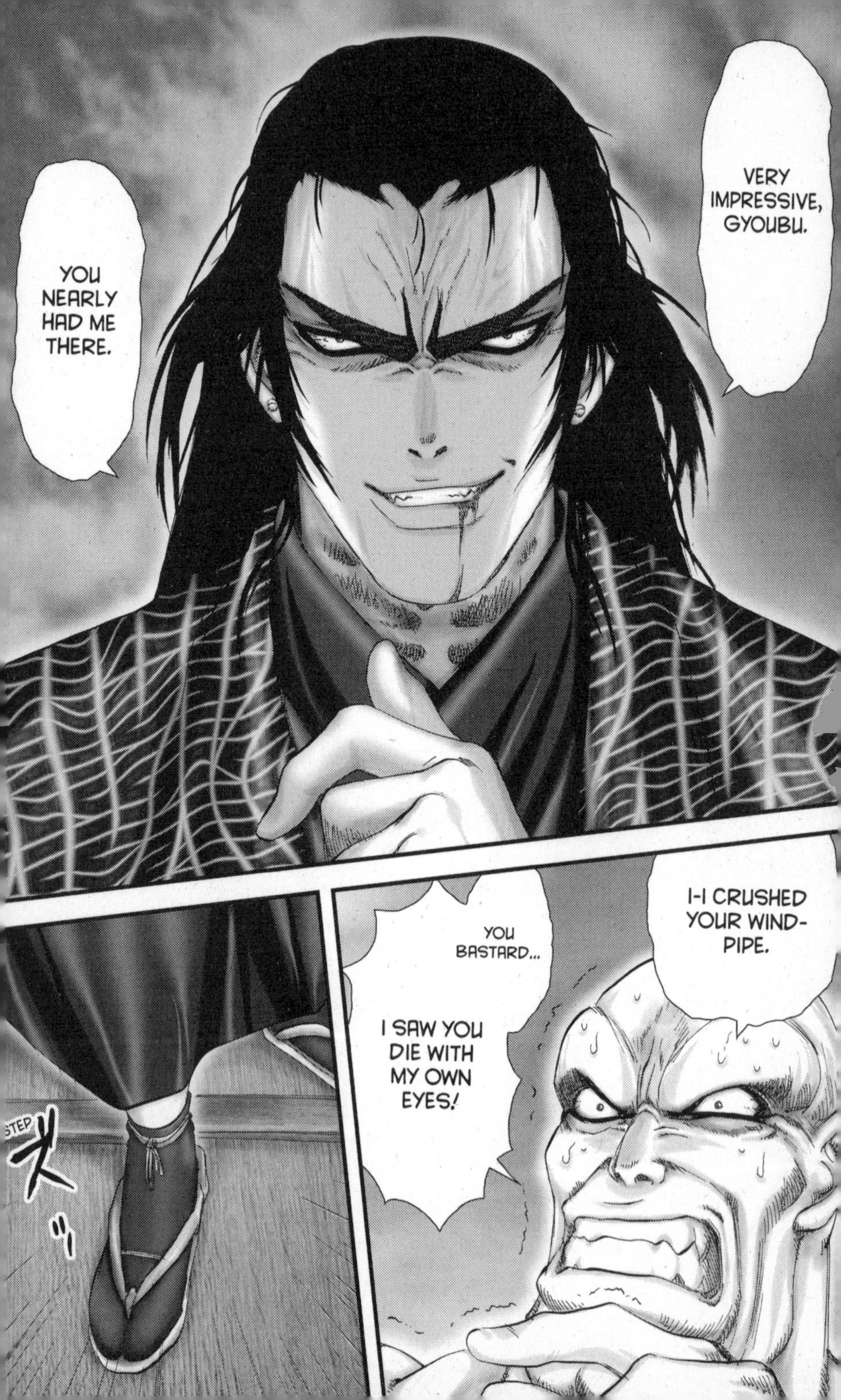
VERY IMPRESSIVE, GYOUBU.
YOU NEARLY HAD ME THERE.
I-I CRUSHED YOUR WIND-PIPE.
YOU BASTARD...
I SAW YOU DIE WITH MY OWN EYES!
STEP

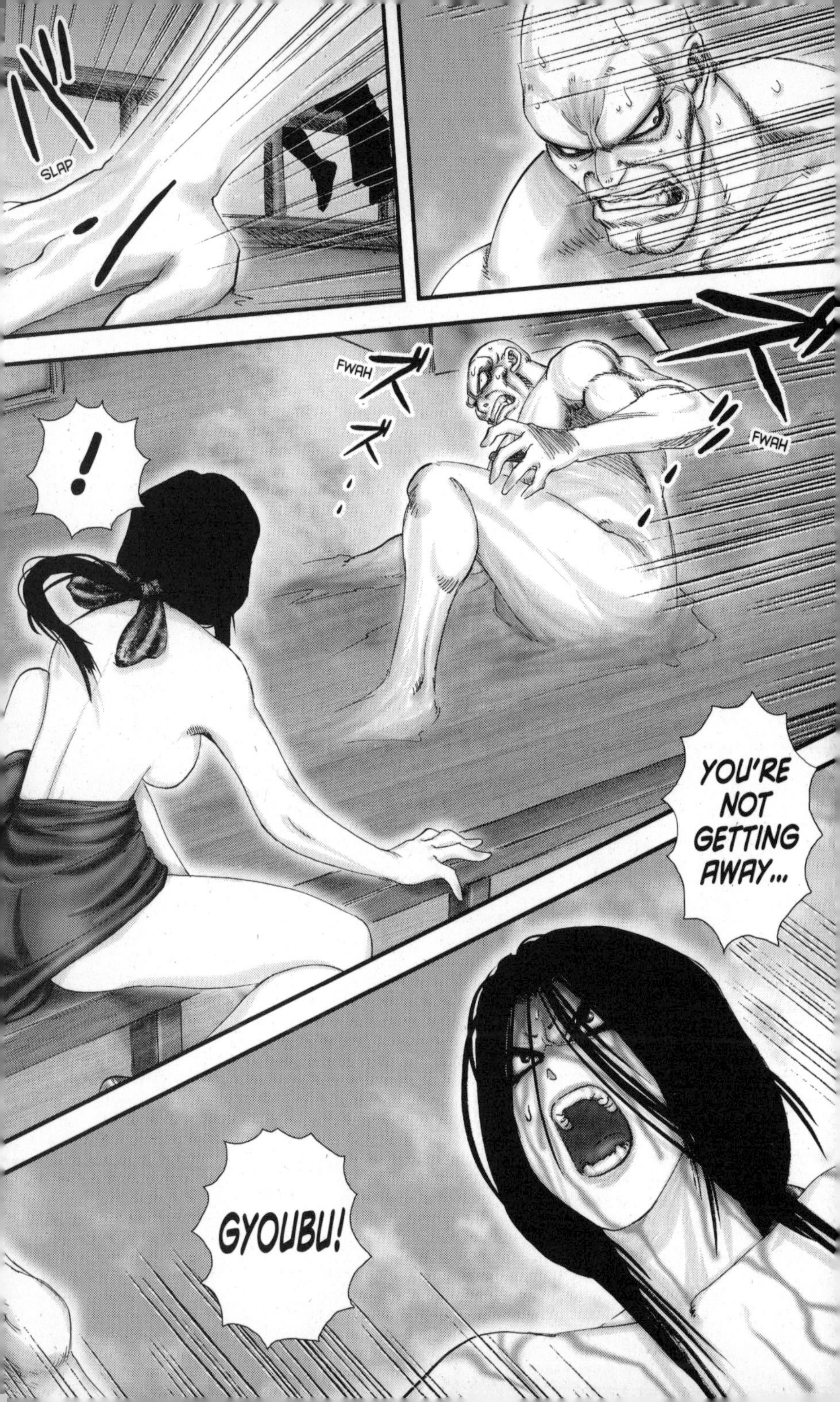
SLAP
FWAH
FWAH
!
YOU'RE NOT GETTING AWAY...
GYOUBU!

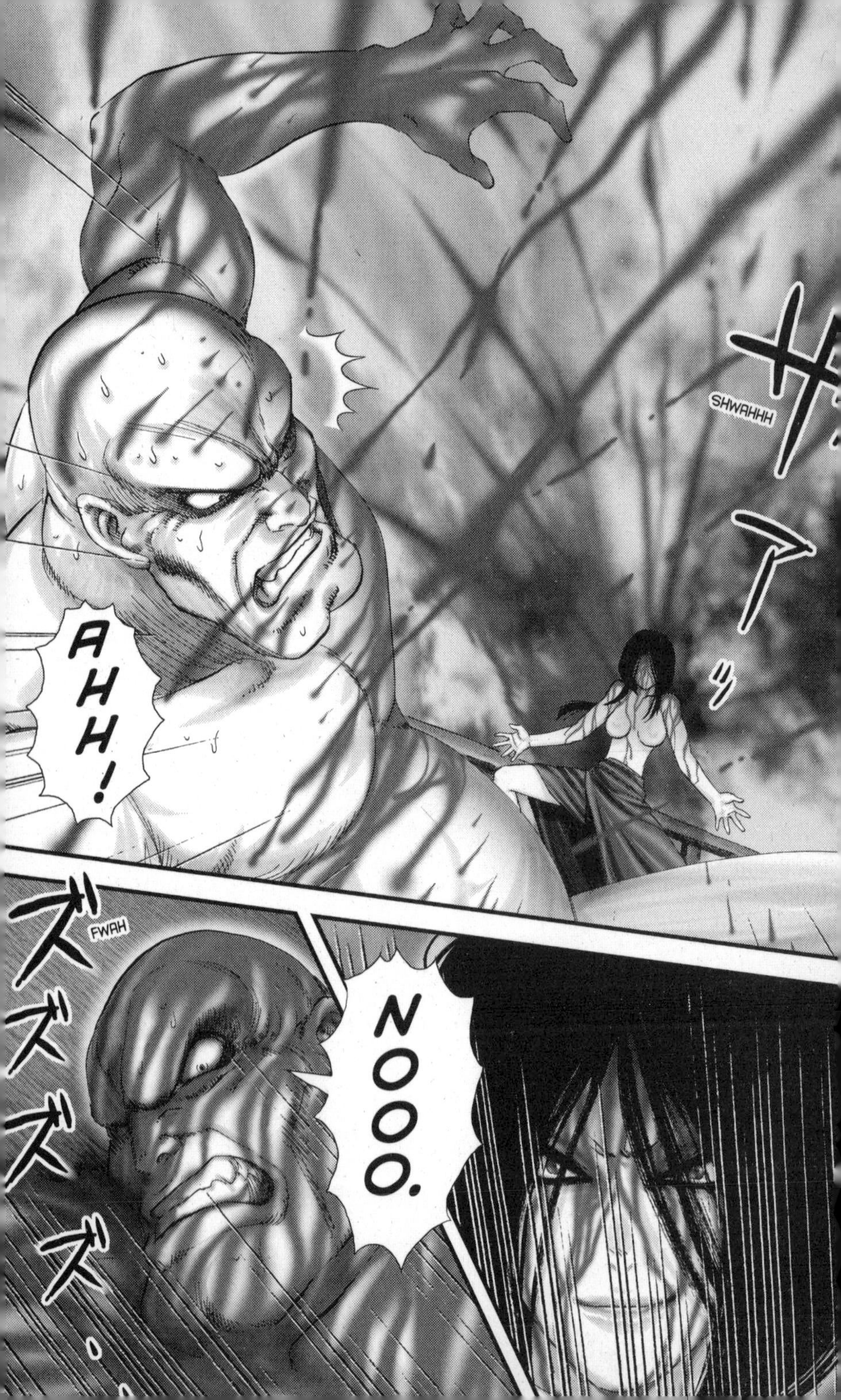

ザァーッ
SHWAHHH
AHHH!
NOOO.
ズズズズ・・
FWAH

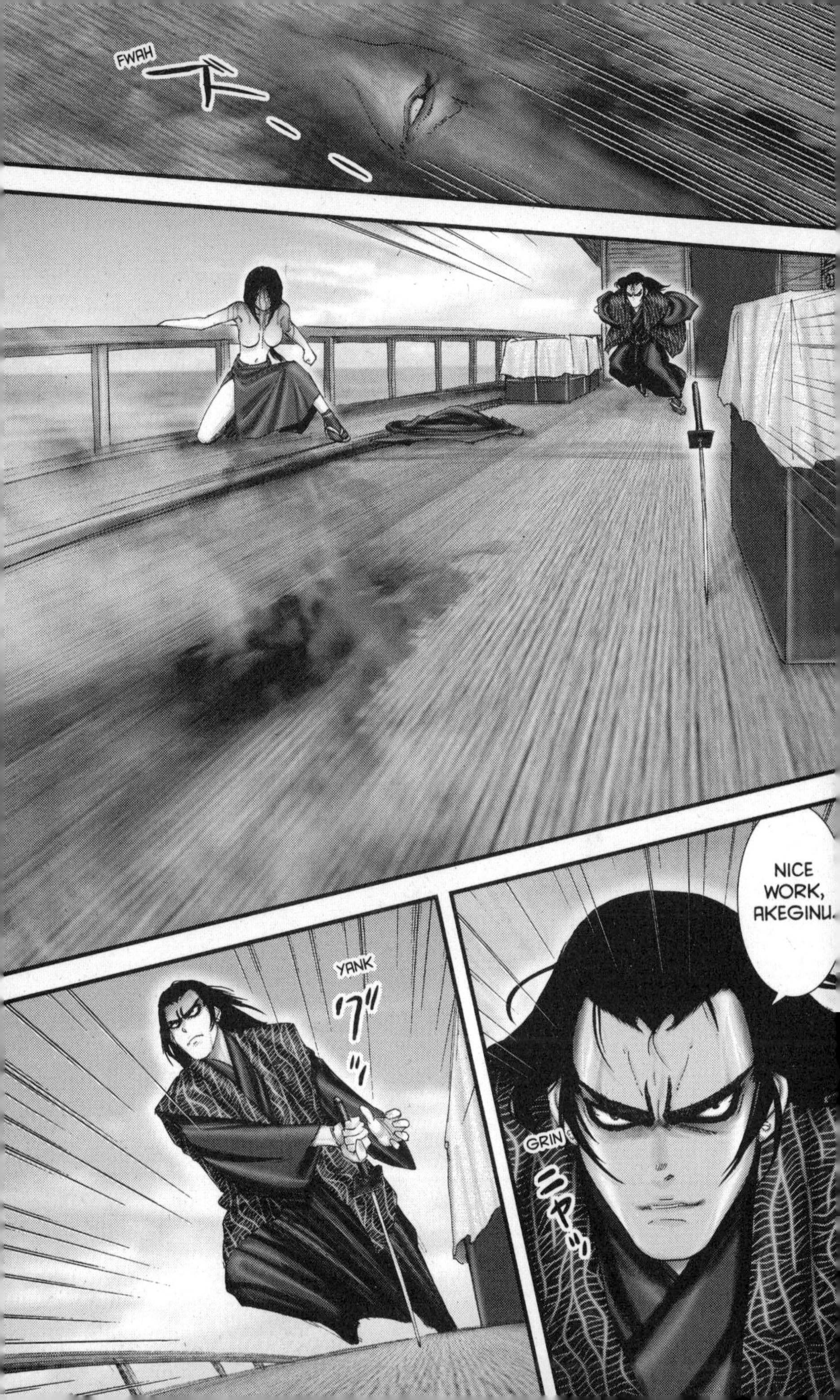
FWAH
NICE WORK, AKEGINU.
GRIN
ニヤッ
YANK
グッ

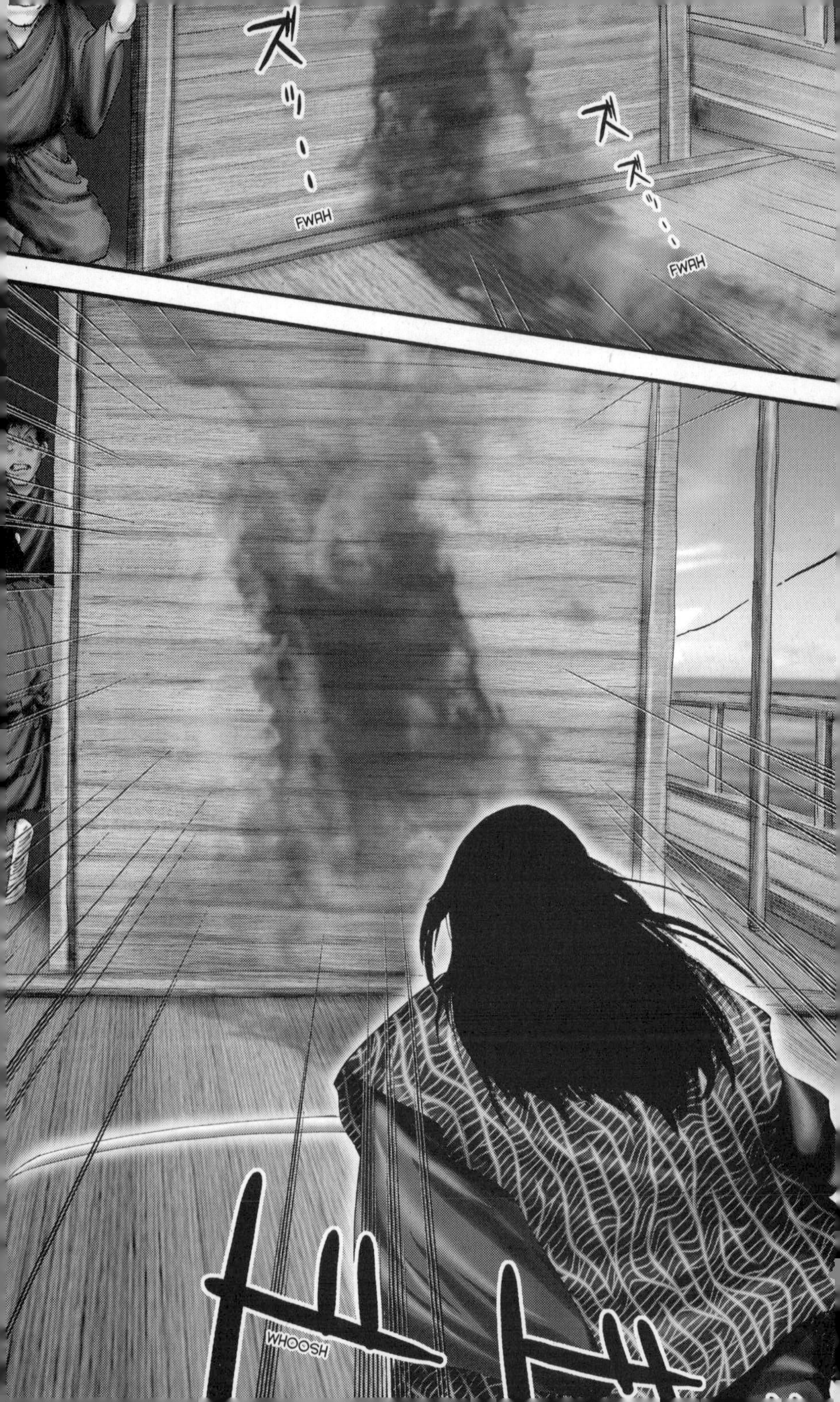

FWAH
FWAH
WHOOSH

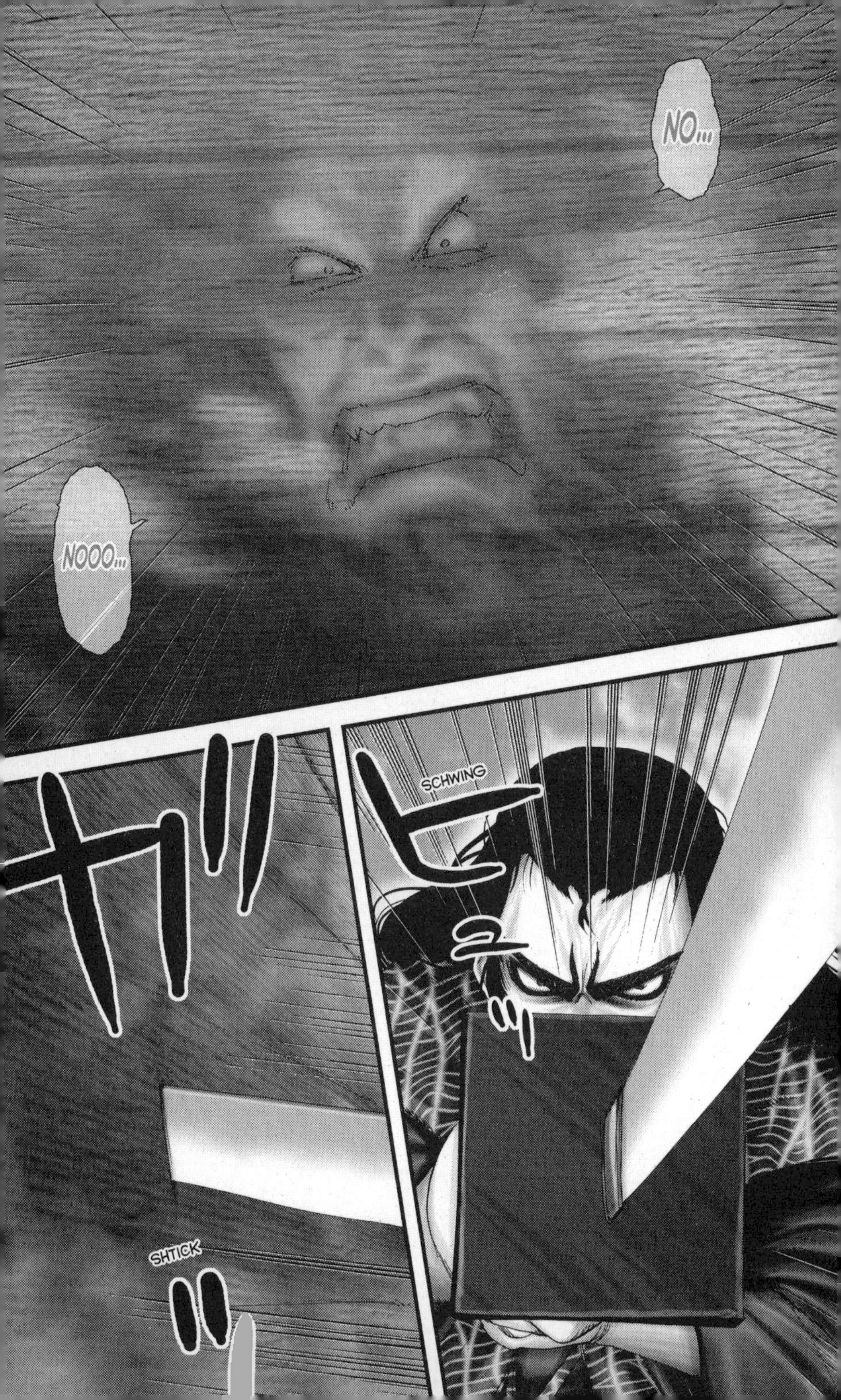

NO...
NOOO...
SCHWING
SHTICK

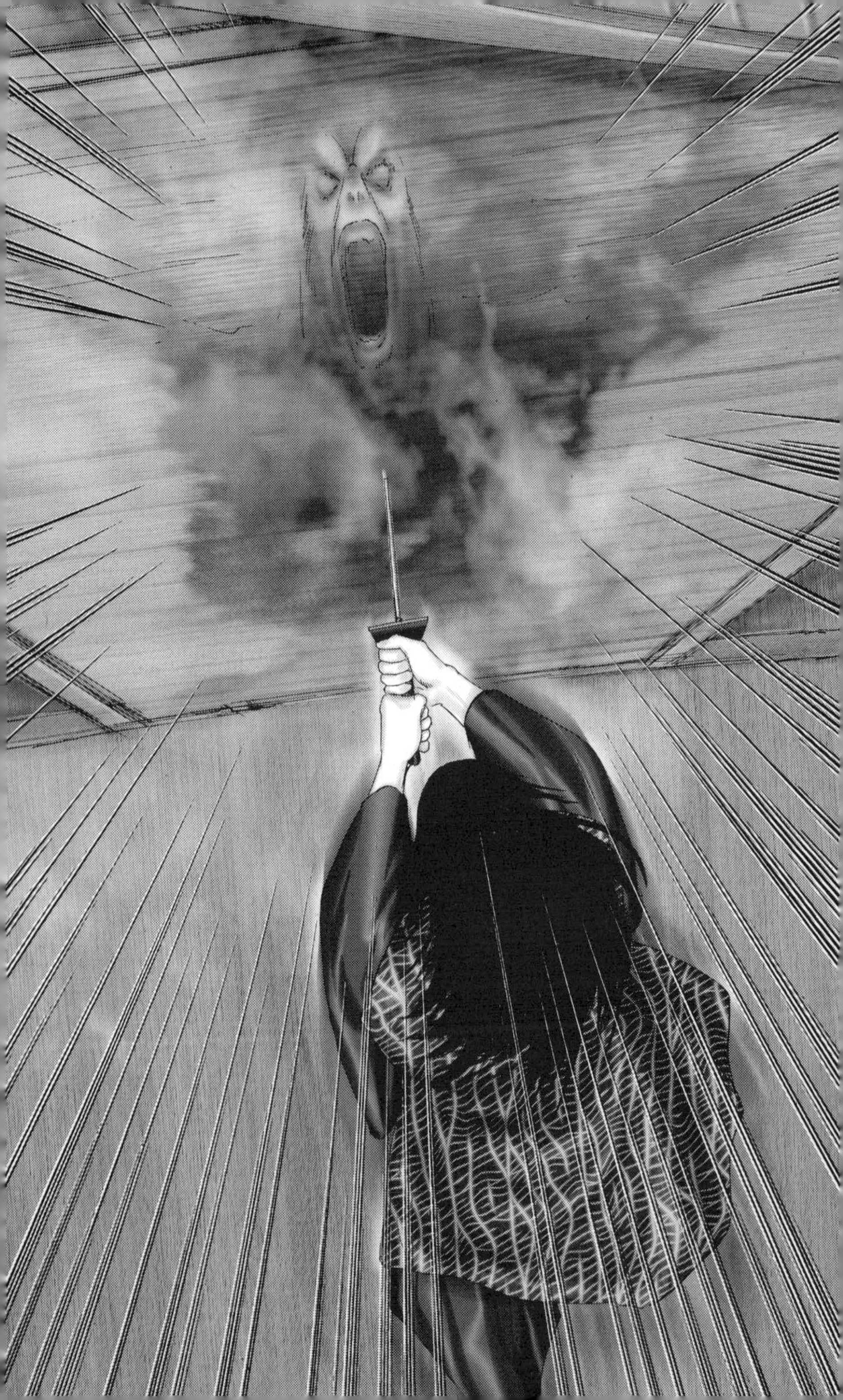

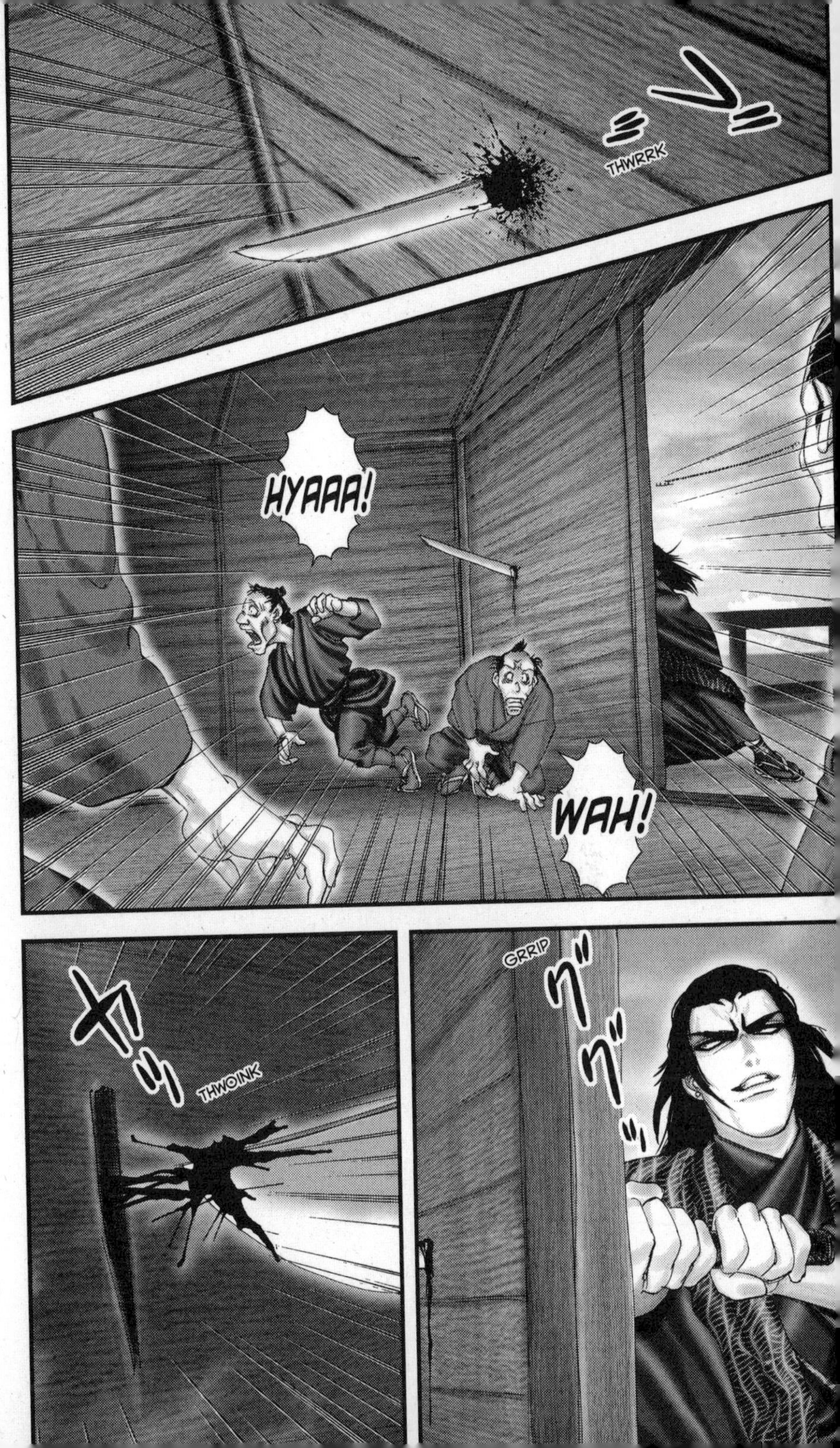
THWRRK
HYAAA!
WAH!
GRRIP
THWOINK

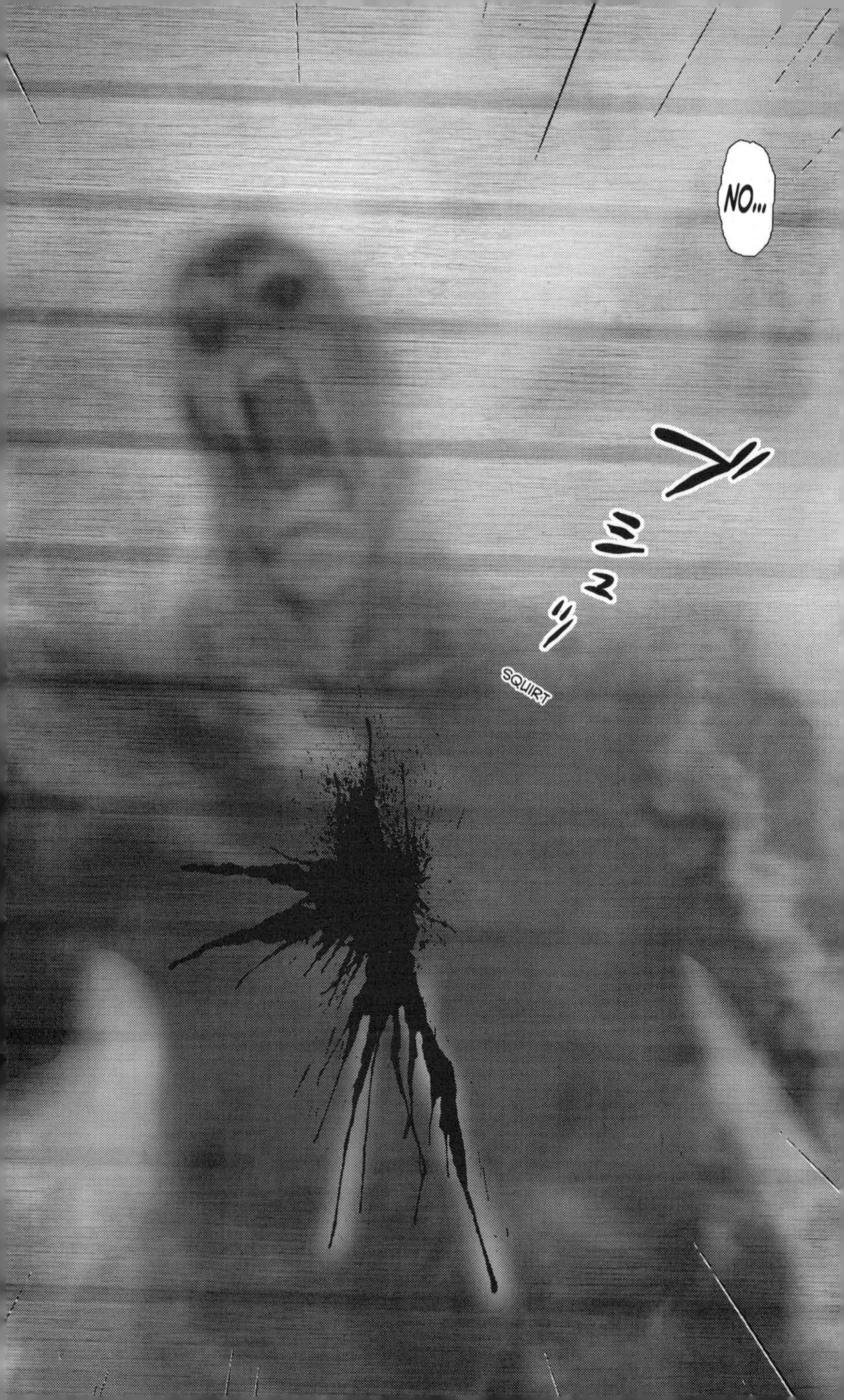
NO...
ジミュッ
SQUIRT

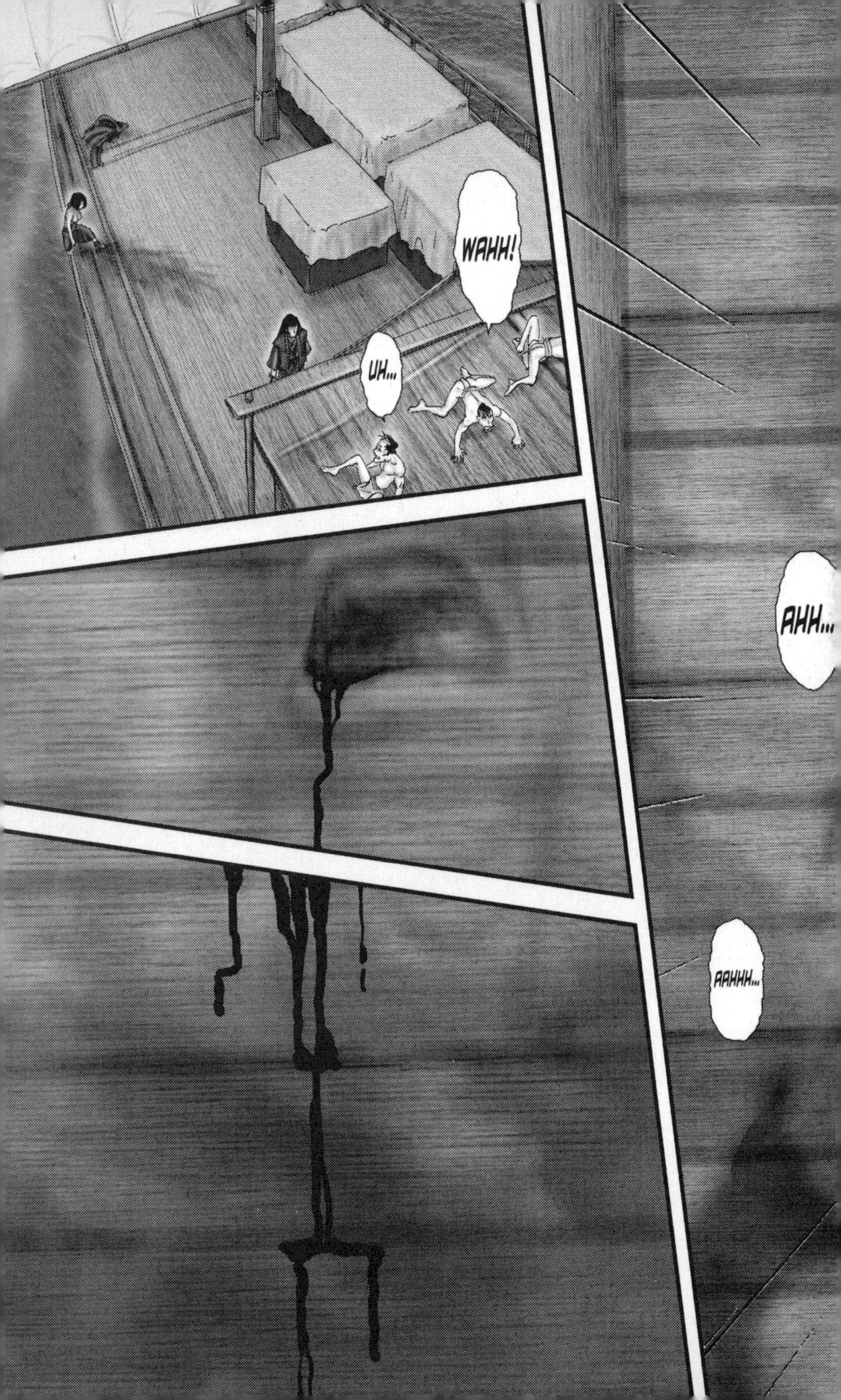
AHH...
AAHHH...
WAHH!
UH...

THAT'S THE END OF...

...GYOUBU KASUMI.

GRIN

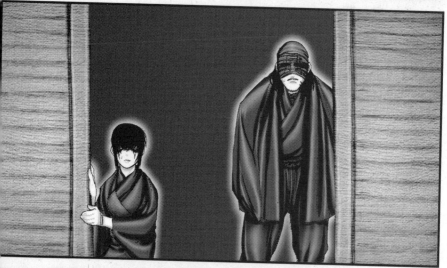

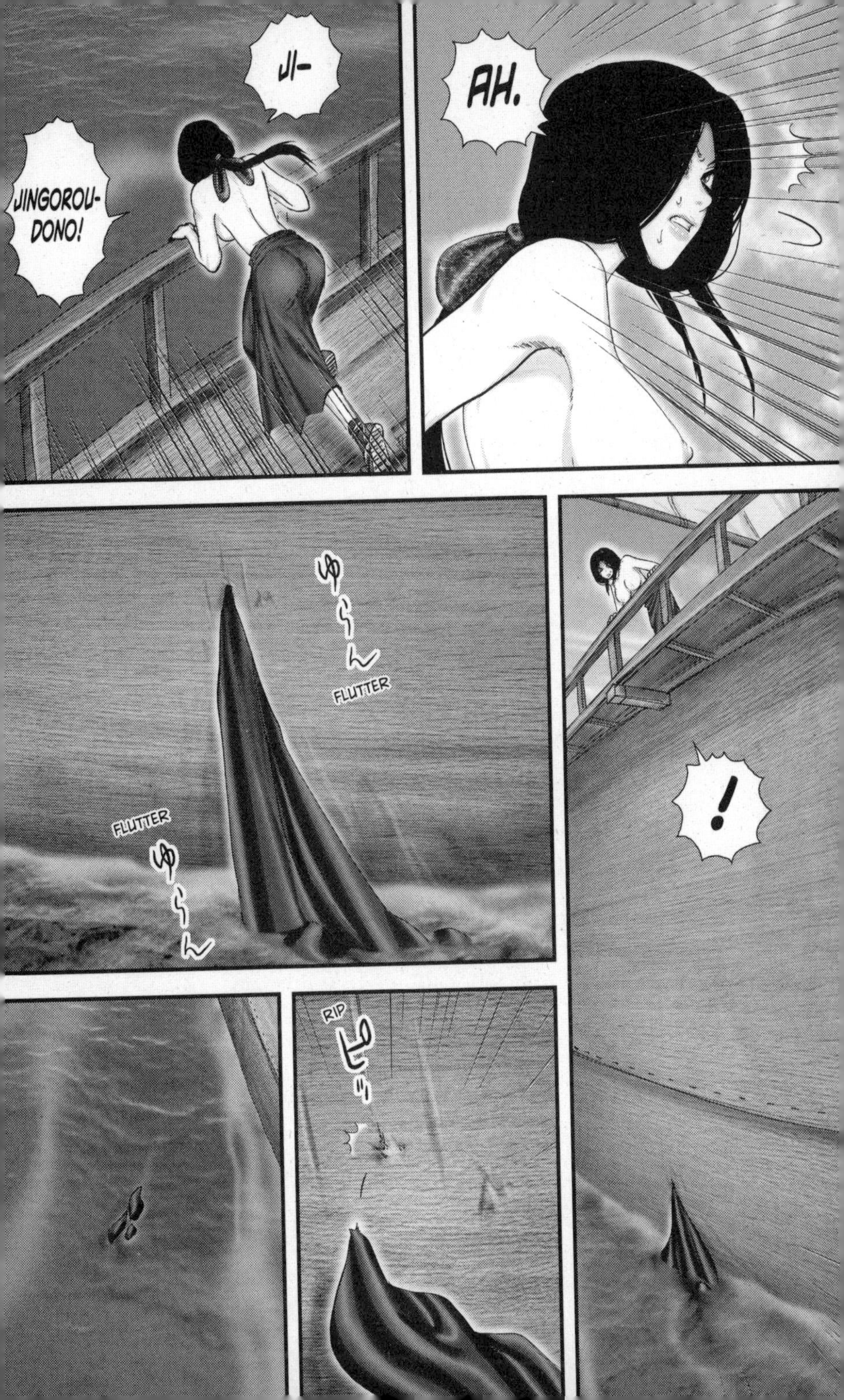
AH.
JI-
JINGOROU-DONO!
!
ゆらん
FLUTTER
FLUTTER
ゆらん
RIP
ピッ

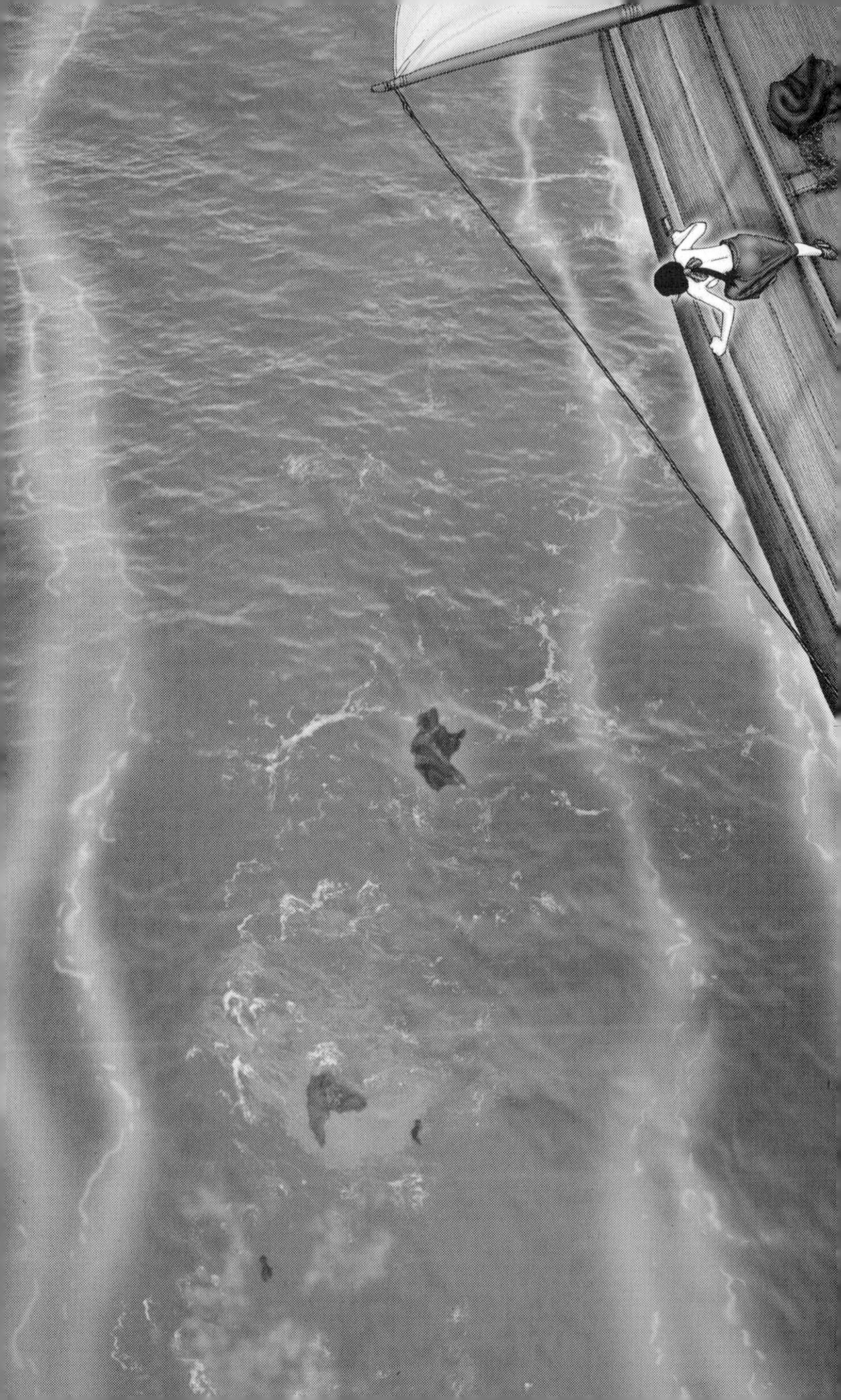

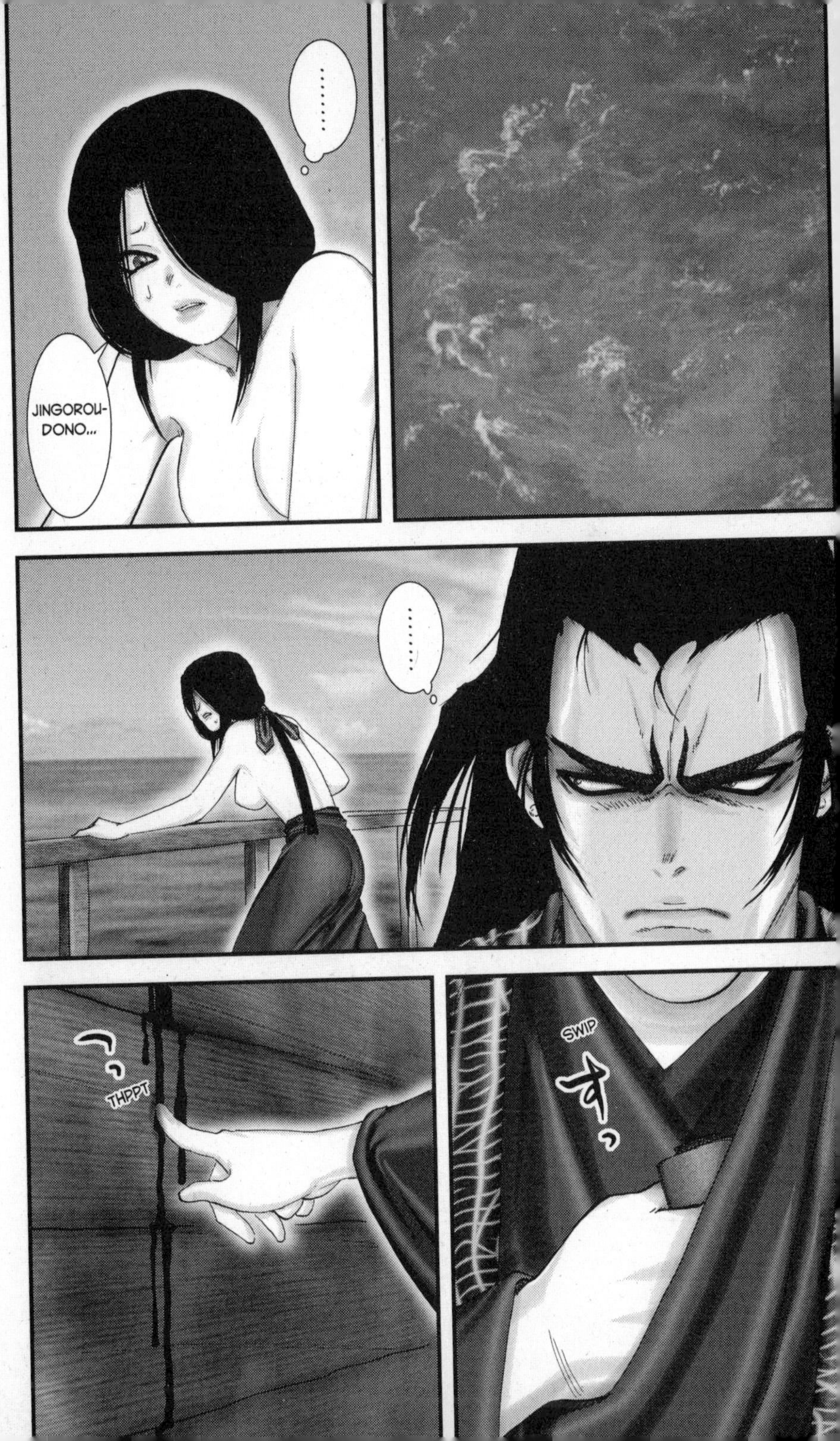
……
JINGOROU-DONO…
……
SWIP
すっ
THPPT

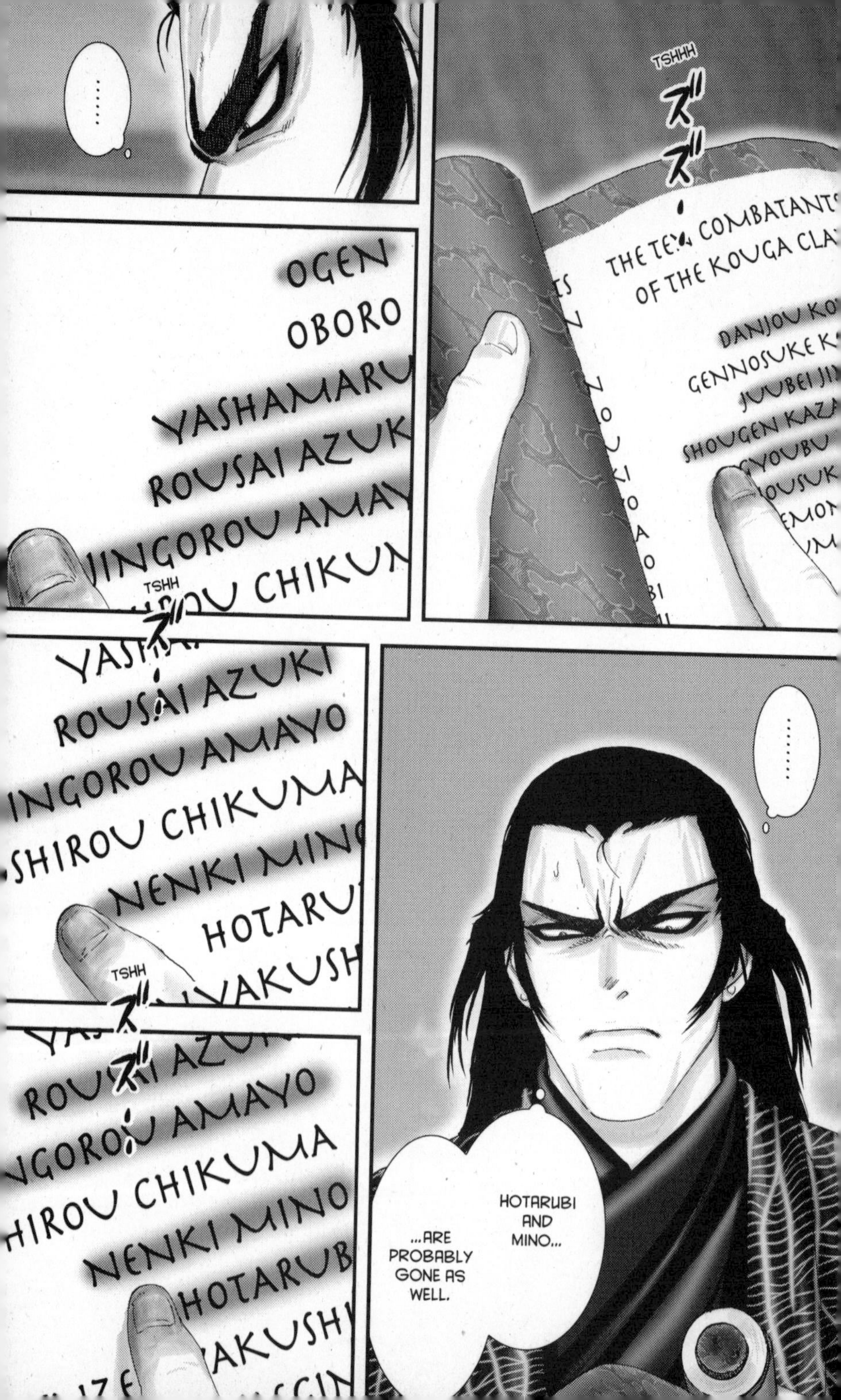
TSHHH
ズズズ
OF THE KOUGA
......
OGEN
OBORO
TSHH
ズ
ROUSAI AZUKI
JINGOROU AMAYO
SHIROU CHIKUMA
HOTARU
TSHH
ズ
......
HOTARUBI AND MINO...
...ARE PROBABLY GONE AS WELL.
TSHH
ズズ
ROUSAI AZUKI
JINGOROU AMAYO
SHIROU CHIKUMA
NENKI MINO
HOTARUBI
YAKUSHI

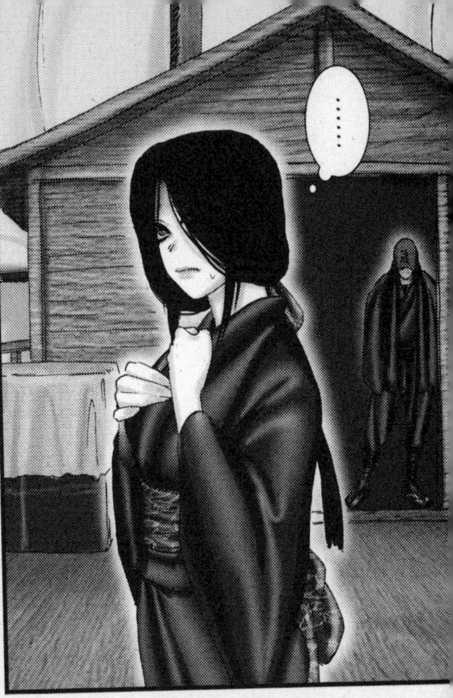
......

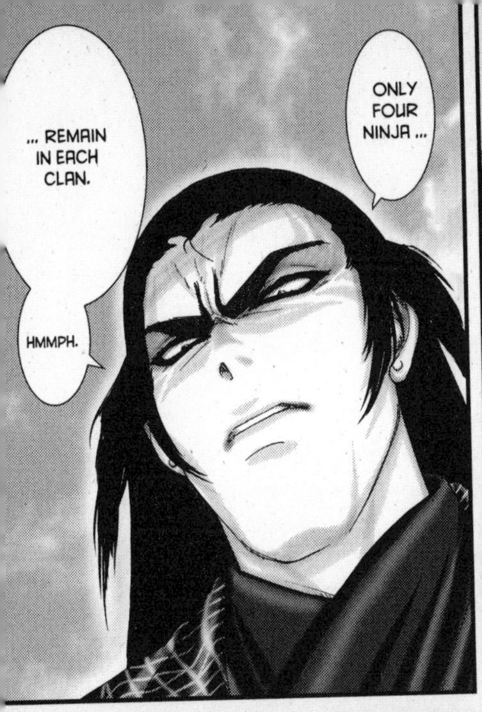
ONLY FOUR NINJA ...
... REMAIN IN EACH CLAN.
HMMPH.

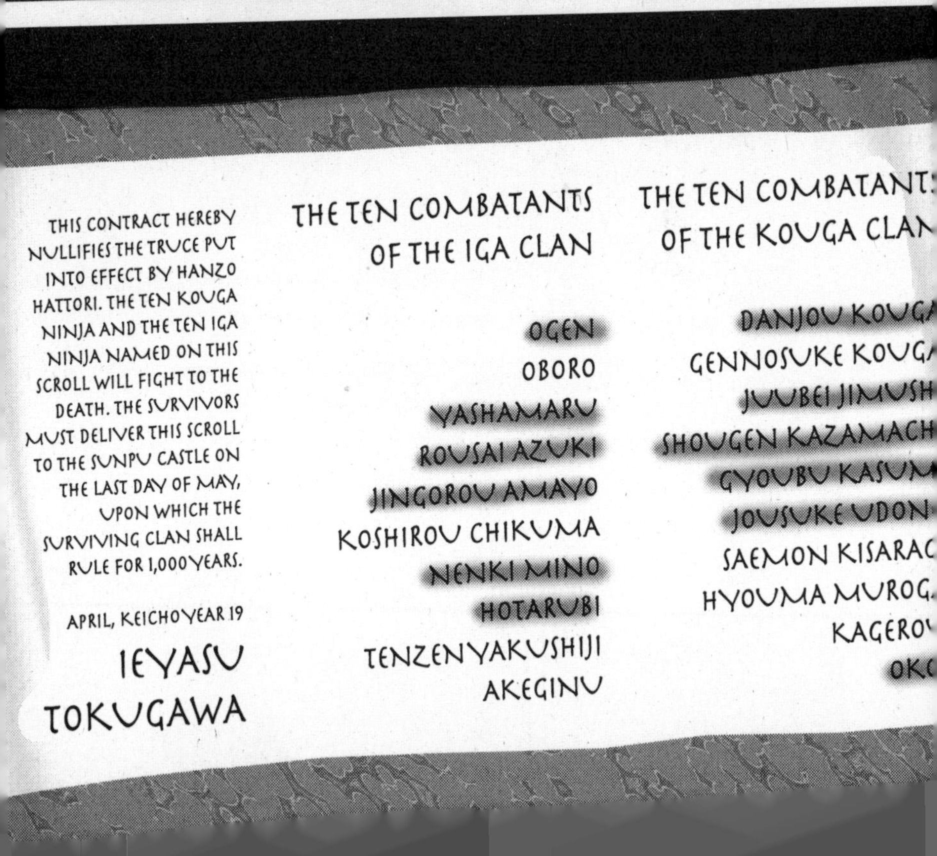
THIS CONTRACT HEREBY NULLIFIES THE TRUCE PUT INTO EFFECT BY HANZO HATTORI. THE TEN KOUGA NINJA AND THE TEN IGA NINJA NAMED ON THIS SCROLL WILL FIGHT TO THE DEATH. THE SURVIVORS MUST DELIVER THIS SCROLL TO THE SUNPU CASTLE ON THE LAST DAY OF MAY, UPON WHICH THE SURVIVING CLAN SHALL RULE FOR 1,000 YEARS.
APRIL, KEICHO YEAR 19
IEYASU TOKUGAWA
THE TEN COMBATANTS OF THE IGA CLAN
OGEN
OBORO
YASHAMARU
ROUSAI AZUKI
JINGOROU AMAYO
KOSHIROU CHIKUMA
NENKI MINO
HOTARUBI
TENZEN YAKUSHIJI
AKEGINU
THE TEN COMBATANT
OF THE KOUGA CLA
DANJOU KOUG
GENNOSUKE KOUG
JUUBEI JIMUSH
SHOUGEN KAZAMACH
GYOUBU KASUM
JOUSUKE UDON
SAEMON KISARA
HYOUMA MUROG
KAGERO
OK

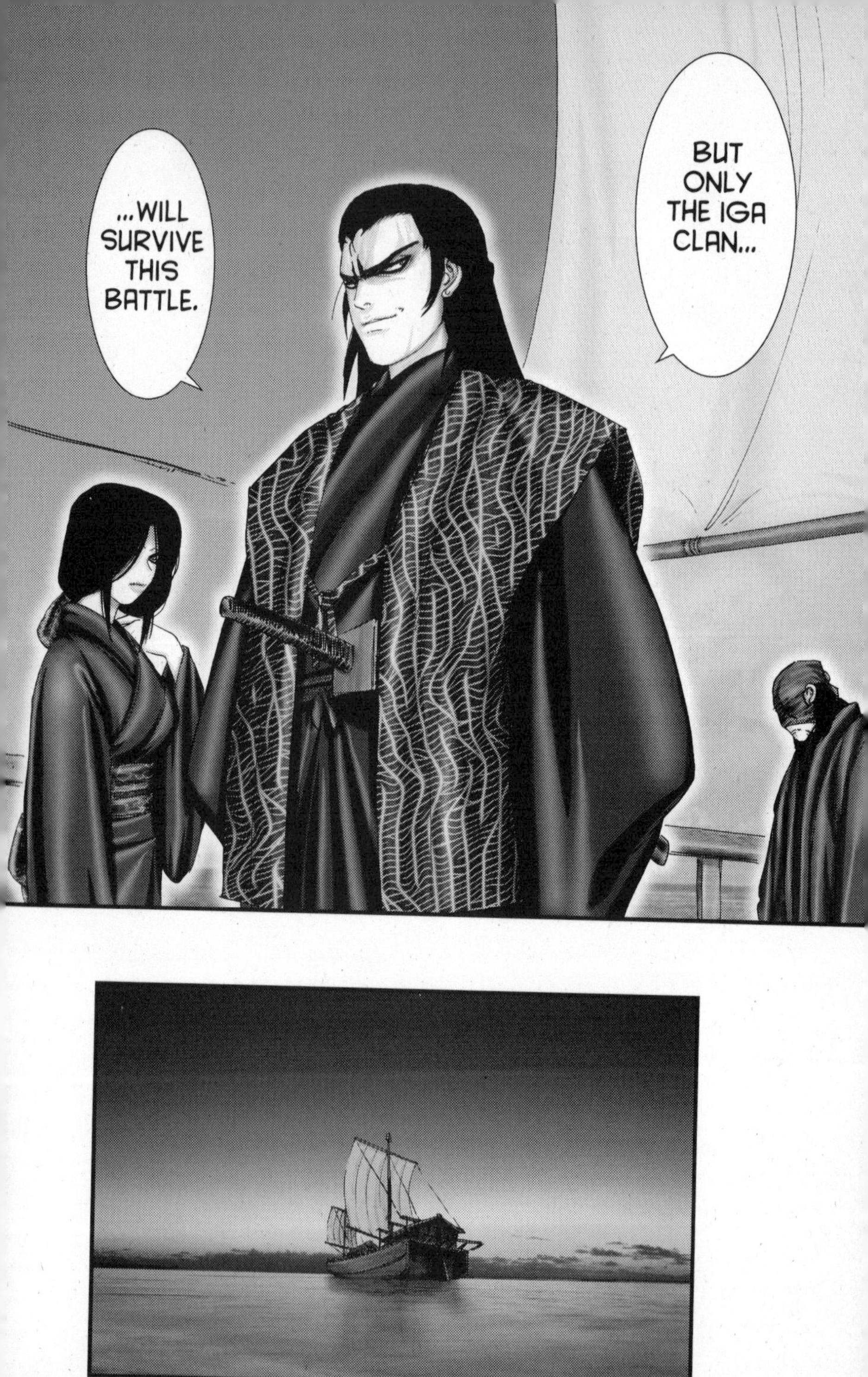
BUT ONLY THE IGA CLAN...
...WILL SURVIVE THIS BATTLE.

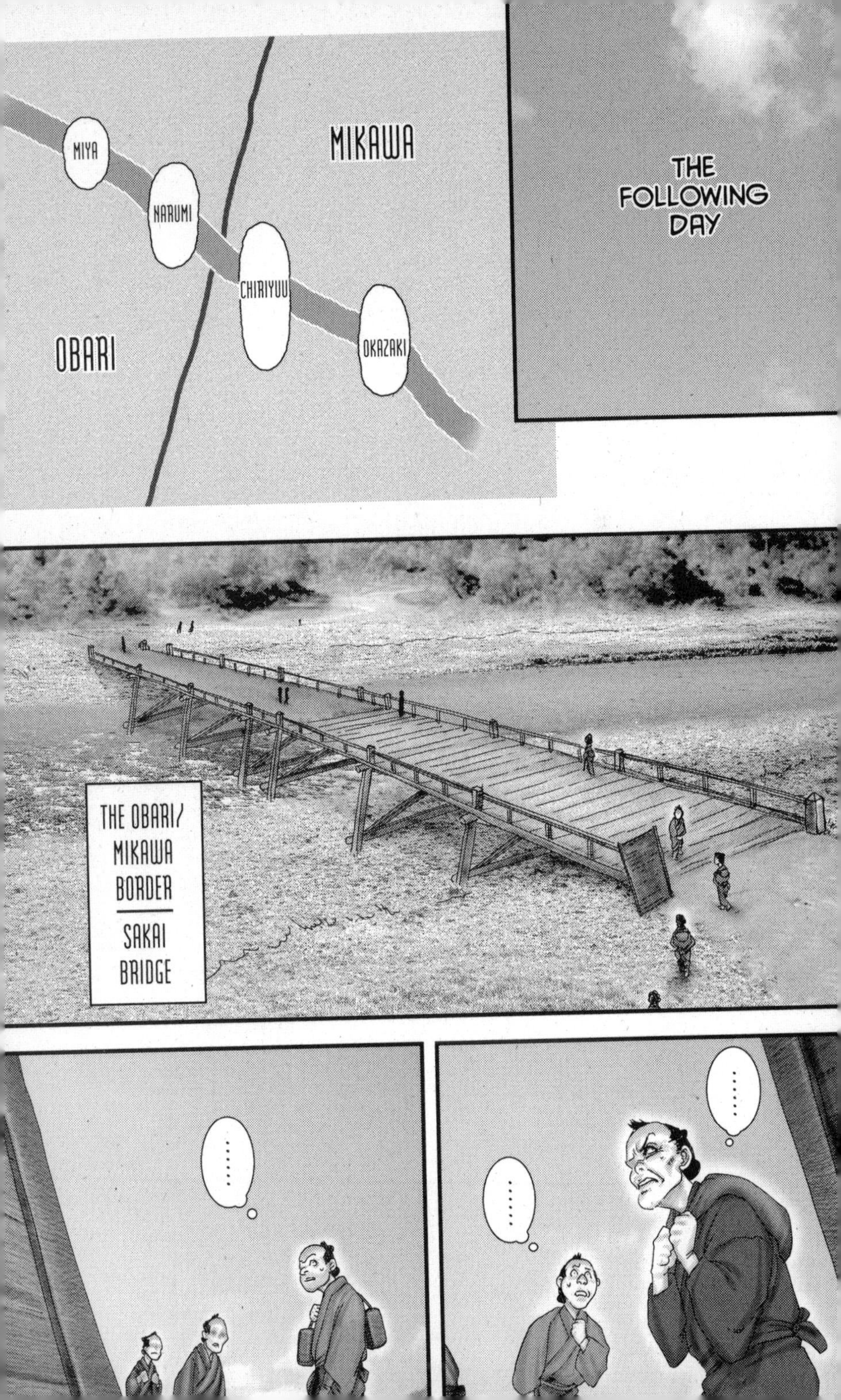

THE FOLLOWING DAY
MIKAWA
MIYA
NARUMI
CHIRIYUU
OKAZAKI
OBARI
THE OBARI/ MIKAWA BORDER
SAKAI BRIDGE
……
……
……

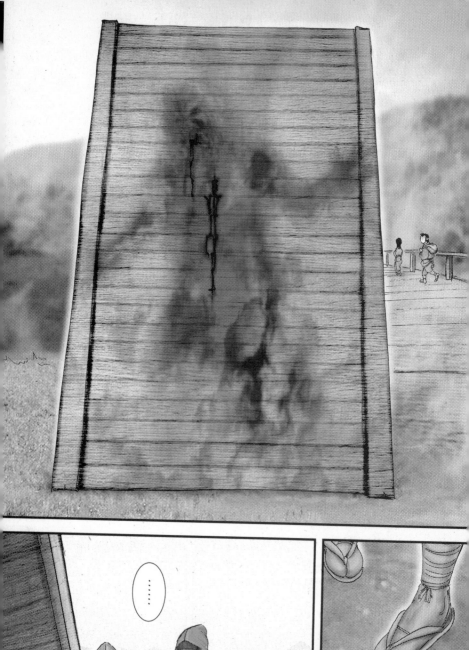

. . . . .

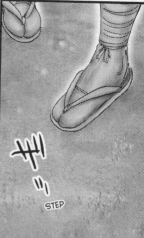

STEP

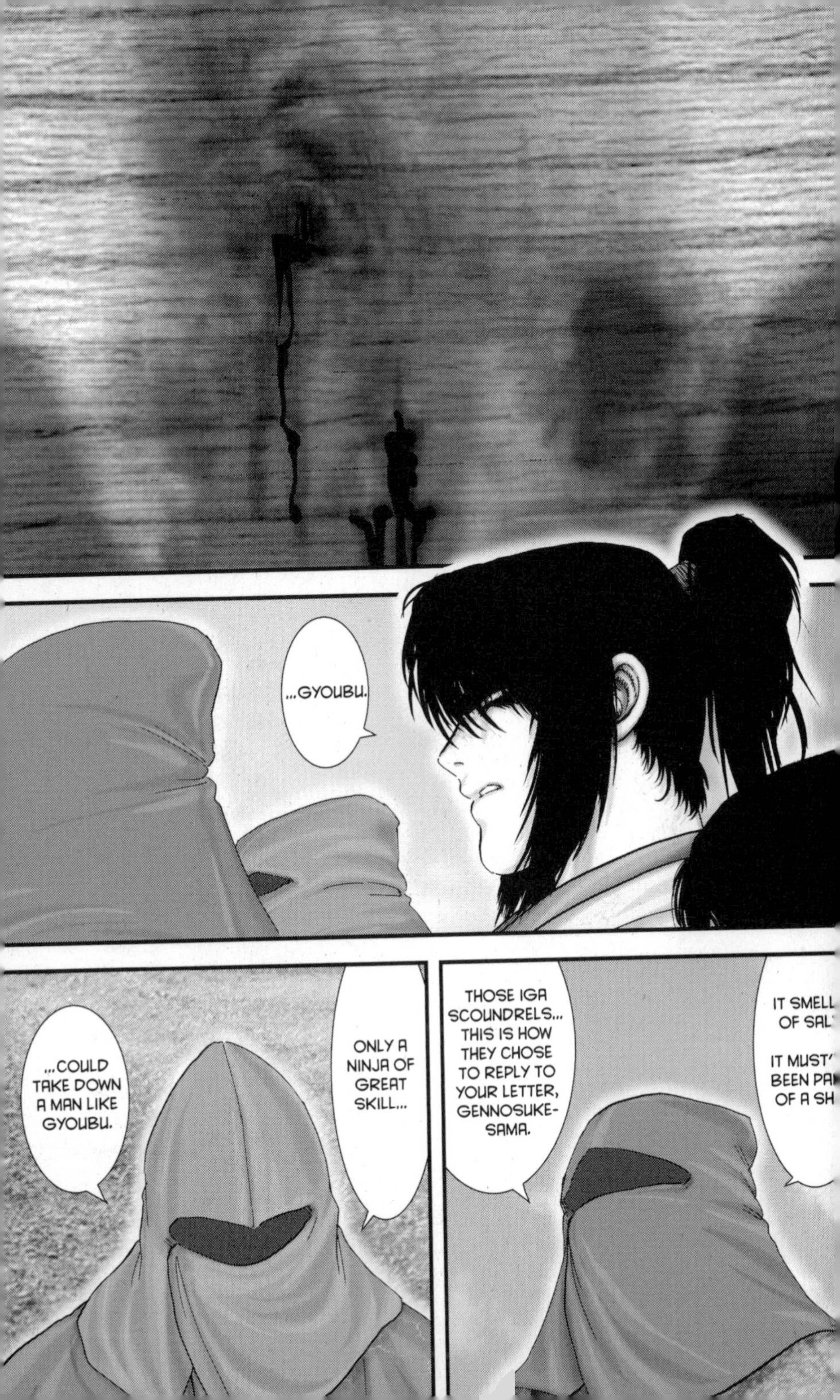
...GYOUBU.
IT SMELL OF SAL
IT MUST BEEN PA OF A SH
THOSE IGA SCOUNDRELS... THIS IS HOW THEY CHOSE TO REPLY TO YOUR LETTER, GENNOSUKE-SAMA.
ONLY A NINJA OF GREAT SKILL...
...COULD TAKE DOWN A MAN LIKE GYOUBU.

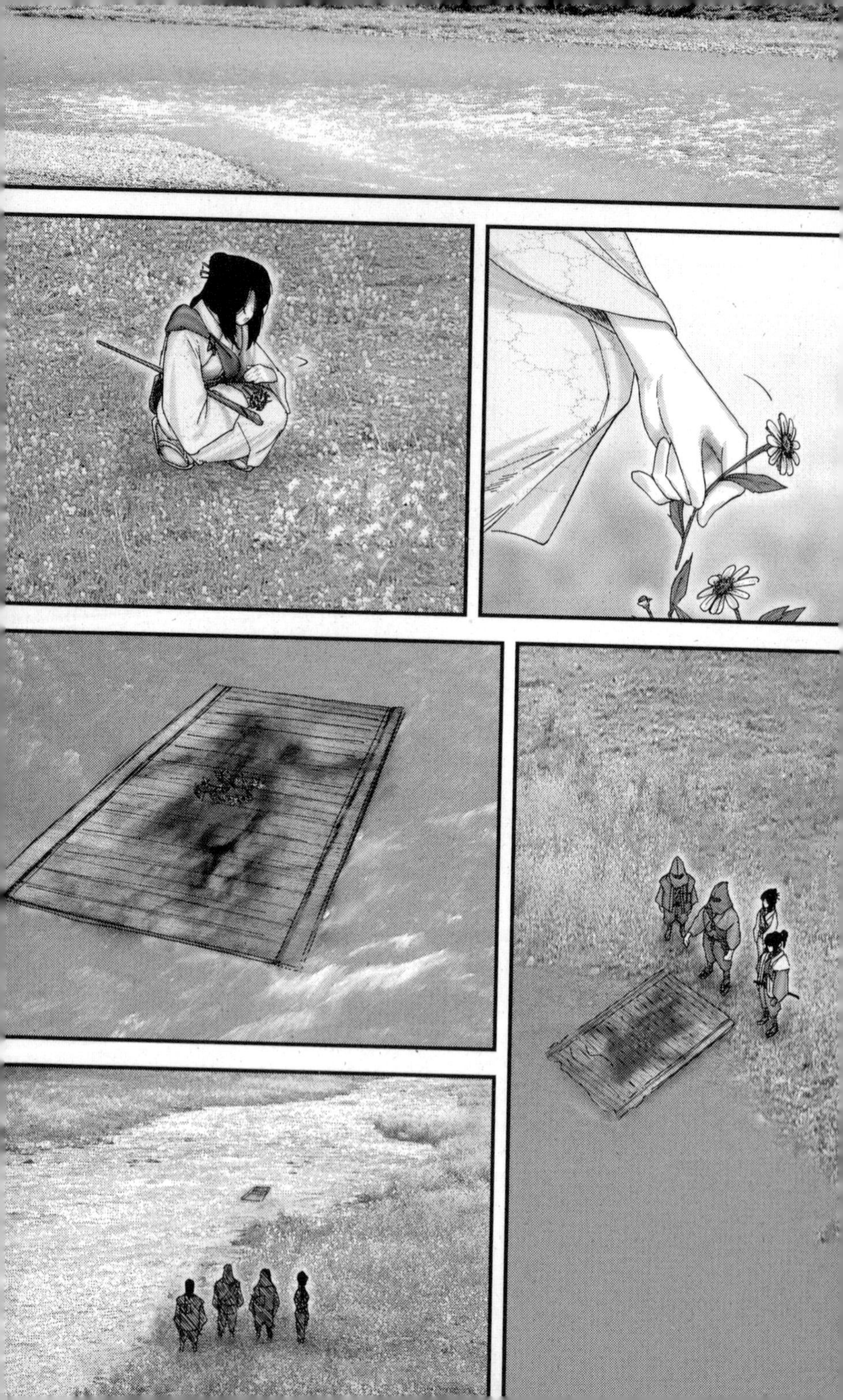

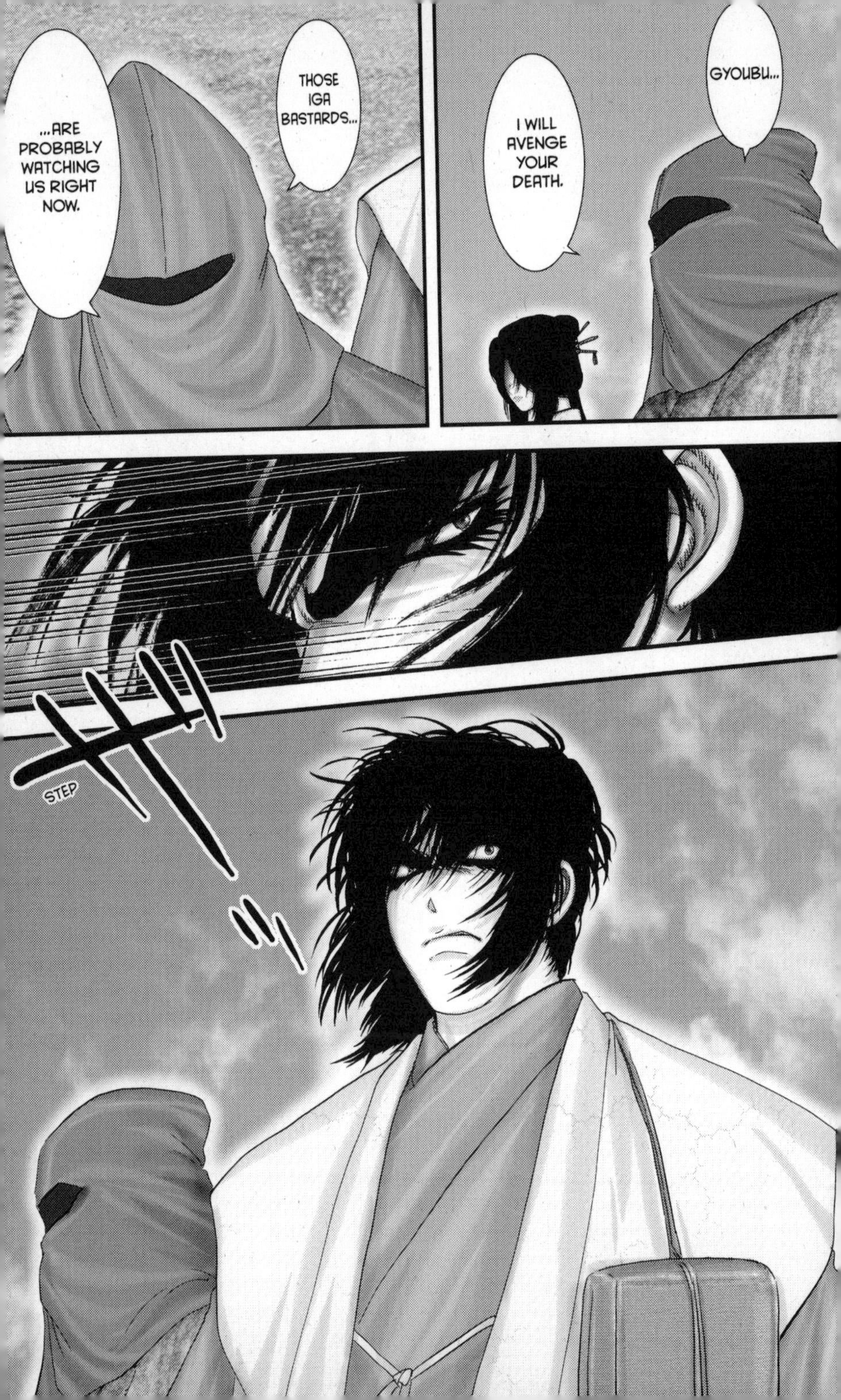
GYOUBU...
I WILL AVENGE YOUR DEATH.
THOSE IGA BASTARDS...
...ARE PROBABLY WATCHING US RIGHT NOW.
STEP

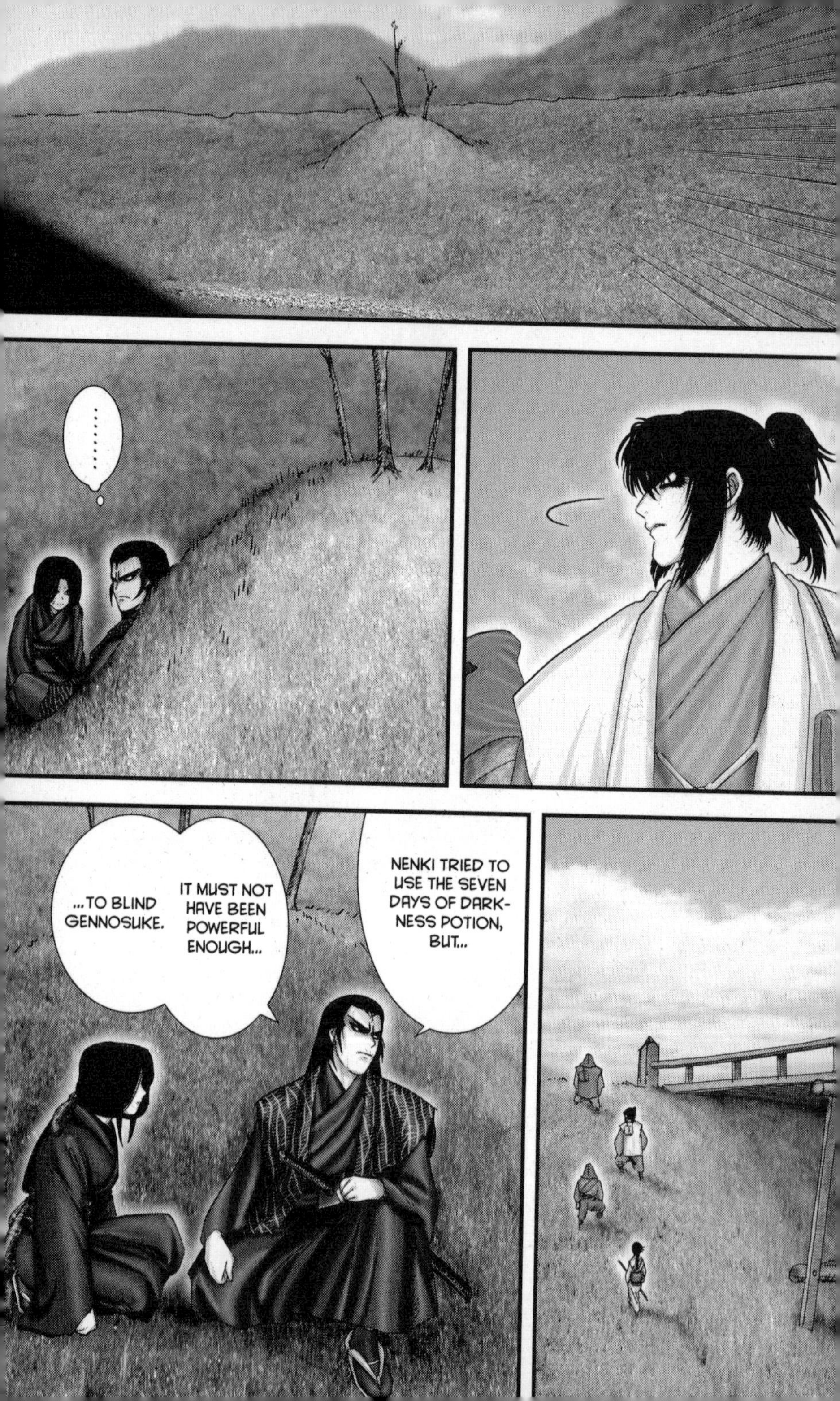
....
NENKI TRIED TO USE THE SEVEN DAYS OF DARK-NESS POTION, BUT...
IT MUST NOT HAVE BEEN POWERFUL ENOUGH...
...TO BLIND GENNOSUKE.

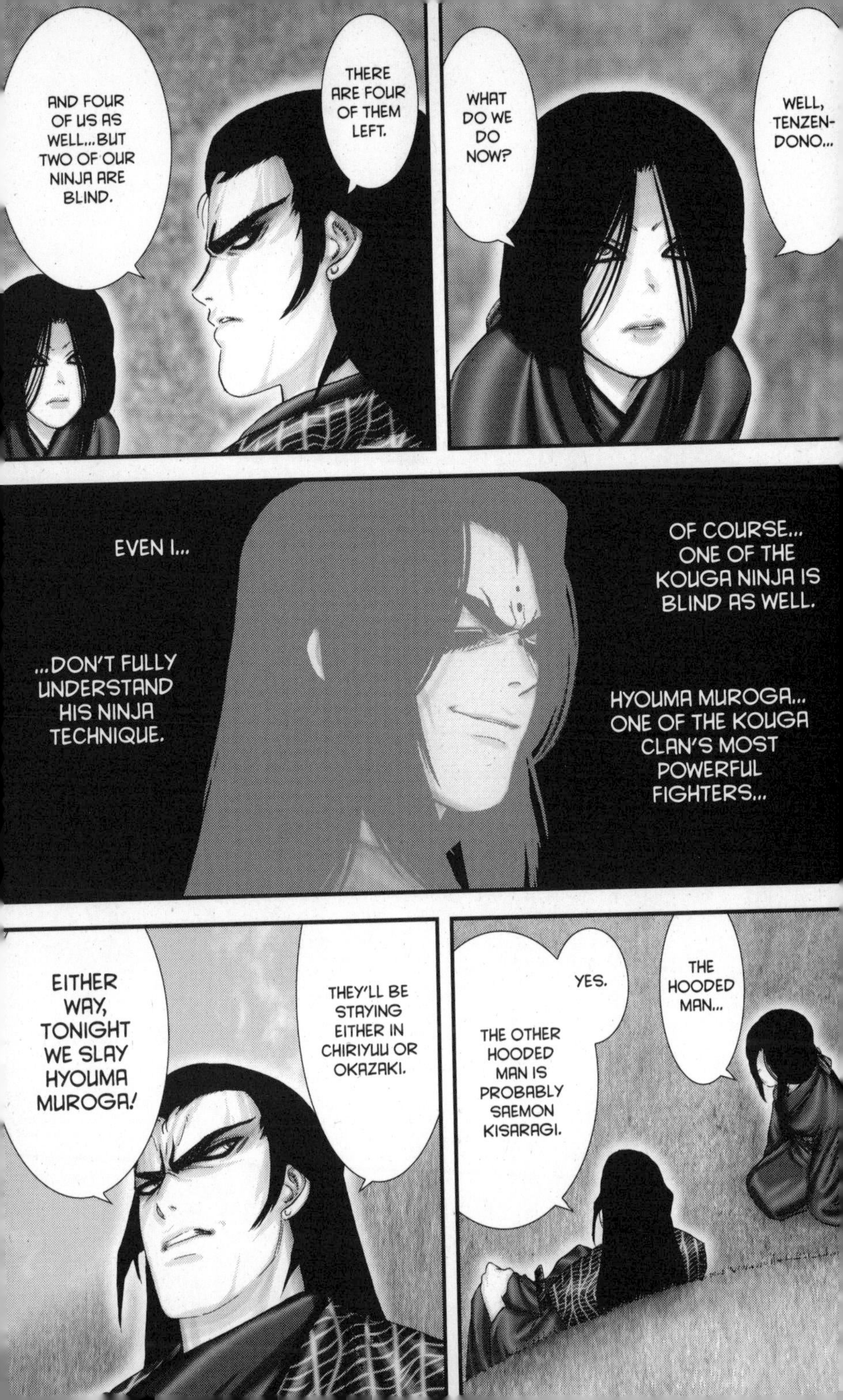
WELL, TENZEN-DONO...
WHAT DO WE DO NOW?
THERE ARE FOUR OF THEM LEFT.
AND FOUR OF US AS WELL...BUT TWO OF OUR NINJA ARE BLIND.
OF COURSE... ONE OF THE KOUGA NINJA IS BLIND AS WELL.
HYOUMA MUROGA... ONE OF THE KOUGA CLAN'S MOST POWERFUL FIGHTERS...
EVEN I...
...DON'T FULLY UNDERSTAND HIS NINJA TECHNIQUE.
THE HOODED MAN...
YES.
THE OTHER HOODED MAN IS PROBABLY SAEMON KISARAGI.
THEY'LL BE STAYING EITHER IN CHIRIYUU OR OKAZAKI.
EITHER WAY, TONIGHT WE SLAY HYOUMA MUROGA!

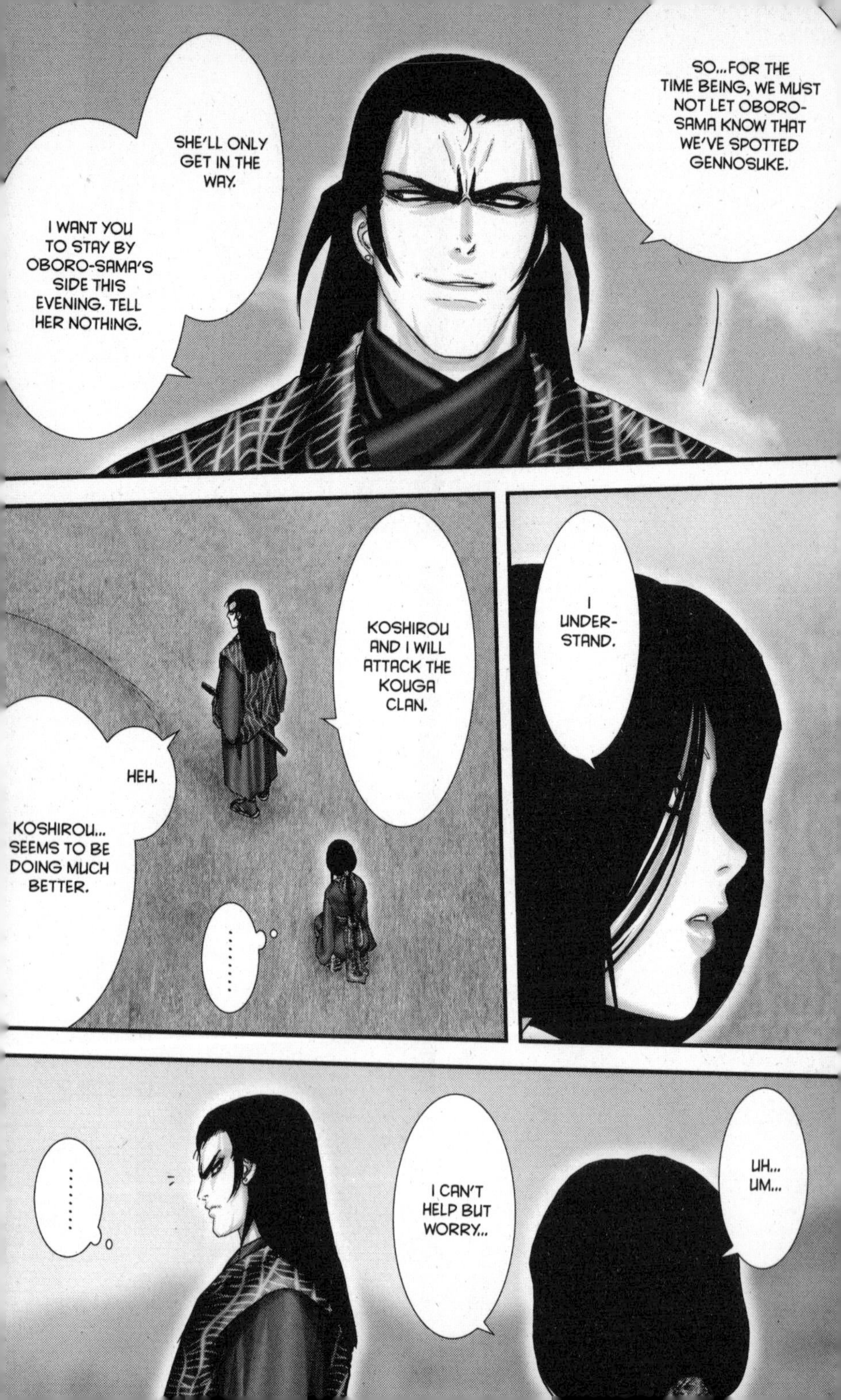
SO...FOR THE TIME BEING, WE MUST NOT LET OBORO-SAMA KNOW THAT WE'VE SPOTTED GENNOSUKE.
SHE'LL ONLY GET IN THE WAY.
I WANT YOU TO STAY BY OBORO-SAMA'S SIDE THIS EVENING. TELL HER NOTHING.
I UNDER-STAND.
KOSHIROU AND I WILL ATTACK THE KOUGA CLAN.
HEH.
KOSHIROU... SEEMS TO BE DOING MUCH BETTER.
......
UH... UM...
I CAN'T HELP BUT WORRY...
......

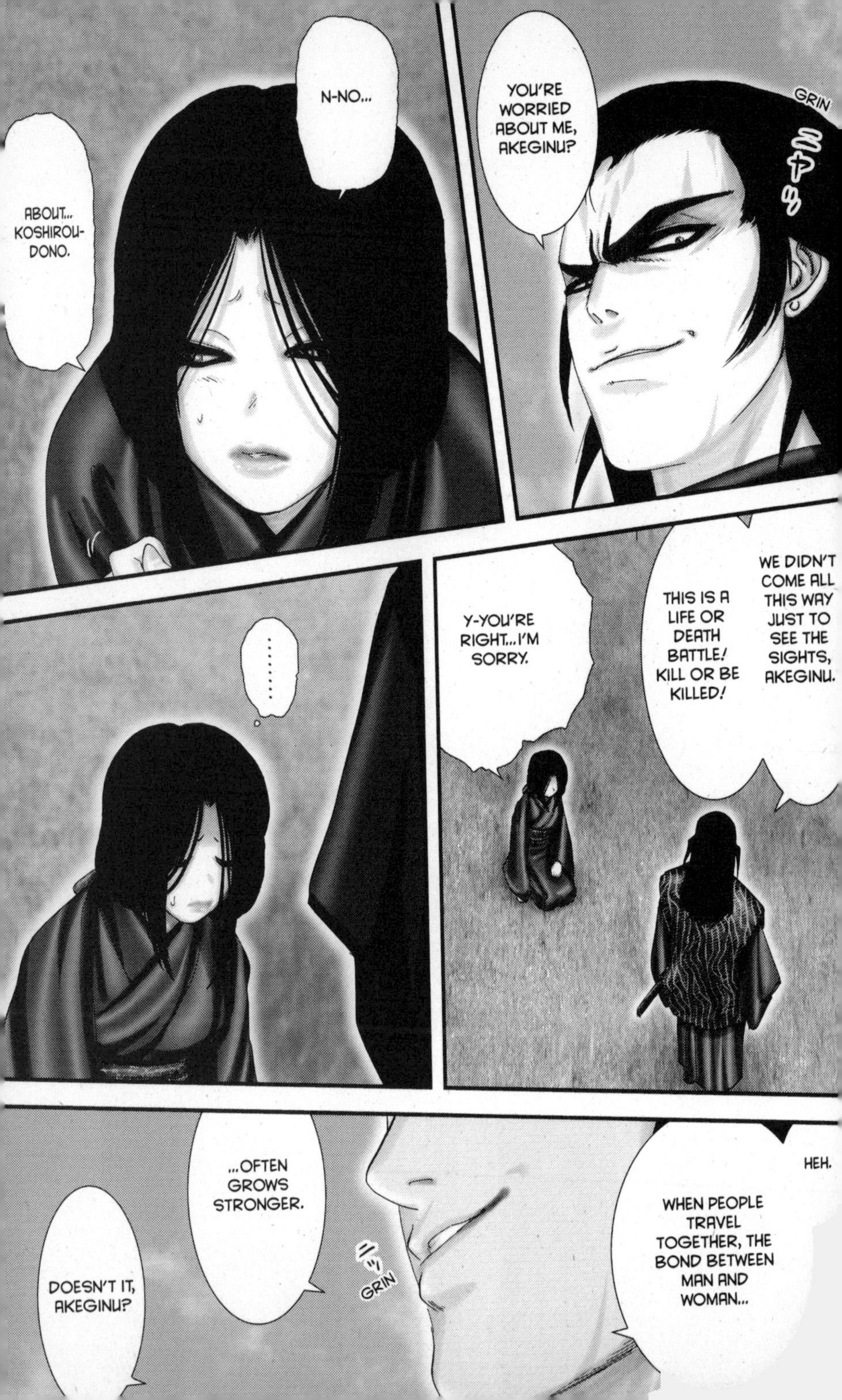
YOU'RE WORRIED ABOUT ME, AKEGINU?
GRIN
ニヤッ
N-NO...
ABOUT... KOSHIROU-DONO.
WE DIDN'T COME ALL THIS WAY JUST TO SEE THE SIGHTS, AKEGINU.
THIS IS A LIFE OR DEATH BATTLE! KILL OR BE KILLED!
Y-YOU'RE RIGHT...I'M SORRY.
......
HEH.
WHEN PEOPLE TRAVEL TOGETHER, THE BOND BETWEEN MAN AND WOMAN...
...OFTEN GROWS STRONGER.
ニッ
GRIN
DOESN'T IT, AKEGINU?

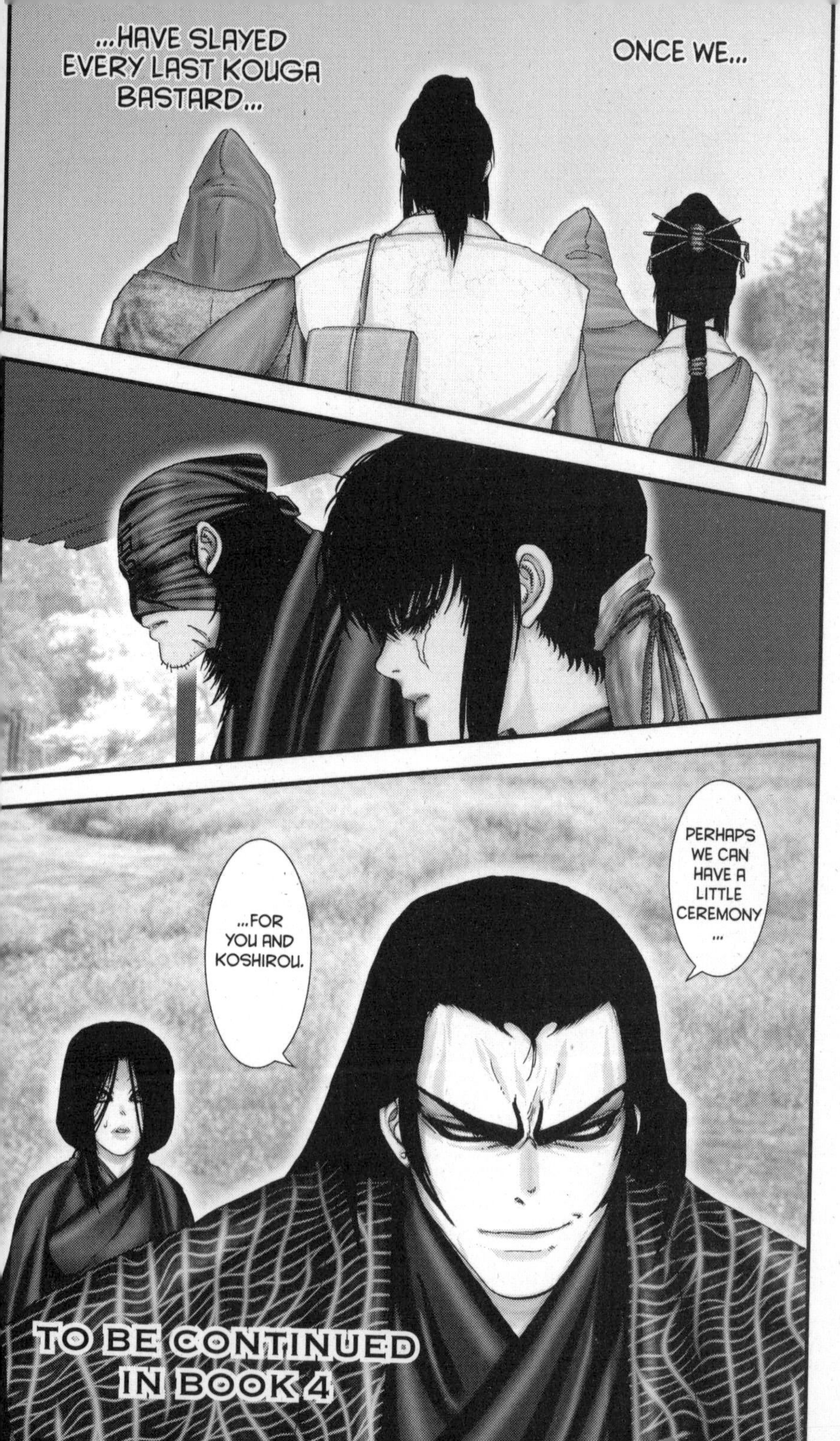
ONCE WE...
...HAVE SLAYED EVERY LAST KOUGA BASTARD...
PERHAPS WE CAN HAVE A LITTLE CEREMONY...
...FOR YOU AND KOSHIROU.
TO BE CONTINUED IN BOOK 4

FŪTARO YAMADA

Born in 1922 in Hyogo Prefecture, Fūtaro Yamada made his debut as a novelist while still a student at Tokyo Medical University. Yamada was known for his mystery novels such as *Ganchuu No Akuma*. Later, his Ninja Scrolls series became wildly popular. He penned a wide body of literature, including the period piece *Makaitensei*, as well as several collections of essays such as *Ato Senkai No Banmeshi* and *Ningen Rinjyuu Zukan*. He passed away on July 28, 2001.

MASAKI SEGAWA

Masaki Segawa made his debut in 1997 with the series Senma Monogatari, which ran in the weekly comic *Morning*. In 1998, he began his long-running *Uppers* magazine series Onigiri Jyuuzou, which ended in the year 2000. This is his second long-running series, and his first adaptation. He loves cats and watermelon. He currently resides in Funabashi.

Translation Notes

Japanese is a tricky language for most Westerners, and translation is often more art than science. For your edification and reading pleasure, here are notes on some of the places where we could have gone in a different direction in our translation of the work, or where a Japanese cultural reference is used.

THE TOKAIDO TRAIL, PAGE 17

The Tokaido Trail was a famous 300-mile coastal road linking Kyoto and Tokyo during the Tokugawa Era. The road was used by the shogun to maintain control over the country, but it soon became a major commercial route. The fifty-three stations along the Tokaido route were depicted in wood block prints by the famous Edo Era artist Hiroshige. Today several train lines make the journey from Kyoto to Tokyo along parts of the Tokaido Trail.

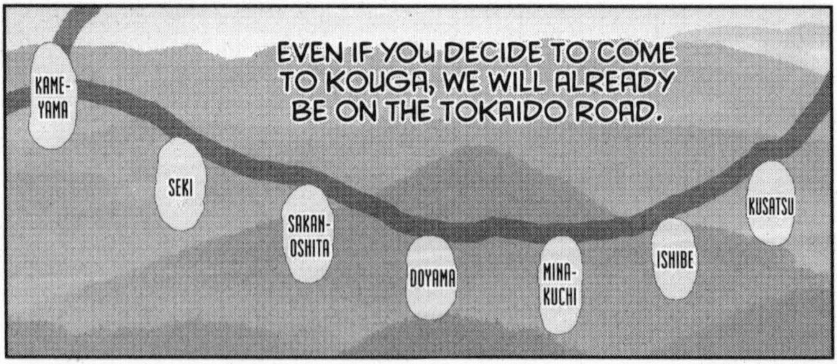
EVEN IF YOU DECIDE TO COME TO KOUGA, WE WILL ALREADY BE ON THE TOKAIDO ROAD.
KUSATSU
ISHIBE
MINA-KUCHI
DOYAMA
SAKAN-OSHITA
SEKI
KAME-YAMA

KASA, PAGE 169

"Kasa" literally means umbrella. In the old days, people wore woven umbrella hats to keep out the sun and rain. Gyoubu wears one on page 134.

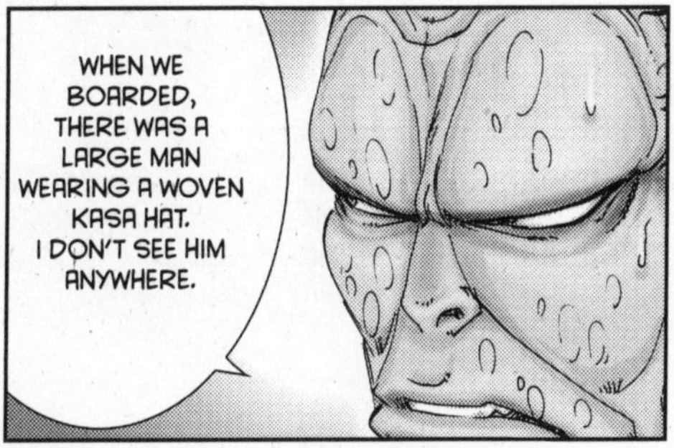
WHEN WE BOARDED, THERE WAS A LARGE MAN WEARING A WOVEN KASA HAT. I DON'T SEE HIM ANYWHERE.

Special Sneak Preview

Here's a sneak peek
at *The Kouga Ninja Scrolls,*
the book that inspired Basilisk!
Coming soon to bookstores
everywhere.

THE CASTLE KEEP STOOD IN THE BACKGROUND, SEVEN STORIES HIGH. FROM A distance, it looked like a heap of dancers' fans piled atop one another.

Two men faced off.

In the blaze of the sun, the men's bodies turned transparent. Clouds dropped their shadows upon them, shifting the men into hazy shadows as well. They nearly faded into nothingness. An audience of countless eyes watched them, but these eyes had to squint more and more to see them, frequently losing sight of the two men.

Even so, nobody looked away. A distance of no more than fifteen feet separated the men, and within that space a charged air of menace billowed back and forth in waves. Everyone strained their eyes upon this spot, so much so that the image of these fighters became branded into their minds. Yet neither man held an unsheathed sword—rather, both of them stood empty-handed. If the audience had not just witnessed the shocking display of ninja skills, the watchers would probably not have recognized the deadly atmosphere surging between the two men now.

One of the men, Kazamachi Shougen, about forty years old, was hideous, with a bumpy forehead and hollow cheeks that contrasted with the shining red dots that served as his eyes. He had a round, swollen hump like a hunchback. His long, narrow, gray limbs had been bloated abnormally at their limits. Every one of his fingers and toes—which poked out from straw sandals—was as large as a lizard.

Moments ago, he had been attacked by five samurai. As they approached him, his arrogant stance said: *You wish to cut me down as if I were a mere novice.* Unimpressed, his attackers advanced in the intimidating *Yagyu* sword-fighting stance. Holding their swords out from their bodies, they looked like scarecrows.

"Aaah!" Two of the five warriors suddenly screamed and staggered back clutching at their eyes. Without a word, Kazamachi Shougen had attacked them. They didn't understand what had happened, or even how it had occurred, but the remaining three men panicked, and their terror sent them into a furious frenzy. Their swords were already drawn, and they had just been attacked, so in a mixture of shock and reflex action the remaining three waved their swords in the air and charged.

Shougen darted to the side, toward the stone wall of the castle keep. Escaping from the onrushing, poorly manufactured swords, he scrambled up the wall. Amazingly, he did so without ever turning his back to his enemies. Spiderlike, with his back to the wall, he clambered up the huge stone wall using his hands and feet. Or, one should say, his *hand* and feet—his right hand continued gripping his sword. Climbing just beyond the men's reach, he looked down at the three pursuing samurai and smirked.

It only seemed to be a smirk. Something flew from his mouth, striking the three remaining soldiers, who all immediately slammed their eyes shut and stumbled in dizziness. The other two soldiers were still writhing and covering their eyes. His back pressing the wall, Kazamachi Shougen noiselessly crept down. The battle was already over.

The object that exploded from Shougen's mouth was no ordinary weapon. It was a glob of mucus the size of a coin from the *Keicho* reign. From anyone else, it would have been nothing more than phlegm, but Shougen could make his mucus extremely thick and sticky. The five soldiers would be unable to get it out of their eyes for days, not before they had torn out all their own eyelashes in the effort.

Meanwhile, Yashamaru—a youth from the province of Iga—had also been pitted against five samurai.

The word "youth" would not adequately describe the handsome brilliance of this young man. Although he was dressed in coarse clothing as if he had come from the mountains, he had cheeks the color of cherry blossoms and his black eyes shined. He looked like the ideal image of a handsome young man.

Stepping toward the five warriors, he chose not to touch the mountain sword that hung from his waist tied to a rattan belt. Instead, he drew out a black ropelike thing. This "rope" had immense power: It was incredibly thin, yet had the strength of steel wire. Even a direct chop from a sword could not cut it. During the day, it shone with dazzling brilliance. But once the sun went down, it became completely invisible.

Suddenly, the mysterious rope twisted around a sword and flung it into the air. A sharp, earsplitting groan erupted as the rope came whistling across horizontally. Two soldiers collapsed, gripping their thighs and backs. Yashamaru used both hands to hurl the ends of the rope in different directions at the same time. He didn't bother to attack the soldiers closest to him; instead, he brought down two soldiers who were ten feet away. He lassoed them around the necks like bellowing beasts.

The rope had been forged through a special technique: Black strands of women's hair had been tied together and sealed with animal oil. A mere touch of the rope upon human flesh had the same effect as a blow from an iron whip. As the rope coiled around the thighs and bodies of the defeated soldiers, their skin burst open as if sharp swords were slicing them. Several dozen feet long, the rope moved like a living creature—spinning, twisting, striking, encircling, and amputating its enemies. And yet, watching it revealed nothing of its next movement—it was inscrutable. Unlike swords and spears, the rope could move autonomously, without regard to Yashamaru's position. Movements of rope and master were unrelated. Enemies had no way to defend themselves, and certainly no chance to attack.

And now, the two mysterious warriors—both of them victors over five attacking samurai—challenged each other, silently, almost magically.

The early summer clouds that hung over the castle keep slowly thinned and dissipated into nothingness. It was as if they were melting in the blue sky. And although it took no more than a few minutes, it seemed to last an eternity. That was the way time flowed...

Kazamachi Shougen's mouth twisted into a smirk. Simultaneously, a groan erupted from Yashamaru's fist, and his rope burst forth, striking at Shougen like an unleashed whirlwind. Shougen dropped to the ground. For a second, all those watching seemed to be witnessing the same mass hallucination—it seemed like a gigantic gray spider was scrambling across the ground. It took another second before the observers realized that this was Kazamachi Shougen, and that, instead of being ensnared by the rope, he had escaped. He landed on all fours and, smirking, spat a light blue sticky clump at Yashamaru.

The round, filmy membrane had nearly struck Yashamaru's face when it vanished in midair—lassoed by Yashamaru's rope. Realizing this, Shougen—for the first time—seemed frightened.

Tsu-tsu-tsu. Shougen scampered backward on all fours. With his head hanging upside down, he scurried up the stone tower of the castle keep in one burst. Everyone watching gasped and the sound echoed off the castle walls.

Shougen's body seemed to fly up the white wall, outracing the tip of Yashamaru's pursuing rope. Shougen glided to the top, then disappeared into the shadows behind an ornamental board at the edge of the curved roof. Using it as his shield, he spat a sticky clump downward. But Yashamaru was no longer there. Yashamaru had lassoed his second length of rope around the edge of the roof, pulled himself up, and his body now floated in midair. Shougen scampered away across the bronze roof tiles. But as soon as he outraced one length of rope, Yashamaru threw another length of rope at him. The battle pitted a trembling bagworm shooting out deadly threads against a scampering spider spitting magical phlegm. The airborne death match that raged against the backdrop of dazzling early summer clouds clearly was not a duel between human beings. This was a fight between monstrous creatures—no, between magical things, far removed from the world of humans.

In the midst of the crowd that watched this nightmarish battle was the elderly lord of the castle. He waved his hand and looked to the side. "Enough. Have them cease, Hanzou. Let's continue this battle tomorrow."

The duel had already ranged over three floors of the castle. The way things were headed, at least one ninja, and maybe both, would end up dead. The old lord of the castle snapped, "This must not become some kind of spectacle for townspeople to gawk at. Sunpu Castle is full of spies from Osaka." The speaker was Tokugawa Ieyasu, lord of the castle—and the man who had nearly conquered and unified Japan.

Tomare!

STOP!

YOU'RE GOING THE WRONG WAY!

MANGA IS A COMPLETELY DIFFERENT
TYPE OF READING EXPERIENCE.

TO START AT THE *BEGINNING*,
GO TO THE *END*!

THAT'S RIGHT!

AUTHENTIC MANGA IS READ THE TRADITIONAL JAPANESE WAY—
FROM RIGHT TO LEFT. EXACTLY THE *OPPOSITE* OF HOW AMERICAN
BOOKS ARE READ. IT'S EASY TO FOLLOW: JUST GO TO THE OTHER
END OF THE BOOK, AND READ EACH PAGE—AND EACH PANEL—
FROM RIGHT SIDE TO LEFT SIDE, STARTING AT THE TOP RIGHT.
NOW YOU'RE EXPERIENCING MANGA AS IT WAS MEANT TO BE.